The **Rough Guide** to

Berlin

written and researched by

John Gawthrop and Christian Williams

ROUGH
GUIDES

www.roughguides.com

Contents

Berlin's architecture colour section following p.112

Ostalgie colour section following p.208

Colour maps following p.328

◄◄ Graffiti on the wall ◄ The Brandenburg Gate

Introduction to

Berlin

Seemingly in a perpetual state of transformation, Berlin is an extraordinary city. For over a century, events here either mirrored or determined what happened in the rest of Europe, and – even twenty years after the world-changing fall of the Berlin Wall – change in the city is brisk. Only now is the process of healing the wounds of half a century of totalitarian blight beginning to come to an end, as it reasserts itself as the capital of Europe's most powerful country.

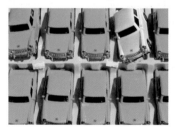

Light-hearted **sightseeing** is difficult in Berlin: this is a profoundly scarred city, with looming symbols of the war years; the remains of the Wall; and several museums that openly and intelligently try to make sense of twentieth-century German history. Even in its flashiest sections the city can still seem half-built, many of its modern buildings – on both sides of the former divide – somehow making it look less finished and more ugly. Unlike Paris, Amsterdam or Munich, Berlin isn't a city where you can simply stroll and absorb the atmosphere: you need to plan your trips and target your points of interest, using the city's excellent transport system to cover what can be longish distances.

Given the range and severity of the events Berlin endured, it's no wonder it emerged far differently from anywhere else in Germany. West Berlin's **unorthodox** character made it a magnet for those seeking alternative lifestyles – hippies and punks, gays and lesbians, artists and musicians all flocked there. Non-Germans came too, attracted by the city's tolerance: Turks, Greeks and Italians, who originally came as "guest workers" in the 1960s, soon made Berlin Germany's most **cosmopolitan** city by far – as reflected in the wide variety of cuisine on offer in the city's restaurants, cafés and bars. Though cut off by the Wall for thirty years, the eastern part of the city has always been Berlin's real centre, and it took only a decade or so for it to reassert itself

in this role. The area east of the Brandenburg Gate, focused around Unter den Linden and the Spandauer Vorstadt neighbourhood just to the north, has emerged as the city's prime magnets for **shopping** and **entertainment**. Sleek chrome and glass have replaced crumbling brick, while Potsdamer Platz, nothing but a barren field straddling the death-strip of the Berlin Wall, is now a bustling entertainment quarter. It's an exciting scene and, for anyone familiar with the forlorn and unkempt eastern streets of the GDR, a slightly unbelievable one. Here especially the rapid **transformation** of Berlin into capital city and economic and cultural powerhouse is evident.

Berlin in a week

Berlin is a 24-hour city, but some things are best done on certain days – check the calendar below to make sure you don't miss a beat.

Tuesdays *Kinotag* in many of Berlin's cinemas means cheap cinema tickets – including at the Sony Center, the main English-language cinema (see p.239).

Thursdays Berlin's state museums waive admission for the last four opening hours of the day. Most museums are open until 6pm, a few until 10pm.

Fridays Join the locals as the city takes all night to unwind from the working week – until dawn in many bars and clubs (see p.223).

Saturdays Get tickets to watch Hertha BSC – the city's best football team – play in the gloriously revamped 1936 Olympic Stadium (see p.250).

Sundays Hit a café for the tremendous buffet brunches that have become so popular in Berlin (see p.207).

Nowhere in the city is more than a stone's throw from a bar, be it a corner *Kneipe* or a slick upscale café – indeed, the variety of bars and restaurants is one of the city's great strengths. Its legendary, pretty much nonstop, **nightlife** is another: Berlin really is a 24-hour city, and you'll never be short of something to do. But beware, the **pace of change** in Berlin, particularly in the eastern part of the city, is such that new cafés and restaurants open (and close) daily and traffic is frequently re-routed around building sites; one of the upsides, however, is that the city's state museums are undergoing radical revamping.

What to see

B erlin is a difficult place to get a handle on, with several main drags and no clear centre. Most visitors begin their exploration in the central Mitte district on the city's premier boulevard **Unter den Linden**, starting at the most famous landmark, the **Brandenburg Gate**, then moving over to the adjacent seat of Germany's parliament, the **Reichstag**. Unter den Linden's most important intersection is with **Friedrichstrasse**, which cuts north–south. At its eastern end Unter den Linden is lined by stately Neoclassical buildings and terminates on the shores of **Museum Island**, home to eastern Berlin's leading museums, but its natural extension on the other side of the island is **Karl-Liebknecht-Strasse**, which leads to a distinctively GDR-era part of the city around **Alexanderplatz**, the eastern city's main commercial and transport hub. Northwest from here, the **Spandauer Vorstadt** was once the heart of the city's Jewish community, and has some fascinating reminders of those days, though today it's best known for the bars and nightlife centred around Oranienburger Strasse.

◀ Helmut Newton Museum

Back at the Brandenburg Gate, a walk south along the fringes of the gigantic **Tiergarten** park takes you to the swish modern **Potsdamer Platz**. Huddled beside Potsdamer Platz is the **Kulturforum**, an

agglomeration of cultural institutions that includes several high-profile art museums. Also fringing the park are Berlin's **diplomatic** and **government** quarters, where you'll find some of the city's most innovative architecture, including the formidable **Hauptbahnhof**. The western fringes of the Tiergarten park are given over to a zoo, which is also the name of the main transport hub at this end of town. This is the gateway to City West, West Berlin's old centre that spreads across the sub-districts of **Charlottenburg**, **Wilmersdorf** and **Schöneberg**. Shopping boulevards radiate out from the church and include the upmarket **Kurfürstendamm**, while northwestern **Charlottenburg** houses the museums and gardens around the baroque **Schloss Charlottenburg**, the impressive 1930s **Olympic Stadium** and **Plötzensee Prison** where the Nazis executed opponents to their regime.

Off-beat Berlin

Berlin's a city in which being quirky counts for a lot. With our offbeat suggestions below you can be as funky as the best of them:

- Sip a cocktail in a beach bar on the River Spree in a *Strandkorb* (beach basket), with sand between your toes (see p.250).
- Learn the basics of graffiti art with Alternative Berlin (see p.28), then find your own bit of wall and do some practising.
- Swim or sweat in the pools and saunas of the converted barges of the Badeschiff, which bob on the inky River Spree: or arrive first thing for an outdoor yoga session (see p.250).
- Career around the Berlin streets in a rented go-kart to see the sights from a new perspective (see p.29).
- Peruse the fleamarkets for a taster of Berlin's history: rummage around for GDR memorabilia, vintage clothes, rare books and old Eastern coins. Trödelmarkt am Arkonaplatz (see p.247) is one of the best.

▼ Riverside bar

Schöneberg and **Kreuzberg** are the two residential districts immediately south of the centre and are home to the most vibrant nightlife in the western half of the city. The former is the smarter of the two and popular as a gay area, while Kreuzberg is grungier. Beyond Kreuzberg's eastern fringes, and back in what used to be East Berlin, **Friedrichshain** and **Prenzlauer Berg** flank the eastern side of the city centre. Friedrichshain offers some unusual architectural leftovers from the 1950s, while the cobbled streets of Prenzlauer Berg are one of the few places in which the atmosphere of prewar Berlin has been preserved, so despite feverish construction in many parts, it's still possible to find side streets that appear unchanged for a century and spot facades

▶ Siegessäule

scarred by wartime bullets. To the north Prenzlauer Berg flows fairly seamlessly into the attractive if sleepy district of **Pankow**.

Surrounding these three districts are the city's **eastern suburbs**, typified by a sprawl of prewar tenements punctuated by high-rise developments and heavy industry in districts such as **Lichtenberg** and **Marzahn-Hellersdorf**, while the area around **Köpenick** at the city's south-eastern edge, with its lakes and woodland dotted with small suburban towns and villages, offers so genuine a break from the city that it's easy to forget that this area still belongs to Berlin.

Though generally overlooked by visitors, the **western suburbs** encompass some of Berlin's most attractive areas. Much of the area comprises woodland (the Grunewald) and lakes (the Havel), a reminder that about a third of the western part of Berlin is either forest or park. It's also where you'll find the **Dahlem museum complex**, displaying everything from German folk art to Polynesian huts, and the medieval town of **Spandau**.

Completely surrounding Berlin is the rather sleepy and provincial state of Brandenburg, which offers some worthwhile **day-trips**, including **Potsdam**, location of Frederick the

▲ Bode flea market

Great's palace and gardens of **Sanssouci**; another major tourist draw is the former concentration camp of **Sachsenhausen**, just to the north of the city in Oranienburg.

When to go

Lying in the heart of Europe, Berlin's climate is continental: winters are bitingly cold, summers hot. April is the soonest you should go if you're after decent weather: any earlier and you'll need to don winter clothing, earmuffs and a decent pair of waterproof shoes; this said, the city (especially the eastern part) does have a particular poignancy when it snows. The best time to visit is in May; June and July can be wearingly hot, though the famed Berlin air (*Berliner Luft* – there's a song about its vitality) keeps things bearable.

Climatic conditions

	Jan	Feb	Mar	Apr	May	Jun	Jul	Aug	Sep	Oct	Nov	Dec
Temperature												
Max/Min (°C)	9/-12	11/-12	17/-7	22/-2	28/2	30/6	32/9	31/8	28/4	21/-1	13/-4	10/-9
Max/Min (°F)	48/10	52/10	63/19	72/28	82/36	86/43	90/48	88/46	82/39	70/30	55/25	50/16
Rainfall												
mm	43	38	38	43	56	71	53	66	46	36	51	56
Sunshine hours	2	3	5	6	8	8	8	7	6	4	2	1

20

things not to miss

It's not possible to see everything that Berlin has to offer on a short trip – and we don't suggest you try. What follows is a subjective selection of the city's highlights, ranging from vibrant nightlife to local cuisine and outstanding architecture, all arranged in colour-coded categories to help you find the very best things to see, do and experience. All entries have a page reference to take you straight to the guide, where you can find out more.

01 **East Side Gallery** Page **147** • The Berlin Wall was always famous for its graffiti, and now, on the longest remaining stretch, murals record its demise.

02 **The Reichstag** Page **48** • Perhaps Germany's most famous landmark, this muscular Neoclassical building now has a magnificent glass cupola you can walk round for free.

03 **Currywurst** Page **208** • Berlin snack bars serve every type of German sausage, but be sure to try *Currywurst*, their speciality.

04 **Berlin Wall Memorial** Page **95** • See the Wall as it once was in the only remaining completely preserved section.

05 **Berliner Weisse** Page **214**
• Few would argue this brew is one of the world's best, but since you order it in either green or red it must be one of the most unusual.

06 **Sony Center** Page **100** •
Corporate architecture let loose along the former death strip of the Berlin Wall with spectacular results.

07 **Sachsenhausen** Page **190**
• The former concentration camp for both the Nazis and Soviets makes for a grim but rewarding day-trip from the city.

08 **Sanssouci** Page **182** • An easy day out to Potsdam brings you to a series of fine palaces.

09 **Sunday brunch** Page **207** • As hedonistic as the nightlife the night before, Sunday brunch buffets are Berlin's best hangover cure.

11 **Tacheles** Page **91** • A taste of Berlin artists' squatter culture is offered in this multistorey countercultural workshop.

10 **Jüdisches Museum** Page **133** • Visitors throng here just to see the Libeskind-designed building, but the excellent museum is worthy of its home.

12 **Brandenburg Gate** Page **44** • Portal to Berlin's most impressive street and witness to several historical episodes: Napoleon stole the quadriga; the Soviets placed the gate within the Berlin Wall and then the world watched as the Wall came down around it.

13 **KaDeWe** Page **245** • A gigantic department store that's all class and has an excellent food court.

14 **Bars and clubs** Page **223** • You can party all night every night in Berlin's bewildering array of bars and clubs.

15 **Tiergarten** Page **97** • The city's green lung is full of attractive lakes and wooded nooks.

17 **Hackeschen Höfe** Page **81** • A series of elegant early-twentieth-century courtyards with stylish cafés and boutiques.

16 **Fernsehturm** Page **72** • Love or loathe its concrete curves, this Eastern-bloc relic has the best views over the city.

Basics

Basics

Getting there

The quickest and generally cheapest way of reaching Berlin from the United Kingdom and Ireland is by air, a journey of around ninety minutes. It is, however, possible to travel by train or by car via a ferry. Direct flights link Berlin to New York, which can also prove a useful route for visitors from Australia and New Zealand, though changing flights at a major European hub such as London, Amsterdam or Frankfurt – the only option for South African travellers – will probably be less expensive.

Airfares also vary considerably according to the **season**, with the highest being around June to August; fares drop during the "shoulder" seasons – September to October and April and May – and you'll get the best prices during the low season, November to March (excluding Christmas and New Year when prices are hiked up and seats are at a premium). Flying at **weekends** will also usually raise the price of a return fare.

Flights from the UK and Ireland

Direct **scheduled flights** to Berlin are available **from London** airports with Air Berlin, BMI, British Airways, easyJet, Germanwings, Lufthansa and Ryanair. Other UK airports with direct flights to Berlin include **Bristol**, **Glasgow** and **Liverpool** with easyJet; **Edinburgh** and **Manchester** with Germanwings; and Edinburgh and **East Midlands** with Ryanair. In Ireland both Ryanair and Aer Lingus offer direct flights **from Dublin**.

The published return fare of the national airlines can cost as much as £300, but in reality booking a week or so in advance and via online booking systems can easily halve this amount. Prices with the budget airlines – Air Berlin, easyJet and Ryanair – can start as low as £50 for a return fare, but you'll often need to book at least a month ahead to secure this.

Flights from the US and Canada

Continental offers direct daily flights to Berlin **from New York**. But if you are beginning your journey from elsewhere in the US, you may well find a cheaper and better connection from Washington, Boston, Chicago, Miami, Los Angeles and Seattle via a major European hub. Canadians are unlikely to make major savings by flying to the US first.

The lowest discounted **scheduled fares** you're likely to get in low/high season flying midweek to Berlin are US$450/1100 from New York, Boston or Washington; US$500/1500 from Chicago; US$800/1700 from Los Angeles or Seattle; US$900/1700 from San Francisco. Canadians have fewer direct-flight options than Americans. The widest selections are out of Toronto and Montreal, with low/high season fares to Berlin from around CDN$900/$1500; from Vancouver expect to pay from CDN$1300/1800.

Flights from Australia, New Zealand and South Africa

There are **no direct flights** to Berlin from Australia, New Zealand or South Africa; most airlines use Amsterdam, Frankfurt, London or Paris as their European gateway. All involve either a transfer or overnight stop en route in the airline's hub city: flying times from the Antipodes are around 24 hours via Asia and thirty hours via the US; from South Africa the shortest flight times, including transfer are around seventeen hours.

Regular return airfares are seasonally adjusted – low season is from mid-January to the end of February and October to November; high season is mid-May to

Four steps to a better kind of travel

At Rough Guides we are passionately committed to travel. We feel strongly that only through travelling do we truly come to understand the world we live in and the people we share it with – plus tourism has brought a great deal of **benefit** to developing economies around the world over the last few decades. But the extraordinary growth in tourism has also damaged some places irreparably, and of course **climate change** is exacerbated by most forms of transport, especially flying. This means that now more than ever it's important to **travel thoughtfully** and **responsibly**, with respect for the cultures you're visiting – not only to derive the most benefit from your trip but also to preserve the best bits of the planet for everyone to enjoy. At Rough Guides we feel there are four main areas in which you can make a difference:

- Travel with a purpose, not just to tick off experiences. Consider **spending longer** in a place, and getting to know it and its people.
- Give thought to how often you **fly**. Try to avoid short hops by air and more harmful night flights.
- Consider **alternatives to flying**, travelling instead by bus, train, boat and even by bike or on foot where possible.
- Make your trips **"climate neutral"** via a reputable carbon offset scheme. All Rough Guide flights are offset, and every year we donate money to a variety of charities devoted to combating the effects of climate change.

August and December to January; the remainder of the year is shoulder season. Flights to Europe are generally cheaper via Asia than the US, and typical economy fares from Australia in low season start at around Aus$2200, in high season at Aus$2800. Low season scheduled fares from Auckland start at around NZ$2500, rising to NZ$3000 in the high season. From South Africa you'll likely pay between R10,000 and R19,000 depending on the season.

Trains

Travelling to Berlin **by train** will rarely save you any money and takes far longer than flying. By far the **fastest** and most popular train route to Berlin begins with **Eurostar** from London St Pancras to Paris Gare du Nord (2hr), and then change stations to Paris Gare de l'Est for the onward overnight train to Berlin (11hr). Return tickets for the complete journey begin at around £120, depending on your fare flexibility and seating or sleeping arrangements. You can get through-ticketing – including the London Underground journey to St Pancras – from mainline stations in Britain; typical add-on prices are £30 from Edinburgh or Glasgow, £20 from Manchester and £15 from

Birmingham. If you plan to use the rail network to visit other regions of Germany, you might consider buying a **rail pass** via **German Rail**, an InterRail or a Eurail pass; for information on these check with the train contacts opposite.

Buses

Travelling to Berlin by **bus** won't bring any major savings over the cheapest air fares, and the journey will be long and uncomfortable, interrupted every three to four hours by stops at motorway service stations. The one advantage is that you can buy an open return at no extra cost.

Services are run by **Eurolines** from Victoria Coach Station in London. There are two buses daily to Berlin; the journey takes around 19 hours and costs £94 return. Starting your journey outside London can add considerably to the time, but little to the cost – the complete journey time from Edinburgh is 37 hours, but tickets start from £111. There's about a twenty percent discount on these rates for those under 26 and if you are travelling elsewhere in Europe you might consider buying a **Europass** or a **Busabout** bus pass; for information see the bus contacts opposite.

Airlines, agents and operators

Airlines

Aer Lingus ⓦ www.aerlingus.com.
Air Berlin ⓦ www.airberlin.com.
Air Canada ⓦ www.aircanada.com.
Air France ⓦ www.airfrance.com.
Air New Zealand ⓦ www.airnz.co.nz.
bmi ⓦ www.flybmi.com.
British Airways ⓦ www.ba.com.
Cathay Pacific ⓦ www.cathaypacific.com.
Continental Airlines ⓦ www.continental.com.
Delta ⓦ www.delta.com.
easyJet ⓦ www.easyjet.com.
Germanwings ⓦ www.germanwings.com.
KLM (Royal Dutch Airlines) ⓦ www.klm.com.
LOT (Polish Airlines) ⓦ www.lot.com.
Lufthansa ⓦ www.lufthansa.com.
Northwest ⓦ www.nwa.com.
Qantas Airways ⓦ www.qantas.com.
Ryanair ⓦ www.ryanair.com.
SAS (Scandinavian Airlines) ⓦ www.flysas.com.
South African Airways ⓦ www.flysaa.com.
Swiss ⓦ www.swiss.com.
United Airlines ⓦ www.united.com.

Agents and operators

British Airways Holidays UK ☎ 0844/493 0787, ⓦ www.britishairways.com. Packages and independent itineraries for both long trips and short city-breaks.
DER Tours UK ☎ 0207/290 1104, ⓦ www .dertravel.co.uk. The German national travel agency, which offers city breaks.
Harvey World Travel New Zealand ☎ 0800/758 787, ⓦ www.holidayshoppe.co.nz. Great deals on flights, hotels and holidays.
Martin Randall Travel UK ☎ 0208/742 3355, ⓦ www.martinrandall.com. Small-group cultural tours, usually accompanied by lecturers: an eight-day Berlin, Potsdam, Dresden package costs around £2080.

North South Travel UK ☎ 01245/608 291, ⓦ www.northsouthtravel.co.uk. Friendly, competitive travel agency, offering discounted fares worldwide. Profits are used to support projects in the developing world, especially the promotion of sustainable tourism.
STA Travel UK ☎ 0871/230 0040, US ☎ 1-800/781-4040, Australia ☎ 134 782, New Zealand ☎ 0800/474 400, South Africa ☎ 0861/781 781; ⓦ www.statravel.co.uk. Worldwide specialists in independent travel; also student IDs, travel insurance, car rental, rail and bus passes, and more. Good discounts for students and under-26s.
Trailfinders UK ☎ 0845/058 5858, Ireland ☎ 01/677 7888, Australia ☎ 1300/780 212; ⓦ www.trailfinders.com. One of the best-informed and most efficient agents for independent travellers.
travel.com.au Australia ☎ 1300/130 483, ⓦ www.travel.com.au. Excellent all-round travel agent.
Travel CUTS Canada ☎ 1-866/246-9762, US ☎ 1-800/592-2887, ⓦ www.travelcuts.com. Canadian youth and student travel firm.
USIT Ireland ☎ 01/602 1906, Northern Ireland ☎ 028/9032 7111; ⓦ www.usit.ie. Ireland's main student and youth travel specialists.

Rail contacts

Deutsche Bahn UK ☎ 0871/880 8066, ⓦ www.bahn.com.
Eurostar UK ☎ 0843/218 6186, ⓦ www.eurostar .com.
Rail Europe UK ☎ 0844/848 4064, US ☎ 1-888/382-7245, Canada ☎ 1-800/361-7245, Australia ☎ 03/9642 8644, New Zealand ☎ 0937/7 5415; ⓦ www.raileurope.co.uk.

Bus contacts

Busabout UK ☎ 0845/026 7514, ⓦ www .busabout.com.
Eurolines UK ☎ 0871/781 8181, ⓦ www .eurolines.com.

Arrival

All points of arrival lie within easy reach of the city centre via inexpensive and efficient public transport; the furthest of the city's two airports is only 25 minutes by train from Berlin's city-centre Hauptbahnhof where trains from all over Europe converge. Some trains also stop at other major stations such as Bahnhof Zoo, Alexanderplatz and the Ostbahnhof, which may be more convenient for your destination. Public transport tickets are valid for the entire system of trams, buses and suburban and underground trains. If you plan to use public transport throughout your stay, then get a ticket that covers several days (see p.26) – all these can be validated to cover your journey from the airport and are available from ticket machines at all points of arrival. A handful of upmarket hotels offer courtesy shuttles.

By air

Until the completion of Berlin Brandenburg International (BBI) airport in 2012, Berlin's air traffic (ⓦwww.berlin-airport.de) will be shared between the **Schönefeld** airport, which lies on an adjacent site, and **Tegel** airport, 7km northwest of the city centre.

Tegel

Many scheduled and charter flights still arrive at the small and manageable **Tegel (TXL)** airport 7km northwest of the centre, where you'll find plenty of shops, currency exchange facilities, left luggage and several car rental companies on the land-side. Once past security it's another story, with only the most rudimentary services.

From Tegel, several buses head into different parts of the city. The TXL JetExpressBus **bus** (daily 5am–11.30pm every 15–20min) heads to Hauptbahnhof (25min) and Alexanderplatz (35min). **Bus X9** (Mon–Fri 4.50am–11pm every 5–10min; Sat & Sun 5.20am–12.30am every 10min) goes to Bahnhof Zoo (20min). **Bus #109** heads to S-Bahn station Charlottenburg and **#128** to U-Bahn station Osloer Strasse. If you intend to buy a Welcome Card, City Tour Card or simply a week ticket (see p.26), do this from the ticket machine just outside the terminal, the bus driver can only sell single and day tickets. **Taxis** cover the distance in half the time (depending on the traffic) and cost about €18.

Schönefeld and Berlin Brandenburg International

Schönefeld lies 20km southeast of the city centre and mostly serves budget airlines and holiday charters, and beside it is its replacement, **Berlin Brandenburg International** which will eventually consume it. The train station is a five-minute walk from the terminal, from where the Airport Express **train** takes 30 minutes to reach the Hauptbahnhof, and the **S-Bahn** about 40 minutes (4.30am–11pm), but may be more convenient since you can get off the service at more stops; the same ticket is valid on either service – see p.26. Long queues at the ticket machines in the underground passageway can usually be avoided by buying tickets from identical machines on the platform. A **taxi** into the town centre from Schönefeld/BBI costs around €35.

By train

Trains from European destinations generally head straight to the swanky Hauptbahnhof, which has late-opening shops and all the facilities you would expect from a major train station. The station is also a stop on the major S-Bahn line, and on the U-Bahn network. Your train ticket may well include use of zones A and B of the city's public transport system (see p.26) to finish your journey: check with the conductor or ticket office.

B

BASICS

23

By bus

Most international **buses** and those from other German cities stop at the **Zentraler Omnibusbahnhof** or **ZOB** (central bus station), Masurenallee, Charlottenburg, west of the centre, near the Funkturm; many buses, including the #M49 service to the city centre or U-Bahn line #2 from Kaiserdamm station, link it to the Ku'damm area, a journey of about fifteen minutes. The bus station has an information booth, a taxi stand and a couple of snack places.

By car

Getting into Berlin **by car** is relatively easy as Germany's famed autobahns (*Autobahnen*) pass reasonably close to the city centre. It may, however, be a long trip – the autobahns are very congested and delays are the norm. From the west you're most likely to approach on autobahn A2, which will turn into A10 (the ring-road around Berlin), from which you turn off onto A115, a highway that eases you onto Kaiserdamm and the west side of the city, and just fifteen minutes from Zoo station. From the south you'll approach on autobahn A9, but the route once you hit the A10 is the same. Drivers coming from the Hamburg area will approach from the north on M24, which also turns into A10, but this time you take the A111 into the Charlottenburg district of Berlin.

City transport

Berlin's public transport network is well integrated, efficient and inexpensive. The cornerstone of the system is the web of fast suburban (S-Bahn) and underground (U-Bahn) trains, which are supplemented on the streets by buses and trams. All are run by the BVG, whose network looks complicated at first glance but quickly becomes easy to navigate. Once onboard, illuminated signs and announcements ensure it's easy to find the right stop. Tickets are available from machines at stations, on trams or from bus drivers – but in all cases be sure to validate them by punching them in a red or yellow machine when you travel; failure to do so will result with fines at spot checks.

Public transport

The mainstay of the transport system is the **U-Bahn**, a subway that's clean, punctual and rarely crowded. Running both under and over ground, it covers much of the centre and stretches into the suburbs: trains run from 4am to around 12.30am, and all night on Friday and Saturday. Once they have closed down for the night their routes are usually covered by night buses – denoted by a number with the prefix "N". The **S-Bahn** system is a separate network of suburban trains, which runs largely overground, and is better for covering long distances fast and effectively and complements the U-Bahn in the city centre.

It runs until 1.30am on weeknights and all night on Friday and Saturday.

You never seem to have to wait long for a **bus** in the city and the network covers most gaps in the U-Bahn system, with buses converging on Zoo Station and Alexanderplatz. Buses #100 and #200, between the two, are particularly good for sightseeing purposes. **Night buses** mostly run every half hour and routes often differ from daytime ones; maps of the night bus routes can be picked up at most U-Bahn ticket booths.

Berlin's quiet and comfortable **trams** are found for the most part in the eastern section of the city, where the network has survived from prewar days. Some buses and

trams are termed **MetroBus** or **MetroTram** and their numbers are preceded by the letter M: these are services that form the core of this network running particularly frequently and all night.

For **more information** about Berlin's public transport system, call or check their website (☎194 49, ⓦwww.bvg.de) which has complete listings and timetables for the U- and S-Bahn systems, plus bus, tram and ferry routes. Most U-Bahn stations also provide simple free maps of the U- and S-Bahn, trams and some bus services at kiosks on the platform. There are also transport information offices at Zoo Station, the Hauptbahnhof, Friedrichstrasse and Alexanderplatz, where you can also buy a complete and highly detailed guide to services, and various souvenirs of the network.

Tickets

All BVG services are served by the same **tickets**, valid for transfers between different modes of transport as well as all other public transport services within the VBB system, which includes buses and trams in Potsdam, Oranienburg and even Regional Express trains (marked RE operating within the city limits). **Tickets** can be bought from the machines on U- and S-Bahn station platforms. These take €5, €10 and €20 notes and all but the smallest coins, give change and have a basic explanation of the ticketing system in English. Though it's tempting to ride without a ticket, be warned that plain-clothes inspectors frequently cruise the lines, meting out on-the-spot **fines** of €40 for those without a valid ticket or pass. You can also buy tickets, including day tickets, directly from the driver on a bus (change given); if you have a ticket already show it to the driver as you board.

The transport network is divided into three **zones** – A, B and C. Basic **single tickets** (**Einzeltickets**) cost €2.10 and allow travel in Zone A and B. Zone C covers the outskirts of town and includes Potsdam, Oranienburg and Schönefeld/BBI airport, and a ticket for zones A, B & C costs €2.80. All tickets are valid for two

hours, enabling you to split your journey as often as you like, but can't be used for a return journey. A **Kurzstrecke**, or **short-trip ticket**, costs €1.30 and allows you to travel up to three train or six bus stops (no return journeys or transfers).

Buying a **day ticket** (**Tageskarte**), valid until 3am the next morning, for €6.50 for the entire network, may work out cheaper, as might the excellent-value **seven-day ticket** (**Sieben-Tage-Karte**), which costs €26.20 for zones A and B and €32.30 for zones A, B and C. A small **group ticket** (**Kleingruppenkarte**) is available for a whole day's travel for up to five people; it costs €15.90 or zones A and B and €16.10 for three zones. Another possibility is the **Welcome Card** (€21.50 for 72 hours), which allows one adult and up to three children 72 hours' unlimited travel, and the **City Tour Card** (ⓦwww.citytourcard.com), which is good for unlimited travel in the AB zone for 48 hours (€15.50) or 72 hours (€20.50). Both cards also give concessionary rates at a host of attractions and discounts at participating tour companies, restaurants and theatres. The main difference between the two are their partners, so check to see which are more appealing. If you're in Berlin for longer than a couple of weeks, you should consider buying a **monthly ticket** (**Monatskarte**); various types are available and explained in full in English via the information buttons on dispensing machines.

By car

Though there's practically no need for a **car** within the city, you might want one to tour outside Berlin. The most important rules to bear in mind when driving in Berlin are simple: you drive on the right; main roads have a yellow diamond indicating who has priority; and if you are driving in built-up areas, traffic coming from the right normally has right of way. This is particularly important to remember in former East Berlin, where **trams** always have the right of way. Unfamiliarity with the traffic system means that unwary visiting drivers are prone to cutting in front of turning trams at junctions – a frightening and potentially lethal error. Also, when trams halt at their designated stops, it's forbidden to overtake until the tram starts moving, to allow passengers time to cross the road and board.

Thanks to a post-unification boom in car ownership and extensive road construction projects, Berlin suffers **traffic snarl-ups** that can compete with the worst any other European city has to offer. Rush-hour jams start at around 5pm and are particularly bad on Friday afternoons: don't be surprised if a journey takes three or four times as long as you'd expect during these periods.

Finding **parking spaces** in central Berlin can be tricky and you'll almost certainly have to pay. Parking meters, identifiable by their tall grey rectangular solar-power umbrellas, generally charge €1–3 per 30min. You're supposed to move after the hour, and stiff fines are handed out to those without tickets; even if you drive a car with foreign plates you can expect it to be towed away. Parking garages generally charge around €2 per hour.

Central Berlin has been designated an Umweltzone – a green zone announced by a sign with the word printed on it – in which all cars must display an emission badge (Umwelt Plakette; ⓦwww.umwelt-plakette .de). These cost around €10 and can be bought from garages that offer TÜV auto-testing (the German equivalent of an MOT). The badges work on the traffic-light system, and currently all vehicles with amber and red badges are banned in central Berlin. In practice this means if you have a pre-'93 petrol car, a pre-'97 diesel vehicle or a diesel van, you will probably have to have an expensive catalytic converter fitted or leave

your vehicle on the fringes of the central city. Fines for having the wrong badge or none at all are currently €40.

Car rental

All the major **car rental** agencies are represented in Berlin, although the best deals are often found through local operators. You can find local car rental firms in the Yellow Pages under "*Autovermietung*"; by phoning around you should be able to get something for under €30 a day, though

Addresses

The street name is always written before the number and all Berlin addresses are suffixed by a five-figure postcode. Street numbers don't always run odd–even on opposite sides of the street – often they go up one side and down the other. Strasse (street) is commonly abbreviated to Str., and often joined on to the end of the previous word. Other terms include Weg (path), Ufer (river bank), Platz (square) and Allee (avenue). Berlin apartment blocks are often built around courtyards with several entrances and staircases: the Vorderhaus, abbreviated as VH in addresses, is as the name suggests, the front building; the Gartenhaus (garden house) and the Hinterhof (HH; back house) are at the rear of the building. EG means the ground floor, 1 OG means the first floor, etc. Dachwohnung means the "flat under the roof" – in other words, the attic.

watch out for hidden extras such as limited mileage. Most rental places do good-value Friday afternoon to Monday morning deals, and most expect to see a credit card and passport.

Car rental agencies

Alamo ⓦ www.alamo.com.
Avis ⓦ www.avis.com.
Budget ⓦ www.budget.com.
Enterprise ⓦ www.enterprise.com.
Europcar ⓦ www.europcar.com.
Hertz ⓦ www.hertz.com.
National ⓦ www.nationalcar.com.
Robben & Wientjes Prinzenstrasse 90–91, Kreuzberg ⓣ 030/61 67 70 (U-Bahn Moritzplatz)

and Prenzlauer Allee 96 ⓣ 030/42 10 36 (U-Bahn Prenzlauer Allee), ⓦ www.robben-wientjes.de. *A good local firm with cars from €15 per day.*
SIXT ⓦ www.sixt.com.
Thrifty ⓦ www.thrifty.com.

Taxis and rickshaws

Berlin's cream-coloured **taxis** are plentiful and always metered: for the first 7km it's €3.10 plus €1.70 per kilometre, after which it's €1.20 per kilometre. Fares rise slightly between 11pm and 6am and all day Sunday. Taxis cruise the city day and night and congregate at useful locations. Short trips, known as *Kurzstrecke*, can be paid on a flat rate of €3.50 for up to two kilometres

Sightseeing tours

Walking and cycling tours

Fierce competition between several English-language **walking tour** companies means that the quality of all of them is very high. All offer general four-hour city tours for around €12 plus more specialized ones such as Third Reich sites; Cold War Berlin; Jewish life; Potsdam; and Sachsenhausen. Companies include Original Berlin Walks (ⓣ 030/301 91 94, ⓦ www.berlinwalks.com); Insider Tours (ⓣ 030/692 31 49, ⓦ www.insiderberlintours.com); and New Berlin Tours (ⓣ 030/510 50 03 01, ⓦ www .newberlintours.com), whose city-centre one is technically free, though generous tips are expected. One company offering something a bit different is Alternative Berlin (ⓣ 0162/81 98 264, ⓦ www.alternativeberlin.com), which tours the graffiti art and squats of Berlin's underbelly.

Insider and New Berlin also run **cycling tours**, as does specialist Fat Tire Bike Tours (ⓣ 030/24 04 79 91, ⓦ www.fattirebiketours.com/berlin), which charges €20 for a guided four-hour pedal around central Berlin astride a beach cruiser bike. If all that sounds too much like hard work, consider hiring a **rickshaw** and driver with Velotaxi tours (ⓣ 030/44 31 94 28) whose tours start at €15.

Bus tours

Bus tours abound, though you may find that buying a day ticket and hopping on and off the #100 and #200 services with a guidebook is more flexible and cheaper. Most depart from the Kurfürstendamm between Breitscheidplatz and Knesebeckstrasse, making the rounds several times every day, though schedules are curtailed in the winter. Companies include Severin + Kühn (ⓣ 030/880 41 90, ⓦ www .berlinerstadtrundfahrten.de) and Tempelhofer Reisen (ⓣ 030/752 30 60, ⓦ www .tempelhofer.de). A basic two-hour tour costs about €19.

Boat tours

Boats cruise Berlin's numerous city-centre canals and suburban lakes regularly throughout the summer, and boat companies offer a variety of short jaunts, including ones through the centre of town and day-trips to the Wannsee or Potsdam. In most cases you can just turn up at quayside stops and buy a ticket on the spot; all city centre companies have central stops around the Spree Island. Among them is Reederei Riedel (March to mid-Dec; ⓣ 030/639 46 46, ⓦ www.reederei-riedel.de), which runs several day-trips on the River Spree, taking in the Reichstag and the Landwehrkanal. Its *Stadtkernfahrt* (€8.50) lasts around an hour, or you can join the three-hour *Brückenfahrt* (€16), which runs a large loop around all of central Berlin, at or five minutes, though this only works when you hail a moving cab, and you must request it on getting into the taxi. Taxi firms include: **City Funk** (☏030/21 02 02), **Funk Taxi Berlin** (☏030/26 10 26) and **Spree Funk** (☏030/44 33 22).

Finally, if you're not in a hurry and want to go only a short distance, you might consider hailing a **cycle rickshaw**. Between April and October they are easy to find at the Brandenburg Gate and other key points. They cost €6 for the first kilometre, then €2.50 for each subsequent kilometre. The drivers double as guides and are usually well informed and chatty, and also offer tours – see box below.

Cycling

An extensive network of bike paths makes **cycling** around the city quick and convenient. You can also take your bike on the U- and S-Bahn; useful to explore the countryside and lakes of the Grunewald. To take your bike on a train you'll need to buy a **Fahrrad ticket** for the underground system (available as a short journey, single journey, day ticket or monthly ticket). One good investment if you're going to explore the city under your own steam is the cycle route map published by the **German bicycle club** ADFC, available from their shop at Brunnenstrasse 28 (Mon–Fri noon–8pm, Sat 10am–4pm; ☏030/448 47 24; U-Bahn

a number of points around the city. The same company also runs day-trips (€18) out to the Pfaueninsel and the Wannsee in the west of the city, to the Müggelsee in the east, and on other lakes surrounding Berlin. Other companies with similar city-centre offerings include Reederei Winker (☏030/349 95 95, ⓦwww.reederei-winkler.de); the cheap and cheerful Berlin Wassertaxi (☏030/65 88 02 03, ⓦwww.berliner-wassertaxi .de); and Stern und Kreis Schiffahrt (☏030/536 36 00, ⓦwww.sternundkreis.de). The latter also runs a number of tours around the lake systems in the Grunewald, including trips to Potsdam, and tours of the waterways around Köpenick starting from Treptower Park, as do several smaller companies whose details can be found at the Reederverband der Berliner Personenschiffahrt (ⓦwww.reederverband-berlin.de).

Unusual tours

If all of these options seem too conventional, try one of Berlin's growing number of wacky tours. One unique to Berlin is exploring the city in a **Trabant**, the cute 26-horse-power fibreglass car of the GDR. This is offered by Trabi Safari (☏030/27 59 22 73, ⓦwww.trabi-safari.de) which shows you how to operate the machine before you set off on a self-driven ninety-minute tour in their fleet of jolly open-top cars. Trips are available daily day and night, start at €79 per person if you're in a group of four, or €89 per person for just a driver and single passenger, and include an excellent commentary via dashboard speakers. A less historically grounded experience is offered by Kart 4 You (☏0800/750 75 10, ⓦwww.kart4u.de) who organize tours of the city by **go-kart** – though it's probably more fun to just take them off by yourself to jet around Berlin's streets at ground-level (three hours cost €49–59). Other unusual vehicles – among them quads and scooters – can be rented via ⓦwww.scooter-rent.de from €6 per hour.

Finally, try taking to the skies in a tethered **hot-air balloon** with Hi-Flyer, Wilhelmstrasse/Zimmerstrasse (April–Oct daily 10am–10pm; Nov–March daily 11am–6pm; ☏030/226 67 88 11), who'll take you up to 150m at a cost of €19 for fifteen minutes. Or trump that with a **flight** over Berlin and Potsdam in a "raisin-bomber", the **DC-3** that supplied the city during its 1948 Blockade (see p.141). Rosinenbomber Sightseeing, Schönefeld Airport (☏030/53 21 53 21) organize these 35-minute trips for €169, including a martini and a short talk about the history and trip at the start (you will hear very little later over the amazing racket of a prop driven DC-3). Both companies are on the Air Service Berlin website (ⓦwww.air-service-berlin.de), where you can also find helicopter and seaplane flights as well as skydives over the capital.

Rosenthaler Platz) as well as most city bookshops. The ADFC can also provide free listings of bike rental and bike shops, with current rates and contact details. For a list of companies offering **bike tours** in and around the city, see box, p.28.

One good company for bike rental is **Fahrradstation** whose six branches in central Berlin include one at Auguststrasse 29a (Mon–Fri 10am–7pm, Sat 10am–3pm; ☎030/22 50 80 70; U-Bahn Weinmeister-strasse), and at Bergmannstrasse 9, Kreuzberg (Mon–Fri 10am–7pm, Sat 10am–4pm; ☎030/215 15 66; U-Bahn Gneisenaustrasse). Rates are €15 per day or €50 per week and can be booked online at ⓦ www.fahrradstation.com.

A convenient innovation introduced and run by railway company Deutsche Bahn (DB)

is **CallBikes**, rental bikes scattered around zone A of the city, found on street corners and at major points like the Brandenburg Gate and Potsdamer Platz. These silver-and-red, full-suspension bicycles can be rented at any time of day for €0.08 per minute (up to €9 for 24hr and €36 for a week), with no deposit or minimum charge. To use one you first need to register a credit card (☎0700/05 22 55 22, ⓦ www.callabike -interaktiv.de). Registering your mobile will mean it will automatically debit your account when you call. Once you've registered, it's just a matter of calling the individual number on the side of a bike and receiving an electronic code to open the lock. To drop it off you can leave it on any street corner then ring up for a code to lock the bike and leave its location as a recorded message.

The media

English is the second language in Berlin, so you won't have a problem finding a good range of English-language newspapers and magazines and – with a little searching – programmes on the TV and radio.

Newspapers

The best place to look for **British and US newspapers** is at the newsagents in the main train stations: Bahnhof Zoo, Hauptbahn-nhof, Alexanderplatz, Friedrichstrasse and the Ostbahnhof.

Berlin has four **local newspapers**. Two of these are from the presses of the right-wing Springer Verlag: the *Berliner Morgenpost* is a staid, conservative publication, and *BZ* is a trashy tabloid. *Berliner Kurier* is another tabloid, less trashy, but less exciting. The other main local paper is the *Berliner Zeitung*, originally an East Berlin publication, which covers national and international news as well as local stories.

Of the **national** dailies, the two best sellers are also from the Springer press: *Die Welt* (ⓦ www.welt.de), once a right-wing

heavyweight, has become somewhat more centrist, while the *Bild* is a sensationalist tabloid. At the other end of the political spectrum are the Berlin-based *Tagesspiegel*, a good, liberal read, and the left-of-centre *Tageszeitung*, known as *taz* (ⓦ www.taz.de) – not so hot on solid news, but with good in-depth articles on politics and ecology, and an extensive Berlin listings section on Friday. It has the added advantage of being a relatively easy read for non-native German speakers. The more conservative *Frankfurter Allgemeine* is also widely available in the city, though its main focus is business and it can be a bit dry. Hamburg-based *Die Zeit* appears every Thursday and, while left-wing in stance, includes a number of independ-ently written reports. For details of Berlin's **listings magazines**, see p.39.

Television

Germany has **two national public TV channels** – ARD and ZDF – which somewhat approximate BBC channels or a down-market PBS; Berlin also has regional public channel RBB. Otherwise major commercial channels dominate, foremost among them Sat, RTL and VOX. All channels seem to exist on a forced diet of US reruns clumsily dubbed into German. With cable TV, available in larger hotels, you'll be able to pick up the locally available **cable channels** (over twenty to choose from, including MTV and BBC World).

Radio

Berlin's radio output is reasonable, and you can find good things on the dial, despite a multitude of stations churning out light music and soft rock, and little else. The only **English-speaking radio** stations are the BBC World Service (90.2FM) and NPR Berlin (104.1FM) with their non-commercial news, talk, and entertainment programmes. For **talk** radio in German try sophisticated Radio Eins (95.8FM). The best **local music** stations, depending on your taste, are Fritz Radio (102.6FM), with some decent dance and hip-hop, and Star FM (87.9FM), with its diet of American rock. For indie music try Motor FM (100.6FM). Best of the classical music stations is Klassik Radio (101.3FM), while Jazz Radio (101.9FM) offers jazz and blues.

Festivals

Berlin's festivals are, in the main, cultural affairs, with music, art and the theatre particularly well catered for. Other events tend to be rather staid; worth looking out for, however, are the *Volksfeste* – small, local street festivals you often come across by chance from July to September. Most city districts, in the east especially, have their own *Volksfeste* (⊛ www.schaustellerverband-berlin.de), which are usually an excuse for open-air music, beer-swilling and Wurst-gnawing.

The best place to find out what's on is the tourist offices (p.39): all mainstream events are well publicized in their leaflets and in brochures like *Berlin Programm*. For a list of public holidays see p.38.

January

Grüne Woche ⊛ www.gruenewoche.de. Late Jan. Berlin's annual agricultural show, held in the Messegelände, with food goodies to sample from all over the world.
Sechstagerennen ⊛ www.sechstagerennen -berlin.de. Late Jan. A Berlin tradition since the 1920s this six-day non-stop cycle race takes place in the Velodrome, Paul-Heyse-Strasse.
Lange Nacht der Museen ⊛ www.lange-nacht -der-museen.de. The last Sat of Jan. Many of Berlin's museums extend their hours – most until midnight – with surprisingly sociable results.

February

Berlinale ⊛ www.berlinale.de. The third largest film festival in the world, with around twelve days of old and new movies, arthouse cinema and more mainstream entertainment. Films are usually shown in the original versions with German (and sometimes English) subtitles. The festival is concentrated around the multiplexes on Potsdamer Platz, though the programme is repeated at various cinemas around town; check *Tip, Zitty* or the festival's own free daily magazine for listings. Tickets are available from booths in the Potsdamer Platz Arcade or Europa Center, or at participating theatres on the day of the screening. A limited number of season tickets go on sale a week before opening.

May

Museum Island Festival ⓦ www.museums inselfestival.info. From May until Sept. Various film screenings, theatre productions, dance performances and music concerts make up an extensive bill, the highlights usually a couple of large open-air concerts.
Theatertreffen Berlin ⓦ www.theatertreffen -berlin.de. Large, mainly German-speaking theatre event held in various theatres, which tends towards the experimental.

June

Fete de la Musique ⓦ www.lafetedelamusique .com. June 21. Bands from all over Europe and beyond come to play in bars, clubs and other venues around the city.
Christopher Street Day ⓦ www.csd-berlin.de. Last Sat in June. Parade with lots of floats, music and costumed dancers celebrating gay pride at the end of the week-long Berlin Pride Festival.
German-French Festival ⓦ www.volksfest -berlin.de. Mid-June to mid-July. Mini-fair with food and music and a reconstruction of a different French town each year.
Köpenicker Sommer ⓦ www.schaustellerverband -berlin.de. Second half of June. Held in Köpenick, this features a re-enactment of the robbery of the Rathaus safe in 1906 (see p.165).

July

Classic Open Air ⓦ www.classicopenair.de. Early July. The Gendarmenmarkt makes the perfect setting for this week-long series of very popular outdoor classical concerts in mid-July.
Gauklerfest ⓦ www.gauklerfest.de. Late July to early Aug. Juggling and street performers' festival on Unter den Linden.
German-American Festival ⓦ www.deutsch -amerikanisches-volksfest.de. Lasts three weeks of July to mid-Aug. One of the most popular events of the year. Eat junk food and gamble away your euros on lotteries and other carnival games.

August

Tanz im August ⓦ www.tanzimaugust.de. Mid- to late Aug. Hebbel Theater. A series of dance performances featuring companies and artists from all over the world.
Lange Nacht der Museen ⓦ www.lange-nacht -der-museen.de. Late Aug. Over one hundred of Berlin's museums stay open until at least midnight and put on various special events in a repeat of the January event.

September

Jewish Culture Days ⓦ www.juedische -kulturtage.org. Early Sept. Various venues. Concerts, lectures, readings and films that focus each year on Jewish culture in a particular country or place.
Popkomm ⓦ www.popkomm.de. Three days in early Sept. Germany's largest independent music tradeshow and festival with both renowned and newly discovered acts playing in many city centre clubs.
Feste an der Panke Mid-Sept. *Volksfest* in Pankow that's often among the city's best.
Berlin Marathon ⓦ www.real-berlin-marathon .com. Late-Sept. The race begins on Strasse des 17 Juni and ends nearly 50km later, after passing through Dahlem and along the Ku'damm, back at the Kaiser-Wilhelm Memorial Church; closing date for entries is one month before the marathon.

October

Tag der Deutschen Einheit Oct 3. Day of German unity is celebrated with gusto, beer, sausages and music at the Brandenburg Gate.
Art Forum Berlin ⓦ www.art-forum-berlin.de. Early Oct. An exposition with an international selection of galleries and dealers representing a broad spectrum of contemporary works.

November

JazzFest Berlin ⓦ www.jazzfest-berlin.de. Early Nov. Longstanding jazz festival that's been running since the 1960s and often attracts big names to venues throughout the city.

December

Christmas Street Markets Twee Christmas markets – with roasted almonds, mulled wine and local handicrafts – dot the city with the most significant on Breitscheidplatz and Alexanderplatz, but the prettiest are around the Staatsoper at Unter den Linden, on the Gendarmenmarkt, where evening performances add to the atmosphere, or outside the city in Spandau's old town.
New Year's Eve Run ⓦ www.scc-events.com. Dec 31. Annual 6.3km run organized by the Berlin Marathon authorities, with free entry and prizes for fancy dress.
Silvester Germany's largest open-air New Year's Eve party takes place again along the Strasse des 17 Juni, between the Brandenburg Gate and the Siegessäule, to the sound of fireworks and top-40 hits while nipping sparkling wine from street stalls.

Culture and etiquette

Berliners are traditionally quite a gruff lot who don't suffer fools gladly, though much of this attitude is laced with a sardonic wit known as *Berliner Schnauze* – literally "Berlin snout". Learn to take all this in your stride: it's nothing personal, just an everyday way of dealing with urban living. Another defining attribute for Berliners is their Prussian sense of orderliness and respect for rules and authority. Jaywalkers will more frequently be reprimanded by bystanders – "what if a child saw you?" – than by the police. Thankfully, despite this, Berlin is a very tolerant place.

This tolerance comes in part from the city's appeal to unconventional Germans who relocate from elsewhere in the country and partly from its large immigrant population with their more relaxed attitude. Staggering around in the small hours, drinking in the street, or being openly gay will neither raise an eyebrow nor turn a head. This open-mindedness also extends to tolerating people **smoking** far more widely than elsewhere in Western Europe – though legislation has begun to curb some of this in restaurants and bars.

Travel essentials

Costs

By the standards of most European capitals, prices in Berlin are reasonable and well short of the excesses of Paris and London and with quality to match. Nevertheless, for those heading out to sample Berlin's famous nightspots, visiting the city has the potential to become expensive.

Assuming you intend to eat and drink in moderately priced places, use public transport sparingly and stay at hostels, the **minimum** you could get by on is €25 (around £23/US$34) a day. For this you would get a sandwich (€3), an evening meal (€10), three beers (€7) and one underground ticket (€2), with around €3 left for museums, entertainment, etc. A more realistic figure, if you want to see as much of the city as possible (and party at night), would be at least twice that amount.

Crime and personal safety

Crime in Berlin is modest in comparison with other European cities of equal size. The type you're most likely to encounter is **petty crime** such as pickpocketing or bag-snatching in one of the main shopping precincts. Sensible **precautions** include carrying bags slung across your neck and not over your shoulder; not carrying anything in pockets that are easy to dip into; having copies of your passport, airline ticket and driving licence, and leaving the originals in your hotel safe; and noting down travellers' cheque and credit card numbers – best of all take digital photos of all these items and store them online or email them to yourself.

As far as **personal safety** is concerned, most parts of the city centre are safe enough. Use common sense, but even the

Emergency numbers

The **emergency phone number** for the police is ℡110; for all non-urgent matters – such as reporting a crime after the event or having your car impounded – call the 24-hour hotline ℡030/46 64 46 64: they will pass you on to the relevant district station.

If you are a woman and have been assaulted sexually or otherwise you might also contact the **Rape Crisis Line** operated by Lara (Mon–Fri 9am–6pm; ℡030/216 88 88, ℠www.lara-berlin.de) or the **Women's Crisis Hotline** (Frauenkrisentelefon) (Mon & Thurs 10am–noon, Tues 3–5pm, Wed 10am–noon & 7–9pm, Fri 7–9pm, Sat & Sun 5–7pm; ℡030/615 42 43, ℠www.frauenkrisentelefon.de), which will also try to help in other crisis situations.

rougher neighbourhoods (say, eastern Kreuzberg or Friedrichshain) feel more dangerous than they actually are: the run-down U-Bahn stations at Kottbusser Tor and Görlitzer Bahnhof (both in largely immigrant districts), or S-Bahn stations Warschauer Strasse and Ostkreuz, look alarming when compared to the rest of the system, but wouldn't stand out in many other European cities. The situation in suburbs is a little trickier with immigrant gangs flexing their muscles in the western half of the city and neo-nazi thugs an issue in the east. With caution it's fine, but all the same it's wise to be wary in **suburbs** like **Lichtenberg**, **Marzahn**, **Wedding or Neuköln**, where muggings and casual violence do occur, particularly to those who stand out. Evasive strategies include working out beforehand exactly where you're going so that you don't look lost and vulnerable, avoiding unlit areas, travelling with a friend if possible and not wearing or carrying anything obviously valuable.

If you do have something **stolen** (or simply lost), or suffer an attack you'll need to register the details at the local police station: this is usually straightforward, but inevitably there's bureaucratic bumph to wade through. Make a note of the crime report number – or, better still, ask for a copy of the statement itself – for your travel insurance company.

The two offences you might unwittingly commit concern identity papers and jaywalking. By law you need to carry **proof of your identity** at all times. A driver's licence or ID card is fine, but a passport is best. It's essential that you carry all your documentation when driving – failure to do so may result in an on-the-spot fine. **Jaywalking** is also illegal and you can be fined if caught. Even in the irreverent atmosphere of Berlin, locals stand rigidly to attention until the green signal comes on – even when there isn't a vehicle in sight. Cars are not required to stop at crossings; although walking on one should give you right of way, use your judgement and be careful.

Electricity

The German electricity supply runs at 220-240V, 50Hz AC; sockets generally require a two-pin plug with rounded prongs. Visitors from the UK will need an adaptor, visitors from North America may need a transformer, though most of those supplied with electrical equipment – like cameras, laptops and mobile phones – are designed to accommodate a range of voltages – it should say on it.

Entry requirements

British and other EU nationals can enter Germany on a valid passport or national identity card for an indefinite period. US, Canadian, Australian and New Zealand citizens do not need a visa to enter Germany, and are allowed a stay ninety days within any six-month period. South Africans need to apply for a visa, from the German Embassy in Pretoria (see opposite), which will cost around R260 depending on the exchange rate. Visa requirements vary for nationals of other countries; contact your local German embassy or consulate for information.

In order to **extend a stay** once in the country all visitors should contact the Ausländeramt (Alien Authorities) in the nearest large town: addresses are in the phone books. For more information on this process and finding a job see p.36.

German embassies abroad

UK 23 Belgrave Square, London SW1X 8PZ ☎0207/824 1300; ◍www.london.diplo.de.
Ireland 31 Trimelston Ave, Booterstown, Blackrock, Co Dublin ☎01/269 3011; ◍www.dublin.diplo.de.
US 4645 Reservoir Rd NW, Washington, DC 20007-1998 ☎202/298-4000; ◍www .germany-info.
Canada 1 Waverley St, Ottawa, Ontario K2P 0T8 ☎613/232-1101; ◍www.ottawa.diplo.de.
Australia 119 Empire Circuit, Yarralumla, Canberra 2600 ☎02/6270 1911; ◍www.germanembassy .org.au.
New Zealand 90–92 Hobson St, Wellington ☎04/736 063; ◍www.wellington.diplo.de.
South Africa 180 Blackwood St, Arcadia, Pretoria 0083 ☎012/427 8900; ◍www.pretoria .diplo.de.

Consulates in Berlin

UK Wilhelmstrasse 70–71 ☎030/20 45 70, ◍www.britischebotschaft.de.
Ireland Jägerstrasse 51 ☎030/22 07 20, ◍www.embassyofireland.de.
US Pariser Platz 2 & Clayallee 170 ☎030/830 50, ◍germany.usembassy.gov.
Canada Leipziger Platz 17 ☎030/20 31 20, ◍www.canadainternational.gc.ca.
Australia Wallstrasse 76–79 ☎030/880 08 80, ◍www.germany.embassy.gov.au.
New Zealand Friedrichstrasse 60 ☎030/20 62 10, ◍www.nzembassy.com.

Health

For immediate medical attention, head for the 24-hour emergency room of a major **hospital**, such as the Charité Universitätsklinikum, Charitéplatz 1, Mitte (☎030/450 50; S-Bahn Hauptbahnhof). For **dental emergencies** get in touch with an emergency dental clinic: Zahnärtzlicher Notdienst (☎030/89 00 43 33, ◍www.kzv .de). In the event of an **emergency**, phone ☎112 for an ambulance (*Krankenwagen*).

If you need a **doctor**, call ☎01805/32 13 03 (◍www.calladoc.com; calls cost €0.14 per

minute), an English-language service that will discuss your symptoms and refer you or send an English-speaking doctor.

As a member of the European Union, Germany has free reciprocal health agreements with other member states, whose citizens can apply for a free **European Health Insurance Card** (EHIC; ◍www.ehic.org.uk), which will give you free or cut-rate treatment, but will not pay for repatriation. The EHIC allows you to claim back costs and is available from post offices in the UK. Without this form you'll have to pay in full for all medical treatment, which is expensive – currently around €30 for a visit to the doctor. Non-EU residents will need to insure themselves against all eventualities, including medical costs, and are strongly advised to take out some form of travel insurance (see below).

To get a prescription filled, go to a **pharmacy** (*Apotheke*), signalled by an illuminated green cross. Pharmacists are well trained and generally speak English. There's a 24-hour pharmacy in the Hauptbahnhof, otherwise outside normal hours (usually 8.30am–6.30pm), a notice on the door of any pharmacy indicates the nearest one open. Calling ☎030/31 00 31 or checking ◍www.kvberlin.de produces the same information. You'll be served through a small hatch in the door, so don't be put off by a closed appearance.

Insurance

Even though EU healthcare privileges apply in Germany and Berlin is a relatively safe city, you'd do well to take out an insurance policy before travelling to cover against theft, loss and illness or injury. Before buying a policy, however, it's worth checking whether you are already covered: some all-risks home insurance policies may cover your possessions when overseas, and many private medical schemes include cover when abroad. In Canada, provincial health plans usually provide partial cover for medical mishaps overseas, while holders of official student/ teacher/youth cards in Canada and the US are entitled to some accident coverage and hospital in-patient benefits. Students will often find that their student health coverage extends during the vacations and for one term beyond the date of last enrolment.

Rough Guides travel insurance

Rough Guides has teamed up with WorldNomads.com to offer great **travel insurance** deals. Policies are available to residents of over 150 countries, with cover for a wide range of **adventure sports**, 24hr emergency assistance, high levels of medical and evacuation cover and a stream of **travel safety information**. Roughguides.com users can take advantage of their policies online 24/7, from anywhere in the world – even if you're already travelling. And since plans often change when you're on the road, you can extend your policy and even claim online. Roughguides.com users who buy travel insurance with WorldNomads.com can also leave a positive footprint and donate to a community development project. For more information go to ⓦ **www.roughguides.com/shop**.

If you need to make a claim, you should keep receipts for medicines and medical treatment.

Internet

Berlin is a very internet-conscious city and online access is excellent. Larger hotels, a growing number of cafés, and all the main train stations have WLAN hotspots – and there's a free one in the Sony Center (see p.100). Access in internet cafés costs about €1–4 per half-hour.

Laundry

All larger hotels generally provide a laundry service – but at a cost. Launderettes scattered throughout the city are generally cheaper, with an average load costing around €5 to wash and dry. Hours tend to be daily 7am–10pm and addresses can be found listed under "Waschsalon" in the Yellow Pages. One popular Berlin chain is Schell und Sauber, Oderberger Strasse 1, (U-Bahn Eberswalder Str.).

Left luggage

There are 24-hour lockers at the Zoo, Friedrichstrasse, Alexanderplatz, Ostbahnhof Schönefeld airport/Berlin Brandenburg International stations; Bahnhof Zoo and the Hauptbahnhof also have left-luggage offices. Charges for lockers range around €1–2 per day.

Living in Berlin

Berlin acts as a magnet for young people from Germany and all over Europe. The capital's reputation as a politicized, happening city with a dynamic arts scene and tolerant attitudes means there is a large English-speaking community: something that will work to your advantage for jobs and housing, and to your disadvantage in competition.

Work permits (*Arbeitserlaubnis*) aren't required for EU nationals, though everyone else will need one – and, theoretically, you should not even look for a job without one.

However, the paperwork and bureaucracy are complicated and tedious, and it's essential to seek advice from an experienced friend, especially when completing official forms. The best official place for advice is the **Auswärtiges Amt** (German Federal Foreign Office; ☎030/01 88 81 70, ⓦ www .auswaertiges-amt.de), whose website has the latest information – in English – on entry into Germany and local contact details.

All those who want to stay in Germany for longer than three months – including EU citizens – must technically first **register** their **residence** (*Anmeldung*) at an Einwohner- meldeamt within a Bürgeramt (of which there are fifty in Berlin) within a week of moving in or face a possible fine. For **non-EU citizens** getting work or an *Anmeldung* is extremely difficult, unless you've secured the job before arriving in Germany. However, citizens of Australia, New Zealand, Canada and Japan between 18 and 30 can apply for a working holiday visa, enabling legal work in Germany for ninety days in a twelve-month period: contact German embassies for details.

While the newspapers advertise apartments and rooms for **long-term accommodation**, it's much quicker and less traumatic to sign on at one of the several **Mitwohnzentralen** – accommodation agencies that specialize in long-term sublets in apartments throughout the city. When you find a place to live, you need to first register your residence (*Anmeldung*) at an Einwohnermeldeamt. The form for this requires a signature from your landlord.

Numerous **job agencies** offer both temporary and permanent work – usually secretarial – but you'll obviously be expected to have a good command of German. Useful internet sources are: ⓦwww.stepstone.de; ⓦwww.mamas.de; ⓦwww.jobs.de; ⓦwww.jobnet.de; ⓦwww.monster.de; and ⓦwww.job-office.com.

Lost property

The Police lost and found department (Fundbüro) is at Platz der Luftbrücke 6, Tempelhof (☎030/75 60 31 01; U-Bahn Platz der Luftbrücke). For items lost on public transport, contact the BVG Fundbüro, Potsdamer Strasse 182, Schöneberg (Mon–Thurs 9am–6pm, Fri 9am–2pm; ☎030/19 44 9; U-Bahn Kleistpark). Tegel airport's lost property department can be contacted on ☎030/41 01 23 15; Schönefeld airport's is on ☎030/34 39 75 33.

Mail

Post offices and unmissable bright yellow postboxes dot Berlin, so that you are never far from either. Central Berlin's most conveniently situated **post office** (*Postämt*), with the longest hours, is at Bahnhof Friedrichstrasse (under the arches at Georgenstrasse 12; Mon–Fri 6am–10pm, Sat & Sun 8am–10pm; ⓦwww.deutschepost.de). Other offices (generally Mon–Fri 8am–6pm, Sat 8am–1pm), tend to have separate parcel offices (marked *Pakete*), usually a block or so away; and you can also buy stamps from the small yellow machines next to some postboxes and at some newsagents.

When posting a letter, make sure you distinguish between the slots marked for various postal codes. Boxes marked with a red circle indicate collections late in the day and on Sunday.

Maps

Having a **map** is essential for getting around Berlin; the city is full of little side streets, its long-running boulevards tend to change names every couple of blocks and Berliners are notorious for giving poor directions. Your best bet is the companion edition to this book: the *Rough Guide Map: Berlin*, produced on waterproof paper, and with the majority of the listings in this book conveniently marked. A more comprehensive map is the convenient and ingeniously folded *Falk Plan*, which contains an excellent gazetteer and enlarged plans of the city centre. It also includes a map of the U- and S-Bahn system and an index of every street in Berlin and Potsdam. It's available at most bookstores and newsagents. Those looking for complete treatment of the public transport system should pick the *BVG & S-Bahn Berlin Atlas*, which has complete listings and timetables for the U- and S-Bahn system, and bus, tram and ferry routes. It's available at the larger U-Bahn and S-Bahn stations.

Money and banks

Germany has the **euro** as its currency, which is split into 100 cents. At the time of writing, the exchange rate was approximately €1.23 to the pound, €0.81 to the US dollar and €0.71 to the Australian dollar. For the latest rates, go to ⓦwww.xe.com.

Banks are plentiful and their hours usually Monday to Friday from 9am to 3pm and two days a week to 6pm. It may be worth shopping around several banks (including the savings banks or Sparkasse), as the rates of exchange offered can vary, as can the amount of commission deducted. The latter tends to be a flat rate, meaning that small-scale transactions should be avoided whenever possible. In any case, the several **Wechselstuben** (bureaux de change) at the main train stations, offer better rates, as well as being open outside normal banking hours and weekends, usually daily 8am–8pm.

Debit and credit cards are becoming a part of everyday life, though their use is not as widespread as in the UK or North America. Cash is still the currency of choice, particularly in bars and restaurants. Major credit and debit cards (such as American Express, Mastercard and Visa) are good in department stores, mid- to upmarket restaurants, and an increasing number of shops and petrol stations. Should you want to get **cash** on your plastic, the best way is from any of the many **ATMs** around town. In addition to credit cards, most bank debit cards, part of either the Cirrus or Plus systems, can be used for withdrawing cash. Most banks will also give an advance against your credit card, subject to a minimum of the equivalent of £60/$100 – stickers in the bank windows indicate which cards they're associated with.

Opening hours and public holidays

Large shops in central Berlin are **open** Monday to Saturday from 10am to 8pm, while smaller shops or those outside the centre usually close two hours earlier, and a few department stores will stay open until 10pm on Thursday, Friday and Saturday. Supermarkets and other shops in main stations, particularly the Hauptbahnhof, are open longer hours, mostly daily 8am to 10pm. Most other shops are closed on Sundays.

Opening hours on **public holidays** generally follow Sunday hours: most shops will be closed and museums and other attractions will follow their Sunday schedules. **Public holidays** fall on January 1, Good Friday, Easter Monday, May 1, Ascension Day (forty days after Easter), Whitsun, October 3, November 3 and December 25 & 26.

Phones

You can make local and **international calls** from most phone boxes in the city – marked international – which are generally equipped with basic instructions in English. Virtually every pay phone you'll find takes coins and **cards**. The latter come in €5, €10 and €20 denominations and are available from all post offices and some shops. Phone boxes with a ringing bell symbol indicate that you can be called back on that phone. Another option is to use one of the many **phone shops** offering cheap international calls, usually alongside internet services, found throughout the city. The cheapest time to call abroad is between 9pm and 8am.

You should be able to use your mobile phone in Berlin if it's been connected via

Calling home from abroad

Note that the initial zero is omitted from the area code when dialling the UK, Ireland, Australia and New Zealand from abroad.

Australia international access code + 61.

Ireland international access code + 353.

New Zealand international access code + 64.

South Africa international access code + 27.

UK international access code + 44.

US and Canada international access code + 1.

the GSM system common to the rest of Europe, Australia, New Zealand and South Africa. If you haven't used your mobile phone abroad before, check with your phone provider whether it will work in Germany, and what the call charges are. If you are in Germany for a while, consider getting a local SIM card for your phone. These are available through Berlin's many phone shops and even corner stores and tend to cost around €15, often including some credit. To use a different SIM card in your phone, it will need to be unlocked, if it isn't already, to accept the cards of different providers. The phone shops will be able to advise where this is possible locally. Expect to pay around €10 for this instant service. Top-up cards can be bought in supermarkets, kiosks and phone shops.

The **international code** for Germany is ☎49. For **directory enquiries** in English call ☎118 37; the service costs an initial €0.20, then €1 per minute.

Time

Germany is one hour ahead of GMT, six hours ahead of US Eastern Standard Time and nine ahead of US Pacific Standard Time.

Tipping

Service is, as a rule, included in the bill. Rounding up a café, restaurant or taxi bill to the next euro or so is acceptable in most cases, though when you run up a particularly large tab you will probably want to add some more.

Tourist information

Before you set off for Berlin, it's worth contacting the German National Tourist Board, which has a lot of useful information on accommodation, what's on in town and a selection of glossy brochures. There's a wealth of resources on the internet too – we've included a selection of general sites with information in English below.

Once in the city, the **tourist office**, Berlin Tourismus Marketing (ⓦ www.berlin-tourist -information.de), can supply a wider selection of bumph than the national offices, including comprehensive listings of cultural events, and help with accommodation. They run four tourist information centres (see opposite) and a call centre (Mon–Fri 8am–8pm, Sat & Sun 10am–6pm; ⓣ030/25 00 25), which provides general information as well as accommodation bookings. BTM also publishes a bilingual events magazine, *Berlin Events*, which details most of the mainstream cultural happenings in the city. In addition, they produce a very handy free map.

For travel information and bookings, as well as general tips and advice, there's also the helpful **EurAide** office in Zoo Station (inside the Reisezentrum; May–Aug daily 10am–7pm, Sept–April Mon–Fri 11am–6pm; ⓦ www.euraide.de), set up specifically for English-speaking travellers.

Berlin has two essential **listings magazines** – *Tip* (ⓦ www.tip-berlin.de) and *Zitty* (ⓦ www.zitty.de) – which come out on alternate weeks. *Zitty* is marginally the better of the two, with day-by-day details of gigs, concerts, events, TV and radio, theatre and film, alongside intelligent articles on politics, style and the Berlin in-crowd, and useful classified ads. Reading copies of these can be found in any bar. A third magazine, also with a good deal of listings information and possibly more useful if you don't speak any German, is the monthly English-language *ExBerliner* (ⓦ www.exberliner.com), which largely caters to Berlin's expat community.

Tourist offices in Berlin

Neuen Kranzler Eck S- and U-Bahn Zoologischer Garten. Kurfürstendamm 21, Passage. Mon–Sat 10am–8pm, Sun 10am–6pm (extended hours April–Oct).
Hauptbahnhof S-Bahn Hauptbahnhof. Daily 8am–10pm.
Alexa Shopping Center S- and U-Bahn Alexanderplatz. Grunerstrasse 20. Mon–Sat 10am–8pm (extended hours April–Oct).
Brandenburg Gate S-Bahn Unter den Linden. Pariser Platz (south wing). Daily 10am–6pm (extended hours April–Oct).

German National Tourist Board offices abroad

UK ⓣ 0207/317 0908, ⓦ www.germany-tourism .co.uk.
US & Canada ⓣ 212/661-7200, ⓦ www .cometogermany.com.
Australia ⓣ 02/9236 8982 ⓦ www.germany -tourism.de.

Useful websites

ⓦ **www.berlin.de** The city's official site, with loads of general information, plus the latest events.
ⓦ **www.berlin-online.de** An excellent, all-purpose source for news, business, politics, entertainment, restaurants, listings and the like.
ⓦ **www.gotoberlin.de** General travel guide geared towards young people.

Travellers with disabilities

Access and facilities for the disabled (Behinderte) are good in Berlin: most of the major museums, public buildings and the majority of the public transport system are wheelchair friendly, and an active disabled community is on hand for helpful advice.

A particularly good meeting place with lots of useful information is the *Hotel MIT-Mensch* Ehrlichstrasse 48 (ⓣ030/509 69 30 ⓦ www.mit-mensch.com; S-Bahn Karlshorst; €82 for a standard double room in peak season), which provides friendly lodging run by and for wheelchair users.

A good source of more formal and in depth information is **Mobidat** (ⓦ www .mobidat.net), an activist group that campaigns for better access for people with disabilities. They have a great wealth of information on wheelchair-accessible hotels and restaurants, city tours for disabled travellers and local transport services. Their online database lists over 40,000 buildings in Berlin, including hotels, restaurants and theatres, indicating their degree of accessibility. Less useful is the tourist office (see p.39), though they have listings of suitable accommodation. Lastly, if you speak German, you might like to browse the online version of the quarterly magazine *Handicap* (⊛www.i-motio.de), for its hundreds of articles and active forums.

The public transport system is disabled-aware: four out of five buses and around half its trams have ramps to allow access – look for a blue wheelchair symbol on the side of vehicles. Trains are generally easy to board, but getting onto the platforms less so – most but not all U- and S-Bahn stations are equipped with lifts. The official U- and S-Bahn map indicates which stations are wheelchair-accessible; for more information check with the BVG (⊛www.bvg.de; see p.24) first.

The City

The City

Mitte: Unter den Linden and around

The natural place to start exploring Berlin is at its most famous landmark, the **Brandenburg Gate**. It lies at the head of its premier boulevard **Unter den Linden** and beside the iconic **Reichstag**, the German parliament. During the Berlin Wall years all three became rather forlorn symbols of malaise: the gate sat in the no man's land of the Wall, the road led nowhere and the building lay largely empty. But now, after reunification, regeneration and Berlin's reinvention as Germany's capital, they again provide a nucleus for a city that lacked a coherent centre for so long.

This revival has helped resurrect an important historical district, which harks back to Berlin's eighteenth-century transformation from relative backwater to its role as capital of Prussia, which had become one of Europe's largest players. With Prussia's rise its architects were commissioned to create the trappings of a capital city – churches, theatres, libraries, palaces and an opera house – all on and around Unter den Linden. Safe **Baroque** and **Neoclassical** styles predominate, and there are no great flights of architectural fancy. These buildings were meant to project an image of solidity, permanence and power, perhaps to allay the latent insecurity of Brandenburg-Prussia as a relatively late arrival on the European stage.

However, almost every one of these symbols of Prussian might was left gutted by the bombing and shelling of World War II. Paradoxically, it was the postwar communist regime that resurrected them from the wartime rubble to adorn the capital of the German Democratic Republic. The result was a pleasing re-creation of the old city, though one motive behind this restoration was to impart the East German state with a sense of historical continuity by tacitly linking it with Prussia.

This **restoration** was so successful that looking at these magnificent eighteenth- and nineteenth-century buildings it's difficult to believe that as recently as the 1960s large patches of the centre lay in ruins. Like archeologists trying to picture a whole vase from a single fragment, the builders took a facade, or just a small fraction of one, and set about re-creating the whole. And even though much of what can be seen today is an imitation, it's often easy to suspend disbelief and imagine an unbroken continuity.

This rejuvenation is at its most amazing on the **Gendarmenmarkt**, a square just south of Unter den Linden where, even in the 1980s, its twin Neoclassical churches – the **Französischer Dom** and **Deutscher Dom** – remained bombed-out shells. Also impressive is the reconstruction of the grand buildings in and around **Bebelplatz**, which under the noble rulers of Prussia – the Hohenzollern – became an impressive prelude to the awesome buildings of the Spreeinsel, which included their palace and Museum Island (see Chapter 2).

By following the sequence of this chapter you can do a **walking tour** of the district that's manageable in a day. It's worth starting early to get to the Reichstag before the big queues form, but if they already have, consider ending your day's exploration here: the building's open until midnight and Berlin's nocturnal cityscape is an attraction itself. South of Brandenburg is the **Holocaust Memorial**, which perversely paves the way to the site of **Hitler's Bunker** – sitting within Berlin's prewar **Regierungsviertel** or "government quarter" along **Wilhelmstrasse** – where the Führer committed suicide. Almost nothing of Regierungsviertel survives today, but along the road there's a small but interesting exhibition on the **Stasi**, the East German secret police.

The Brandenburg Gate

Heavily laden with meaning and historical association, the **Brandenburg Gate** (Brandenburger Tor; S-Bahn Unter den Linden) has come to mark the very centre of Berlin. Built as a city gate-cum-triumphal arch in 1791, it was designed by Carl Gotthard Langhans and modelled after the Propylaea, the entrance to the Acropolis in Athens. The Gate became, like the Reichstag later, a symbol of German solidarity, looking out to the monolithic Siegessäule, a column celebrating Prussian military victories and guarding the city's grandest thoroughfare. In 1806 Napoleon marched under the arch and took home with him the **Quadriga**, the horse-drawn chariot that tops the Gate. It was returned a few years later, and the revolutionaries of 1848 and 1918 met under its form; later the Gate was a favoured rallying point for the Nazis' torch-lit marches.

After the building of the Wall placed the Gate in the Eastern sector, nearby observation posts became the place for visiting politicians – John F. Kennedy included (see p.46) – to look over the Iron Curtain from the West in what became a handy photo opportunity; the view was apparently emotive enough to reduce

▲ The Quadriga

Margaret Thatcher to tears. With the opening of a border crossing here just before Christmas 1989, the east–west axis of the city was symbolically re-created. The GDR authorities, who rebuilt the Quadriga following wartime damage, had removed the Prussian Iron Cross from the Goddess of Victory's laurel wreath, which topped her staff, on the grounds that it was "symbolic of Prussian-German militarism". When the border was reopened, the Iron Cross was replaced, which some, mindful of historical precedent, still viewed with a frisson of unease – but now it certainly seems harmless enough and is used as a popular backdrop for photos of posing tourists.

Pariser Platz

The Brandenburg Gate looms over **Pariser Platz**, whose ornamental gardens have been restored to reproduce the prewar feel, if not exact look, since the square is now surrounded by modern buildings. However, the millions of euros that have gone into this redevelopment have had some interesting results despite the stringent building guidelines: windows have to be vertical in format and facades can only be a maximum of 49 percent glass, with stone the only permissible material for the exterior cladding – a few buildings obey this rule, while the Acadamie der Künste deliberately flaunts it.

DZ Bank

Described as the "best thing I've ever done" by Canadian-born architect Frank O. Gehry, the DZ Bank is worth a second look, even if you can't do much more than crane your neck at its curvaceous interiors from the lobby. While the building's plain exterior almost mockingly follows the exacting building codes – it's only just fifty percent stone, its windows only slightly taller than wide – inside, beyond the huge blocks of Portuguese marble in the entrance, thousands of individually formed metal panels give the conference rooms at its heart an aquatic, undulating curvaceousness. The structure is also unusual in that it moves from a height of five storeys at the front to ten at the rear. Though owned by a bank, the building is mostly used as offices and event space; one of the thirty super-luxurious private apartments at the back is owned by Gerhard Schröder, the former German Chancellor (1998–2005).

Acadamie der Künste

Shoulder-to-shoulder with the DZ Bank and every bit as eye-catching is the glassy **Acadamie der Künste** (Academy of Art; Tues–Sun 11am–8pm; €8 for exhibitions, free on first Sun of the month; Ⓦ www.adk.de). The building somehow slithered through local building codes by ostensibly copying the design of the prewar building that was here – though reconstructing it in glass and steel. Naturally a storm raged over how the building had been approved, but sensibly the courts upheld permission for it to stay. Inside you can see the last original structure from prewar Pariser Platz, tucked away at the back of building, and wander across sweeping concrete expanses for first-floor views of the Platz. The building holds half-a-dozen temporary contemporary art exhibitions per year; the rest of the building includes offices, a café and a private club.

Hotel Adlon

On the southeast corner of the Platz, the legendary **Hotel Adlon** (see p.195), once one of Europe's grandest hotels, has been rebuilt. The original was host to luminaries from Charlie Chaplin to Lawrence of Arabia and Kaiser Wilhelm II,

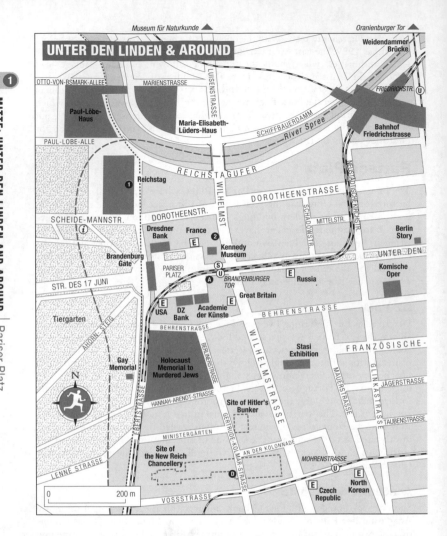

and was regarded throughout the continent as the acme of luxury and style. The building was destroyed in the closing days of the war, and this new version, modelled loosely on its predecessor – the lobby fountain, for example, was salvaged from the original – attempts the same heights of opulence. Even if you can't afford a drink here, let alone a room, have a look at the lobby and imagine the late eighteenth century when Berlin was the cultural capital of Europe. Culture of a very different sort graced the building in 2002, when Michael Jackson, who was staying in the bullet-proof presidential suite, dangled his youngest child over the balcony in front of the world's press.

Berlin Kennedy Museum

For an intriguing homage to John F. Kennedy visit the **Berlin Kennedy Museum** (daily 10am–6pm; €7; ☎030/20 65 35 70, ⓦwww.thekennedys.de), in the

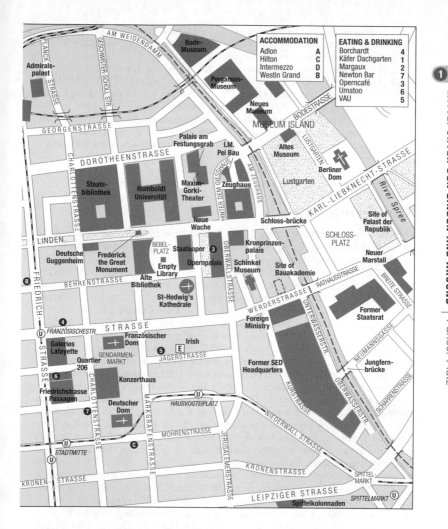

ACCOMMODATION

Adlon	A
Hilton	C
Intermezzo	D
Westin Grand	B

EATING & DRINKING

Borchardt	4
Käfer Dachgarten	1
Margaux	2
Newton Bar	7
Operncafé	3
Umatoo	6
VAU	5

northeast corner of Pariser Platz, which documents his special relationship with the media and his internationally significant visit to the front lines of the Cold War in 1960s Berlin.

John F. Kennedy understood, as no other politician before him, the power of photos and then television – partly thanks to his former-photojournalist wife Jackie. As Norman Mailer put it: "America's politics…(became)…America's favorite movie, America's first soap opera, America's bestseller." Evidence of this carefully orchestrated media campaign (which included a ban on photos showing Kennedy wearing glasses) and resultant cult of personality abounds in the museum's **three hundred photos** and magazine covers. The dozens of other 1960s relics include JFK's old ties, cufflinks, phonebook and some preserved presidential doodles – twirling shapes casually interspersed with words like Cuba, Berlin, Eastern Europe – as well as the crocodile-skin briefcase that accompanied him on his fateful trip to Dallas. Also here is a brilliant **photomosaic** of Kennedy by American artist Rob Silvers who invented the technique: it uses hundreds of pictures from his life to build a mask.

But the real highlight of the museum, and the reason for it being here, are exhibits relating to JFK's eight-hour **Berlin visit** on June 26, 1963. The Berlin Wall had been built just two years earlier, so the city's emotions ran high, and there's wonderful footage here of ecstatic crowds – people breaking free of security cordons to shake hands with the passing president. Kennedy's city parade included a stop at the viewing platform in front of the Brandenburg Gate – draped for the occasion by the Russians in enormous red flags and communist placards – before he retreated to Schöneberg to deliver his impassioned "Berliner" speech (see p.130). The day proved so emotional that at the end of it JFK commented to his aides "we'll never have another day like this one as long as we live".

The Reichstag

Directly behind the Brandenburg Gate a line of cobbles marks the course of the Berlin Wall where for 28 years it separated the Gate from the other great emblem of national unity, the **Reichstag** – now once again the seat of Germany's parliament. The imposing nineteenth-century Neoclassical Reichstag immediately impresses, its stolid, bombastic form wholly in keeping with its pivotal role in history. It was built to house a sham parliament answerable only to the Kaiser, but in November 1918, Philipp Scheidemann declared the founding of the German Republic from a window here, paving the way for the Weimar Republic, which lasted just fourteen years before the Nazis claimed power. Their coup came partly as a result of a fire in the Reichstag in 1933, seen across the world in flickering newsreels, which gave the Nazis an excuse to introduce an emergency decree suspending civil rights and effectively instigating a dictatorship. Debate as to who actually started the fire began immediately and continues to this day. In a show trial, an itinerant ex-communist Dutch bricklayer, **Marius van der Lubbe**, was successfully charged with arson and executed the following year, but it's more likely that the Nazis began the fire themselves. Equally famously, the Reichstag became a symbol of the Allied victory at the end of World War II, when soldiers raised the Soviet flag on its roof – even though heavy fighting still raged below. The building was left in tatters by the conflict, and only in 1971 was its reconstruction completed to house a museum of its own and Germany's history, but in 1990 the government of a reunified Germany decided to move its parliament back, though that didn't happen until April 19, 1999 – once all its interiors had been refashioned and a new **cupola** (daily 8am–midnight; last admission 10pm; free; Ⓦwww.bundestag.de) set atop the building. Designed by British architect Sir Norman Foster, this giant glass **dome** supported by a soaring mirrored column has become the building's main visitor attraction. A circular ramp spirals up the inside to a **viewing deck** with stunning 360-degree views of the city. In the foreground the Regierungsviertel buildings (see p.112) and the massive Tiergarten park dominate, but the Sony Center (see p.100), the Fernsehturm (see p.72) and the shimmering golden roof of the Synagogue on Orianienburgerstrasse (see p.87) are other obvious landmarks. Expect to queue for entry for at least an hour, though if you arrive early or late in the day it can be a bit quicker – or, for immediate entry, make a reservation at the *Käfer Dachgarten* restaurant (see p.215).

Having explored the inside of the Reichstag, wander around the building and try to spot the scores of patched bullet holes around some of its windows from the last days of the Battle of Berlin. At the back of the building, beside the River Spree and the nearest corner of the Tiergarten, there are also a poignant series of **plaques** and **crosses** with the names (where known) of those who later died attempting to swim or climb the East German border here.

The Holocaust Memorial

The block of land immediately south of the Brandenburg Gate and Pariser Platz is officially dedicated to the National Memorial to the Murdered Jews of Europe. It is generally known as the **Holocaust Memorial** (℡030/2639 43 36, ⓦwww .holocaustmahnmal.de; S-Bahn Unter den Linden) and was unveiled in May 2006 after almost seventeen years of planning and controversy (see box, p.50), and six years of designing and building. The monument is the work of New York architect Peter Eisenman, who was inspired by the densely clustered gravestones in Prague's Jewish graveyard. It involves 2711 dark grey oblong pillars of varying heights evenly and tightly spaced over the entire site – which is about the size of three football pitches. With no single entrance, visitors make their own way through the maze to the centre where the blocks are well above head height, tending to convey a sense of gloom, isolation and solitude, even though Eisenman insists he has created a "place of hope". At night, 180 lights illuminate the space, creating a sombre yet stunning spectacle.

The underground **information centre** (April–Sept Tues–Sun 10am–8pm, last admission 7.15pm; Oct–March Tues–Sun 10am–7pm, last admission 6.15pm; free; tours in English Sat 11am & 2pm, Sun 11am, 2pm & 4pm, €3) in the southeast corner of the monument, relates the life stories and plight of some Jewish victims of the Holocaust. Carefully researched and expertly presented, the small exhibition outlines the overall history of the Nazi hounding and extermination of Jews before moving on to the personal stories that lurk behind the monstrous statistics. Among them are notes left by those on their way to their death – including some thrown from the cattle wagons as they were transported to death camps. The exhibition **audio tour** (€4) is largely unnecessary, but does help

▲ Holocaust Memorial

Memorial controversy

Even by the standards of Berlin, which is well used to hotly debating almost every bricks-and-mortar city centre project, the **Holocaust Memorial** was one of Berlin's most **controversial** projects ever. It was criticized for its unnecessarily large scale and location, on prime real estate with little historical significance. And in a city where finances are tight, the price tag made it unpopular, as did the way the project was forced on Berliners by the Federal government, with an attitude that tended to dismiss any criticism as simply anti-Semitic. One criticism was that the rectangular stones were too reminiscent of SS militarism, but more compelling were arguments that memorials at former camps, like Sachsenhausen (see p.190), are more relevant, and that the brass cobbles (*Stolpersteine*) commemorating victims outside their former homes are more poignant and all-pervading.

One particularly contentious twist in the tale of the memorial's construction concerns **Degussa**, the company that provided anti-graffiti paint for the blocks. As a daughter company of IG-Farben – who produced Cyclon-B, the gas used in the Nazi gas chambers – some thought it wasn't appropriate for them to be involved in the project. After much debate, their tender was confirmed: it was argued that the whole nation was building the monument and that no organization or company should be hindered from contributing.

flesh things out a little and acts as a donation to the foundation that built and runs the memorial, whose spiralling costs – the final tab was €27.6m – have landed it in some financial trouble.

The Gay Holocaust Memorial

Over the road from the Holocaust Memorial, the fringes of the Tiergarten park hold another concrete oblong, dedicated as a **Gay Holocaust Memorial**. Officially called "The Memorial to Homosexuals persecuted by Nazis", it remembers the 54,000 people who were convicted of homosexual acts under the regime; of which an estimated 8,000 died in concentration camps. Inaugurated by Berlin's gay mayor Klaus Wowereit (see p.252) in 2008, the four-metre high monument mimics those commemorating Jewish victims, but is different in that it also contains a window behind which plays a film of two men kissing.

Hitler's bunker and around

A minutes' walk south of the Holocaust Memorial, along Gertrude-Kolmar-Strasse, is its oddest possible bedfellow: the site of **Hitler's bunker**, where the Führer spent his last days, issuing meaningless orders as the Battle of Berlin raged above. Here Hitler married Eva Braun and wrote his final testament: he personally was responsible for nothing; he had been betrayed by the German people, who had proved unequal to his leadership and deserved their fate. On April 30, 1945, he shot himself, and his body was hurriedly burned by loyal officers. A roadside sign at the end of the **Ministergärten** (see p.51) provides a plan of the bunker detailing its rooms and their functions. Though it's often assumed that the bunker was glamorously furnished, the diagram accurately reveals how spartan the facility was. With fitting irreverence, the spot where Hitler breathed his last breath is now below a clothing bank.

The sign also maps the astonishing number of other bunkers that were once in the vicinity, the largest one being under the **Neues Reichskanzlei** (New Reich Chancellery), the vast building designed by Albert Speer in 1938 as part of the

Nazi remodelling of the government area around Wilhelmstrasse. This gigantic complex ran to the north of and almost the length of Vossstrasse. Today nothing remains, for even though the Chancellery building survived the war, it was torn down in a fit of revenge by the conquering Soviet army, who used its marble to fashion the memorial on Strasse des 17 Juni (see p.110) and the huge war memorial at the Soviet military cemetery in Treptower Park (see p.144).

The Ministergärten

The lands immediately west of Hitler's bunker were, during the Wall years, part of the death strip separating East and West Berlin. On reunification it was decided to resuscitate this part of the Regierungsviertel again, by inviting the government ministries from Germany's sixteen states to build on a street named the **Ministergärten** in their honour. However, only seven took up the offer – the rest chose to avoid the historically charged site – with all opting for similarly dynamic modern designs replete with imposing entrances, atria and exhibitions spaces. For the most part, however, they simply house offices and ministerial accommodation.

Wilhelmstrasse

The next road south of the Ministergärten, An der Kolonnade leads east to **Wilhelmstrasse** which, from 1871 to the end of the Third Reich, was Imperial Berlin's Whitehall and Downing Street rolled into one. Its many ministries and government buildings included the Chancellery and, after the Republic was established in 1918, the Presidential Palace. Today little remains, but trying to figure out what was where can be compelling (see map, p.272), and information boards with photos and descriptions of the former buildings have helpfully been placed along the street. Today though, most of Wilhelmstrasse is lined by fairly dull apartment buildings that once housed high-ranking East Germans, and the only structure that stands out is an apparent airport control tower that turns out to be the **Czech Embassy**. Moving north along the street is an exhibition on the **Stasi** (see p.160) and beyond it a road closure that announces the presence of the **British Embassy**. This counter-terrorism measure allows you to properly appreciate the eye-pleasing, quirky building by Michael Wilford; its austere stone facade is broken up at the centre by a riot of shapes in cool grey and violent purple – playful elements thought to reflect the British sense of humour and style.

Stasi: Die Ausstellung

Accessed via a pathway opposite the junction of Wilhelmstrasse with Hannah-Arendt-Strasse, **Stasi: Die Ausstellung** (Stasi: The Exhibition; Mon–Sat 10am–6pm; free; Ⓦ www.bstu.bund.de) provides a sobering display on the feared East German Secret Police. The material is presented by the government commission responsible for sifting through and reconstructing Stasi files, and whose work includes the painstaking reassembly of documents hastily shredded as the GDR's regime came to an end. The exhibition is briefer than the similar one at the former Stasi headquarters on Normannenstrasse (see p.160), but it does nevertheless contain several intriguing intelligence devices, including hidden cameras, tiny tape recorders, a big toolbox for producing counterfeit documents and even the proverbial toothpaste tube with a secret compartment. Aside from these cunning tools, however, the exhibit relates (in German only – ask to borrow a free transcript in English) just what a powerful and frightening organization the Stasi was, and the amazing degree of observation, infiltration and control they practised in the GDR.

Unter den Linden

Berlin's grandest boulevard, **Unter den Linden**, runs due east from the Branden-burg Gate towards the Spreeinsel and once formed the main east–west axis of Imperial Berlin. The street – "beneath the lime trees" – was named after the trees on its central island; the first saplings were planted by Friedrich Wilhelm, the Great Elector, during the seventeenth century to line the route from his palace to his hunting grounds in the Tiergarten (see p.108). The original trees were replaced by crude Nazi totem poles during the 1930s, so the present generation dates from a period of postwar planting.

Until 1989 the western end of Unter den Linden also marked the end of the road for East Berliners: a low barrier ran a hundred metres or so short of the Branden-burg Gate. From here it was possible to view the gate, beyond which the discreet presence of armed border guards and the sterile white concrete of the Wall signalled the frontier with West Berlin. This reduced Unter den Linden to little more than a grand blind alley, which – lined by infrequently visited embassies – gave it a strangely empty and decorative feel. Revitalization since 1989 has helped the boulevard reassume something of its old role and today it's busy and bustling, fringed by shops and cafés, though their presence is relatively muted.

The Russian Embassy

One of the first buildings you'll see as you head east from Pariser Platz is the massive **Russian Embassy**, rearing up on the right. Built in 1950 on the site of the prewar (originally Tsarist) embassy, it was the first postwar building to be erected on Unter den Linden and an example of the much maligned *Zuckerbäckerstil* or "wedding-cake style": a kind of blunted, monumental Classicism characteristic of Stalin-era Soviet architecture. Berlin has a number of such buildings, the most spectacular being those along Karl-Marx-Allee (see p.147).

Friedrichstrasse

Halfway along Unter den Linden, you come to its most important intersection as it crosses the busy shopping street of Friedrichstrasse. Before the war this was one of the busiest crossroads in the city, with Friedrichstrasse a well-known prosti-tutes' haunt lined by cafés, bars and restaurants. Nazi puritanism dealt the first blow to this thriving *Vergnügungsviertel* (Pleasure Quarter), and the work was finished by Allied bombers, who effectively razed the street. Rebuilt considerably wider, what had once been a narrow, slightly claustrophobic street became a broad, desolate road. Since reunification, Friedrichstrasse has been extensively revamped. Bland modern edifices now house offices, malls and a series of fairly high-end boutiques that rub shoulders with more everyday shops, including several good bookshops.

The Staatsbibliothek

A block east of the intersection with Friedrichstrasse, Unter den Linden passes south of the **Staatsbibliothek zu Berlin** (State Library; Mon–Fri 9am–9pm, Sat 9am–5pm; free; 90min tours first Sat of the month 10.30am, also free; ⓦstaatsbibliothek-berlin.de; U-Bahn Französische Strasse). First the Prussian, then GDR state library, it is now twinned with the Staatsbibliothek in the Kulturforum (see p.102). A typically grandiose edifice dating from the turn of the twentieth century, its facade was extensively patched up after wartime shrapnel damage, and is now mainly the haunt of Humboldt University students. Visitors who don't feel like delving into the volumes within can sit in the ivy-clad courtyard by the fountain. As you do so, admire a GDR-era sculpture showing a member of the proletariat apparently reading a didactic Brecht poem on a relief at the other side of the fountain.

The Deutsche Guggenheim

Housed in a former bank and a far cry from the museum's architectural landmarks in New York and Bilbao, the German branch of the **Deutsche Guggenheim** (daily 10am–8pm, Thurs until 10pm; €4, Mon free; free tours 6pm; Ⓦwww .deutsche-guggenheim.de; U-Bahn Französische Strasse) sits at the southern side of Unter den Linden, at the intersection with Charlottenstrasse. The disappointingly small, but well-lit gallery shows around four temporary exhibitions per year, focusing on top-drawer modern and contemporary art. Recent exhibitions have included the works of such international artists as Robert Mapplethorpe, Julie Mehretu, Anish Kapoor and Jackson Pollock. There's a small museum shop and a sleek, quiet café on site.

The Gendarmenmarkt

A five-minute walk south along Charlottenstrasse from beside the Deutsche Guggenheim lies the immaculately restored square, **Gendarmenmarkt**, one of the architectural highlights of Berlin, where it's hard to imagine that all the buildings were almost obliterated during the war and that rebuilding lasted until well into the 1980s.

The Gendarmenmarkt's **origins** are prosaic. It was originally home to Berlin's main market until the Gendarme regiment set up their stables on the site in 1736 and gave the square its name (readopted after its GDR-era hiatus as Platz der Akademie). With the departure of the military, the Gendarmenmarkt was transformed at the behest of Frederick the Great, who ordered an architectural revamp of the two churches that stood here – the **Französischer Dom** and **Deutscher Dom** – in an attempt to mimic the Piazza del Popolo in Rome. The grid-like street pattern that survives around it is testament to the area's seventeenth-century origins when a number of city extensions took Berlin beyond its original walled core. This area, once known as Friedrichstadt, became a Huguenot stronghold thanks to Prussian guarantees of religious freedom and rights which attracted them in numbers.

The Französischer Dom

Frederick the Great's revamp is at its most impressive and eye-catching in the **Französischer Dom** at the northern end of the square. Originally built as a simple place of worship for Berlin's influential Huguenot community at the beginning of the eighteenth century, the building was transformed by the addition of a Baroque tower, turning it into one of Berlin's most appealing churches.

The **Dom tower** was built some eighty years after the church and has the attraction of some fine tower bells – which ring out automatically every day at noon, 3pm and 7pm, providing a near-deafening experience to those on the balcony at the time. Concerts are sometimes performed by bell-ringers at other times – ask at the desk for details. You can climb up (daily 10am–7pm; €2.50) via a longish spiral of steps to an outside balcony with good views over the square.

At the base of the tower is the entrance to the **Hugenottenmuseum** (Tues–Sun noon–5pm; €2), detailing the history of the Huguenots in France and Brandenburg. There are sections dealing with the theological background of the Reformation in

France, the Revocation of the Edict of Nantes leading to the flight of the Huguenots from their native country, their settling in Berlin and the influence of the new arrivals on trade, science and literature. The museum also has a short section on the destruction and rebuilding of the Dom.

The tower is so striking that a lot of visitors don't actually notice the church proper, the **Französischen Friedrichstadtkirche** (French Church in Friedrichstadt; Tues–Sun noon–5pm), which is modest enough in appearance that it looks more like an ancillary building for the tower. The main entrance to the church is at the western end of the Dom, facing Charlottenstrasse. The church, re-consecrated in 1983 after years of restoration work, has a simple hall-like interior with few decorative features and only a plain table as an altar.

The Deutscher Dom

At the southern end of the square, the **Deutscher Dom**, built in 1708 for the city's Lutheran community, is the stylistic twin of the Französischer Dom. The Dom now hosts the "Wege-Irrwege-Umwege" exhibition (May–Sept Tues–Sun 10am–7pm; Oct–April Tues–Sun 10am–6pm; free), which looks rather exhaustedly at Germany's democratic history, and is consequently fairly dull. The exhibition is in German, but a free English-language audio guide is available at the front desk (ID required as deposit). A wander up through the Dom with its labyrinth of galleries is the highlight, and the reward for reaching the top is the chance to see a few scale-models of some early Norman Foster designs for the reconstruction of the Reichstag (see p.54).

Konzerthaus Berlin

Between the two churches on Gendarmenmarkt stands Schinkel's Neoclassical **Konzerthaus Berlin** (formerly called the Schauspielhaus). Dating from 1817, it was built around the ruins of Langhans' burned-out National Theatre, retaining the latter's exterior walls and portico columns. A broad sweep of steps leads up to the main entrance and into an interior of incredible opulence, where chandeliers, marble, gilded plasterwork and pastel-hued wall paintings all compete for attention. Gutted during a raid in 1943, the building suffered further damage during heavy fighting as the Russians attempted to root out SS troops who had dug in here. It reopened in October 1984 and during Christmas 1989, Leonard Bernstein conducted a performance of Beethoven's Ninth Symphony here to celebrate the *Wende*, with the word *Freiheit* ("Freedom") substituted for *Freude* ("Joy") in Schiller's choral finale.

The Schiller statue

The **statue of Schiller** outside the Konzerthaus was repositioned here in 1988, having been removed by the Nazis over fifty years earlier, returned to what was then East Berlin from the West in exchange for reliefs originally from the Pfaueninsel (see p.175) and a statue from a Tiergarten villa. Outside Germany, Friedrich Schiller (1759–1805) is best known for the *Ode to Joy* that provides the words to the final movements of Beethoven's Ninth Symphony, but in his homeland he is venerated as one of the greatest German poets and dramatists of the Enlightenment. His works, from early *Sturm und Drang* dramas like *Die Räuber* ("The Thieves") to later historical plays like *Maria Stuart*, were primarily concerned with freedom – political, moral and personal – which was probably the reason why the Nazis were so quick to bundle him off the Gendarmenmarkt.

Jägerstrasse and around

Leading west from the Gendarmenmarkt, **Jägerstrasse** was the site of particularly heavy fighting during the 1848 revolution, but is best known as the centre of Berlin's nineteenth-century **banking quarter**. It was from here that the Mendelssohn Bank, a huge Jewish concern founded by the sons of philosopher Moses Mendelssohn, bankrolled much of Berlin's industrial revolution and a plaque on the north side of the street, outside number 51, tells its story. A few steps west, the Berlin extension of the **Nolde Stiftung** (Nolde Foundation; daily 10am–7pm; €8; ℡030/40 00 46 90, ⓦwww.nolde-stiftung.de), Jägerstrasse 55, showcases the work of leading German expressionist painter Emil Nolde. His vivid paintings and awkward lithographs were predictably banned by the Nazis, but he defiantly continued to work in secret in his home on Germany's Baltic coast, producing the wonderful work that's revealed in the changing temporary exhibitions here.

A block south of Jägerstrasse, beside U-Bahn Hausvogteiplatz is the **Infocenter Wiederaufbau Berliner Schloss**, Hausvogteiplatz 3-4 (Information Centre for the Reconstruction of the Berlin Palace; daily 9.30am–6pm; free; ⓦberliner-schloss.de), which is chock-full of fundraising propaganda in support of the controversial rebuilding of Schloss (see p.62). Pop in to see the delightful scale model of Unter den Linden, Museum Island and the Schloss, all circa 1930: a tremendous amount of work has gone into getting the historical details correct and statues have even been reconstructed using aluminium foil. The centre also offers the chance to see some original palace stonework and detailed plans for the proposed reconstruction, buy postcards of old Berlin and donate to the rebuilding project.

Bebelplatz and around

Some two blocks northeast of the Gendarmenmarkt, the lime trees no longer define Unter den Linden as it opens out into the imposing Neoclassical **Bebelplatz** that marks the start of Berlin's eighteenth century showpiece quarter. Bebelplatz itself was conceived by Frederick the Great as both a tribute to ancient Rome and a monument to himself. He and the architect **Georg Wenzeslaus von Knobelsdorff** drew up plans for a space that would recall the great open squares of the Classical city and be known as Forum Fridericianum. It never quite fulfilled such lofty ambitions, although the architecture of many of the buildings did receive acclaim at the time. The centrepiece square is rather bleak and unimpressive, suggesting it might not be a bad idea to replant the gardens that graced it in the late eighteenth century. Yet the square has only just recovered from a spate of building work that put in an underground car park and gutted the **Dresdner Bank** on its south side, which has been converted to house the luxurious *Hotel de Rome*; the interiors of which were used for sequences of the film *Run Lola Run* (see p.301).

The Empty Library

At the windswept and otherwise featureless centre of Bebelplatz lies the **Empty Library**, a monument to the most infamous event to happen on the square. It was here that on May 10, 1933, the infamous **Büchverbrennung** took place, demonstratively in front of the university, on what was then called Opernplatz. On the orders of Joseph Goebbels, Hitler's propaganda minister, 20,000 books that conflicted with Nazi ideology went up in flames. Among them were the works of "un-German" authors like Erich Maria Remarque, Thomas and Heinrich Mann,

Stefan Zweig and Erich Kästner, along with volumes by countless foreign writers, H.G. Wells and Ernest Hemingway among them. The most fitting comment on this episode was made with unwitting foresight by the Jewish poet Heinrich Heine in the previous century: "Where they start by burning books, they'll end by burning people." The ingenious monument itself, by Micha Ullmann, is simply a room with empty shelves set in the ground under a pane of glass; it is at its most spectacular at night when a beam of light streams out.

The Alte Bibliothek

The **Alte Bibliothek**, a former royal library, crowds the western side of Bebelplatz with a curved Baroque facade that has given it the nickname *Die Kommode* ("the chest of drawers"). Built between 1775 and 1780, its design was based on that of the Michaelertrakt in Vienna's Hofburg. Lenin spent some time here poring over dusty tomes while waiting for the Russian Revolution, and, even though only the building's facade survived the war, it has all been immaculately restored.

The Frederick the Great monument

Just north of the **Alte Bibliothek** and in the middle of Unter den Linden is a statue of **Frederick the Great**, a nineteenth century work by Christian Rauch, showing Frederick astride a horse. Around the plinth, about a quarter of the size of the monarch, are representations of his generals, mostly on foot and conferring animatedly.

After World War II, the statue of *Der alte Fritz*, as Frederick the Great is popularly known, was removed from Unter den Linden and only restored to its city-centre site in 1981 after a long exile in Potsdam. Its reinstalling reflected an odd revaluation by Erich Honecker's GDR of the pre-socialist past: no longer were figures like Frederick the Great, Blücher, Scharnhorst et al to be reviled as imperialistic militarists, but were to be accorded the status of historic figures worthy of commemoration. Even Bismarck, the Iron Chancellor of Wilhelmine Germany, was recognized as having "in his *Junker* way played a progressive historical role".

The Humboldt Universität

Over Unter Den Linden from the Frederick statue, the restrained Neoclassical **Humboldt Universität** was designed in tandem with the buildings around Bebelplatz and originally built in 1748 as a palace for Frederick the Great's brother. In 1809 the philologist, writer and diplomat Wilhelm Humboldt founded a school here that was to become the University of Berlin, and later be renamed in his honour. Flanking the entrance gate are statues of Wilhelm and his brother Alexander, famous for their exploration of Central and South America. Wilhelm is contemplating the passing traffic, book in hand, and Alexander is sitting on a globe above a dedication to the "second discoverer of Cuba" from the University of Havana. Humboldt Universität Alumni include Karl Marx, Friedrich Engels and Karl Liebknecht, the socialist leader and proclaimer of the first German Republic who was murdered in 1919 (see p.269). The philologists Jacob and Wilhelm Grimm (better known as the Brothers Grimm) and Albert Einstein are some of the best-known former members of staff.

The Staatsoper

Knobelsdorff's Neoclassical **Staatsoper**, on the east side of Bebelplatz, is among its plainer buildings, though it represented the pinnacle of the architect's career and was Berlin's first theatre. The building is best viewed from Unter den Linden, where an imposing portico marks the main entrance. Just under two centuries after its construction it became the first major building to fall victim to World War II bombing, on the night of April 9–10, 1941. The Nazis restored it for its bicentenary in 1943, but on February 3, 1945, it was gutted once again. Now totally reconstructed, like virtually everything else in the area, it is one of Berlin's leading opera houses.

Sankt-Hedwigs-Kathedrale

Just behind the Staatsoper is another Knobelsdorff creation, the stylistically incongruous **Sankt-Hedwigs-Kathedrale** (Mon–Sat 10am–5pm, Sun 1–5pm; free), which was built as a place of worship for the city's Catholic minority in 1747 and is still in use. According to popular legend it owes its circular shape and domed profile to Frederick the Great's demand that it be built in the form of an upturned teacup. This probably stems from the fact that the monarch "advised" Knobelsdorff; in truth, the building's shape was inspired by the Pantheon in Rome. Reduced to a shell on March 2, 1943, the cathedral was not reconstructed until 1963, a restoration that left it with a slightly altered dome and a modernized interior.

The **interior**, once past the hazy biblical reliefs of the entrance portico, is perhaps the most unusual aspect of the whole building. The greatest feature of the vast main hall is the split-level double altar – the upper one is used on Sundays and special occasions, while the sunken altar in the crypt, reached by a flight of broad stairs, is used for weekday masses. All this is complemented by the stainless-steel pipes of the ethereal-sounding organ above the entrance, and 1970s-style globe-lamps hanging from the ceiling. If you've survived the combined effects of all this, the crypt with its eight grotto-like side chapels and near-abstract charcoal drawings is a further attraction.

The Opernpalais

East of the cathedral lies a lawn dotted with dignified **statues of Prussian generals**. Among them are Scharnhorst, Yorck and Gneisenau, though it's Blücher, whose timely intervention turned the day at Waterloo, who looks most warlike – sabre in hand and with his foot resting on a cannon. The baroque building behind all this martial prowess is the eighteenth-century **Opernpalais**. Known as the Prinzessinpalais (Princesses' Palace) before the war, for its role as the swanky town house of Friedrich Wilhelm III's three daughters, it's now home to a couple of pricey restaurants and the genteel *Operncafé* (see p.207).

The Friedrichwerdersche Kirche

By ducking under two sets of arches beside the Opernpalais, in the square's southeast corner, you'll come to the **Friedrichwerdersche Kirche** in which the **Schinkel Museum** (daily: 10am–6pm; free; ⓦwww.smb.spk-berlin.de; S-Bahn Hausvogteiplatz) fittingly celebrates the work of the man, who, more than anyone, gave nineteenth-century Berlin its distinctive Neoclassical stamp (see box, p.58). The church itself is a rather plain neo-Gothic affair, a stylistic departure for Schinkel, who was infatuated with the Classical styles he had encountered on trips to Italy. Here, however, the inspiration for the Friedrich-werdersche Kirche came from churches he had seen on a visit to England in 1826. A detailed history of the church is provided in the upper gallery of the museum, which also gives a full rundown of Schinkel's achievements, setting his work in the context of the times. A jumble of nineteenth-century German Neoclassical statuary crowd the ground floor.

Karl Friedrich Schinkel (1781–1841)

The incredibly prolific architect **Karl Friedrich Schinkel** was without doubt one of the most influential German architects of the nineteenth century. Nearly every town in Brandenburg has a building that Schinkel had, at the very least, some involvement in. His first ever design, the **Pomonatempel** in Potsdam, was completed while he was still a nineteen-year-old student in Berlin. Despite this auspicious beginning, his architectural career did not take off immediately and for a while he worked as a landscape artist and theatre-set designer. Towards the end of the first decade of the nineteenth century he began submitting architectural designs for great public works, and, in 1810, he secured a job with the administration of Prussian buildings.

In 1815 he was given a position in the new Public Works Department, and during the years between 1815 and 1830 he designed some of his most renowned buildings such as the Grecian-style **Neue Wache** (see p.60), the elegant **Schauspielhaus** (see p.54) and the **Altes Museum** (see p.66) with its striking Doric columns: all vital to enhancing the ever-expanding capital of Brandenburg-Prussia. Later in his career Schinkel experimented with other architectural forms, a phase marked by the Romanesque **Charlottenhof** in Potsdam (see p.188).

The Bauakademie

Before World War II the block to the east of the **Friedrichwerdersche Kirche**, on the banks of the Spree, was the site of the **Bauakademie** – Karl Friedrich Schinkel's architectural school. This 1836 building is widely considered one of modern architecture's true ancestors, with its rejection of the Classicism around it in favour of brick exterior and terracotta ornamentation. The building spoke of industrialisation and a changing view towards design and construction, and even at the time it was thought to be one of Schinkel's finest creations; he seemed to agree, moving in and occupying a top-floor apartment until his death in 1841. The Kaiser however, hated it, referring to it as the horrible red box that blots the view from the palace (see p.62). The GDR regime also had no time for it, demolishing it in 1962 – despite its relatively light war damage – in favour of a prefab for its foreign ministry, which became one of the first buildings to be demolished after the *Wende*. It was replaced by a grassy field with a statue of Schinkel in the middle looking a little lost, but there are proposals to rebuild the Bauakademie. As an advertisement and incentive, a corner section of the building has been reconstructed on its original site. The rest of the building has been recreated using scaffolding, wrapped in a canvas facade – in an attempt to stimulate enthusiasm and raise funds for reconstruction.

The Foreign Ministry

Behind the Bauakademie and beside the River Spree lies the heavily guarded **Foreign Ministry**. The structure, though massive, projects an unassuming aspect by means of its plain glass facade, through which you can see a serene covered courtyard, complete with trees and fountain. It illustrates one answer to a common problem facing architects for the new German capital: how to create large and significant civic buildings whilst avoiding any hints of Nazi monumentalism? A good example of the latter, and now also occupied by the Foreign Office, lies directly behind: the immense and imposing **Central Bank** built between 1934 and 1938. Having survived the war, it became the SED (Socialist Unity Party of Germany) headquarters and so the nerve centre of the East German Communist party.

The Kronprinzenpalais

The Baroque **Kronprinzenpalais** on Unter den Linden dates from 1663, but is really defined by a 1732 facelift that gave it a more grandiose appearance to reflect its role as a residence for Prussian princes. With the demise of the monarchy in 1918 it became a national art gallery and a leading venue for modern art. In 1933 the Nazis closed it, declaring hundreds of Expressionist and contemporary works housed here to be examples of *entartete Kunst* or "degenerate art". Most of these were either sold off abroad or destroyed, and a number were bought at knock-down prices by leading Nazis, Göring among them. The Kronprinzenpalais has since played host to a variety of organizations and temporary exhibitions.

The Zeughaus and the Deutsches Historisches Museum

The sturdy Baroque building opposite the Kronprinzenpalais was once built as the old Prussian Arsenal or **Zeughaus**. Many of the building's decorative elements are the work of Andreas Schlüter, notably the walls of the **Schlüterhof**, the museum's inner courtyard, where reliefs depict the contorted faces of dying warriors. There was much excitement at the Zeughaus on June 14, 1848, when, during revolutionary upheavals, the people of Berlin stormed the building looking for arms. A number of citizens were killed, and no weapons were found, but the incident gave the authorities an excuse to bring troops into the city and ban various newspapers and democratic organizations.

Just over thirty years later the Zeughaus was turned into a Prussian army museum. During the Nazi period it exhibited propaganda on World War I, portraying it as an undeserved defeat and making much of the dishonest conduct of enemies in the peace treaties – as well as being used for Remembrance Day speeches. At the March 1943 speech there was a failed attempt on Hitler's life; the Führer changed his plans, giving the suicide bomber, Rudolf von Gersdorff, only just enough time to rush to the lavatory and defuse the bomb.

From 1953, the heavily damaged building became a museum of German history first offering the GDR's version of events, then, after reunification, a progressively more balanced, Western view as the **Deutsches Historisches Museum** (daily 10am–6pm; €5; ☎030/203 04 44 44, ⓦwww.dhm.de; S-Bahn Hackescher Markt). Now the museum's immense collection is put to use to chart German history from the Dark Ages to the present – though the opportunity to reflect on the changing way in which the museum itself has portrayed and perverted history in the past has been missed. Be sure to allow at least two hours to do the place justice and with only a relatively small proportion of the exhibition in English, the **audio guide** is recommended.

The **history** produced by the museum focuses overwhelmingly – perhaps inevitably – on military escapades, though it does make an effort to show how big events or "epochs of change" affected the masses. It's all attractively set out and deals cleverly with difficult or contentious areas – such as the rise of nationalism and concepts of German nationhood – by simply providing a balanced summary of the main facts and avoiding interpretation.

Highlights from the early collection include an extraordinary assemblage of **armour** from the old Zeughaus days – including a 15kg jousting helmet – and an impressive collection of early sixteenth-century **bibles**, some of the first books to be printed anywhere. But the most engrossing exhibits are of later periods, following the French Revolution, where the museum offers a balanced view of Prussia, attempting to explain how it slid from being one of the most progressive parts of Europe to one of its most militarized powers. On display are several **helmets** of those killed in action in World War I, gruesomely memorable for the holes left by the bullets that killed their owners.

The exhibition goes on to examine Weimar Germany and the rise of philosophical extremes, particularly communism and fascism, with displays of propaganda art and leaflets helping to provide a useful insight into the mindset of the times. The **Nazi Third Reich** is then explored in every deplorable detail – including the depiction of the war in Russian and American and Nazi **propaganda films**, the latter showing the *Blitzkrieg* arrive in Poland and also mocking Jewish captives in chain gangs. It also covers the GDR years, where the exhibition splits to tell the parallel stories of the two Germanys.

I.M. Pei Bau

The eye-catching swirling glass building behind the Zeughaus is another part of the Deutsches Historisches Museum (see p.59; same hours and entry ticket), and the work of American-Chinese architect I.M. Pei – most famous for his glass pyramid at the entrance to the Louvre in Paris. Pei's hallmark geometric glass is here too, with the resulting play of light perhaps the most important factor in making the building work. The temporary exhibitions here usually delve into German social history in the last couple of centuries, and vary widely, though all seem to share first-class display techniques and even-handedness in the treatment of what are often difficult subject matters.

The Neue Wache

Schinkel's most celebrated surviving creation, the **Neue Wache**, is on Unter den Linden beside the Deutsches Historisches Museum. Built between 1816 and 1818 as a guardhouse for the royal watch, it resembles a stylized Roman temple and served as a sort of Neoclassical police station until 1918. In 1930–31 it was converted into a memorial to the military dead of World War I, and in 1957 the GDR government extended this concept to include those killed by the Nazis, dedicating the building as a "Memorial to the Victims of Fascism and Militarism". Until 1990 one of East Berlin's most ironic ceremonies was played out in front of the Neue Wache – the regular changing of the Nationale Volksarmee (National People's Army – the GDR army) honour guard, a much-photographed goose-stepping ritual that ended with the demise of the East German state. These days it serves as the "National Memorial to the Victims of War and Tyranny", and inside it a granite slab covers the tombs of an unknown soldier and an unknown concentration camp victim. At the head of this memorial stone is a statue, depicting a mother clutching her dying son, an enlargement of a small sculptural piece by Käthe Kollwitz (see p.121).

Palais am Festungsgrab

The grand-looking building behind the Neue Wache, the **Palais am Festungsgrab** has had a chequered career. Built during the eighteenth century as a palace for a royal gentleman of the bedchamber, it later served as a residence for Prussian finance ministers, and during GDR days it was the Zentrale Haus der Deutsch-Sowjetischen Freundschaft or "Central House of German-Soviet Friendship". Today it houses the *Tadschikische Teestuben*, a tearoom serving Russian specialities, and the **Theater im Palais** (see p.237). West beside the **Palais**, the **Maxim-Gorki-Theater** (see p.237) is a one-time singing academy converted into a theatre after World War II.

Mitte: Museum Island and around

At its eastern end, Unter den Linden leads to the **Spreeinsel**, the island in the middle of the River Spree that formed the core of the medieval twin towns of Berlin-Cölln. From the fifteenth century onwards, by virtue of its defensive position, it became the site of the Hohenzollern *Residenz* – the fortress-cum-palace and church of the family who controlled Berlin and Brandenburg. Centred on present-day **Schlossplatz**, this was originally a martial, fortified affair, as much for protection from the perennially rebellious Berliners as from outside enemies, but over the years domestic stability meant that the *Residenz* could be reshaped on a slightly more decorative basis.

In a demonstrative break with Prussia's Imperial past the GDR tore down the war-damaged palace to make way for a huge parade plaza and some of its most important civic buildings, the **Palast der Republik** and the **Staatsrat**. Then, in another demonstrative break, this time with its communist past, Berlin's current administration decided to tear down the former and rebuild the palace – this project is ongoing.

Grand building projects are also in progress on the northern tip of the island where in the nineteenth century the Hohenzollerns added a museum quarter; the

Bridges to Museum Island

Unless you're hopping off bus #100 from Bahnhof Zoo or Alexanderplatz (alight at Schlossplatz) the best way to get to Museum Island is to take the S-Bahn to Hackescher Markt. From there walk west through the square, then through Monbijoupark to **Monbijoubrücke** beside the Bode-Museum or, by ducking under the railway arches, cross the Spree to the Alte Nationalgalerie on **Friedrichsbrücke**, another pedestrian bridge. Both bridges are replacements for ones destroyed by the German army during the Battle of Berlin – more interesting are a couple of the bridges that survived the war intact. Schinkel's **Schlossbrücke** at the eastern end of Unter den Linden is particularly impressive. It first opened on November 28, 1823 when not fully completed, lacking among other things a fixed balustrade, and 22 people drowned when temporary wooden barriers collapsed. Eventually cast-iron balustrades were installed, featuring graceful dolphin, merman and sea-horse motifs designed by Schinkel. The other noteworthy bridge to Museum Island is the **Jungfernbrücke**, tucked away behind the former Staatsrat, Berlin's oldest surviving bridge, built in 1798 and actually a drawbridge.

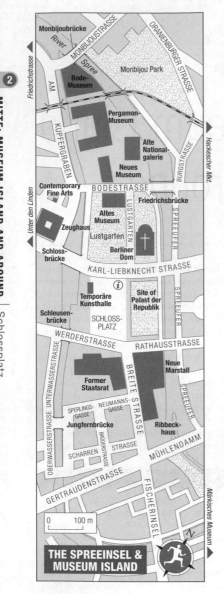

THE SPREEINSEL & MUSEUM ISLAND

building took over eighty years, and eventually created an area known as Museumsinsel or **Museum Island**. Some of the world's greatest museums reside here: the **Pergamonmuseum**, with its jaw-dropping collection of antiquities; the **Altes Museum**, with its selection of superlative Greek vases; the **Neues Museum**, with its extraordinary Ancient Egyptian antiquities; the **Altes Nationalgalerie** and its world-class assortment of nineteenth-century European paintings; and the **Bode-Museum**, with one of Europe's most important sculpture collections.

Schlossplatz

East of Unter den Linden, beyond the Schlossbrücke, is **Schlossplatz**, the former site of the Berliner Schloss, the old Imperial Palace, the remains of which were demolished by the communists after the war, and which, along with the Berliner Dom (see p.65), formed the Imperial *Residenz*. Work began on the palace in 1443 and the Hohenzollern family were to live there for nearly half a millennium. Over the centuries the Schloss was constantly extended and reshaped, the first major overhaul coming in the sixteenth century when it was transformed from a fortress into a Renaissance palace. Later it received a Baroque restyling, and subsequently virtually every German architect of note, including Schlüter, Schinkel and Schadow, was given the opportunity to add to it. For centuries the Schloss dominated the heart of Berlin, and until the 1930s no city centre building was allowed to stand any higher.

On November 9, 1918, the end of the Hohenzollern era came when Karl Liebknecht proclaimed a "Free Socialist Republic" from one of the palace balconies (now preserved in the facade of the Staatsrat building, see opposite), following the abdication of the Kaiser. Almost simultaneously, the Social Democrat Phillip Scheidemann announced a democratic German republic from the Reichstag, and it was in fact the latter that prevailed, ushering in the pathologically unstable Weimar Republic of the 1920s.

After the war the Schloss, a symbol of the still recent Imperial past, was an embarrassment to the GDR authorities who dynamited its ruins in 1950, even

The Palast der Republik and the Humboldt Forum

It was no coincidence that the GDR authorities chose the site of the Imperial Schloss for their **Palast der Republik**, a piece of brutal 1970s modernism in glass and concrete, to house the Volkskammer, the GDR's parliament. This huge angular building with its bronzed, reflective windows was completed in under a thousand days, and became a source of great pride to Erich Honecker's regime. As well as the parliament, it also housed an entertainment complex: restaurants, cafés, a theatre and a bowling alley. It would host craft fairs, discos, folk nights and Christmas festivities, and going there on a day out – something that all East German children were entitled to do once they'd turned 14 – was considered a highlight of growing up.

The interior was at once a showcase of East German design and a masterpiece of tastelessness, the hundreds of lamps hanging from the ceiling of the main foyer giving rise to the nickname, *Erich's Lampenladen* – "Erich's lamp shop". Shortly before unification asbestos was discovered, and on October 3, 1990, the building closed for almost thirteen years while it was stripped out. With only the glass and a skeleton of steel beams left inside, the Palast then became the chic venue for a guerrilla combination of **exhibitions**, **concerts** and **installations**, as well as a **nightclub** on the night of the fifteenth anniversary of the fall of the Wall.

In 2006, by order of the German Parliament, work started to dismantle the Palast. In its place a version of the original Prussian palace, dubbed the **Humboldt Forum**, will be built, to house a mix of cultural and scientific institutions, probably including all the state museums in Dahlem (see p.169). The new palace is to copy the original's dimensions and facade, but due to budget constraints, sadly not its central dome – which in truth made the building. Construction starts in 2010, taking until at least 2018, and will cost between €670 million and €1.2 billion. However, neither the Federal government nor the city of Berlin has cash to spare, nor can they agree how to split the bill, and an independent foundation (see p.55) set up to raise money has collected little. But Berlin is being honest about the difficulties and time-consuming grandeur of the vision, commissioning a local team of landscape architects to fill the gap with an array of lawns on different levels.

though it was no more badly damaged than a number of other structures that were subsequently rebuilt. In its place came the Palast der Republik (see above), which outlasted the regime that created it for almost a decade before it was dismantled to make way for transitional projects and ultimately a recreation of the Schloss. An information booth and lookout tower in the square informs of the plans and progress, but for more detailed information visit the visitor centre near the Gendarmenmarkt (see p.55).

The Staatsrat

With the Palast der Republik gone, the only reminder of the GDR on Schlossplatz is the one-time **Staatsrat**, or State Council, an early 1960s building on the southern side of the platz, with some stylistic affinities to the *Zuckerbäcker* architecture of the Stalin era. Its facade incorporates a large chunk of the Berliner Schloss, notably the balcony from which Karl Liebknecht proclaimed the German revolution in 1918. The building is now the campus for the European School of Management and Technology (Ⓦ www.esmt.org).

Neue Marstall and Breite Strasse

Immediately east of the Staatsrat lies the **Neue Marstall**, an unimaginative turn-of-the-twentieth-century construction, built to house the hundreds of royal coaches and horses used to ferry the royal household around the city. During the

November Revolution of 1918, when it was headquarters of the revolutionary committee, revolutionary sailors and Spartacists beat off government forces from it. A couple of plaques commemorate this deed of rebellious derring-do and Liebknecht's proclamation of the socialist republic. One shows Liebknecht apparently suspended above a cheering crowd of sailors and civilians, while the other, to the left of the entrance, has the head of Marx hovering over some excited but purposeful-looking members of the proletariat.

Breite Strasse sweeps south beside the Neue Marstall, but before it arrives at the intersection with Mühlendamm – just over the Spree from the Nikolaiviertel (see p.76) – it passes the delicately gabled **Ribbeckhaus**. This late-Renaissance palace from the seventeenth century is one of the city's oldest surviving buildings and now houses a branch of Berlin's public library.

The Berliner Dom

Opposite the Palast der Republik and adjacent to the Lustgarten, The **Berliner Dom** (daily: April–Sept Mon–Sat 9am–8pm, Sun noon–8pm; Oct–March Mon–Sat 9am–7pm, Sun noon–7pm; €5, audioguide €3; ⓦ www.berlinerdom .de) is a hulking symbol of Imperial Germany that managed to survive the GDR era. It was built at the turn of the twentieth century, on the site of a more modest cathedral, as a grand royal church for the Hohenzollern family. Fussily ornate with a huge dome flanked by four smaller ones, it was meant to resemble that of St Peter's in Rome, but somehow comes across as little more than a dowdy neo-Baroque imitation.

The Berliner Dom served the House of Hohenzollern as a family church until 1918, and its vault houses ninety sarcophagi containing the remains of various members of the line. The building was badly damaged during the war, but has undergone a long period of reconstruction, leaving it looking like a simpler version of its prewar self, with various ornamental cupolas missing from the newly rounded-off domes.

The main entrance leads into the extravagantly overstated **Predigtkirche**, the octagonal main body of the church. From the marbled pillars of the hall to the delicate plasterwork and gilt of the cupola, there's a sense that it's all meant to reflect Hohenzollern power rather than serve as a place of worship. As if to confirm this impression, six opulent Hohenzollern sarcophagi, including those of Great Elector Wilhelm I, and his second wife, Dorothea, are housed in galleries at the northern and southern ends of the Predigtkirche. The spiritual underpinnings of the society they ruled are less ostentatiously represented by statues of Luther, Melanchthon, Calvin and Zwingli, along with four German princes favourable to the Reformation, in the cornices above the pillars in the main hall.

For an overhead view, head for the **Kaiserliches Treppenhaus** (Imperial Staircase), a grandiose marble staircase at the southwest corner of the building, which leads past pleasantly washed-out paintings of biblical scenes to a balcony looking out onto the Predigtkirche. Here you'll also find a small exhibition on the history of the building. Back downstairs and to the south of the Predigtkirche is the restored **Tauf- and Traukirche**. At first sight this appears to be a marbled souvenir shop, but it is in fact a side chapel used for baptism and confirmation ceremonies.

Lustgarten

A large flat green expanse leading up to the Altes Museum on the northern side of the Schlossplatz, the **Lustgarten** was originally a garden built by the Great Elector. Later King Friedrich Wilhelm I, Prussia's "Soldier-King", turned it into a parade ground as part of his general attempt to transform the city into vast barracks. In 1942 resistance fighters under the Jewish communist Herbert Baum set fire to an anti-communist exhibition that was being held here, an action that cost them their lives. It is commemorated by a stone cube at the centre of the greenery that, despite the inscription "forever bound in friendship with the Soviet Union", still attracts wreath-layers. At the northern end of the Lustgarten, at the foot of the steps leading up to the Altes Museum (see p.66), is a saucer-shaped rock, carved from a huge glacier-deposited granite boulder found near Fürstenwalde, just outside Berlin, and brought here in 1828 to form part of the Altes Museum's rotunda. A mistake in Schinkel's plans meant that its seven-metre diameter made it too large, so, for want of a better plan, it was left here to become an unusual decorative feature.

Museum Island

The northern tip of the Spreeinsel is known as **Museum Island** (Museumsinsel) and is the location of Berlin's most important museums, whose origins go back to 1810, when King Friedrich Wilhelm III decided Berlin needed a museum to house the then rather scant collection of royal treasures. He ordered the reclamation of a patch of Spree-side marsh and commissioned Schinkel to come up with a suitable building, which resulted in the Altes Museum at the head of the Lustgarten.

Things really started to take off when German explorers and archeologists began plundering the archeological sites of Egypt and Asia Minor. The booty brought back by the Egyptologist Carl Richard Lepsius during the 1840s formed the core of what was to become a huge collection, and the Neues Museum was built to house it at the behest of King Friedrich Wilhelm IV. Later that century the Imperial haul was augmented by treasures brought from Turkey by Heinrich Schliemann, for which the vast Pergamonmuseum was constructed.

During World War II the contents of the museums were stashed away in bunkers and mine shafts for protection from bombing, and in the confusion of 1945 and the immediate postwar years it proved difficult to recover the scattered works. Some had been destroyed, others ended up in museums in the Western sector and others disappeared to the East with the Red Army. Gradually, though, the various surviving pieces were tracked down and returned to Berlin – with the notable exception of the

---

Visiting the state museums

The state-run museums of Museum Island exhibit only part of Berlin's collections, which also has groups of museums in the Kulturforum (p.102), Charlottenburg (p.123) and Dahlem (p.169). In all these groupings, the basic ticket to enter a museum (€4–8) is sometimes also a *Standortkarte* (literally "area ticket") which is also good for all the other museums in that grouping on the same day.

For Museum Island you have a choice of tickets: individually most museums cost €8 or €10; but a one-day **Bereich-karte** for all the museums in this chapter costs €14; or there's the better-value Drei-Tage-Karte (three-day ticket: €19), which covers all permanent exhibitions in state museums and a selection of the city's private museums too – a total of around sixty museums. Entry to all state museums is **free** during the last four hours of opening on Thursdays, but these and other museum opening hours regularly change so best check the website Ⓦ www.smb.museum first. In all cases **special exhibitions** cost extra. Most exhibits are only in German, but some collections do provide explanations and information sheets in English and many have excellent, multilingual **audio tours** included in the entrance price – though these usually cost €4 at times when admission is free.

Priam's Treasure, Schliemann's most famous find, which allegedly came from the ruins of the fabled city of Troy. This collection of nine thousand gold chains, elaborate silver pictures, gold coins and other amazing artefacts hit the front pages in 1993 when it finally resurfaced in Moscow, where it remains today.

Reunification has brought together the impressive and long-divided collections of Museum Island, which is being completely **restored and partially remodelled** in an ambitious plan, begun in 1999 and due for completion in 2015 (ⓦwww .museumsinsel-berlin.de). Plans include the creation of a single main entrance and the development of an underground exhibition space that connects all the museums, similar to that at the Louvre in Paris. This is gradually producing one of the world's greatest museum complexes and, with the worst of the general reshuffling over, most of the collections are already fully accessible.

The Altes Museum

At the head of the Lustgarten the **Altes Museum** (daily 10am–6pm except Wed 10am–10pm; €8; ⓦwww.smb.museum; U- & S-Bahn Friedrichstrasse), is perhaps Schinkel's most impressive surviving work, with an 87-metre-high facade fronted by an eighteen-column Ionic colonnade. Along with the Konzerthaus Berlin (see p.54), this is one of Berlin's most striking Neoclassical buildings. Opened as a home for the royal collection of paintings in 1830, the Altes Museum is now host to the **Collection of Classical Antiquities**: small sculpture and pottery from the city's famed Greek and Roman collections. These small works may lack the power and drama of the huge pieces on view at the Pergamon, but there are some captivating items well presented here: *The Praying Boy*, a lithe and delicate bronze sculpture from Rhodes dating back to 300 BC, is the collection's pride and joy. Look, too, for the vase of Euphronios, decorated with an intimate painting of athletes in preparation – the series of Greek vases here is considered to be among the finest in the world.

The Neues Museum

Between the Altes Museum and the Pergamonmuseum is the **Neues Museum** (Mon–Wed & Sun 10am–6pm, Thurs–Sat 10am–8pm; €10; ⓦwww.neues -museum.de; U- & S-Bahn Friedrichstrasse), originally opened in 1855 to house the Egyptian collection. Bombed out in the war, the building was slowly rebuilt and renovated to the highest standard under British architect David Chipperfield, who took great pains to preserve as many original museum features as possible, including fluted stone columns and battered faux-Egyptian ceiling frescos. Entire wings had been destroyed in the War, including the central staircase, but rather than imitating every detail, plain concrete, bare brick and huge wooden rafters have been used for repairs, creating both a sense of history and an effective contrast to the original sections. Finally reopened in 2009, the building houses Berlin's **Egyptian Collection** and **Museum for Pre- and Early History**.

The result of innumerable German excavations in Egypt from the early part of the twentieth century, the most prized exhibit of the **Egyptian Collection** is the 3300-year-old *Bust of Queen Nefertiti*, a treasure that has become a symbol for the city as a cultural capital. There's no questioning its beauty – the queen has a perfect bone structure and gracefully sculpted lips – and the history of the piece is equally interesting. Created around 1350 BC, the bust probably never left the studio in Akhetatenin in which it was created, acting as a model for other portraits of the queen (its use as a model explains why the left eye was never drawn in). When the studio was deserted, the bust was left there, to be discovered some 3000 years later in 1912 and then officially unveiled in Berlin in 1924; which also marked the beginning of an ongoing diplomatic struggle by the Egyptian authorities to have it returned to Egypt.

▲ Exhibit at the Neues Museum

Elsewhere in the collection, atmospheric lighting complements the uniformly high standard of the exhibits. The light is used to particularly good effect on the Expressionistic, almost Futuristic, *Berlin Green Head* of the Ptolemaic period. Don't miss the interesting pieces from the Schliemann excavations of Troy, though the best pieces (some represented here as replicas) remain in Russia, carted away as spoils of war; while delicate negotiations for their return continue.

A bit of a comedown after all the Egyptian excitement below is the **Museum für Vor- und Frühgeschichte**, in the attic of the museum, encompassing a rather underwhelming collection of archeological discoveries from the Berlin area.

The Alte Nationalgalerie

Tucked just behind the Neues Museum is the **Alte Nationalgalerie** (Fri–Wed 10am–6pm, Thurs 10am–10pm; €8; ⓦ www.smb.museum; U- & S-Bahn Friedrichstrasse), a slightly exaggerated example of post-Schinkel Neoclassicism that contains the **nineteenth-century** section of Berlin's state art collection. The main body of the museum, built in 1876, resembles a Corinthian temple and is fronted by an imposing equestrian statue of its royal patron, Friedrich Wilhelm IV.

Particularly noteworthy among the Alte Nationalgalerie's collection are several works of the "**German Romans**", mid-nineteenth-century artists like Anselm Feuerbach and Arnold Böcklin, who spent much of their working lives in Italy; Böcklin's eerie, dreamlike *Isle of the Dead* retains its power even today. A highlight of this school is the Casa Bartholdy **frescoes**, softly illuminated paintings by Peter Cornelius, Wilhelm Veit and others that illustrate the story of Joseph. The broad canvases of Adolph von Menzel strike a rather different note: though chiefly known during his lifetime for his detailed depictions of court life under Frederick the Great, it's his interpretations of Berlin on the verge of the industrial age, such as *The Iron Foundry*, that make more interesting viewing today.

Other rooms contain important **Impressionist** works by van Gogh, Degas, Monet and native son Max Liebermann, plus statues by Rodin. But it's on the top floor, in the **Galerie der Romantik**, with its collection of nineteenth-century paintings from the German Romantic, Classical and Biedermeier movements, that the collection is at its most powerful. The two central rooms on this floor contain work by **Karl Friedrich Schinkel** and **Caspar David Friedrich**. Schinkel was the architect responsible for the Neoclassical design of the Altes Museum (see p.66) and his paintings are meticulously drawn Gothic fantasies, often with sea settings. *Gothic Church on a Rock by the Sea* is the most moodily dramatic and didactic in purpose: the medieval knights in the foreground ride next to a prayer tablet – Schinkel believed that a rekindling of medieval piety would bring about the moral regeneration of the German nation. But more dramatic are the works of **Caspar David Friedrich**, all of which express a powerful elemental and religious approach to landscape. Particularly evident of the brooding and drama of his Romantic sensibility is the *Abbey Among Oak Trees* of 1809, perhaps the best known of his works.

The Pergamonmuseum

The **Pergamonmuseum** (Fri–Wed 10am–6pm, Thurs 10am–10pm; €10; Ⓦwww .smb.museum; U- & S-Bahn Friedrichstrasse) is accessible from Am Kupfergraben on the south bank of the River Spree. It's a massive structure, built in the early part of the twentieth century in the style of a Babylonian temple to house the treasure trove of the German archeologists who were busy plundering the ancient world, packaging it up and sending it back to Berlin.

The museum is divided into three sections, the most important one being the **Department of Antiquities** on the main floor, which contains the **Pergamon Altar**. A huge structure dedicated to Zeus and Athena, dating from 180 to 160 BC, it was unearthed at Bergama in western Turkey by the archeologist Carl Humann and brought to Berlin in 1903. The **frieze** shows a battle between the gods and giants and is a tremendously forceful piece of work, with powerfully depicted figures writhing in a mass of sinew and muscle. To the rear of the Altar is the **Telephos Frieze**, another amazing Pergamon find, which originally adorned the interior of the Pergamon Altar; its depiction of the life story of Telephos, the legendary founder of Pergamon, is a bit more sedate. The section also contains other pieces of Hellenistic and Classical architecture, including the two-storey **market gate** from the Turkish town of Miletus. Built by the Romans in 120 AD, the gate was destroyed by an earthquake just under a thousand years later and brought to Berlin in fragmentary form for reconstruction during the nineteenth century.

The **Middle Eastern Section**, also on the main floor, has items going back four thousand years to Babylonian times. The collection includes the enormous **Ishtar Gate** (see box below), the **Processional Way** and the facade of the **Throne Room** from Babylon, all of which date from the reign of Nebuchadnezzar II in the sixth century BC. It's impossible not to be awed by the size and the remarkable state of preservation of the deep-blue enamelled bricks of the Babylon finds, but at the same time bear in mind that much of it is a mock-up, built around the original finds.

A thirteen year-long facelift

At over 2600 years old, it's perhaps high-time that the **Ishtar Gate** – one of the eight fabled gates of the ancient city of Babylon, and one of the Pergamonmuseum's biggest draws – got a face lift. Partly because of the museum's humidity and lack of air conditioning, the thirteen-metre-high gate needed work in around a thousand places, mainly on the glaze that seals the enamel tiles, about one-tenth of which are original. The process involves cleaning each section then slowly injecting chemicals into it, and this will happen in front of an average of 2000 visitors a day. Completing the entire process is expected to take until 2019.

Pride of place in the museum's **Islamic Section** goes to the relief-decorated facade of a Jordanian **Prince's Palace** at Mshatta, from 743 AD, presented to Kaiser Wilhelm II by the sultan of Turkey. On a slightly more modest scale is a thirteenth-century **prayer niche** decorated with turquoise, black and gold tiles, from a mosque in Asia Minor. Also worth seeking out is the **Aleppo Room**, a reception chamber with carved wooden wall decorations, reassembled in Berlin after being removed from a merchant's house in present-day Syria.

The Bode-Museum

The stocky, neo-Baroque **Bode-Museum** (Fri–Wed 10am–6pm, Thurs 10am–10pm; €8; Ⓦwww.smb.museum; U- & S-Bahn Friedrichstrasse) at the northern tip of Museum Island suffered such heavy damage during World War II that it was scheduled for demolition in the late 1940s, until Berliners took to the streets in protest.

The result of expensive renovation over the years is impressive, having created opulent entrances and stairways, a swish first-floor **café**, and, most importantly providing a seamless backdrop for one of Europe's most impressive **sculpture collections**. Wilhelm von Bode, the first director of the museum that now bears his name, would probably have approved: his ambition was to present as complete a history of European sculpture as possible, and place them in a proper context. This led to his scouring Europe for items like fireplaces, frescoes and even whole ceilings for the museum. The present set-up doesn't go quite that far but despite wartime losses the collection represents a good tour of European sculpture between the third and nineteenth centuries. A particular strength is the early **Italian Renaissance** with pieces by Luca della Robbia, Donatello, Desiderio da Settignano, Francesco Laurana and Mino da Fiesole among the highlights. Also from Italy is the unusual attraction of the **Tiepolo-Kabinett**, a small white and pastel room rich in stucco ornamentation and immaculate frescoes by Giovanni Battista Tiepolo, in a 1759 work originally located in a north Italian village.

The **German collection** is equally authoritative, particularly in sections detailing the Middle Ages – including work by masters like the late fifteenth-century woodcarver Tilman Riemenschneider, along with Hans Multscher, Hans Brüggemann, Nicolaus Gerhaert van Leyden and Hans Leinberger. Equally — significant, particularly in the local context, are sculptures of several proud and imposing Prussian generals by Andreas Schlüter, created for Wilhelmplatz – a square that used to abut Wilhelmstrasse and Berlin's government quarter (see p.57); the imposing statue of Friedrich Wilhelm I sitting astride a horse in the museum lobby is also his work.

The collection suffered greatly during the war, with many pieces in storage being irreparably damaged, such as the early sixteenth-century bust by Antonio della Porta, damaged by fire and now resembling a gruesomely disfigured figure or traumatized victim of war, which is displayed in the museum as a memorial to the others.

Also in the building is a collection of **Byzantine Art**, said to be second only to that of Istanbul's archeological museum. It's particularly strong on early Christian religious items, as well as featuring ornamental Roman sarcophagi and several intricate mosaics and ivory carvings that stand in testament to the sophistication of Byzantium.

Finally, the Bode-Museum is also home to an extraordinary **Numismatic collection**. Though mainly appealing to those with a specialist interest, it's worth a quick look for its gigantic size – around half-a-million coins – and the prize possessions, which include seventh-century coins that were among some of the first to have ever been minted.

Mitte: Alexanderplatz and around

With the gigantic TV tower looming over all Berlin, the adjacent, dreary **Alexanderplatz** – an unmistakeable product of the old East Germany – is easy to find. And as a major U-Bahn, S-Bahn and tram station it's also easy to get to. During East Berlin's forty-year existence, while Unter den Linden was allowed to represent the glories of past Berlin, Alexanderplatz and its environs were meant to represent the glories of a modern socialist capital. However, it's hard to imagine that the concrete gigantism of the GDR era will wear as well as the efforts of Schinkel and his contemporaries. This is one part of town where there's little point in trying to spot prewar remains, as there's almost no trace of what stood here before 1945. Whole streets have vanished – the open area around the base of the **TV tower**, or Fernsehturm, for example, used to be a dense network of inner-city streets – and today only a few survivors like the **Marienkirche** and **Rotes Rathaus** remain standing amid the modernity.

This is not to say that Alexanderplatz should be passed by. If you can let your aesthetic sensibilities take a back seat, it's worth exploring not only the area's handful of historic buildings but also the ugly East German creations that have their own place in Berlin's architectural chronology.

If it all gets too much, relief from the concrete is on hand in the nearby **Nikolaiviertel**, a pedestrian area that recreates a portion of Berlin's destroyed medieval heart and is home to the **Zille Museum**, which sketches out the life and work of cartoonist and satirist Heinrich Zille. The Nikolaiviertel backs onto a stretch of the **River Spree** that's lined by attractive riverside paths which join up to form a loop past some interesting modern buildings, including the **Dutch Embassy**, a clutch of secluded old buildings beside a stretch of Berlin's medieval first wall (built to keep people out rather than in), some private **art galleries** and **workshops** and the **Märkisches Museum**, where you can flesh out some of the city's history.

Alexanderplatz

Though long an important business and traffic centre, today's **Alexanderplatz** – a sprawling, windswept, pedestrianized plaza surrounded by high-rises – is largely the product of a 1960s GDR vision of what the centre of a modern, socialist metropolis should look like. During the eighteenth century routes to

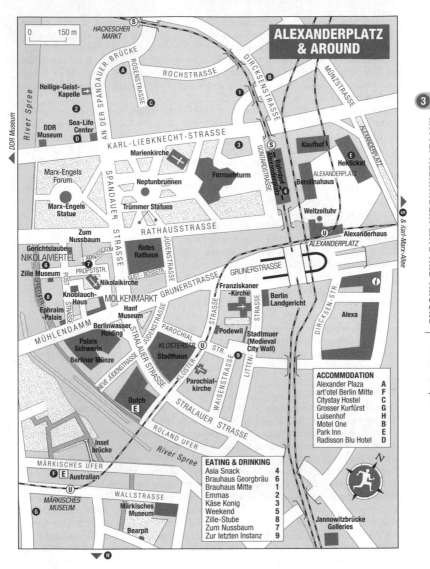

Map labels:

ALEXANDERPLATZ & AROUND

0   150 m

HACKESCHER MARKT

River Spree

DDR Museum

Heilige-Geist-Kapelle

Sea-Life Center

DDR Museum

ROCHSTRASSE

ROSENSTRASSE

AN DER SPANDAUER BRÜCKE

DIRCKSENSTRASSE

MÜNZSTRASSE

ALEXANDERPLATZ

KARL-LIEBKNECHT-STRASSE

Marienkirche

Marx-Engels Forum

Neptunbrunnen

Fernsehturm

Kaufhof

Hekticket

ALEXANDERPLATZ

Berolinahaus

Marx-Engels Statue

Trümmer Statues

SPANDAUER STRASSE

RATHAUSSTRASSE

GONTARDSTRASSE

Bahnhof Alexanderplatz

Weltzeituhr

Alexanderhaus

& Karl-Marx-Allee

Zum Nussbaum

Gerichtslaube

NIKOLAIVIERTEL

Zille Museum

Rotes Rathaus

JUDENSTRASSE

AM NUSSBAUM

PROPSTSTR.

Nikolaikirche

GUST.-BÖSSSTR.

ALEXANDERPLATZ

GRUNERSTRASSE

Knoblauch-Haus

Ephraim-Palais

POSTSTRASSE

MOLKENMARKT

Hanf Museum

Franziskaner-Kirche

Berlin Landgericht

GRUNERSTRASSE

DIRCKSEN-STR.

Alexa

SPREEUFER

Berlinwasser Holding

Palais Schwerin

Berliner Münze

MÜHLENDAMM

STRALAUER STRASSE

NEUE JUDENSTRASSE

JUDENSTRASSE

PAROCHIAL STRASSE

KLOSTERSTR.

Stadthaus

Parochial-kirche

KLOSTER STR.

Podewil

Stadtmuer (Medieval City Wall)

WAISENSTRASSE

LITTEN-STR.

Dutch

STRALAUER STRASSE

ROLAND UFER

River Spree

Insel brücke

MÄRKISCHES UFER

Australian

WALLSTRASSE

MÄRKISCHES MUSEUM

Märkisches Museum

Bearpit

Jannowitzbrücke Galleries

N

ACCOMMODATION
Alexander Plaza	A
art'otel Berlin Mitte	F
Citystay Hostel	C
Grosser Kurfürst	G
Luisenhof	H
Motel One	B
Park Inn	E
Radisson Blu Hotel	D

EATING & DRINKING
Asia Snack	4
Brauhaus Georgbräu	6
Brauhaus Mitte	1
Emmas	2
Käse Konig	3
Weekend	5
Zille-Stube	8
Zum Nussbaum	7
Zur letzten Instanz	9

all parts of Germany radiated from here, and a cattle and wool market stood on the site. It acquired its present name after the Russian tsar Alexander I visited Berlin in 1805. Today, in addition to the S-Bahn line running overhead, three underground lines cross beneath the platz, various bus routes converge on the area, and several tram lines course through it, making it one of central Berlin's busiest corners.

Alexanderplatz has figured prominently in city upheavals ever since revolutionaries (including the writer Theodor Fontane) set up barricades here in 1848. In 1872 it was the site of a demonstration by an army of homeless women and children, and nearly half a century later, during the revolution of 1918, sailors occupied the Alexanderplatz police headquarters (a feared local landmark that lay just to the southeast of the platz – a plaque marks the spot) and freed the prisoners. More recently, it was the focal point of the million-strong city-wide **demonstration** of November 4, 1989, which formed a prelude to the events of November 9, when hundreds of thousands of people crammed into the square to hear opposition leaders speak.

Throughout its existence, the face of Alexanderplatz has undergone many transformations. A major reshaping at the end of the 1920s cleaned up what had turned into a rather sleazy corner of the city and turned it into one of its main shopping centres, with two expensive department stores in the vicinity: Hermann Tietz and Wertheim. Both were Jewish-owned until "Aryanized" by the Nazis. The Kaufhof department store facing the fountain was, as Centrum, one of the best-stocked shops in East Germany, though these days it's just another run-of-the-mill big store, now joined by several other chain stores around the square.

From the main doors at the southern end of the train station – which looks much the same as it did before the war despite being a 1960s rebuild – the route onto "Alex" leads through a gap between a couple of prewar survivors: the **Alexanderhaus** and the **Berolinahaus**, two buildings designed at the beginning of the 1930s by the architect and designer Peter Behrens, whose ideas influenced the founders of the Bauhaus movement. With their opaque glass towers beautifully lit at night, these are the only Alexanderplatz buildings not to have been destroyed in the war. The most intriguing communist-era landmark on the square is the **Weltzeituhr** ("World Clock") in front of the Alexanderhaus. Central Berlin's best-known rendezvous point, it tells the time in different cities throughout the world, and is a product of the same architectural school responsible for the Fernsehturm.

The Fernsehturm

Overshadowing every building in the vicinity, the gigantic **Fernsehturm**, or TV tower (daily: March–Oct 9am–midnight; Nov–Feb 10am–midnight; €10.50; ⓦ www.berlinerfernsehturm.de), just southwest of the Alexanderplatz S-Bahn station, looms over the eastern Berlin skyline like a displaced satellite sitting on top of a huge factory chimney. The highest structure in Western Europe, this 365-metre-high transmitter was built during the isolationist 1960s, a period when the eastern part of the city was largely inaccessible to West Germans, and intended as a highly visible symbol of the permanence of East Berlin and the German Democratic Republic. Its construction was watched with dismay and derision by West Berliners (and many in the East), who were heartily amused by the fact that sunshine reflecting off the globe on the tower forms a cross visible even in western Berlin; they dubbed it the "pope's revenge", much to the reported chagrin of the old GDR authorities. Nevertheless, after completion in 1969 the tower soon became a popular stop-off on the East Berlin tourist circuit.

These days, having outlasted the regime that conceived it, the Fernsehturm has become part of the scenery, and though few would champion it on the grounds of architectural merit, it does have a certain retro appeal. Along with being an unmissable orientation point, the tower also provides a tremendous **view** (40km on a rare clear day) from the observation platform – reached by a very fast lift. Above the observation platform is the *Tele-café*, whose main attraction is that it revolves on its own axis twice an hour. If you want to go up, bear in mind that there are sometimes long queues (evening is your best bet).

▲ The Fernsehturm from Alexanderplatz

The Marienkirche

Once hemmed in by buildings, and now oddly alone in the shadow of the huge Fernsehturm, stands the **Marienkirche** (daily: April–Oct 10am–9pm; Nov–March 10am–4pm; free; U- & S- Bahn Alexanderplatz), Berlin's oldest parish church. The Gothic stone and brick nave dates back to about 1270, but the tower is more recent, having been added in 1466, with the verdigris-coated upper section tacked on towards the end of the eighteenth century by the designer of the Brandenburg Gate, Carl Gotthard Langhans. This uncontrived combination of architectural styles somehow makes the Marienkirche one of Berlin's most appealing churches, its simplicity a reminder of the city's village origins.

The **interior** is an excellent place to escape the increasingly frenetic street life of the area and listen to a free organ recital (Sat 4.30pm). Near the main entrance at the western end of the church is a small cross erected by the citizens of Berlin and Cölln as penance to the pope, after a mob immolated a papal representative on a nearby marketplace. There are five holes in the cross and, according to tradition, during the Middle Ages convicted criminals wishing to prove their innocence could do so by inserting the fingers of one hand into the holes simultaneously – not too many escaped punishment, though, as the feat is virtually an anatomical impossibility. Just inside the entrance, look out for the fifteenth-century *Totentanz*, a twenty-two-metre frieze showing the dance of death. It's very faded, but accompanied by a representation of how it once looked, with Death shown as a shroud-clad mummy popping up between people from all levels of society.

The vaulted nave is plain and white but enlivened by some opulent decorative touches. Foremost among these is Andreas Schlüter's magnificent **pulpit**, its canopy dripping with cherubs and backed by a cloud from which gilded sunrays radiate. Complementing this are the white marble altar with a huge triptych altarpiece and the eighteenth-century organ, a riot of gilded filigree and yet more cherubs, topped by a sunburst.

The Neptunbrunnen

Walking a short way south across the large open plaza from the **Marienkirche** brings you to the **Neptunbrunnen**, an extravagantly imaginative fountain incorporating a statue of a trident-wielding Neptune sitting on a shell. A serpent, seal and alligator spray the god of the sea with water, and he is supported by strange fish and eel-draped aquatic centaurs with webbed feet instead of hooves. Around the rim of the fountain sit four female courtiers, symbolizing what were at the time the four most important German rivers: the Rhine, the Vistula, the Oder and the Elbe. The statue was built in 1891 and was originally on Schlossplatz.

The Rotes Rathaus

Across Rathausstrasse from the Neptunbrunnen is a rare survivor of Hohenzollern-era Berlin in the shape of the **Rotes Rathaus**, Berlin's "Red Town Hall". So called because of the colour of its bricks rather than its politics, the Rotes Rathaus has a solid angularity that contrasts sharply with the finicky grandeur of contemporaries like the Dom. This is perhaps because it's a symbol of the civic rather than the Imperial Berlin of the time – a city in the throes of rapid commercial expansion and industrial growth. The building has lost some of its impact now that it's been hemmed in by new structures, but it remains a grandiose, almost Venetian-looking edifice; look out for the intricate bas-relief in terracotta, illustrating episodes from the history of Berlin, that runs around the building at first-floor level. The Rathaus was badly knocked around in 1945, but made a good comeback following restoration during the 1950s. During GDR days it was headquarters of the East Berlin city administration, and since October 1991 it has housed the united city's administration.

The reconstruction of the Rathaus and thousands of other Berlin buildings is largely due to the *Trümmerfrauen* or "rubble women", who set to work in 1945 clearing up the 100 million tons of rubble created by wartime bombing and shelling. Their deeds are commemorated by the **statue** of a robust-looking woman facing the eastern entrance to the Rathaus on Rathausstrasse. Women of all ages carried out the bulk of the early rebuilding work, since most of Berlin's adult male population was dead, disabled or being held in PoW camps by the Allies. Despite this, the male contribution to the work is also marked by a statue of a man looking wistfully towards his *Trümmerfrau* counterpart from the western end of the Rathaus.

Sea-life Center

Spandauer Strasse, once one of the city's more important streets, cuts through the plaza beside the Rathaus. Though almost all its historic buildings were destroyed during the war, it is still worth a quick exploration. At its northwestern corner stands a large modern colossus that incorporates the *Radisson Hotel* (see p.196), a touristy mall and Berlin's **Sea-life Center**, Spandauer Strasse 3 (daily 10am–7pm, last admission 6pm; €16.95; ☎030/99 28 00, ⓦwww.sealifeeurope.com; S-Bahn Hackescher Markt), a fiercely commercial aquarium that displays the fairly dreary aquatic life of the region's rivers and the North Atlantic. But at least the species here, highlights of which include sea horses, jellyfish, small sharks and manta rays, are elegantly displayed, particularly in the **Aquadom**. This gigantic tubular tank, located in the lobby of the *Radisson* next door, has an elevator through which Sea-life visitors can slowly rise. Others might sneak a peek at it from the hotel lobby, with its swish bar and comfy chairs.

Heilige-Geist-Kapelle

Northwest of the Sea-life Center, en route to Hackescher Markt (see Chapter 4), is the red-brick Gothic **Heilige-Geist-Kapelle** (Holy Ghost Chapel), one of Berlin's oldest surviving buildings. A remnant of the fourteenth century, it's now quaintly incongruous dwarfed as it is by the larger, newer building (part of Humboldt University) that was grafted onto it at the turn of the twentieth century. The original interior has not survived, but it's a miracle that the chapel is still standing at all: it has endured the huge city fire of 1380, an enormously destructive explosion of a nearby gunpowder magazine in 1720, and, above all, wartime bombing.

The DDR Museum

On the same city block as the Heilige-Geist-Kapelle, but tucked into the banks of the Spree, is the popular **DDR Museum**, Karl-Liebknecht-Strasse 1 (Mon–Fri & Sun 10am–8pm, Sat 10am–10pm; €5.50; ☎030/847 12 37 31, ⓦwww .ddr-museum.de), a homage to *Ostalgie* (see the *Ostalgie* colour section). By focusing almost entirely on daily life, it glosses over the GDR's gloomiest issues – like censorship and repression – and is consequently quite upbeat. The collection isn't big, but addresses a wide range of themes, mostly using hands-on displays. There are memories of the school system, pioneer camps and the razzmatazz with which the feats of model workers were celebrated. Less impressive were the GDR's awkward attempts to rival western fashions, as its collection of polyester clothing and bleached jeans shows. Small wonder then that one big craze in the GDR was nudism – as one very revealing display explains – which was considered as healthy as the many sports that the state unceasingly supported.

The section devoted to travel is particularly good, and includes the chance to sit behind the wheel of a Trabi, where you'll quickly appreciate the "fewer parts mean less trouble" principle upon which the fibreglass car was built. The car is parked in front of video footage of East Berlin streets; for journeys further afield you can consult an Eastern Bloc road atlas, which clearly defines where you can find the freedom of the open road.

But the museum's highlight is the chance to mooch around a tiny reconstructed GDR apartment, ablaze with retro browns and oranges, where you're invited to nose through cupboards and cosy up on a sofa to watch speeches by Erich Honecker: "*Vorwärts immer, rückwärts nimmer*" ("always forwards, never backwards").

The Marx-Engels-Forum

South down Spandauer Strasse on the southern side of Karl-Liebknecht-Strasse, is the **Marx-Engels-Forum**, a severely well-ordered patch of city-centre greenery. At its heart sits a lumpen bronze representation of the founders of the "scientific world view of the working class", as pre-*Wende* guidebooks referred to Karl Marx and Friedrich Engels. Facing the monument are eight steel pillars bearing photogravure images of uplifting scenes from Soviet and East German life and events from various revolutionary struggles. These have been partly vandalized, and someone has made a determined effort to scratch out the face of Erich Honecker on one of them. Nearby are blurred bronze reliefs of men and women doing nothing in particular, and between the Marx-Engels statue and the Palast der Republik are some similarly unclear stone reliefs showing muscular men standing around.

The Nikolaiviertel

Slightly to the southwest of the Rotes Rathaus lies the compact network of streets of the **Nikolaiviertel**, a district razed overnight on June 16, 1944 and rebuilt by the GDR authorities in the early 1980s in an attempt to re-create some of the old heart of Berlin on the site of the city's **medieval** core. One or two original buildings aside, the Nikolaiviertel consists partly of exact replicas of historic Berlin buildings and partly of stylized buildings not based on anything in particular, but with a vaguely "old Berlin" feel. Sometimes it doesn't quite come off, and in places the use of typical East German *Plattenbau* construction techniques, with prefabricated pillars and gables, isn't too convincing, but all in all the Nikolaiviertel represents a radical and welcome architectural departure from the usual East German response of levelling an area and building enormous concrete edifices.

Sadly, the district has barely taken seed, having the sterile feel of a living history museum that attracts only tourists and those Berliners who work in the restaurants and *Gaststätten* which, in keeping with their surroundings, tend to specialize in heavy traditional German food – a good place to come if that's what you're looking for.

Some of the most attractive Nikolaiviertel houses – mostly pastel-facaded town houses four or five storeys high – are around the Nikolaikirche, along Propststrasse, and on the southern side of Nikolaikirchplatz, behind the church itself, where they are particularly convincing – it's hard to believe that these are fakes dating back only as far as the beginning of the 1980s. To compare these with an original head to the Knoblauch-Haus on Poststrasse.

The Nikolaikirche

At the centre of Nikolaiviertel, on Nikolaikirchplatz, just off Propststrasse, is the Gothic **Nikolaikirche** (Tue & Thurs–Sun 10am–6pm, Wed noon–8pm; €5; Ⓦ www.stadtmuseum.de), a thirteenth-century church, restored to its twin-towered prewar glory. The Nikolaikirche is one of the city's oldest churches and it was from here on November 2, 1539, that news of the Reformation was proclaimed to the citizens of Berlin. The distinctive needle-like spires date from a nineteenth-century restoration, or rather their design does – the building was thoroughly wrecked during the war, and what you see today is largely a rebuild, as extensive patches of lighter, obviously modern masonry show.

The church is now a **museum** that traces the building's history, although it is often given over to temporary exhibitions. An unusual feature of its interior is the bright colouring of the vault ribbings: the orange, purple, green and other vivid lines look like a Sixties Pop Art addition, but actually follow a medieval pattern discovered by a restorer in the 1980s.

Zum Nussbaum and the Zille Museum

Propststrasse runs past the side of Nikolaikirche all the way down to the River Spree and ends in a rather clichéd statue of St George and the Dragon. Along it are a couple of places associated with Heinrich Zille – the Berlin artist who produced earthy satirical drawings of Berlin life around the turn of the twentieth century. One of his favourite watering holes – along with another Berlin artist Otto Nagel – was the sixteenth-century **Zum Nussbaum** (see p.208) pub, though in those days it stood on the opposite side of the Spree on the Spreeinsel before it was destroyed by wartime bombing. The replica is a faithful copy, right down to the walnut tree in the tiny garden. Many of Zille's drawings of early twentieth-century proletarian life were based on stories overheard in this pub, and you can explore the results further down the street at the excellent little **Zille Museum** (April–Oct daily 11am–7pm; Nov–March Tues–Sun 11am–6pm; €5; ☎030/24 63 25 00, Ⓦwww.heinrich-zille-museum.de). The museum gives a good insight into the artist's life and attitude, though it makes no allowances for non-German speakers. But if you can understand German, or know a little of Zille's background, it's easy to enjoy the three rooms and short video on the artist's life, and to appreciate his economical style and ability to portray squalid working-class life humorously and vividly.

The Gerichtslaube and the Knoblauch-Haus

Crossing Propststrasse is Poststrasse, the only other main street in the Nikolaiviertel. At its northern end is the **Gerichtslaube**, a replica of Berlin's medieval courthouse. The original was dismantled in 1870 in order to create the space needed for the building of the Rotes Rathaus, and was removed to the grounds of Schloss Babelsberg in Potsdam where it can still be seen (see p.189).

The southern end of Poststrasse is more rewarding, thanks to the presence of the **Knoblauch-Haus** at no. 23 (Tues & Thurs–Sun 10am–6pm, Wed noon–8pm; free; Ⓦwww.stadtmuseum.de), a Neoclassical town house built in 1759 and a rare survivor of the war. It was home to the patrician Knoblauch family, who played an important role in the commercial and cultural life of eighteenth- and nineteenth-century Berlin, and now contains an exhibition (with nothing in English) about their activities. While the careers of Eduard Knoblauch, Berlin's first freelance architect, and Armand Knoblauch, founder of a major city brewery, are only mildly interesting, the real appeal here is the **interior** of the house, with its grand-bourgeois furnishings, which gives a good impression of upper middle-class life in Hohenzollern-era Berlin. The ground floor and vaulted basement of the Knoblauch-Haus are home to the *Historische Weinstuben*, a reconstruction of a nineteenth-century wine-restaurant once favoured by the playwrights Gerhart Hauptmann, August Strindberg and Henrik Ibsen.

The Ephraim-Palais

With its curving elegant Rococo facade and mainstream art exhibits the **Ephraim-Palais**, Poststrasse 16 (Tues & Thurs–Sun 10am–6pm, Wed noon–8pm; €5; Ⓦwww.stadtmuseum.de), is far more in step with its surroundings. A rebuilt eighteenth-century merchant's mansion, this is another relic of Berlin bourgeois high life and now houses a museum of Berlin-related art from the seventeenth to the beginning of the nineteenth centuries, with numerous pictures, prints and maps giving a good impression of the city in its glory days.

The Ephraim-Palais was built by Veitel Heine Ephraim, court jeweller and mint master to Frederick the Great, and all-round wheeler-dealer. He owed his lavish lifestyle primarily to the fact that – on Frederick's orders – he steadily reduced the silver content of the Prussian *thaler*. This earned a great deal of money for Frederick and Ephraim himself but ruined the purchasing power of the currency.

The Molkenmarkt

The busy but soulless square just east of the Nikolaiviertel, the **Molkenmarkt,** is one of Berlin's oldest public spaces. On its eastern side Jüdenstrasse – "Jews' Street" was Berlin's original Jewish ghetto, until they were driven out of Brandenburg in 1573. When allowed back into Berlin in 1671 they mainly settled near today's Hackescher Markt (see Chapter 4). Glowering over the road, the large domed **Stadthaus** is reminiscent of the Französischer Dom (see p.53) but dates from as recently as 1911, a relic of the days when the area served as the administrative district of Wilhelmine Berlin. Also on the Molkenmarkt is the smooth zinc-clad **Berlinwasser Holding** building, with its fiercely angular arches and windows, which belongs to the local water company. The work of highly acclaimed local architect Christoph Langhof, it cleverly plays on the **Palais Schwerin**, the traditional building next door – one of two pompous buildings that make up the **Berliner Münze** (Berlin Mint), whose most impressive feature is a replica of a frieze depicting coining techniques by Gottfried Schadow, designer of the Brandenburg Gate Quadriga.

The Dutch Embassy

A couple of minutes' walk along the north bank of the Spree from the Berlin Mint sits the striking **Dutch Embassy** building, designed by Rem Koolhaas. The concept for it was to blend the security and formality of the civil service with something that projects Dutch openness. The resulting building has a slightly unfinished look but is clever in the way that it circulates light and air and with its use of a cube housing the ambassadorial accommodation, which stands apart from the rest. The embassy staff's habits were used to inspire the building: in the previous embassy, the entrance hall was popular for informal meetings so the designers created an enormous hallway as a centrepiece that extends up to all eight storeys and shapes the building's internal communication and ventilation.

Klosterstrasse and around

Named after a long-gone local monastery, **Klosterstrasse** leaves the banks of the Spree and the Dutch Embassy to link several minor points of interest. The **Parochialkirche**, a Baroque church that dates back to the sixteenth century, lies near its junction with **Parochialstrasse**. The bare brick interior (legacy of the usual wartime gutting) is a venue for changing, but often low-key and dull, art exhibitions (free). Parochialstrasse itself had a brief moment of importance in the city's history when the building at **Parochialstrasse 1** hosted the first meeting of Berlin's post-Nazi town council, headed by future SED chief Walter Ulbricht, even as fighting still raged a little to the west. Ulbricht and his comrades had been specially flown in from Soviet exile to sow the seeds of a communist civil administration, and they moved in here, having been unable to set up shop in the still-burning Rotes Rathaus.

The northern end of Klosterstrasse is worth a quick look for the gutted thirteenth-century **Franziskaner-Kirche**, destroyed by a landmine in 1945 and left a ruin by GDR authorities as a warning against war and fascism. Another ruin from Berlin's history is behind it on Littenstrasse where a fragment of **Stadtmauer**, the original thirteenth-century Berlin wall, survives. Behind it is the atmospheric old pub **Zur letzten Instanz**, Berlin's oldest (see p.216).

The Jannowitzbrücke galleries

From Klosterstrasse, head east to the increasingly industrialized neighbourhood and U- and S- Bahn station **Jannowitzbrücke**. It's here, under the red-brick arches of the S-Bahn viaducts, that some of Berlin's most dynamic artists and avant-garde gallerists have settled. These unkempt spaces provide rough-and-ready studios in an edgy location for those who have tired of the increasingly gentrified area around Auguststrasse (see p.91) that attracted bohemian artists in the immediate post-*Wende* years. It's worth ducking into one or two of those that are open to the public to see what some of the contemporary Berlin art scene is up to; the entrance to the studios is rather hidden behind a petrol station.

The Märkisches Museum

With the appearance of a red-brick neo-Gothic cathedral, the **Märkisches Museum**, Am Köllnischen Park 5 (Tues & Thurs–Sun 10am–6pm, Wed noon–8pm; €5, free on first Wed every month; Ⓦ www.stadtmuseum.de; U-Bahn Märkisches Museum), dates from before reunification and shows its age in the dated treatment of the history of Berlin and the Mark Brandenburg, with lots of small rooms crammed with paintings, gadgets and glass vitrines. The displays are also incomplete and episodic: eighteenth- and nineteenth-century culture is definitely the museum's forte.

Following the tour laid out by the museum, one of the first rooms deals with Berlin's late nineteenth-century role as a centre of **barrel organ** production, an industry established by Italian immigrants. Many of these music-makers are on display, as well as their increasingly large and more intricate progeny. Organ-grinding performances are given every Sunday at 3pm.

The rooms that follow are more engaging, and devoted to themes such as "Industrialization", "Intellectual Life", "Woman", and "the Military". Also noteworthy is the **Gottische Kapelle**, a room resembling a small chapel and filled with wonderful pieces of medieval sacred art from (usually) unknown local artisans, including the expressive sculpture, *Spandauer Madonna*.

More secular is the room devoted to the "Panorama", a huge arcade-like machine, built over a hundred years ago: as you peer through the eyepiece, a huge drum rotates to show you in turn dozens of fascinating **3D photographs** of 1890s Berlin.

The **ground floor** is the least rewarding section, covering early history from pottery pieces of the first prehistoric settlers to copies of royal proclamations from Friedrich Wilhelm, the Great Elector, who died in 1688. The highlight here – on the way out of the exhibition – is a bronze statue of Bismarck dressed as a blacksmith manfully forging German unity.

More Berliniana is on view outside the museum: a statue of Heinrich Zille and behind him in the Köllnischer, a leafy park, a **bearpit**, the depressing home of a couple of sleepy brown bears, here for being the symbol of the city and gracing its flag.

Mitte: The Spandauer Vorstadt

The **Spandauer Vorstadt**, the crescent-shaped area running north of the River Spree between Friedrichstrasse and Alexanderplatz, emerged after the *Wende* as one of the most intriguing parts of the unified city. Its appeal is based on both its history as Berlin's prewar **Jewish quarter**, and the fact that it now boasts a booming **shopping**, **restaurant** and **nightlife** scene, with the added advantage that the district is easily navigable on foot.

The Spandauer Vorstadt originated as one of a number of suburbs built beyond Berlin's walled centre during the seventeenth century when the city population swelled with persecuted French Huguenots. These were later joined by large numbers of persecuted Jews from Eastern Europe (see box, pp.88–89), so that by the turn of the twentieth century the district had become the cultural and spiritual centre of a well-established, wealthy and influential Jewish community.

Deportation of the Jews under the Nazis took much of the soul out of the Spandauer Vorstadt; it was further decimated during the GDR era when what little business life remained was largely shut down. From the 1950s until the *Wende* the quarter became little more than a network of decrepit prewar streets punctuated by the occasional slab of GDR-era housing. Few visitors strayed here from Unter den Linden, and apart from a couple of pockets of restoration the area was allowed to decay quietly. Since then the area has undergone a dramatic revival, with squatters and artists as pioneers and restoration projects following hard on their heels, putting the infrastructure to rights and renovating the backstreets to usher in a tide of bars, boutiques, cafés and restaurants.

The S-Bahn station and convivial square of **Hackescher Markt** provide the district's main focus, along with the surrounding attractively restored streets, like **Sophienstrasse**. The area to the east of here was once known as the **Scheunenviertel** when it was Berlin's most squalid and colourful district, though Nazi demolition of this heavily Jewish and unruly enclave removed all evidence from today's residential streets. The Nazis too left an indelible imprint on the area to the west – the heart of Berlin's prewar **Jewish district**, which is focused around **Grosse Hamburger Strasse** and the busy **Oranienburger Strasse**. Here the past is as much recalled by the absence of landmarks than their presence. At least the **Neue Synagoge** has been restored, not as a working synagogue, but as a museum of Jewish culture. Further down Oranienburger Strasse sits the dank and graffiti-covered **Tacheles**, an anarchic 1990s artists' squat whose vibe has been preserved in several ad hoc bars. Opposite is

Auguststrasse, a vital part of Berlin's contemporary art scene, with studios and galleries dotted along its length.

At its western end, around **Oranienburger Tor**, the district becomes more functional and forgettable, though it was once the hub of Berlin's industrial revolution. But almost all points of interest in the vicinity mostly appeal to fans of **theatre**, particularly of **Bertolt Brecht**, whose house, grave and some of the theatres where he worked dot the area. Finally, just beyond the district's northern fringes are a couple of Berlin's most important sights: the **Berlin Wall Memorial**, the only place in the city where a section of the Berlin Wall has been preserved in its entirety – complete with border defences and a "death strip" between two parallel walls; and a **World War II bunker** within the Gesundbrunnen U-Bahn station.

S-Bahnhof Hackescher Markt

Running the entire southern length of **Hackescher Markt** is its **S-Bahnhof**, a nineteenth-century construction retaining an original red-tile facade with mosaic decorative elements and rounded windows typical of the period. Now a protected building, its architectural features are best appreciated by walking through the station itself and taking a look at the northern facade. On both sides the arches under the S-Bahn tracks have been renovated and house trendy restaurants, bars and clothes shops.

The Hackesche Höfe

Among the most significant forces of revitalization in the area and one of the main draws of the neighbourhood are the **Hackesche Höfe**, a series of nine courtyards built between 1905 and 1907 to house businesses, flats and places of entertainment. Restored to their former Art Deco glory, the *Höfe* (courtyards) bustle with crowds visiting the several cafés, stores, galleries, theatres and cinemas within. The first courtyard, decorated with blue mosaic tiles, is home to the Chamaleon Varieté, a venue at the forefront of the revival of the city's interwar cabaret tradition. The second courtyard contains the Hackesche Höfe Theater, which regularly hosts klezmer concerts and Jewish-themed theatre pieces.

Though thoroughly beautified today, these courtyards preserve a layout that was common in this district and much of prewar Berlin, where daily life was played out in a labyrinth of the *Hinterhöfe*, or courtyards that were hidden from the shops and offices on the main road. Within the *Hinterhöfe* were a warren of small-scale workshops – with housing above and to the rear – together producing a microcosm of the city, with rich and poor, housing and commerce crammed together for better or worse, forming the squalid turn-of-the-twentieth-century urban culture that was satirized by Heinrich Zille (see p.77).

Just east of the Hackesche Höfe begins a concentration of shops pedalling young and fashionable clothing and footwear. **Rosenthaler Strasse** and **Neue Schönhauser Strasse** are both good places to browse, as is **Münzstrasse**, which has become an important centre of Berlin's small-time fashion boutiques.

Stolpersteine

Look at the ground around the entrances to some Hackesche Höfe and you'll find brass-plated cobblestones known as **Stolpersteine**, or "stumbling-blocks". These are some of the nine thousand laid into footpaths around Germany as a memorial to the victims of Nazi persecution: each carries a name, birth-date and their fate.

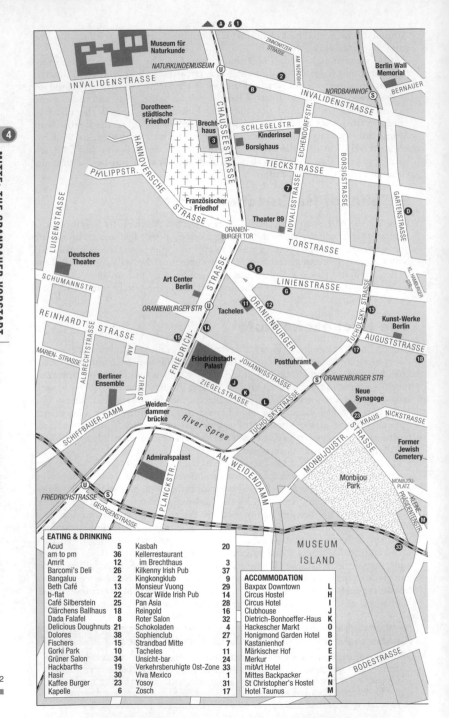

Museum für
Naturkunde

NATURKUNDEMUSEUM

Berlin Wall
Memorial

BERNAUER

INVALIDENSTRASSE

ZINNOWITZER
STRASSE

AM NORDBHF

NORDBAHNHOF

INVALIDENSTRASSE

Dorotheen-
städtische
Friedhof

Brecht-
haus

SCHLEGELSTR.

Kinderinsel

Borsighaus

EICHENDORFFSTR.

BORSIGSTRASSE

GARTENSTRASSE

PHILIPPSTR.

HANNOVERSCHE

STRASSE

CHAUSSEESTRASSE

TIECKSTRASSE

Französischer
Friedhof

NOVALISSTRASSE

Theater 89

ORANIEN-
BURGER TOR

TORSTRASSE

LUISENSTRASSE

Deutsches
Theater

SCHUMANNSTR.

REINHARDT

STRASSE

ORANIENBURGER STR

Art Center
Berlin

Tacheles

ORANIENBURGER

LINIENSTRASSE

TUCHOLSKY-STRASSE

KL. HAMBURGER
STR.

Kunst-Werke
Berlin

AUGUSTSTRASSE

MARIEN- STRASSE

ALBRECHTSTRASSE

AM

ZIRKUS

FRIEDRICH-

STRASSE

Berliner
Ensemble

Weiden-
dammer-
brücke

Friedrichstadt-
Palast

JOHANNISSTRASSE

ZIEGELSTRASSE

Postfuhramt

ORANIENBURGER STR

Neue
Synagoge

KRAUS

NICKSTRASSE

Former
Jewish
Cemetery

SCHIFFBAUER-DAMM

River Spree

TUCHOLSKYSTRASSE

MONBIJOUSTR.

STRASSE

Admiralspalast

AM WEIDENDAMM

Monbijou
Park

MONBIJOU-
PLATZ

KLEINE
PRÄSIDENTENSTR.

FRIEDRICHSTRASSE

GEORGENSTRASSE

PLANCKSTR.

MUSEUM
ISLAND

BODESTRASSE

EATING & DRINKING			
Acud	5	Kasbah	20
am to pm	36	Kellerrestaurant	
Amrit	12	im Brechthaus	3
Barcomi's Deli	26	Kilkenny Irish Pub	37
Bangaluu	2	Kingkongklub	9
Beth Café	13	Monsieur Vuong	29
b-flat	22	Oscar Wilde Irish Pub	14
Café Silberstein	25	Pan Asia	28
Clärchens Ballhaus	18	Reingold	16
Dada Falafel	8	Roter Salon	32
Delicious Doughnuts	21	Schokoladen	4
Dolores	38	Sophienclub	27
Fischers	15	Strandbad Mitte	7
Gorki Park	10	Tacheles	11
Grüner Salon	34	Unsicht-bar	24
Hackbarths	19	Verkehrsberuhigte Ost-Zone	1
Hasir	30	Viva Mexico	1
Kaffee Burger	23	Yosoy	31
Kapelle	6	Zosch	17

ACCOMMODATION	
Baxpax Downtown	L
Circus Hostel	H
Circus Hotel	I
Clubhouse	J
Dietrich-Bonhoeffer-Haus	K
Hackescher Markt	O
Honigmond Garden Hotel	B
Kastanienhof	C
Märkischer Hof	E
Merkur	F
mitArt Hotel	G
Mittes Backpacker	A
St Christopher's Hostel	N
Hotel Taunus	M

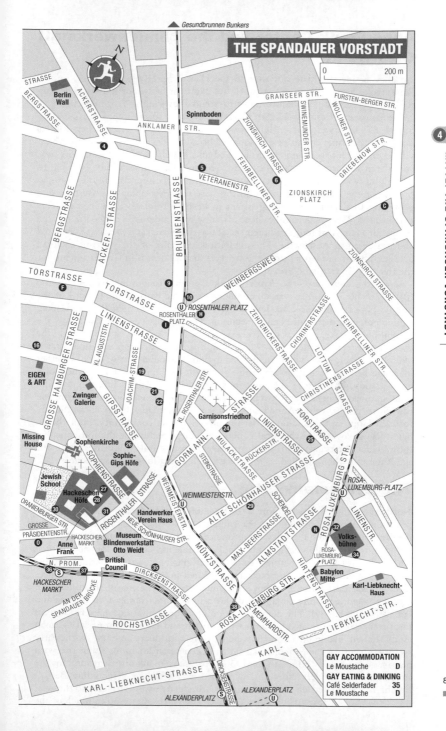

▲ Gesundbrunnen Bunkers

THE SPANDAUER VORSTADT

0 ————— 200 m

STRASSE

Berlin Wall

BERGSTRASSE

ACKERSTRASSE

ANKLAMER STR.

Spinnboden

GRANSEER STR.

FURSTEN-BERGER STR.

SWINEMÜNDER STR.

WOLLINER STR.

④

⑤

ZIONSKIRCH STRASSE

⑥

FEHRBELLINER STR.

VETERANENSTR.

ZIONSKIRCH PLATZ

GRIEBENOW STR.

ⓒ

BRUNNENSTRASSE

BERGSTRASSE

ACKER - STRASSE

WEINBERGSWEG

ZIONSKIRCH STRASSE

TORSTRASSE

ⓕ

TORSTRASSE

⑨

⑩

Ⓤ *ROSENTHALER PLATZ*

ROSENTHALER PLATZ

Ⓗ

ZEHDENICKERSTRASSE

CHORINERSTRASSE

FEHRBELLINER STR.

LINIENSTRASSE

ⓘ

LOTTUM STRASSE

CHRISTINENSTRASSE

GROSSE HAMBURGER STRASSE

KL. AUGUSTSTR.

JOACHIM-STRASSE

⑯

EIGEN & ART

⑳

Zwinger Galerie

⑲

GIPSSTRASSE

㉑

㉒

KL. ROSENTHALER STR.

STRASSE

Garnisonsfriedhof

㉔

LINIENSTRASSE

㉕

TORSTRASSE

Missing House

Sophienkirche

Sophie-Gips Höfe

㉖

SOPHIENSTRASSE

GORMANN-STRASSE

STEINSTRASSE

MULACKSTRASSE

RÜCKERSTR.

ROSA-LUXEMBURG-PLATZ

Ⓤ

Jewish School

Hackeschen Höfe

㉗

㉘

ROSENTHALER STRASSE

NEUE SCHÖNHAUSER STR.

WEINMEISTERSTR.

WEINMEISTERSTR. Ⓤ

ALTE SCHÖNHAUSER STRASSE

㉙

SCHENDELG.

ALMSTADTSTRASSE

Ⓝ

ROSA-LUXEMBURG STR.

㉜

Volks-bühne

㉞

㉛

Handwerker Verein Haus

ⓞ

ORANIENBURGER STR.

GROSSE PRÄSIDENTENSTR.

Anne Frank

HACKESCHER MARKT

Museum Blindenwerkstatt Otto Weidt

MAX.-BEERSTRASSE

MÜNZSTRASSE

ROSA-LUXEMBURG PLATZ

Babylon Mitte

HIRTENSTRASSE

Karl-Liebknecht-Haus

British Council

㊱ Ⓢ

N. PROM.

㊲

DIRCKSENSTRASSE

㉟

LIEBKNECHT-STR.

HACKESCHER MARKT

AN DER SPANDAUER BRÜCKE

ROCHSTRASSE

㊳

ROSA-LUXEMBURG

MEMHARDSTR.

DIRCKSENSTRASSE

KARL-

KARL - LIEBKNECHT-STRASSE

ALEXANDERPLATZ

Ⓢ *ALEXANDERPLATZ*

Ⓤ

GAY ACCOMMODATION	
Le Moustache	D
GAY EATING & DINKING	
Café Selderfader	35
Le Moustache	D

Anne Frank Center and the Blindenwerkstatt Otto Weidt

An alley beside the main entrance to the Hackesche Höfe, accessed at no. 39 Rosenthaler Strasse, leads to two small but excellent first-floor museums dealing with the depressing personal stories of persecuted Jews in the Third Reich.

The **Museum Blindenwerkstatt Otto Weidt** (daily 10am–8pm; free; ℡030/28 59 94 07, ⓦwww.museum-blindenwerkstatt.de; S-Bahn Hackescher Markt) occupies the former rooms of a broom and brush factory run by one Otto Weidt, whose employees were mostly deaf, blind and Jewish. Luckily the factory was considered important to the war effort, so for a long time Weidt was able to protect his workers from deportation to concentration camps. But in the 1940s, as pressure grew, he resorted to producing false papers, bribing the Gestapo and providing food and even hiding places to keep them alive, all at considerable personal risk. One small room, whose doorway was hidden by a cupboard, was the refuge for a family of four until their secret was discovered and they were deported and murdered in Auschwitz. The exhibition has relics of the wartime factory: brushes, photos and letters from the workers, but all of it is in German so ask for the free English translation on entry.

Across the courtyard, the **Anne Frank Center** (Tues–Sun 10am–6pm; €5; ℡030/288 86 56 10, ⓦwww.annefrank.de), tells the world-famous story of the bright, popular, middle-class Jewish girl who died in Bergen-Belsen, leaving behind poignant diaries of Nazi persecution. The familiarity of the tale allows the exhibition to take only a relatively superficial look at it, starting with the background to the persecution – including diagrammatic representations of the 1935 Nuremberg laws, which delineated in pointless and obsessive detail whether marriage between people is admissible based on the amount of Jewishness of a great-grandparent, before sketching out the basics of Anne's life, wonderfully photographed by her father Otto Frank. Anne had no connection with Berlin, and the centre, partner to the Anne Frank House in Amsterdam, simply chose this site for its location in the middle of Berlin's prewar Jewish community. Nonetheless her story is woven into the local context in a large section of the museum that shows video interviews with Berlin teenagers, from ethnic minorities about the age Anne was when she died, as they relate their aspirations and experiences.

The Scheunenviertel

Northeast of the Hackesche Hofe is the **Scheunenviertel** ("barn quarter"), now a fairly unremarkable residential area enclosed between Rosenthaler Strasse and Alexanderplatz. Despite today's appearance, its history is a fairly lively one: founded in 1672, following a decree that flammable hay could no longer be stored within the city limits, Scheunenviertel was originally a base for Berlin's poorest peasants; in later years it attracted impoverished political and religious refugees from all over Europe, with its heyday coming towards the end of the nineteenth century when it became a magnet for Jewish migrants from eastern Europe and Russia (see pp.88–89). The neighbourhood's melting-pot atmosphere made it an ideal refuge for those at odds with the Prussian and later the Imperial German establishment, making it a notorious centre of revolutionary activity. By the early twentieth century the Scheunenviertel had become an infamous slum, rife with deprivation and petty crime. In the 1930s it became a regular battleground for the street gangs of the left and right, while artists and writers – including Bertolt Brecht, Marlene Dietrich and actor Gustav Gründgens – were attracted to the area, quick to create their own bohemian enclave. The Nazis put a stop to much of the activity in the Scheunenviertel by pulling chunks of it down, ostensibly to make way for a U-Bahn station. But at the same time they played on the district's unsavoury reputation by extending the term Scheunenviertel to include the affluent and bourgeois Jewish areas around the Oranienburger Strasse – an attempt to tar all Jews with the same brush.

The Garnisonsfriedhof

At the eastern end of Auguststrasse, on Kleine Rosenthaler Strasse, lies the leafy **Garnisonsfriedhof**, a military cemetery dating from the eighteenth century, full of rusting cast-iron crosses with near-obliterated inscriptions commemorating officers and men of the Prussian army. Also here is the rather grander tomb of Adolph von Lützow, a general who found fame during the Napoleonic Wars, contrasting sharply with the overgrown wooden crosses commemorating victims of the Battle of Berlin, hidden away in a far corner. Information about the history of the cemetery is available from the administration offices near the entrance, which also house a small **exhibition** (Mon–Thurs 10am–5.50pm, Fri 10am–3.30pm; free).

The Volksbühne and Karl-Liebknecht-Haus

On the eastern side of what was once the Scheunenviertel lies Rosa-Luxemburg-Platz where the most prominent landmark is the **Volksbühne** theatre, built in 1913 with money raised by public subscription. Under the directorship of the ubiquitous Max Reinhardt, it became Berlin's people's theatre and, daringly for that time, put on plays by Hauptmann, Strindberg and Ibsen. Erwin Piscator continued the revolutionary tradition from 1924 to 1927, and immediately after the war in September 1945 a production of Lessing's plea for tolerance, *Nathan the Wise*, was put on here. The theatre was officially reopened in 1954 and became one of the ex-GDR capital's best theatres. These days it's still one of the most exciting and innovative theatres in the city (see p.237).

Nearby, at Weydingerstrasse 14 and Kleine Alexanderstrasse 28, is the **Karl-Liebknecht-Haus**, the former KPD central committee headquarters, which also housed the editorial offices of the communist newspaper *Rote Fahne* ("Red Flag"). From the late 1920s onwards this was an important centre of resistance to the increasingly powerful Nazis: 100,000 pro-communist workers demonstrated here on January 25, 1933, just days before Hitler came to power. After the Reichstag fire in February 1933 the KPD was broken up and its headquarters ransacked.

Sophienstrasse

Sophienstrasse was first settled at the end of the seventeenth century and was once the Spandauer Vorstadt's main street. Extensively restored in the 1980s it's now the best-looking street in the Hackescher Markt district and features a mix of retailers and arts workshops. In places, however, the restoration is only skin-deep and the pastel frontages of the old apartment houses conceal rundown, crumbling courtyards.

At Sophienstrasse 21 a doorway leads to the **Sophie-Gips Höfe**, a renovated retail and office complex that houses the **Sammlung Hoffman**, a private art collection which can be visited on ninety-minute tours on Saturdays by appointment (11am–4pm; €8; ☎030/28 49 91 20, ⓦwww.sammlung-hoffmann .de) – some of the larger pieces are on display outside – and *Barcomi's Delicatessen*, a fashionable coffee-and-cake establishment. A walk through the colourful, neon-lit passageway brings you to neighbouring Gipsstrasse, a rather quiet side street but a night-time favourite, with a couple of trendy bars.

North up Sophienstrasse, the vaguely Gothic-looking **Handwerkerverein-shaus** at no. 18 used to be the headquarters of the old craftsmen's guild. Until the founding of the German Social Democrat Party (SPD), this had been the main focus of the Berlin workers' movement, and continued to play an important role as a frequent venue for political meetings, including, on November 14, 1918, the first public gathering of the Spartakusbund (Spartacus League), the breakaway anti-war faction of the SPD that later evolved into the KPD (Communist Party of Germany).

Beyond here, and some turn-of-the-twentieth-century neo-Baroque apartment buildings, lies the **Sophienkirche**. Built in 1712, this is one of the city's finest Baroque churches, and the only central Berlin church to survive the war more or less undamaged. Its clear, simple lines come as a welcome change after the monumental Neoclassicism and fussy Gothic revivalism of so much of Berlin's architecture. The church's seventy-metre-high tiered tower, added during the 1730s, is one of the area's most prominent landmarks. The ground on which the church was built was a gift from the Jewish community to the Protestant community, who at the time were slightly financially embarrassed. The church itself was paid for by Princess Sophie Louise in order to provide a parish church for the neighbourhood. The **interior**, in washed-out shades of green and grey, is a simple but pleasing affair. The one note of aesthetic exuberance is a pulpit with a crown-like canopy, set on a spiral pillar, which makes it look exactly like a chalice.

Grosse Hamburger Strasse

Sophienstrasse ends westwards at **Grosse Hamburger Strasse**, a road dotted with several poignant reminders of the area's Jewish past. It's home to Berlin's oldest **Jewish cemetery**, established in 1672, and the first **Jewish old people's home** to be founded in the city. The Nazis used the building as a detention centre for Jews, and 55,000 people were held here before being deported to the camps. A memorial tablet, on which pebbles have been placed as a mark of respect (following the Jewish practice for grave-site visits), and a sculpted group of haggard-looking figures, representing deportees, mark the spot where the home stood. The grassed-over open space behind is the site of the cemetery itself. In 1943 the Gestapo smashed most of the headstones and dug up the remains of those buried here, using gravestones to shore up a trench they had excavated through the site. A few cracked headstones with Hebrew inscriptions line the graveyard walls. The only freestanding monument was erected after the war to commemorate Moses Mendelssohn, the philosopher and German Enlightenment figure. Also adorned with pebbles, it's on the spot where he is thought to have been buried, with an inscription in German on one side and in Hebrew on the other. Just to the north of the cemetery at **Grosse Hamburger Strasse 27** is a former Jewish boys' school, now a Jewish secondary school for both sexes. Above its entrance a still-visible sign from prewar days reads, in German, "Jewish Community Boys' School". On the facade a plaque pays homage to Mendelssohn, who was a founder of Berlin's first Jewish school here in 1778, and who, until 1938, was commemorated by a bust in the school's garden.

On the other side of the street, the **Missing House** is a unique and effective monument to the wartime destruction of Berlin. A gap in the tenements marks where house number 15–16 stood until destroyed by a direct hit during an air raid. In the autumn of 1990 the French artist Christian Boltanski put plaques on the side walls of the surviving buildings on either side as part of an installation, recalling the names, dates and professions of the former inhabitants of the vanished house.

Oranienburger Strasse and around

Before the war Oranienburger Strasse was the centre of Berlin's affluent Jewish community and still bears some reminders from this time. During its spell in East Berlin it was one of the city centre's more desolate streets, but after 1989 it became an atmospheric bar-crawling strip, and is now principally known for its **restaurants** and stylish watering holes, which attract locals and tourists in equal numbers. After dark, prostitutes openly solicit along the entire road, their presence alongside gawping visitors a little reminiscent of Amsterdam's red-light district.

Sedate **Monbijouplatz** sits at the eastern end of Oranienburger Strasse and is of interest for a couple of modern buildings, at numbers 3 and 5, designed by innovative local architects Grüntuch/Ernst. Though radically different in look, the two buildings share a harmony in their geometric facades and an attention to detail, such as in the intricacy of the small mosaic tiles on the detailing between the vertical bands at number 5, and in the play of light and shadow allowed by the aluminium louvres on the balconies of number 3. Adjacent **Monbijoupark** was once the grounds of a Rococo royal palace, reduced to rubble by the war and, like so many Hohenzollern relics, never rebuilt. The park makes an unexpected and shady refuge from urban pursuits and is a good place to picnic or lie out with a book. The pleasant promenade that separates it from the Spree leads to a footbridge to Museum Island (see Chapter 2).

The Neue Synagoge

During the initial waves of Jewish immigration from the seventeenth century onwards the area around Oranienburger Strasse was a densely populated and desperately poor ghetto, but by the nineteenth century Berlin's Jews had achieved a high degree of prosperity and assimilation. This was reflected in the building of the grand **Neue Synagoge**, to a design by Eduard Knoblauch, halfway down Oranienburger Strasse just off the corner of Krausnickstrasse. The synagogue was inaugurated in the presence of Bismarck in 1866, a gesture of official recognition that, coming at a time when Jews in Russia were still enduring officially sanctioned pogroms, must have made many feel that their position in German society was finally secure. The acceptance that they had enjoyed in Wilhelmine Germany contributed to the sense of disbelief many Jews felt at the rise of Nazism during the 1920s and 1930s.

The Neue Synagoge was built in mock-Moorish style, particularly apparent it its bulbous gilt and turquoise dome. It was Berlin's central synagogue for over sixty years, serving also as a venue for concerts, including one in 1930 by Albert Einstein in his lesser-known role as a violinist. A Jewish museum was opened next door on January 24, 1933, just six days before the Nazi takeover. Neither museum nor synagogue survived the Third Reich. Both were damaged on *Kristallnacht* (see p.89), though the synagogue wasn't actually destroyed thanks to the intervention of the local police chief who chased off SA arsonists and called the fire brigade to extinguish the flames. It remained in use as a place of worship until 1940 when it was handed over to the Wehrmacht, who used it as a warehouse until it was gutted by bombs on the night of November 22, 1943.

After the war the synagogue remained a ruin, and in 1958 the main hall, which was thought to be on the verge of collapse, was demolished, leaving only the building's facade and entrance rooms intact. For many years these stood here

Jews have been part of Berlin's make-up since the earliest days of the twin towns of Berlin-Cölln. As elsewhere in Europe, their history has been studded by **episodic persecution**, though nothing comes close to their ruthless extermination by the Third Reich. Nevertheless, the Jewish community also has a history of determinedly and repeatedly rising to **prominence** against the odds: punching well above its weight in the city's prewar entrepreneurial and cultural scene and again today with the numbers of Jews in Berlin doubling over the past two decades.

Berlin's earliest Jewish settlers gravitated to a tight-knit area around today's Jüden-strasse (see p.77) where, banned from most other trades, they successfully traded and lent money and slowly built a community. But in difficult times – of economic hardship or epidemics – they frequently became scapegoats. Bouts of persecution included during the plague of 1349; 1446, when they were driven from the city; and the **witch hunts** of 1510 when fifty Jews were tortured to death or burnt at the stake, with the rest again barred from the city. Though readmitted thirty years later, they found themselves barred once again in 1573 following a spate of pogroms after Joachim II was murdered and his much-disliked Jewish finance minister was accused of the crime.

Jews were permitted to return to Berlin in 1671, following the expulsion of several rich families from Vienna and given the economic woes of Brandenburg which, in the wake of the detrimental thirty-years war, sought powerful people to help with its rebuilding. Despite suffering personal restrictions and extra taxes, the Jewish population grew, so that by 1700 the city had 117 Jewish families, and in 1712 its **first synagogue** was built near today's Rosenstrasse.

The numbers of Jews in the Spandauer Vorstadt and particularly in the **Scheunenviertel** slum was greatly bolstered by a 1737 order that all Berlin's non-home-owning Jews must move there and that Jews could only enter the city through its northern gates. From that point on, and particularly in the nineteenth century, the area became a refuge for Jews fleeing pogroms in eastern Europe and Russia.

A big part of Berlin's draw was the loosening of Prussia's restrictions and the growing equality of its Jewish population, relative to the rest of Europe. By 1869 German Jews had full rights, and within years Jews rose to prominence in government, one influential group, dubbed the *"Kaiserjuden"*, becoming close advisors to the Kaiser. By the 1920s Jewish department stores, such as **Wertheim**, had become part of the landscape and Jews were also highly active in the cultural scene with musicians such as the **Comedian Harmonists** extremely popular.

By 1933, when the **Nazis** assumed power and state-backed persecution started, there were 160,564 Jews in Berlin: around four percent of the population and one third of those in the German Reich. The process of persecution began with an SA-enforced boycott of Jewish shops, businesses and medical and legal practices on April 1 of that year; many of the wealthiest Jews left the same year, as a series of laws banning them from public office, the civil service, journalism, farming, teaching, broadcasting and acting were introduced. Then in September 1935 the **Nuremberg laws** effectively deprived Jews of their German citizenship, by introducing apartheid-like classifications of "racial purity". There was a brief respite in 1936 when Berlin hosted the Olympic Games and the Nazis, wishing to show an acceptable face to the outside world, eased up on overt anti-Semitism, but by the following year large-scale expropriation of Jewish businesses began. Jews who could see the writing on the wall, and had money, escaped while they could (even though other European countries, the US and Palestine all restricted Jewish immigration), but the majority stayed put, hoping things would improve, or simply because they couldn't afford to emigrate. However, after the violent escalation of Nazi anti-Semitism of **Kristallnacht** – the night of November 9, 1938 – their already beleaguered position became intolerable. "Crystal Night" – named for the shattered glass from **the attacks on Jewish shops and institutions** – resulted in the deaths of at least 36 Berlin Jews, many beaten on the streets while passers-by looked on; the destruction of 23 of the city's 29 synagogues; and wrecking of hundreds of shops and businesses. Afterwards the Nazi government fined the German-Jewish community one billion marks – ostensibly to pay for the damage – and then forcibly "Aryanized" all remaining Jewish businesses, effectively excluding Jews from economic life. With the outbreak of war in September 1939, Jews were forced to observe a night-time curfew and forbidden to own radios. Forced transportation of Jews to the East (mainly occupied Poland) began in February 1940, and September 1941 saw the introduction of a law requiring Jews to wear the yellow Star of David, heralding the beginning of mass deportations.

In January 1942, the **Wannsee conference**, held in a western suburb of Berlin (see p.176), discussed the *Endlösung* or "Final Solution" to the "Jewish Question", drawing up plans for the removal of all Jews to the East and, implicitly, their extermination. As the Final Solution began to be put into effect, daily life for Berlin's Jews grew ever more unbearable: in April they were banned from public transport, and in September their food rations were reduced. By the beginning of 1943 the only Jews remaining legally in Berlin were highly skilled workers in the city's armaments factories, and in February deportation orders began to be enforced for this group too. Most Berlin Jews were sent to Theresienstadt and Auschwitz concentration camps, and only a handful survived the war. By the end of the war the combined effects of emigration and genocide had reduced Berlin's Jewish population by around 96 percent to about 6500; around 1400 had survived as "U-boats", hidden by gentile families at great personal risk, and the rest had somehow managed to evade the final round-ups in precariously legal conditions, usually by having irreplaceable skills vital to the war effort, or by being married to non-Jews.

Since the war Berlin's Jewish population has doubled to around **twelve thousand today** – largely by émigrés from the former Soviet Union. It's now the world's fastest growing Jewish community and the largest in Germany, boasting eight synagogues. With the renovation of the **Neue Synagoge** as a cultural centre and the opening of several Jewish cafés, Oranienburger Strasse has regained a little of its pre-Nazi identity, yet some Jews complain that the tourist interest in this area and their community has led to a Disneyfication and faux celebration of Jewish life. Jewish insignias have begun to appear where there was never a link, and restaurants and cultural events pop up simply to provide visitors with stereotypes – local toy shops even sell *menorah*, the Jewish candelabra. They also argue that although sympathy and interest in sites associated with Jewish culture and persecution is welcome, if their reason is to understand the Holocaust rather than simply indulge a ghoulish interest, then the focus should be on the perpetrators, not the victims.

Meanwhile, **anti-Semitism** in Berlin, especially towards young Jews, appears to be on the rise, with the number of incidents increasing every year – in one swastikas were scrawled on the walls of a Jewish nursery school before a smoke bomb was thrown in, though thankfully the building was empty. These days it is most often the work of disaffected children of immigrant Muslim families, but all the same, Gideon Joffe, widely regarded as head of the city's Jewish community, invites "Germans who say they want an end to the debate about the Nazi past to wear the...Star of David, so they can experience the anti-Semitism that German Jews confront on a daily basis."

▲ The Neue Synagoge

largely overlooked, a plaque on the shattered frontage exhorting the few passers-by to *Vergesst es nie* – "Never forget". The Jewish community pressed for what was left to be turned into a museum, but the authorities did not respond until 1988, when it was decided to resurrect the shell as a "centre for the promotion and preservation of Jewish culture".

A new plaque was affixed to the building amid much official pomp on November 9, 1988, the fiftieth anniversary of *Kristallnacht* and work began on restoring the facade and reconstructing the gilded dome, which, visible from far and wide, has once again become a Berlin landmark.

In 1995, the extensive renovation work was completed and the building was reopened as a museum and cultural centre, officially called **Centrum Judaicum – Neue Synagoge** (March & Oct Mon & Sun 10am–8pm, Tues–Thurs 10am–6pm, Fri 10am–2pm; April–Sept Mon & Sun 10am–8pm, Tues–Thurs 10am–6pm, Fri 10am–5pm; Nov–Feb Mon–Thurs & Sun 10am–6pm, Fri 10am–2pm; €4.60; ⓦ www.cjudaicum.de). Inside there are two permanent exhibitions, one on the history and restoration of the synagogue itself and another on the Jewish life and culture that could once be found in the area. You'll have to pass through airport-style security to get in – a sad reflection of the continuing threat to Jewish institutions from terrorist attack.

The Postfuhramt

Beside S-Bahnhof Oranienburger Strasse, is an important-looking building that turns out to be the **Postfuhramt**, a nineteenth-century post office administration building. Like the synagogue, it's built in the mock-Moorish style so favoured by Berlin civic architects during the nineteenth century. They decked out everything from stations to breweries in alternating bands of orange and yellow brick, with generously arched doorways and windows and fanciful turrets with decorative cupolas. It's now home to **C/O Berlin** (Wed–Sun 11am–8pm; €8; ⓦwww .co-berlin.com), a photographic gallery that's often worth a look for its avant-garde temporary exhibitions.

Tacheles

The revitalization of Oranienburger Strasse began with **Tacheles** (ⓦwww .tacheles.de), a group of young international artists who took over a spectacularly ruined building on the southern side of the street, just beyond the Oranienburger Tor junction, in early 1990. The exterior is usually festooned with works-in-progress, and the building has become home and workplace to an ever-changing band of painters, sculptors, kindred spirits and hangers-on. Inside is a café-bar, and regular gigs and events take place here (see p.225).

The Tacheles building itself has an interesting past, reflecting the history of the city in which it stands. Built in 1907, it was one of the first reinforced concrete structures in Europe, originally housing the Friedrichstrassepassagen shopping centre, then between the wars it became the AEG's exhibition hall for all its electrical products. From 1934 onwards the building was used by the SS and the Deutsche Arbeitsfront, a Nazi labour organization. After the war it housed a cinema and work space for art students, before suffering partial demolition and standing vacant for many years until the Tacheles collective moved in. Rumours of its demise have been rampant in the last few years, as speculators eager to swallow up a big chunk of prime real estate (which it helped bring to life) have honed in on the building, but, after much political wrangling, it seems that Tacheles has ensured its future as a permanent fixture in the cultural landscape. Indeed, it's come a long way since its anarchic beginnings, much to the disappointment of those involved in the early days, who inevitably claim the new-look Tacheles with its plate-glass windows is not the place it once was.

Auguststrasse

Auguststrasse was the epicentre of the 1990s Berlin art scene, and though much of it has now been renovated, it still features various workspaces and commercial galleries. The breathtaking transformation of the street from decrepit inner-city district to thriving arts scene began in 1989 and was given legitimacy in June 1992 when city authorities stumped up enviable financial support for the "37 Rooms Exhibition", during which the whole of Auguststrasse was turned into a giant gallery. Since then the visual arts have flourished here, even if the street may now be past its heyday. But the galleries on and around Auguststrasse still attract artists from all over the world and feature some of the most interesting and controversial work you're likely to see in Berlin. One place worth seeking out is **Kunst Werke Berlin** (see p.235), at number 69, a former margarine factory whose central courtyard is graced by an innovative building that serves as *Café Bravo* and is the work of New York artist Dan Graham, who specializes in distorting light and perception using mirrors, refraction and interference. Made from gas-filled solar panels, the café's walls partially reflect the exterior, while still allowing vague interior outlines to show through.

The theatre district

There's not all that much to see in Berlin's **theatre district**, though you can't fail to notice the giant **Friedrichstadt Palast** on Friedrichstrasse, a clumsy GDR-era Jugendstil pastiche that rears up just south of U-Bahn Oranienburger Tor. It's perfect if you're into big, splashy, scantily clad revues.

Most impressive among the more high-brow theatres dotted about is the elegant **Deutsches Theater**, at Schumannstrasse 13, founded in 1883. Max Reinhardt took over as director in 1905, thereafter dominating the theatre scene for nearly three decades. In 1922 a young and unknown Marlene Dietrich made her stage debut here, and a couple of years later Bertolt Brecht arrived from Munich to begin his energetic conquest of Berlin's theatre world. Even more significant for its associations with Brecht is the **Berliner Ensemble**, tucked away on Bertolt-Brecht-Platz. Built in the early 1890s, its rather austere exterior hides a rewarding and opulent neo-Baroque interior. This is where, on August 31, 1928, the world premiere of his *Dreigroschenoper* ("The Threepenny Opera") was staged, the first of 250 consecutive performances in a ritualistic tribute to one of the few world-famous writers East Germany could later claim as its own. After exile in America during the Nazi era, Brecht returned in 1949 with his wife, Helene Weigel, to take over direction of the theatre, marking his return by painting a still-visible red cross through the coat of arms on the royal box. During box office times (Mon–Fri 8am–6pm, Sat & Sun 11am–6pm) you can view the foyer, but the rest of the theatre is only open to the public during performances, which still include regular performances of Brecht.

A walk over the Spree on Weidendammer Brücke towards Bahnhof Friedrichstrasse brings you to the Jugendstil **Admiralspalast**. Built as a variety theatre in 1910, its partly gilded facade, fluted columns and bas-reliefs come as a real surprise amid the predominantly concrete architecture of the immediate area. As one of the few buildings in the area to have survived bombing, it became an important political meeting hall in the immediate postwar years and on April 22 and 23, 1946, it was the venue for the forced union of the social democratic SPD with the prewar Communist party, the KPD. This resulted in the birth of the SED (Sozialistische Einheitspartei Deutschlands), the GDR Communist Party that controlled the country until March 1990. The building houses Die Distel theatre, a satirical cabaret whose performances sometimes daringly highlighted the paradoxes and frustrations of the pre-*Wende* GDR.

For details of theatres and their performances see p.236.

Bahnhof Friedrichstrasse

Opposite the Admiralspalast lies the grubby edifice of **Bahnhof Friedrichstrasse** with its mediocre shopping arcade and budget eateries. But before the *Wende,* the train station was of real consequence as the main border crossing point for western visitors to East Berlin, and probably the most heavily guarded train station in Europe. There was always a regular flow of main-line and S-Bahn traffic between Friedrichstrasse and West Berlin (except during the Berlin Blockade of 1948–49, see p.141), but until late 1989 the East German government did all it could to keep its own citizens from joining it. A tangle of checkpoints, guard posts and customs controls and, more discreetly, armed guards separated westbound platforms from the rest of the station.

Of particular note in all this was the **border crossing entrance** in the glass and concrete construction between the Bahnhof and the River Spree. Until 1990 an estimated eight million westbound travellers – visitors and tourists and occasionally East German citizens with exit visas – annually queued inside to get through passport and customs controls before travelling by U- or S-Bahn to West Berlin. With visitors to the East needing to return to the West by midnight, the functional building – grimly nicknamed the Tränenpalast or "Palace of Tears" by Berliners – was the scene of many a poignant farewell as people took leave of relatives, friends and lovers here. A few reminders of this era still survive within, including a cubicle with blackened glass windows overlooking the main hall, from which border guards watched those leaving the country. But times have thankfully changed and these days the Tränenpalast is an arts venue, with the arches under the railway tracks just southeast of the station holding a series of antiques stores selling a fascinating assemblage of old art, jewellery, books and curios.

Chausseestrasse

Chausseestrasse was, during the nineteenth century, the location of one of Berlin's densest concentrations of heavy industry. Development began here during the 1820s with the establishment of a steam-engine factory and iron foundry and in 1837 August Borsig built his first factory – by the 1870s his successors were churning out hundreds of steam engines and railway locomotives each year.

Other industrial concerns were also drawn to the area, earning it the nickname *Feuerland* – "Fireland". However, by the end of the century most had outgrown their roots and relocated en masse to the edges of the rapidly expanding city. A reminder of the past, and of Borsig's local influence, is the **Borsighaus** at Chausseestrasse 9. Once the central administration block of the Borsig factories, this sandstone building, its facade richly decorated with bronze figures, looks like a displaced country residence.

The Dorotheenstädtische Friedhof

Roughly opposite the Borsighaus lies the **Dorotheenstädtische Friedhof** (daily: Jan & Dec 8am–4pm, Feb & Nov 8am–5pm, March & Oct 8am–6pm, April & Sept 8am–7pm, May–Aug 8am–8pm; U-Bahn Oranienburger Tor), eastern Berlin's VIP cemetery. Here you'll find the graves of Bertolt Brecht and Helene Weigel; the architect Karl Friedrich Schinkel, his last resting place topped by an appropriately florid monument; John Heartfield, the Dada luminary and interwar photomontage exponent, under a headstone decorated with a runic H; the philosopher Georg Hegel, whose ideas influenced Marx; the author Heinrich Mann; former president Johannes Rau; journalist Günter Gaus; and many Berlin worthies. A plan detailing who lies where is located beside the cemetery administration offices (on the right at the end of the entrance alley). The Dorotheenstädtische Friedhof also encloses the **Französischer Friedhof** (entrance on Chausseestrasse and closer to Oranienburger Tor), originally built to serve Berlin's Huguenot community.

The Brecht-Haus

The **Brecht-Haus** (Tues & Sat 10am–3.30pm Wed & Fri 10–11.30am, Thurs 10–11.30am & 5–6.30pm, Sun 11am–6pm, guided tours on the hour; €3; U-Bahn Oranienburger Tor), at Chausseestrasse 125, was the final home and workplace of Brecht and his wife and collaborator Helene Weigel. The guided tours take in the seven simply furnished rooms – an absolute must for Brecht fans, but not so fascinating if you're only casually acquainted with his works. The Brecht-Haus

Bertolt Brecht (1898–1956)

4

Bertolt Brecht is widely regarded as one of the leading German dramatists of the twentieth century. Born in Augsburg, the son of a paper-mill manager, he studied medicine, mainly to avoid full military service in World War I. Working as an army medical orderly in 1918, his experiences helped shape his passionate anti-militarism. Soon he drifted away from medicine onto the fringes of the theatrical world, eventually winding up as a playwright in residence at the Munich Kammerspiele in 1921. It wasn't until the 1928 premiere of the *Dreigroschenoper* ("The Threepenny Opera"), co-written with the composer Kurt Weill, that Brecht's real breakthrough came. This marked the beginning of a new phase in Brecht's work. A couple of years earlier he had embraced Marxism, an ideological step that had a profound effect on his literary output, leading him to espouse a didactic "epic" form of theatre. The aim was to provoke the audience, perhaps even move them to revolutionary activity. To this end he developed the technique of **Verfremdung** ("alienation") to create a sense of distance between spectators and the action unfolding before them. By using effects such as obviously fake scenery, monotone lighting and jarring music to expose the sham sentimentality of love songs, he hoped to constantly remind the audience that what they were doing was watching a play – in order to make them judge, rather than be drawn into, the action on stage. The result was a series of works that were pretty heavy-going. In 1933, unsurprisingly, Brecht went into self-imposed exile, eventually ending up in the States. His years away from Germany were among his most productive. The political message was still very much present in his work, but somehow the dynamic and lyrical force of his writing meant that it was often largely lost on his audience. Returning to Europe, he finally settled in East Berlin in 1949, after a brief period in Switzerland. His decision to try his luck in the Soviet-dominated Eastern sector of Germany was influenced by the offer to take over at the Theater am Schiffbauerdamm, the theatre where the *Dreigroschenoper* had been premiered more than twenty years earlier. However, before heading east, Brecht first took the precaution of gaining Austrian citizenship and lodging the copyright of his works with a West German publisher. The remainder of Brecht's life was largely devoted to running what is now known as the Berliner Ensemble and facing up to his own tensions with the fledgling GDR.

also has a Bertolt Brecht **archive** (Tues, Wed & Fri 9am–5pm, Thurs 9am–7pm) and the basement is home to the *Kellerrestaurant im Brechthaus* (see p.218), which dishes up Viennese specialities, supposedly according to Weigel's recipes.

A little way past the Brecht-Haus stands a brutal pillar commemorating the Spartakusbund, the breakaway antiwar faction of the SPD formed by Karl Liebknecht in 1916, which later evolved into the KPD, Germany's Communist party. The inscription, a quote from Liebknecht, says, "Spartakus means the fire and spirit, the heart and soul, the will and deed of the revolution of the proletariat."

Museum für Naturkunde

Just west of its crossroads with Chausseestrasse, Invalidenstrasse soon leads to the **Museum für Naturkunde** (Natural History Museum; Tues–Fri 9.30am–6pm, Sat & Sun 10am–6pm; ⓦ www.naturkundemuseum-berlin.de; €6; U-Bahn Naturkundemuseum), one of the world's largest natural history museums. The museum's origins go back to 1716, though the present building and the nucleus of the collection it houses date from the 1880s.

The museum is home to a skeleton of a brachiosaurus, fossil remains of an archaeopteryx (the oldest known bird), and some entertaining rooms devoted to the evolution of vertebrates and the ape family; there's also an interesting if slightly ghoulish section on how the numerous stuffed animals were "prepared for exhibition", as the commentary delicately puts it. Finally, the museum boasts a vast mineralogy collection, including a number of meteorites.

The Berlin Wall Memorial

Opposite S-Bahn Nordbahnhof, on Bernauer Strasse, is the first of two buildings dedicated to the **Berlin Wall Memorial** (Gedenkstätte Berliner Mauer; Tues–Sun: April–Oct 9.30am–7pm; Nov–March 9.30am–6pm; free; Ⓦwww .berliner-mauer-gedenkstaette.de; S-Bahn Nordbahnhof), which contains a bookshop and screens an introductory film. Bernauer Strasse was literally bisected by the Wall; before the Wall was built you could enter or exit the Soviet Zone just by going through the door of one of the buildings, which is why, on August 13, 1961, some citizens, who woke up to find themselves on the wrong side of the newly established "national border", leapt out of windows to get to the West. Over the years, the facades of these buildings were cemented up and incorporated into the partition itself, until they were knocked down and replaced by the Wall proper in 1979. A short section of Wall as it once was – both walls and a death-strip between – remain preserved at the corner of Bernauer Strasse and Ackerstrasse. Down the road, at Bernauer Strasse 111, the **Wall Documentation Centre** (same hours) keeps the story of the Wall alive using photos, sound recordings and information terminals and has a useful viewing tower that you can climb to contemplate the barrier and the way in which it once divided the city.

The Gesundbrunnen bunkers

Immediately north of the Spandauer Vorstadt – and two stops north on the S-Bahn from the Nordbahnhof – lies U- and S-Bahn **Gesundbrunnen,** around which several underground passages and **bunkers** are open for fascinating and unusual tours. The non-profit organisation **Berliner Unterwelten** (Ⓣ030/49 91 05 17, Ⓦberlinerunterwelten.de), organizes these tours, and their ticket office is in the southern entrance hall of the Gesundbrunnen U-Bahn station. The company offers some nine tours at different locations around Berlin, but all their core tours, as listed below, are in the vicinity of the Gesundbrunnen. Tickets for all these tours are available from 10am on the day; the tours start within easy walking distance of the office. **English–language tours** are listed below, but further tours take place in German and Spanish, listed on the website.

The tour of the main Gesundbrunnen bunker, **Tour 1: Dark Worlds** (daily; 90min; 11am), explores a large, well-preserved World War II bunker, one of hundreds of public bunkers that were used towards the end of the war by Berliners waiting out the Allied bombing raids. It was here also where many women committed suicide rather than be raped by advancing Russians. As a valuable part of the U-Bahn network the Gesundbrunnen bunker was one of the few spared from destruction during Germany's demilitarization, and today its rooms and passages contain countless artefacts from the time. Among them are various items cleverly crafted from military waste immediately after the war: helmets became pots, gas masks became oil lamps and tyres were used to sole shoes. Equally interesting are the finds from the Nazi bunker beneath the Reichskanzlei (see p.51), including paintings by SS artists and an enigma machine. Other remnants unearthed from around town and displayed here come from the Battle of Berlin and include the contents of the pockets of two Volksturm recruits – a 15 year old and a 69 year old – killed in the fray. These items all come from modern-day excavations of Berlin, and weapons and bombs are still regularly found by building crews, sometimes with deadly consequences – as one display shows.

If Tour 1 has whetted your appetite, you might like to try the other tours. **Tour 2: From the Flak Towers to a Mountain of Debris** (April–Oct Thurs 1pm, Sun 4pm; 90min; €9) goes into the park opposite the Gesundbrunnen station to explore two of the seven levels of the **Humboldthain** anti-aircraft gun tower that proved too beefy for the Soviets to destroy. Be aware that its cold down there, even in summer, and you won't be welcome on the tour in flip-flops or sandals. **Tour 3: Subways, Bunkers & Cold War** (90min English tours Mon–Fri 1pm; €9) investigates another World War II bunker, but also goes into Cold War-era tunnels and bunkers, including refuges that were equipped for West Berliners in case of a nuclear strike, and underground labyrinths that were blocked to prevent East Germans escaping to the West. Finally, **Tour M – Breaching the Berlin Wall** (2hr English language tours April–Oct Wed 1pm; €12), concerns itself with exploring tunnels dug under the Berlin Wall by would-be escapees and relates stories of success – 300 people managed to escape the GDR like this – and failures.

Mitte: Tiergarten

A huge swathe of peaceful green parkland, smack in the middle of Berlin, the **Tiergarten** stretches west from the Brandenburg Gate and Reichstag, its beautifully landscaped meadows, gardens and woodlands a great antidote to the bustle and noise of the city. The park and its immediate surroundings form a sub-district of the city's central Mitte district whose eastern edge, long occupied by the Berlin Wall, has flourished since the *Wende*. Huge building projects have mushroomed here, some the result of the German Federal government's move to Berlin, but most simply reclaiming death-strip lands in prime locations at the centre of a unified city. The result is a formidable showcase of **modern architecture** around the fringes of the Tiergarten, arguably at its most breathtaking when illuminated at night.

The skyscrapers of **Potsdamer Platz** at the Tiergarten's southeastern corner is Berlin at its most thrustingly commercial and modern. Just west of here are the district's most high-profile attractions: a superb agglomeration of art museums and venues known as the **Kulturforum**. Highlights of this are the Gemäldegalerie, with its internationally renowned collection of European art, the twentieth-century art of the Neue Nationalgalerie and the applied arts of the Kunstgewerbemuseum.

Adjacent to the Kulturforum is a **diplomatic district**, where many of Berlin's embassies have congregated and where the **Bendlerblock**, site of several July Bomb Plot executions (see p.106), houses the interesting Gedenkstätte Deutscher Widerstand, a museum of German resistance against the Nazis. Further west, one architecturally impressive embassy flanks another as far as the Bauhaus Archive, a homage to that influential art and design movement. This is as good a place as any to begin an exploration of the **Tiergarten** park itself. Walk or cycle west to a couple of beer gardens or take a bus a couple of quick stops north to the park's proud centrepiece: the **Siegessäule**, a huge column that celebrates Prussian military victories and delivers fine views over the park and Berlin.

The northeastern corner of the Tiergarten is occupied by the **Reichstag** (see p.48) and a host of other institutions that form Berlin's modern-day Regierungsviertel, or government quarter, where various modern buildings with cutting-edge designs cling to a bend in the River Spree known as the **Spreebogen**. Surveying all this is the monumentalist, glass and steel **Hauptbahnhof Lehrter Bahnhof**, Berlin's new main train station. It occupies a rather desolate, underdeveloped patch of town, though it's near the **Hamburger Bahnhof**, a top-notch modern and contemporary art museum.

Potsdamer Platz, with its U- and S-Bahn station, and the Hauptbahnhof are the main **transport** hubs for the Tiergarten district, but the extremely frequent #100 and #200 **buses** between Bahnhof Zoo and Alexanderplatz are best for navigating around the district. The #200 stops at the Kulturforum, while #100 stops at all

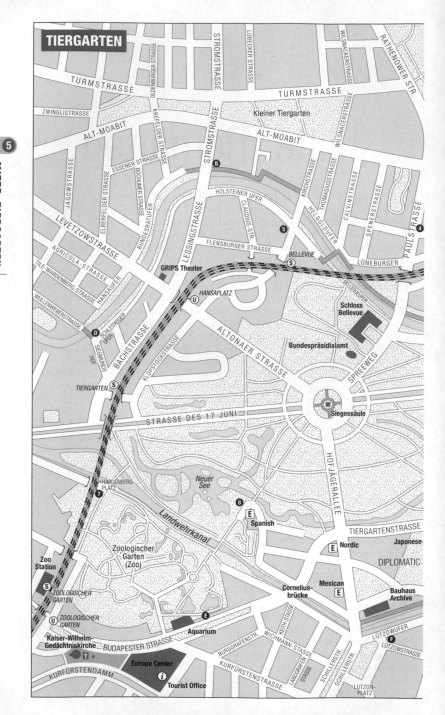

TIERGARTEN

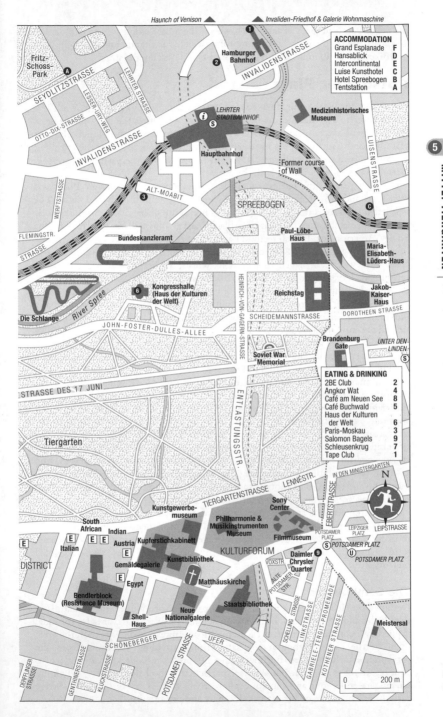

Haunch of Venison ▲   ▲ Invaliden-Friedhof & Galerie Wohnmaschine

ACCOMMODATION
Grand Esplanade   F
Hansablick   D
Intercontinental   E
Luise Kunsthotel   C
Hotel Spreebogen   B
Tentstation   A

Fritz-
Schoss-
Park   Ⓐ

SEYDLITZSTRASSE

LEHRTER STRASSE

LESSER-URY-WEG

OTTO-DIX-STRASSE

INVALIDENSTRASSE

❶
❷ Hamburger
   Bahnhof

INVALIDENSTRASSE

Medizinhistorisches
Museum

LUISENSTRASSE

ⓘ Ⓢ LEHRTER
     STADTBAHNHOF

Hauptbahnhof

Former course
of Wall

WERFTSTRASSE

ALT-MOABIT

❸

SPREEBOGEN

Ⓒ

FLEMINGSTR.

STRASSE

Bundeskanzleramt

Paul-Löbe-
Haus

Maria-
Elisabeth-
Lüders-Haus

River Spree

Kongresshalle
(Haus der Kulturen
der Welt)

❻

HEINRICH-VON-GAGERN-STRASSE

Reichstag

Jakob-
Kaiser-
Haus

Die Schlange

JOHN-FOSTER-DULLES-ALLEE

SCHEIDEMANNSTRASSE

DOROTHEEN STRASSE

Brandenburg
Gate

UNTER DEN
LINDEN
Ⓢ

STRASSE DES 17 JUNI

ENTLASTUNGSSTR.

Soviet War
Memorial

EATING & DRINKING
2BE Club   2
Angkor Wat   4
Café am Neuen See   8
Café Buchwald   5
Haus der Kulturen
  der Welt   6
Paris-Moskau   3
Salomon Bagels   9
Schleusenkrug   7
Tape Club   1

Tiergarten

TIERGARTENSTRASSE

LENNÉSTR.

IN DEN MINISTERGARTEN

N

EBERTSTRASSE

LEIPZIGER
PLATZ   LEIPSTRASSE

Kunstgewerbe-
museum

Sony
Center

South
African Indian

Ⓔ Ⓔ Ⓔ
Ⓔ   Austria
Italian   Ⓔ

Kupferstichkabinett

Philharmonie &
Musikinstrumenten
Museum

Filmmuseum

POTSDAMER
PLATZ

Ⓢ POTSDAMER PLATZ

Ⓤ POTSDAMER PLATZ

DISTRICT

Gemäldegalerie

Kunstbibliothek

KULTURFORUM

Daimler
Chrysler
Quarter ❾

VOXSTR.

ALTE
POTSDAMER
STR.

SCHELLING STRASSE

LINKSTRASSE

GABRIELE-TERGIT-PROMENADE

KÖTHENER STRASSE

Ⓔ

Ⓔ Egypt

Bendlerblock
(Resistance Museum)

✝ Matthäuskirche

Shell-
Haus

Neue
Nationalgalerie

Staatsbibliothek

Meistersal

SCHÖNEBERGER

UFER

POTSDAMER STRASSE

DEFFLINGER
STRASSE

GENTHINERSTRASSE

KLUCKSTRASSE

0   200 m

the major points in the Tiergarten. However, the most flexible way to explore the area, particularly the park itself, is by **bike** (see p.29 for rental information), with CallBikes (see p.30) in invariably good supply at Potsdamer Platz.

Potsdamer Platz

Pulverized during the war, then forced into hibernation by the Berlin Wall, it is only thanks to two decades of frantic building work that the busy junction of **Potsdamer Platz** has re-emerged as a temple of commercialism. Nonetheless the platz is worth visiting for its **modern architecture** alone, and for the excellent **Filmmuseum,** which will appeal to anyone with even a passing interest in German cinema.

Said to have been the busiest square in prewar Europe, **Potsdamer Platz** was once surrounded by stores, bars and clubs and pulsed with life day and night. The war left it severely battered, though it regained some of its vitality in the chaotic years immediately after the war as a black-market centre at the junction of the Soviet, American and British sectors. Later, West Berliners watched from their side of the dividing line as the Soviets put down the East Berlin uprising of 1953. The Cold War was then played out here in words, with the Western authorities relaying their version of the news to East Berliners by means of an electronic newsboard – countered by an Eastern billboard exhorting West Berliners to shop in cheap East Berlin stores. This ended with the coming of the Wall, which finally put a physical seal on the ideological division of Potsdamer Platz. On the Eastern side all the buildings (which were mostly war vintage wrecks) were razed to give the GDR's border guards a clear field of fire, while in the West only a couple of battered survivors, including the hulk of the fine old *Hotel Esplanade*, were left as a reminder of the way things used to be.

The dismantling of the Wall produced one of Europe's most valuable lots, a huge empty site in the middle of the city. It was no surprise, therefore, that – despite earlier plans for a more flexible use – in the end huge multinational corporations won out – Sony, DaimlerChrysler and A&T in particular – purchasing the land and creating equally huge sprawling **commercial complexes**. Building this mini-city from scratch represented a feat of engineering. An entire power, water and sewage infrastructure was created; subway tunnels drilled and new S- and U-Bahn stations built; the surviving Weinhaus Huth, a landmark building, was picked up and trundled to another spot; and the remaining interior portions of the *Hotel Esplanade* were incorporated into a new restaurant.

Now, after years of construction work, almost everything around Potsdamer Platz is complete. Dominated by the offices and apartments of the rich, it's the most muscular display of multinational power in the city – so not to everyone's taste – but probably exactly what Berlin needed to compete as a global metropolis.

The Sony Center

Designed by Helmut Jahn, the **Sony Center** is based around several similar glass-sheathed buildings grouped around a capacious, circular courtyard. Its rotunda, topped by a conical glass roof, is easily the most impressive showpiece in the area, open to the elements but at the same time providing a remove from the surrounding urban racket. Berliners have adopted the courtyard as a place to congregate for major sporting events – particularly football matches – when big screens are rolled out and the atmosphere rivals that of many stadiums. Arrive early for a seat at one of the many cafés, bars and restaurants.

Filmmuseum Berlin

The **Filmmuseum Berlin** (Tues, Wed & Fri–Sun 10am–6pm, Thurs 10am–8pm; €6; Ⓦwww.filmmuseum-berlin.de) provides an excellent introduction to the history of German cinema and television, with a free audio guide that is especially useful to those with limited German. Using a bevy of clips, reconstructions and artefacts, it plots the course of German cinema via various technical innovations, stars and major releases. Things more-or-less start with clips from Berlin's first public screening in 1895 (see p.298) – the first in the world – then focuses on **pioneers** like Oskar Messter, who started the first wave of equipment production as well as distributing and directing his own films. The earliest colour films, in which thousands of frames were laboriously inked by hand, are shown here, as is the rise of the world's first film stars. Among them was Henny Porten, a sturdy blond often portrayed in 1920s Germany as an ideal German woman, but who fell from grace under the Nazis when she refused to leave her Jewish husband.

The turmoil of the **Weimar years** produced some of the highpoints of German cinema, including *The Cabinet of Dr Caligari* (1920), Fritz Lang's *Metropolis* (1927) and *The Blue Angel* (1930), which launched **Marlene Dietrich** internationally. The museum is particularly strong on Dietrich, since it inherited much of her estate on her death in 1992 – and quite a haul it was too: over 3000 documents, 15,000 photos and some 3000 clothes stuffed into 60 valises. Interesting threads include her continual manipulation and mistreatment by Joseph von Sternberg who discovered her and claimed that she "was his myth"; her relationship with her great love Jean Gibson; feelings of never quite belonging in the US; and her bitter opposition to the Nazis and their attempts to lure her back into Germany by matching her exorbitant US salary.

The museum's treatment of the **Nazi era** is both clever and circumspect. There's slender detail on the most famous filmmaker of the time **Leni Riefenstahl**, known for her magnificent portrayal of the 1936 Olympics in *Olympia*, but infamous for her willingness to glorify the Nazis in **propaganda** films like *Triumph des Willens*. The museum plays this and other propaganda films, including the deplorable *Jud Süss*, a tale of a dishonest Jew, on TV sets in unmarked drawers that line the walls of the room; you'll probably need to try a few drawers to find these ones. Propaganda was obviously a part of the Nazi era, but far more numerous, particularly during the war, were **escapist** films – Hitler himself was a big fan of Mickey Mouse.

Cinema in the **postwar period** receives less attention, perhaps understandably given its partial replacement by **television** in the 1960s. However, television fans will enjoy the overwhelming video retrospective in which thousands of images from German television are simultaneously shown on a big screen. There's also a formidable back catalogue accessible in private viewing booths.

The DaimlerChrysler quarter

DaimlerChrysler hired, among others, Renzo Piano and Richard Rogers to create an ensemble of mostly red-brick but otherwise disparate buildings that house several restaurants, a theatre, a film multiplex, a 3D big-screen cinema and the obligatory shopping mall. The use of a variety of forms and facades is successful, but not all that stimulating at street level. Rise above all this, though, to the **Panorama Punkt** (Tues–Sun 11am–8pm; €5), at the top of the complex's largest skyscraper via Europe's stomach-churning fastest elevator, and the views are among the best in the city. This is mainly due to the immense height and ideal central location, but the exposed nature of the outdoor viewing deck gives an immediacy of experience that you won't find in the Fernsehturm, the other main contender.

The only other interesting attraction in the vicinity is the **Meistersaal**, a five-minute walk south at Köthener Strasse 38, the former theatre became a West Berlin recording studio for record label Hansa, known as "Hansa by the Wall". It has been used by both David Bowie and U2, with Bowie recording three albums here while he lived in Schöneberg, and is commemorated by a small plaque on the wall outside.

Leipziger Platz

Created by Berlin's expansion in the early 1700s, the civilized and beautiful **Leipziger Platz** was once almost as busy as Potsdamer Platz, thanks to the presence of shops like Alfred Messel's **Wertheim** department store. What little of the platz that hadn't been destroyed by the war was levelled in 1961 for the death-strip of the Berlin Wall, leaving behind only an octagonal footprint as a reminder. Its ongoing reconstruction involves a series of dreary seven-floor office blocks in monotonous light colours, and looks like it will be a missed opportunity to create something interesting.

The Kulturforum

The **Kulturforum** offers a mixture of museums and cultural spaces that could easily fill a day. Many of the buildings were designed in the 1960s by Hans Scharoun – with the exception of Mies van der Rohe's impressive Neue National-galerie – but mostly the area lay dormant on the fringe of West Berlin, until after the *Wende* when building work was completed.

The Staatsbibliothek

As you walk west from Potsdamer Platz, the first building on your left is the **Staatsbibliothek** (Mon–Fri 9am–9pm, Sat 9am–7pm; free 90min tours in German 10.30am on 3rd Sat of month; Ⓦstaatsbibliothek-berlin.de), which has over three and a half million books, occasional exhibitions, a small concert hall, a reasonable café and a wide selection of British newspapers. The final building to be designed by Hans Scharoun, the *Staabi* is the most popular of his works among his fans, and its most recent claim to fame came when it was used as an important backdrop in Wim Wenders' poetic film elegy to the city, *Wings of Desire*.

The Philharmonie

At the northeast corner of the Kulturforum the honey-coloured **Philharmonie** is home to the Berlin Philharmonic orchestra, frequently considered the world's best. Conducting here is a huge privilege, and to be the resident conductor – as supremo Austrian conductor **Herbert von Karajan** (1908–89) was between 1955 and his death in 1989 – the ultimate accolade, since it's the members of the orchestra themselves that vote for this. Looking at the gaudy gold-clad building, designed in the 1960s by Hans Scharoun, and bearing in mind von Karajan's

---

Entrance to the Kulturforum

A *Bereichskarte* (€8), available at any of the museums in the Kulturforum – the Gemäldegalerie, Kunstbibliothek, Kunstgewerbemuseum, Kupferstichkabinett, Neue Nationalgalerie and Musikinstrumenten museum – will give you entry to all on the same day and includes their excellent audio tours. You will be automatically sold this ticket at all museums except the Musikinstrumenten museum. For information on tickets valid at all of Berlin's municipal museums see p.65.

famously short temper with artists and rigid discipline that alienated many who worked under him – yet proved fabulously successful in the field of popularizing classical music – it's easy to see why Berliners nicknamed it "Karajan's circus". However, Scharoun's complicated floor plan around the orchestra offers top-notch acoustics and views, regardless of your seat. Other than going to a performance (see p.236), you can also view the interior of the building on free tours (in German), held daily at 1pm. Also free are classical concerts given most Tuesdays at 1pm in the foyer – food is available then, but there's no seating.

Musikinstrumenten museum

Continuing the musical theme, the **Musikinstrumenten museum** (Tues, Wed & Fri 9am–5pm, Thurs 9am–10pm, Sat & Sun 10am–5pm; €4 or see box, p.102; Ⓦwww.sim.spk-berlin.de), in the same building as the Philharmonie, comes as something of a disappointment, but there are a few high points in the comprehensive collection of (mostly European) keyboards, wind and string instruments from the fifteenth century to the present day, including the flute Frederick the Great played to entertain his guests. Pre-recorded tapes give a taste of the weird and wonderful sounds of the instruments, the most memorable of which are the seventeenth-century cembalo, a nineteenth-century glass harmonica, consisting of liquid-filled glasses, and a three-storey-high 1929 Wurlitzer organ.

The Kunstgewerbemuseum

Over the road from the Philharmonie is the **Kunstgewerbemuseum** (Museum of Applied Arts; Tues–Fri 10am–6pm, Sat & Sun 11am–6pm; €8, see box, p.102; Ⓦwww.smb.museum) with its encyclopedic, but seldom dull, collection of European arts and crafts. The top floor contains Renaissance, Baroque and Rococo pieces (wonderful silver and ceramics), along with Jugendstil and Art Deco objects, particularly furniture. Among the many impressive pieces is a massive silver buffet that once resided in the Berliner Schloss, one of the very few surviving artefacts from the palace, and, of course, the museum has a superb collection of Meissenware and KPM porcelain. The ground floor holds the Middle Ages to Early Renaissance collections, with some sumptuous gold pieces. Highlights are Lüneburg's municipal silver and the treasures from the Stiftskirche in Westphalian town Enger, which include an eighth-century purse-shaped **reliquary** that belonged to Duke Widikund, leader of the Saxon resistance to Charlemagne. The basement holds a small but great assembly of Bauhaus furniture, glittering contemporary jewellery and a display on the evolution of product design.

The Gemäldegalerie

The nearby **Gemäldegalerie** (Picture Gallery; Tues, Wed & Fri–Sun 10am–6pm, Thurs 10am–10pm; €8, see box, p.102; Ⓦwww.smb.museum) holds a stupendous collection of early European paintings, making it the real jewel of the Kulturforum. Almost nine hundred paintings are on display, arranged in chronological order, and subdivided by region.

German work from the Middle Ages and Renaissance includes the large *Wurzach Altar* of 1437, made in the workshop of the great Ulm sculptor Hans Multscher; its figures' exaggerated gestures and facial distortions make it an ancient precursor of Expressionism. Otherwise some of the best works here are by Albrecht Altdorfer, one of the first fully realized German landscape painters, and Holbein the Younger, represented by several superbly observed portraits. Notable among the many examples of Cranach are his tongue-in-cheek *The Fountain of Youth*, and his free reinterpretation of Bosch's famous triptych *The Garden of Earthly Delights*.

MITTE: TIERGARTEN | The Kulturforum

Religious subjects receive a lighter treatment in the **Netherlandish section**, featuring fifteenth and sixteenth century work. Jan van Eyck's beautifully lit *Madonna in the Church*, is crammed with architectural detail and has the Virgin lifted in the perspective for gentle emphasis. Petrus Christus is thought to have been his pupil, and certainly knew his work, as *The Virgin and Child with St Barbara and a Carthusian Monk* reveals; in the background are tiny Flemish houses and street scenes, carefully locating the event in Bruges. The parts of the collection from the sixteenth century include the works of Bruegel the Elder, whose *Netherlandish Proverbs* is an amusing, if hard-to-grasp, illustration of over a hundred sixteenth-century proverbs such as armed to the teeth, banging a head against a brick wall and casting pearls before swine.

The later **Dutch and Flemish collections**, with their large portraits of Van Dyck and fleshy canvases of Rubens, are another strong point in the gallery. The paintings of Vermeer are the most easily identifiable, by his usual technique of placing furniture obliquely in the centre of the canvas, the scene illuminated by window light. But the high points of this section are several paintings by **Rembrandt**: though *The Man in the Golden Helmet* has been proved to be the work of his studio rather than the artist himself, this does little to detract from the elegance and power of the portrait, its reflective sorrow relieved by the bright helmet.

Finally, the **Italian section** spans from the Renaissance to the eighteenth century, and is particularly strong on works from the Florentine Renaissance, including, most importantly, two paintings by Botticelli: *Madonna with Saints* and *Mary with the Child and Singing Angels*. Other noteworthy painters represented in the museum include Caravaggio (*Cupid Victorious*, heavy with symbolism and homoeroticism), Poussin (the important *Self-Portrait*), Claude and Canaletto.

The Kupferstichkabinett

Sharing its main entrance with the Gemäldegalerie, the **Kupferstichkabinett** (Engraving Cabinet; Tues–Fri 10am–6pm, Sat & Sun 11am–6pm; €8, see box, p.102; ☎030/266 42 30 40; ⓦwww.smb.museum), holds an extensive collection of European medieval and Renaissance prints, drawings and engravings, many kept under protective lighting. Founded by William Humboldt in 1831, the collection includes Botticelli's exquisite drawings for Dante's *Divine Comedy*. The museum hosts temporary exhibitions on all aspects of print-making, drawing and related design.

Kunstbibliothek

Also beside the Gemäldegalerie is the **Kunstbibliothek** (Art Library; Tues, Wed & Fri–Sun 10am–6pm, Thurs 10am–10pm; €8, see box, p.102; ☎030/266 42 30 40, ⓦwww.smb.museum), a gigantic resource for those with an interest in art, photography and graphic design, thanks to its 350,000 volumes and over 1300 international periodicals. The library also has its own galleries for temporary exhibitions, which are almost always worth at least a quick look.

Matthäuskirche

The clear odd-man-out in the Kulturforum is the brick neo-Romanesque **Matthäuskirche** (Matthias Church; Tues–Sun noon–6pm; free), built between 1844 and 1846 and the only survivor of the war in the area. It now houses temporary exhibitions and you can climb the tower for some aerial views of the other, far more modern and angular, Kulturforum buildings.

The Neue Nationalgalerie

By far the finest building here – architecturally speaking – is the **Neue Nationalgalerie** (Tues, Wed & Fri 10am–6pm, Thurs 10am–10pm, Sat & Sun

10am–8pm; €8, see box, p.102; Ⓦ www.smb.museum), behind the Matthäuskirche. A black-rimmed glass box, its ceiling seems almost suspended above the ground, its clarity of line and detail having all the intelligent simplicity of the Parthenon. Designed by Mies van der Rohe in 1965, the upper section is used for temporary exhibits, often of contemporary art, while the underground galleries contain paintings from the beginning of the twentieth century onwards. Included among the permanent collection are the paintings of the "Brücke" group, such as Ernst Kirchner and Karl Schmidt-Rottluff. **Kirchner** spent time in Berlin before World War I, and his *Potsdamer Platz* dates from 1914, though given the drastic changes to it since then it might as well be in another country instead of just down the road. The galleries move on to the portraits and Berlin cityscapes of **Grosz** and **Dix**, notably Grosz's *Gray Day* and Dix's *Maler Family*. Cubism is represented by work from **Braque**, **Gris** and **Picasso** (though the latter is seen in greater number and to better effect in the Berggruen Collection in Charlottenburg; see p.124). There are also pieces by Klee, Max Beckmann and Lyonel Feininger, among others.

The diplomatic district

Immediately west of the Kulturforum is an area once filled by the ostentatious residences of the well-heeled: fine villas with long, narrow gardens overlooking the Tiergarten, before the Nazis forcibly acquired them to generate a **diplomatic district**, with many of the best plots going to close allies like Japan, Italy and Spain. The war saw most of the district comprehensively destroyed, and while the West German government was in Bonn, few countries made much of their plots. But with the government back in Berlin many re-established their presence here, in preference to their East Berlin embassies, producing another of Berlin's stimulating showcases of modern architecture. It's best admired by walking along Tiergartenstrasse – which conveniently lines the way to the **Bauhaus Archive**.

The Bendlerblock and the Gedenkstätte Deutscher Widerstand

Along the eastern edge of the diplomatic district is Stauffenbergstrasse, which takes its name from Count Claus Schenk von Stauffenberg, one of the instigators of the July Bomb Plot (see box, pp.106–107). At no. 13–14 stands the **Bendlerblock**, once the home to the Wehrmacht headquarters – where Stauffenberg was chief of staff – and now the German Defence Ministry. The floors where Stauffenberg worked are occupied by the absorbing exhibition **Gedenkstätte Deutscher Widerstand** (Memorial to German Resistance; Mon–Wed & Fri 9am–6pm, Thurs 9am–8pm, Sat & Sun 10am–6pm; free; Ⓦ www.gdw-berlin.de), a huge collection of photos and documents covering the many and wide-ranging groups who actively opposed the Third Reich – an eclectic mix which included communists, Jews, Quakers and aristocrats. Most of the exhibition is in German, though the free English audio tour (ID required as deposit) gives a good taste by covering the highlights in around forty minutes.

Shell-Haus

At the southern end of Stauffenbergstrasse, beside the Landwehrkanal, the **Shell-Haus** – also called the BEWAG (Berlin Electric Company) building – is one of Berlin's few great modernist buildings to largely survive World War II intact. This office building's tiered levels and undulating facade attempts to reproduce elements of the adjacent canal, and was designed by Emil Fahrenkamp in 1931 and became a leading piece of modernist architecture. The building underwent an elaborate and extraordinarily complicated restoration process in 2001. The inner structure had to be shrunk first to make way for a stonework facade that complied with contemporary regulations – simply adding it to the outside was out of the question as it would have changed the appearance of this protected building.

Anti-Nazi resistance and the July Bomb Plot

Anti-Nazi resistance in Germany was less overt than in occupied Europe, but existed throughout the war, particularly in Berlin, where a group of **KPD-run communist cells** operated a clandestine information network and organized acts of resistance and sabotage. But the odds against them were overwhelming, and most groups perished. More successful for a while was the **Rote Kapelle** (Red Orchestra), headed by Harold Schulze-Boysen, an aristocrat who worked in the Air Ministry, with agents in most of the military offices, who supplied information to the Soviet Union. The **Kreisau Circle**, a resistance group led by Count Helmut von Moltke, and the groups around Carl Goerdeler (former mayor of Leipzig) and General Beck (ex-chief of staff) talked about overthrowing the Nazis and opening negotiations with the western Allies. However, the most effective resistance came from within the military. There had been attempts on Hitler's life since 1942, but it wasn't until late 1943 and early 1944 that enough high-ranking officers had become convinced defeat was inevitable, and a wide network of conspirators established.

The **July Bomb Plot** that took place in the summer of 1944 at Hitler's Polish HQ, the "Wolf's Lair" in Rastenburg, was the assassination attempt that came closest to success. The plot was led by the one-armed **Count Claus Schenk von Stauffenberg**, an aristocratic officer and member of the General Staff, with the support of several high-ranking members of the German army. Sickened by atrocities on the eastern front, and rapidly realizing that the Wehrmacht was fighting a war that could not be won, Stauffenberg and his fellow conspirators decided to kill the Führer, seize control of army headquarters on Bendlerstrasse and sue for peace with the Allies. Germany was on the precipice of total destruction; only such a desperate act, reasoned the plotters, could save the Fatherland.

On July 20, Stauffenberg was summoned to the Wolf's Lair to brief Hitler on troop movements on the eastern front. In his briefcase was a small bomb, packed with high explosive: once triggered, it would explode in under ten minutes. As Stauffenberg approached the specially built conference hut, he triggered the device. Stauffenberg then positioned the briefcase under the table, leaning it against one of the table's stout legs less than two metres away from the Führer. Five minutes before the bomb exploded, the Count quietly slipped unnoticed from the room. One of the officers, Colonel Brandt, then moved closer to the table to get a better look at the campaign maps and, finding the briefcase in the way of his feet under the table, picked it up and moved it to the other side of the table leg. This put the very solid support of the table leg between the briefcase and Hitler.

At 12.42pm the bomb went off. Stauffenberg, watching the hut from a few hundred metres away, was shocked by the force of the explosion; he didn't doubt that the Führer, along with everyone else in the room, was dead.

Stauffenberg hurried off to a waiting plane and made his way to Berlin to join the other conspirators. Meanwhile, back in the wreckage of the conference hut, Hitler and the survivors staggered out into the daylight. Four people were killed, including Colonel Brandt, who had unwittingly saved the Führer's life. Hitler himself, despite being badly shaken, suffered no more than a perforated eardrum and minor injuries. After being attended to, he prepared himself for a meeting with Mussolini later that afternoon.

It quickly became apparent what had happened, and the hunt for Stauffenberg was on. Hitler issued orders to the SS in Berlin to summarily execute

The embassies

The **diplomatic district** kicks off at the northern end of Stauffenbergstrasse, site of the dignified **Egyptian Embassy**, with its polished stonework and detailed engravings, and the flamboyant **Austrian Embassy**, the work of Viennese architect Hans Hollein. West along Tiergartenstrasse, the bulky building hewn

anyone who was slightly suspect, and dispatched Himmler to the city to quell the rebellion.

Back in the military Supreme Command headquarters in Bendlerstrasse, the conspiracy was in chaos. Word reached Stauffenberg and the two main army conspirators, Generals Beck and Witzleben, that the Führer was still alive. They had already lost hours of essential time by failing to issue the carefully planned order to mobilize their sympathizers in the city and elsewhere, and had even failed to carry out the obvious precaution of severing all communications out of the city. Goebbels succeeded in telephoning Hitler, who spoke directly to the arrest team, ordering them to obey his propaganda minister. Then Goebbels set to work contacting SS and Gestapo units, and reminding army garrisons of their oath of loyalty to the Führer. After a few hours of tragicomic scenes as the conspirators tried to persuade high-ranking officials to join them, the Bendlerstrasse HQ was surrounded by SS troops, and it was announced that the Führer would broadcast to the nation later that evening. The attempted coup was over. At 9pm, Hitler broadcast on national radio, saying he would "settle accounts the way we National Socialists are accustomed to settle them".

The conspirators were gathered together, given paper to write farewell messages to their wives, taken to the courtyard of the HQ (a memorial stands on the spot) and, under the orders of one General Fromm, shot by firing squad. Stauffenberg's last words were "Long live our sacred Germany!" Fromm had known about the plot almost from the beginning, but had refused to join it. By executing the leaders he hoped to save his own skin – and, it must be added, save them from the torturers of the SS.

Hitler's revenge on the conspirators was severe even by the ruthless standards of the Third Reich. All the colleagues, friends and immediate relatives of Stauffenberg and the other conspirators were rounded up, tortured and taken before the "People's Court" (the building where the court convened, the Kammergericht building, still stands – see p.129), where they were humiliated and given more or less automatic death sentences, most of which were brutally carried out at **Plötzensee Prison** (see p.127). Many of those executed knew nothing of the plot and were found guilty merely by association. As the blood lust grew, the Nazi party used the plot as a pretext for settling old scores, and eradicated anyone who had the slightest hint of anything less than total dedication to the Führer. General Fromm, who had ordered the execution of the Bendlerstrasse conspirators, was among those tried, found guilty of cowardice and shot by firing squad. Those whose names were blurted out under torture were quickly arrested, the most notable being Field Marshal Rommel, who, because of his popularity, was given the choice of a trial in the so-called People's Court – or suicide and a state funeral. He chose suicide, but other high-ranking conspirators were forced before the court for a public show trial. All were sentenced to death by the Nazi judge Ronald Freisler and hanged on meat-hooks at Plötzensee Prison, their death agonies being filmed for Hitler's private delectation.

The July Bomb Plot resulted in the deaths of at least five thousand people, including some of Germany's most brilliant military thinkers and almost all of those who would have been best qualified to run the postwar German government. (Freisler himself was killed by an American bomb.) Within six months the country lay in ruins as the Allies advanced; had events at Rastenburg been only a little different, the entire course of the war – and European history – would have been altered incalculably.

from rough-cut red sandstone is the **Indian Embassy**, a clever design that attempts to symbolize India's complexities in architectural terms. The entrance is through a gap in a cylinder that starts a contrast of void and solid that continues throughout the building, though the public can only get a closer look during rare exhibitions (check ⓦ www.indischebotschaft.de for details).

Further west down Tiergartenstrasse are the two unmistakable Nazi-era edifices of Germany's closest prewar allies. The **Japanese** completed their embassy in 1942 as many other buildings in Berlin started to collapse in bombing raids. Though it has been restored and remodelled since reunification, the architects carefully respected the original design, preserving stone cladding and only removing some ornamentation – replacing it with sleek lines that tend to add to the monumentalism. The **Italian Embassy** has a similar look, as does the beautifully restored **Spanish Embassy**, though that's a little out of the way – a five-minute walk west to the corner of Lichtensteinallee and Thomas-Dehler-Strasse.

Providing a sharp contrast are the bold bright lines of the area's most exciting modernist buildings around the corner on Klingelhöferstrasse. Here the stunning **Nordic Embassy** provides offices for Denmark, Sweden, Finland, Iceland and Norway. Each occupies a separate building but they share an outer skin of pre-oxidized copper panels that playfully reflect changes in light or weather. Though each country employed different architects, all have stone and timber designs that share a lightness and simple elegance, the natural wood and raw concrete creating contrasts between unfinished and polished elements. The compound includes an exhibition hall (Mon–Fri 10am–7pm, Sat & Sun 11am–4pm) and a canteen (Mon–Fri 10–11.30am & 1–6pm), where visitors can enjoy herring, meatballs and other Nordic specialities.

Another tribute to the simplicity and beauty of modernism is provided by the avant-garde **Mexican Embassy**, next door. Its main features are slanting supports that create a vertical blind effect and a massive concrete and marble entranceway. The public exhibition area (Mon–Fri 9am–1pm) in the atrium is a homage to a Mayan observatory, the first cylindrical construction in the Americas. Like the Nordic Embassy, the Mexican Embassy building is worth a trip at night when it's **floodlit** to tremendous effect.

Bauhaus Archive

Further south down the road, at Klingelhöferstrasse 14, and the #100 bus route between the Tiergarten and Bahnhof Zoo, is the **Bauhaus Archive** (Wed–Mon 10am–5pm; Wed–Fri €6, Sat–Mon €7; ⓦ www.bauhaus.de). The Bauhaus school of design, crafts and architecture was founded in 1919 in Weimar by Walter Gropius. It moved to Dessau in 1925 and then to Berlin, to be closed by the Nazis in 1933 (see box opposite). The influence of Bauhaus has been tremendous, but you only get a very small impression of this from the modest collection here, in a building designed by Gropius and completed in 1979. Marcel Breuer's seminal chair is still (with minor variations) in production today, and former Bauhaus director Mies van der Rohe's designs and models for buildings show how the modernist Bauhaus style has changed the face of today's cities. There's work, too, by Kandinsky, Moholy-Nagy, Schlemmer and Klee, all of whom worked at the Bauhaus.

Tiergarten

Flanking the north sides of both the Kulturforum and the diplomatic district is the **Tiergarten** park, a restful expanse of woodland and lakes which was originally designed by Peter Lenné as a hunting ground under Elector Friedrich III. Largely

Bauhaus, a German word whose literal meaning is "building-house", has become a generic term for the aesthetically functional design style that grew out of the art and design philosophy developed at the Dessau school, in Saxony-Anhalt. The origins of the Bauhaus movement lie in the Novembergruppe, a grouping of artists founded in 1918 by the Expressionist painter Max Pechstein with the aim of utilizing art for revolutionary purposes. Members included Bertolt Brecht and Kurt Weill, Emil Nolde, Eric Mendelssohn and the architect **Walter Gropius**. In 1919 Gropius was invited by the new republican government of Germany to oversee the amalgamation of the School of Arts and Crafts and the Academy of Fine Arts in Weimar into the **Staatliche Bauhaus Weimar**. It was hoped that this new institution would break down the barriers between art and craft, creating a new form of applied art. It attracted over two hundred students who studied typography, furniture design, ceramics, wood-, glass- and metalworking under exponents like Paul Klee, Wassily Kandinsky and Laszlo Moholy-Nagy.

By the end of the 1920s, the staff and students of the Bauhaus school had become increasingly embroiled in the political battles of the time, and throughout the early 1930s Nazi members of Dessau town council called for an end to subsidies for the Bauhaus. Their efforts finally succeeded in the summer of 1932, forcing the school to close down. The Bauhaus relocated to the more liberal atmosphere of Berlin, setting up in a disused telephone factory in Birkbuschstrasse in the Steglitz district. However, after the Nazis came to power, police harassment reached such a pitch that on July 20, 1933, director **Ludwig Mies van der Rohe** took the decision to shut up shop for good. He and many of his staff and students subsequently went into exile in the United States.

destroyed during the 1945 Battle of Berlin, after the war it was used as farmland, largely to grow potatoes for starving citizens, but since then replanting the park has been so successful that these days it's hard to tell it's not original.

The park is most easily accessed by bus #100, which cuts through it on its way from Bahnhof Zoo to Alexanderplatz via all the main sights, but the best way to appreciate it is on foot or by bike. At the very least, try wandering along the Landwehrkanal, an inland waterway off the River Spree that separates the park from the zoo. It's an easy hour's walk between **Corneliusbrücke** – just up Corneliusstrasse from the Bauhaus Archive (see opposite) – and Bahnhof Zoo, via a popular beer garden *Schleusenkrug* (see p.214). At Corneliusbrücke a small, odd sculpture commemorates the radical leader **Rosa Luxemburg**. In 1918, along with fellow revolutionary Karl Liebknecht, she reacted against the newly formed Weimar Republic and especially the terms of the Treaty of Versailles, declaring a new Socialist Republic in Berlin along the lines of Soviet Russia (she had played an important part in the abortive 1905 revolution). The pair were kidnapped by members of the elite First Cavalry Guards: Liebknecht was gunned down while "attempting to escape", Luxemburg was knocked unconscious and shot, her body dumped in the Landwehrkanal.

Just to the north of the Landwehrkanal, and deeper inside the park, a pretty little group of ponds makes up the grand-sounding **Neuer See**. In summer there's another popular beer garden here, the *Café am Neuen See*, and it's possible to rent **boats** by the hour.

The Siegessäule

In the midst of the park and approached by four great boulevards stands the **Siegessäule** (April–Oct Mon–Fri 9.30am–6.30pm, Sat & Sun 9.30am–7pm;

Nov–March daily 10am–6pm; €2.50; bus #100), a column celebrating Prussia's military victories (chiefly that over France in 1871). It was shifted to this spot on Hitler's orders in 1938 from in front of the Reichstag. The move was part of a grand design for Berlin as capital of the Third Reich, and with the same forethought Hitler had the monument raised another level to commemorate the victories to come in what became World War II. Though the boulevard approaches exaggerate its size, it's still an eye-catching monument: 67m high and topped with a gilded winged victory that symbolically faces France. The summit offers a good view of the surrounding area, but climbing the 585 steps to the top is no mean feat. Have a look, too, at the mosaics at the column's base, which show the unification of the German peoples and incidents from the Franco-Prussian War. The four bronze reliefs beside them on the four sides depict the main wars and the victorious marching of the troops into Berlin; these were removed after 1945 and taken to Paris, only to be returned when the lust for war spoils had subsided.

Dotted around the Siegessäule are **statues** of other German notables, the most imposing being that of Bismarck, the "Iron Chancellor", under whom the country was united in the late nineteenth century. He's surrounded by figures symbolizing his achievements; walk around the back for the most powerful.

Strasse des 17 Juni

East and west of the Siegessäule, the **Strasse des 17 Juni** is the broad, straight avenue that cuts through the Tiergarten to form the continuation of Unter den Linden beyond the Brandenburg Gate (see p.44). Originally named Charlottenburger Chaussee, it was also once known as the East–West Axis and was a favourite strip for Nazi processions. Indeed, Hitler had the stretch from the Brandenburg Gate to Theodor-Heuss-Platz (formerly Adolf-Hitler-Platz; see p.125) widened in order to accommodate these mass displays of military might and Nazi power; on his birthday in 1938, 40,000 men and 600 tanks took four hours to parade past the Führer. Later, in the final days of the war, Charlottenburger Chaussee became a makeshift runway for aeroplanes ferrying Nazi notables to and from the besieged capital. Its current name commemorates the day in 1953 when workers in the East rose in revolt against the occupying Soviet powers (see p.138), but today it is better known for demonstrations of a very different sort: it formed the main venue for the hedonistic Love Parade and the focus for celebrations during the 2006 football World Cup. Usually though it's simply a busy thoroughfare by day, while by night prostitutes line its western end and the Siegessäule becomes a prime gay cruising spot.

Schloss Bellevue and the Kongresshalle

From the Siegessäule it's a long hike to the Brandenburg Gate and Reichstag, so it's worth hopping on the #100 bus. En route, look out for **Schloss Bellevue**, an eighteenth-century building that was once a guesthouse for the Third Reich and is today the Berlin home of the Federal President. You might also catch a glimpse of the **Bundespräsidialamt** – a polished granite oval of presidential administrative offices that plays with the reflections of surrounding trees.

Further east, on John-Foster-Dulles-Allee, sits the oyster-shaped **Kongresshalle**, an exhibition centre whose concept couldn't be matched by available technology: its roof collapsed in 1980, and it has since been rebuilt and reopened as the **Haus der Kulturen der Welt**, a venue for theatre, music, performance art and exhibitions – chiefly from Africa, South America and the Far East (Ⓦwww.hkw .de; see p.231). South from here, on the north side of Strasse des 17 Juni, is the **Soviet War Memorial** (Sowjetisches Ehrenmal) to the Red Army troops who

▲ The Haus der Kulturen der Welt

died in the Battle of Berlin. Built from the marble of Hitler's destroyed Berlin HQ, the Reich's Chancellery, it's flanked by two tanks that were supposedly the first to reach the city.

The Spreebogen

The sharpest bend in central Berlin's River Spree, known as the **Spreebogen**, runs through one of Berlin's newest and quietest city quarters just northwest of the Reichstag (see p.48). Here the German government has built a **Regierungsviertel**, or government quarter, and this is also the location of Berlin's new space-age **Hauptbahnhof** train station. But a lot is still missing on a human scale, with visitors left to potter across huge empty plazas in front of giant buildings. The only exception to this is alongside the Spree where a new hangout of sorts is emerging as deckchairs colonize its banks and bars and cafés do a brisk trade, making it a pleasant place to while away an hour or two in the summer as boats cruise by.

Before the war this part of town was known as the **Alsenviertel**, an area of luxurious apartments that overlooked Königsplatz and a much shorter Siegessäule, which stood midway between the Reichstag and the Kroll Opera House, until it was moved to its present position (see p.109) to make way for a "Great Hall of the People". This giant structure, loosely based on Rome's Parthenon, was to be the centrepiece of Hitler and Speer's World Capital Germania, with a cupola so large that it would have been impossible to build with the technology of the time. Instead, the war left the area gutted and largely levelled, its proximity to the East Berlin border deterring any redevelopment. It became an area where West Berliners came to barbecue or learn to drive in empty car parks, while boats from the East – mainly Polish freighters delivering coal to West Berlin's power stations – sailed through the only river checkpoint; all were meticulously scanned underwater for possible escapees.

The Regierungsviertel

New and strikingly well-designed modern buildings form Berlin's **Regierungsviertel** (government quarter), a district built largely in the 1990s to give the German Federal government a home. When planning the new quarter, central concepts included having structures that straddled the Spree, symbolically linking East and West; connecting the main buildings to one another to underline the correlation of government; and to design accessible and transparent buildings as a metaphor for the necessary openness of government. This is best appreciated, in the first instance, by getting an overview from the top of the Reichstag (see p.48).

The biggest but least attention-grabbing building is administrative **Jakob-Kaiser-Haus**, immediately east of the Reichstag, whose 1750 offices make it one of Europe's largest office blocks. However, despite its size, it avoids becoming too monstrous or monotonous by following Berlin's traditional courtyard principle – almost creating a neighbourhood – and by integrating well into its surroundings.

More elegant are the offices and conference rooms of the **Paul-Löbe-Haus** and **Maria-Elisabeth-Lüders-Haus**, just north of the Reichstag and west and east of the Spree respectively. Symbolically joined to one another via a footbridge across the river and over the former East–West border, both were designed by Stefan Braunfels and completed in 2001. Of note are the large windows that form part of the building's energy-efficient heating system by collecting heat – along with the roof – while interior ceilings double as cooling mechanisms.

With its comb-like layout, the Paul-Löbe-Haus plays on design themes present in the imposing Bundeskanzleramt (Federal Chancellery), opposite. A pet project of Helmut Kohl, it was cleverly designed by Axel Schultes and Charlotte Frank to contain subtle references to Le Corbusier and Luis Kahn in the studied detailing and structure. The centrepiece is a nine-storey white cube – earning the building the nickname "the washing machine" – which contains the chancellor's accommodation. Originally the building was to be connected with Paul-Löbe-Haus, to reinforce symbolic relationship between chancellor, administration and parliament but the project ran short of money, so that the only connections are those running underground between the Reichstag and Paul-Löbe-Haus.

The **Bundeskanzleramt** is best appreciated from the northern banks of the Spree; walking there you'll likely pass the **Swiss Embassy** just northeast of the Chancellery. One of few Neoclassical buildings to survive the war intact, its modern extension caused some outrage, even though experts judge the two buildings to be a clever play of opposites – not even the floor levels line up – and praise the careful exterior concreting, done in one pour so that no shuttering or expansion joints are visible.

The final piece of intriguing government-quarter architecture lies at its western end, and is best seen from the Spree. Called **Die Schlange** (The Snake) for its unusual zigzag layout, this brick-clad apartment block has proved rather unpopular among the parliamentarians it was designed for, as some apartments stare into one another and because of the odd-shaped rooms – not to mention high rents and dull surroundings.

The Hauptbahnhof

After almost a decade of planning and construction, Berlin's latest landmark and superlative piece of architecture – the glass and steel five-level **Hauptbahnhof** – opened in time for the 2006 football World Cup. The bold design by two Hamburg-based architects, Meinhard von Gerkan and Volkin Marg, and its capacity – it's Europe's biggest-ever train hub and can handle 300,000 travellers on

Berlin's architecture

"Berlin is a new city; the newest I have ever seen," remarked Mark Twain in 1891. A curious thing for an American to say, but the statement still rings true. Certainly, by European standards the city is relatively young – founded in the thirteenth century and only blossoming from the late sixteenth – but it's the obliterating destruction of World War II that has made it so new. Few buildings hark back to before this time (those that appear to are mostly replicas), and the city has become a haven for modern architecture and experimentation.

Schloss Charlottenburg ▲

The Brandenburg Gate ▲

Haus der Kulturen der Welt ▼

Berlin Dom ▼

Prussia's imperial capital

A chronological tour of Berlin's architecture kicks off in the Nikolaiviertel, with the medieval **Nikolaikirche** (see p.76). This is followed by the ornate Baroque buildings of the seventeenth century – the best examples are the grand **Schloss Charlottenburg** (see p.121) and the **Brandenburg Gate** (see p.44). South of here, magnificent churches with splendid domes stand on the **Gendarmenmarkt** (see p.53). These and many other buildings – such as the **Neue Wache** (see p.60) and the **Altes Museum** (see p.66) – were later adorned by Karl Friedrich Schinkel (1781–1841), with his unmistakable Neoclassical touch. As all these grand edifices were assembled, the industrial revolution in Berlin's suburbs was leading to an explosion in the population: to combat the need for housing a system of tenements around a series of courtyards was developed – the **Hackeschen Höfe** (see p.81) are a good example of this design.

The founding of the German empire in 1871 ushered in *Gründerzeit* architecture, whose premise was largely to recycle earlier styles, but add ostentatious flourishes – the **Reichstag** (see p.48) and the **Berliner Dom** (see p.64) are models of the style.

Nicknames

Change is part of the landscape in Berlin, but one constant seems to be the enthusiasm of Berliners for giving nicknames to their architectural gems. Here are a few examples:

▶▶ **Tele-asparague** Fernsehturm
▶▶ **Eric's lamp shop** Palast der Republik
▶▶ **The commode** Alte Bibliothek
▶▶ **Karajan's circus** Philharmonie
▶▶ **Pregnant oyster** Haus der Kulturen der Welt

Modernism to Third Reich

As a backlash against all this meaningless nostalgia, **Modernism** arrived in Berlin in the early twentieth century. Foremost among the Modernist architects was Peter Behrens (1868–1940), who removed ornamentation and favoured glass, concrete and steel building materials. One of the finest buildings from the period is Emil Fahrenkamp's **Shell-Haus** (see p.105). The Nazis brought any Modernist enterprises to an end, preferring powerful-looking Neoclassical buildings for their **Third Reich**. An imposing remodelling of Berlin was envisaged but defeat in the war scuppered the plans – however a few Nazi buildings remain, including the magnificent **Tempelhof airport** (see p.140) and the **Olympic Stadium** (see p.126).

The divided city

Postwar town planners and architects on both sides of the divided city were presented with a relatively blank canvas. East Berlin continued monumentalist traditions with its enormous **Karl-Marx-Allee** (see p.147) housing schemes built in Stalin's favourite *Zuckerbäckstil* (wedding cake style), while its top project was the **Fernsehturm** (see p.72). Meanwhile, planners in West Berlin did the opposite, in an effort to project a modern yet sensitive image: the use of greenery around buildings was as important as the architecture itself, as at the **Kongresshalle** (see p.110), and Scharoun's **Philharmonie** (see p.102). Prestige projects aside, both Berlins needed affordable housing and both approached this in similarly dismal ways, illustrated by the high-rises of Marzahn. More sensitive **regeneration projects** followed in areas like Prenzlauer Berg in the east and Kreuzberg in the west.

▲ The Olympic Stadium

▲ Nazi motif on Tempelhof airport

▼ Fernsehturm

Hauptbahnhof ▲

Holocaust Memorial ▲

The Reichstag ▼

Jüdisches Museum ▼

Reunification

After the *Wende*, attention shifted to the building projects in areas where the Berlin Wall once stood. The Sony Center and skyscrapers of **Potsdamer Platz** (see p.100) are the most striking, but impressive too are the developments on **Pariser Platz** (see p.45), in the **Regierungsviertel** (Government quarter; see p.112), and those that fringe the Tiergarten, such as the Nordic and Mexican **embassies** (see p.108) and the immense **Hauptbahnhof** (see p.112). Most recent are monuments and museums designed to help Berlin address its past, including Daniel Libeskind's **Jüdisches Museum** (see p.133) and the **Holocaust Memorial** (see p.49).

Though the pace of building work in Berlin is slowing, there's much more to do. The **Brandenburg international airport** is the largest of the projects, but the reconstruction of the **Schloss** is likely to be the most eye-catching. Campaigns are also being waged to reconstruct various historic buildings – cranes will be an integral part of the city's skyline for some time yet.

Berlin's beauties

Everyone has an opinion about what constitutes a wonderful building, but these ones are sure to stun:

▶▶ **Reichstag** A stirringly patriotic and meaningful building, even disregarding its historical associations.

▶▶ **Hackeschen Höfe** Imagine these courtyards teeming with nineteenth-century life.

▶▶ **The Olympic Stadium** Designed to rival Rome's Colosseum.

▶▶ **Sony Center** The Roman atrium reinvented for the 21st century.

▶▶ **Jüdisches Museum** The ideal backdrop for a difficult subject.

1100 trains per day – are impressive. Yet it remains an oddity thanks to the barren immediate surroundings, devoid of Berlin's usual endless graffiti and the normal mix of late-night bars, gambling dens and sex shops that surround most of Europe's major train stations. Here cleanliness, sterility and peacefulness rule, escalators move noiselessly and even the bins shine.

Like London, Berlin had a historic ring of terminus stations, but as early as the 1930s plans were drawn up to make a cross out of the impractical ring. After reunification, the opportunity was seized, and this central station at the crossing point of the two main west-east and north-south lines planned. This was the one-time location of the old Lehrter Bahnhof, which operated from 1871 to 1952 before it was left to rot alongside Berlin's Cold War dividing line. It is now being hailed as a symbolic central point of Europe, with trains running through between Rome and Copenhagen, Moscow and Paris.

The **east-west** track already existed, following an 1882 viaduct that wends its way through the city from Charlottenburg via the Zoo, Friedrichstrasse and Alexanderplatz stations to the Ostbahnhof, giving rail travellers a wonderful Mitte sightseeing tour. The **north-south** line is new and runs four levels further down and fifteen metres under the Spree. However, the architects have expressed the crossing-point in architectural terms: the glass hall follows the east-west line, while the gap between two huge administrative tracts that cross it indicate the direction of the underground north-south track.

Inside, the building works well. Always quick with a nickname, Berliners soon christened it the "glass cathedral", and the basic principles of Gothic-style construction really are in evidence: supports and weights; the space's upward thrust; braces resembling Gothic clustered piers; and a series of "vaults". Though to a casual observer it may seem more like an airy shopping mall criss-crossed by trains, the main hall, with its many-layered staircase systems, elevator tubes, skylights and aperture windows, is also said to be a formal analogy to the feverish spatial fantasies of the Italian Baroque.

Hamburger Bahnhof

North across Invalidenstrasse from the Hauptbahnhof lies Berlin's premier contemporary art museum, the Museum für Gegenwart, located in the **Hamburger Bahnhof** at Invalidenstrasse 50–51 (Museum for Contemporary Art; Tues–Fri 10am–6pm, Sat 11am–8pm, Sun 11am–6pm; €8, free Thurs 2–6pm; Ⓦ www .hamburgerbahnhof.de; U-Bahn Naturkundemuseum or S-Bahn Lehrter Stadtbahnhof). Like the Anhalter Bahnhof, the Hamburger station was damaged in the war, though it had ceased functioning as a station as early as 1906. Fortunately, it didn't suffer its twin's fate in postwar redevelopment, and is today home to this impressive art collection, which represents a thorough survey of postwar art: from Rauschenberg, Twombly, Warhol, Beuys and Lichtenstein right on up to Keith Haring and Donald Judd. And the old train station makes a spacious, effective setting, particularly the main hall, where large sculptures by Anselm Kiefer and Richard Long, among others, are displayed.

Since 2004, the collection has expanded into a series of renovated industrial halls, once in use by a shipping company, where Friedrich Christian **Flick**, a wealthy industrialist with a penchant for contemporary art, shows changing pieces from his heavyweight collection. The exhibition has proved controversial, more because much of Flick's money comes from his family, which had Nazi connections, than the pieces themselves.

There's a good **bookstore** and **café** on the premises, and look out too for the calendar of concerts, lectures and artist appearances.

Invalidenfriedhof

On the opposite bank of the Humboldthafen canal from the Hamburger Bahnhof, there's the opportunity for a pleasant offbeat walk along a towpath to the **Invalidenfriedhof**, a one-time important Prussian military cemetery that spent the latter half of the twentieth century within the death-strip of the Berlin Wall. The path begins alongside the Humboldthafen, which runs beside the Hamburger Bahnhof, and soon leads to the cemetery. The earliest graves date from the mid-eighteenth century, but the most impressive ones belong to prominent Prussian figures, like Count Tauentzien and Generals Winterfeldt and Scharnhorst. These all remained largely undisturbed until the building of the Berlin Wall, when parish boundaries dictated that the death strip would surround the graves. Some of the graveyard was levelled and given over to access tracks, which remain, but a good number of memorials – all those here today – were preserved and provided a surreal and macabre touch to the death strip. This section of the Berlin Wall was also famed for another depressing reason, since it was here that Günter Litfin, the first victim of the Wall, was shot and killed on 24 August, 1961 as he attempted to swim across the canal. A modest information board commemorates the event.

Medizinhistorisches Museum

Medical textbook horrors come alive at the **Medizinhistorisches Museum** (Medical Museum; Tues & Thurs, Fri & Sun 10am–5pm, Wed & Sat 10am–7pm; €5; ⓦ www.bmm.charite.de) on the southern side of Invalidenstrasse. Here two floors of a working hospital are dedicated to a museum with a really old-fashioned feel – thanks to the dusty shelves that harbour the pickled collection of one Rudolf Virchow (1821–1902), a local doctor and professor, that form the main part of the exhibition. Far from being dull, this surreal and disquieting collection is captivating for its freakish qualities. You won't learn much here, thanks to the almost universal lack of signs and explanations (particularly for those without German), but some displays – like the smoker's tarred lungs or the alcoholic's fatty liver – need little explanation. But the grisly highlights of the collection – which will likely remain with you for some time – are the deformed foetuses and babies. As vivid as any horror filmmaker's imagination, these rows of disturbing deformities include conjoined twins, babies absurdly swollen by hydrocephalus and elephantiasis and even a cyclops. Clearly not one for expectant mothers, and, sensibly, children under twelve are barred – under-sixteens require adult accompaniment.

6

Charlottenburg, Wilmersdorf and Schöneberg

mmediately southwest of Berlin's Tiergarten, the districts of **Charlottenburg**, **Wilmersdorf** and **Schöneberg** are all predominantly moneyed, white and rather sedate middle-class residential areas, where you may end up staying if you've taken pension accommodation or found a private room via the tourist office. Attractions may be spread a little more thinly in this part of town, and the distances between them further, but many are well-worth your time.

The core area here is West Berlin's old centre, now known as **City West**, since the term "centre" no longer fits. This neighbourhood's always been a shopping district, particularly along the ritzy **Kurfürstendamm**, and **Tauentzienstrasse**, which is the location of the noble giant **KaDeWe**, Berlin's best-known department store. Typified by modern architecture, the area is a showcase for glitzy Cold War building-projects, yet its most famous building – and the district hub – is the iconic semi-ruined church tower of the **Kaiser-Wilhelm-Gedächtniskirche**, one of few remaining prewar buildings. Besides shops galore, City West also has a smattering of good **museums** – particularly those devoted to photographer Helmut Newton, artist Käthe Kollwitz – and a lively multimedia museum on the city's history.

Moving out of town, the borough of **Charlottenburg-Wilmersdorf** runs all the way west to the forests of the Grunewald (see p.172), but passes several major attractions en route. Among them is the **Schloss Charlottenburg** – Berlin's pocket Versailles with its opulent chambers, attractive gardens and several excellent museums on its doorstep. Further out the wealthy residential **Westend** district is particularly significant for reminders of 1930s and wartime Berlin, including the **Funkturm**, **Olympic Stadium** and the **Plötzensee Prison Memorial**.

Back in town, and just east of City West, the district of **Schöneberg** contains Berlin's oldest **gay village**, but precious few sights; though its city hall witnessed John F. Kennedy's "Berliner" speech.

City West is easily explored on **foot**, as is much of Schöneberg, where most points of interest are an easy walk from Nollendorfplatz. However, Rathaus

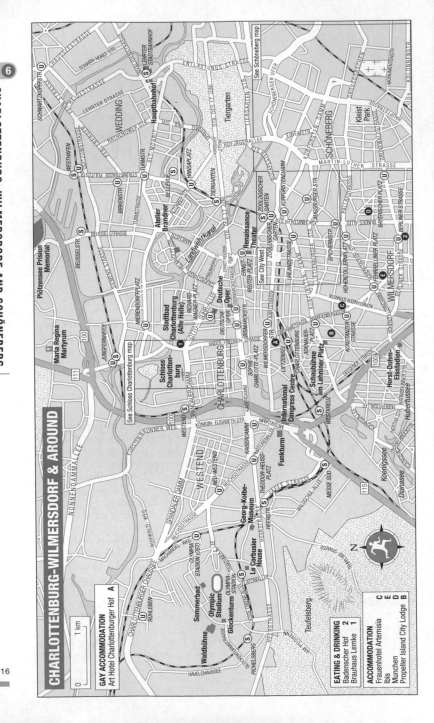

CHARLOTTENBURG-WILMERSDORF & AROUND

0   1 km

GAY ACCOMMODATION
Art Hotel Charlottenburger Hof   A

EATING & DRINKING
Badenscher Hof   2
Brauhaus Lemke   1

ACCOMMODATION
Frauenhotel Artemisia   C
Ibis   E
Munchen   D
Propeller Island City Lodge   B

Schöneberg is best reached by U-Bahn or bus #M46 from **Bahnhof Zoo**, the main transport hub in this part of Berlin from which buses radiate to all the sights in the west.

City West

Long before the term **City West** was coined for the old centre of West Berlin, its main role was as a shopping district, particularly along **Kurfürstendamm** (universally called **Ku'damm**). Even in the grim first few years after the war, a few retailers managed to struggle on here, but it was with the coming of the Berlin Wall that the area got a real boost. With Berlin's true centre snatched away by the GDR, this area quickly became an awkward surrogate. Large amounts of modern building work aimed to transform the area into the heart of a great late twentieth-century metropolis, but the work was largely in vain. Once the Wall came down the city hastily shifted back to its old centre, leaving West Berlin's old centre to years in the doldrums. But lately its iconic avenues have been resurgent, its renaissance based on a mix of big labels – Marc O'Polo, Stefanel, Valentino, Gucci, Cartier, Chanel, Bulgari, Hermès and Louis Vuitton – and a fairly bland mix of affordable high-street shops.

Bahnhof Zoo

Squeezed between a couple of scruffy shopping precincts and surrounded by third-rate modern architecture, **Bahnhof Zoo** is the district's unprepossessing main transport hub. Pulling into Bahnhof Zoo by train still somehow conjures up images of prewar steam trains. But that's as far as the nostalgia goes: the station is comparatively small, without a large lobby or grand entrance portal and its many entrances mostly harbour a retinue of urban casualties. At least a recent makeover and the presence of a few glossy and late-opening stores have helped make the station reasonably smart; it's certainly a far cry from the days, just a couple of decades ago, when it was a marketplace for heroin dealing and child prostitution.

Museum für Fotografie

Behind Bahnhof Zoo, and best reached through its back door, is another of Berlin's excellent municipal museums, the **Museum für Fotografie**, Jebenesstrasse 2 (Tues, Wed & Fri–Sun 10am–6pm, Thurs 10am–10pm; €8 or see p.65, free Thurs 6–10pm; ☎030/31 86 48 25, ⓦwww.smb.museum). The home of the **Helmut Newton Foundation**, it exhibits the work of this world-famous fashion and nude photographer and also sometimes has temporary exhibitions of lesser-known photographers on its upper floors.

The collection was Newton's gift to his home city shortly before his untimely death in 2004, and it divides into two levels of exhibits. The ground floor is a museum to the man and includes a reconstruction of his quirky Monaco office and his oversized made-to-measure beach-buggy – complete with monogram on the steering wheel, no doubt perfect for cruising around Monte Carlo. Old passports, letters, calendars and covers are among the rest of the memorabilia, but none as intriguing as his camera collection, which spans several decades. The upper floors show Newton's work in regularly changing exhibits, but all focus on his unique and heavily stylized portrait, glamour and nude photography, his celebrity portraiture and penchant for Amazonian women. Some of the most intriguing pieces, which often make an appearance in exhibitions, are from his personal collection of unpublished photos. Both Newton and his wife (who worked under the pseudonym Alice Springs) always seem to have cameras to hand to chart every aspect of their life together and obsess over each other's naked forms. Self-portraits

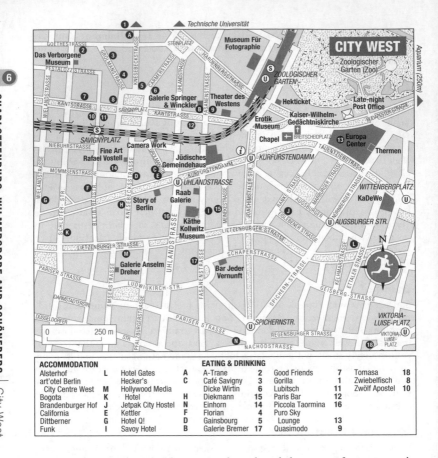

ACCOMMODATION				EATING & DRINKING					
Alsterhof	L	Hotel Gates	A	A-Trane	2	Good Friends	7	Tomasa	18
art'otel Berlin		Hecker's	C	Café Savigny	3	Gorilla	1	Zwiebelfisch	8
City Centre West	M	Hollywood Media		Dicke Wirtin	6	Lubitsch	11	Zwölf Apostel	10
Bogota	K	Hotel		Diekmann	15	Paris Bar	12		
Brandenburger Hof	J	Jetpak City Hostel	N	Einhorn	14	Piccola Taormina	16		
California	E	Kettler	F	Florian	4	Puro Sky			
Dittberner	G	Hotel Q!	D	Gainsbourg	5	Lounge	13		
Funk	I	Savoy Hotel	B	Galerie Bremer	17	Quasimodo	9		

give revealing insights into their state of mind, and the images from Newton's deathbed are particularly stark.

The ground-floor photography **shop** is exceptional, with a coverage that goes well beyond Newton, and with many books at reduced prices.

The Zoo

Step out east through the main entrance of Zoo Station and you're in a maelstrom of bright lights, traffic and high-rise buildings, but walk over the area occupied by the bus station to the other side of the plaza and you'll find yourself at the gates of the **Zoologischer Garten**, containing a zoo (daily: late March to mid-Sept 9am–7pm; mid-Sept to late Oct 9am–6pm, late Oct to late March 9am–5pm; €12; Ⓦwww.zoo-berlin.de) and aquarium (daily 9am–6pm; €12). Laid out in 1844 on the basis of Friedrich Wilhelm IV's private zoo from Pfaueninsel (see p.175), this survived the destruction of World War II, and subsequent pressure from a local starving populace, to become one of Europe's most important zoos, with over 1500 species represented. It's a pleasantly landscaped place with reasonably large compounds for the animals, some peaceful nooks for quietly observing animal behaviour, and lots of benches that make it ideal for picnicking. Unusual highlights are the **Nachttierhaus**, an underground nocturnal environment, whose principle attraction is the bat cave, and a large glass-sided hippo-pool. In addition, amid all the usual cast of characters there's the chance to see a couple of rare giant pandas – both gifts from China.

In 2007 Berlin's most famous celebrity was **Knut**, a rather adorable polar bear cub. Rejected by his mother – a one-time GDR circus bear – and reared by a zoo keeper, his popularity outstripped all expectations, and in true celebrity fashion he appeared on the cover of the German edition of *Vanity Fair*, photographed by Annie Leibovitz. Nowadays a lot less cute, he nevertheless promises to become the living, breathing emblem of the city.

The zoo's **aquarium** lives up to its international reputation, with more species than any other in the world. The large, humid crocodile hall is the most memorable part, though almost all of the tanks are well cared for and appealingly laid out, making it an excellent rainy-day option. Despite the attractive price of the **combined day ticket** (€18), trying to get around both the zoo and aquarium in a day can be quite a rush.

The Erotik-Museum

Wildlife of a different sort is on show at the **Erotik-Museum** (Mon–Sat 9am– midnight, Sun 11am–midnight; €14 or €10 before noon and €25 for couples in the afternoon, over-18s only; Ⓦwww.erotikmuseum.de), a short block south of Bahnhof Zoo, at the end of a strip of sleazy sex shops. It's run by Beate Uhse, a household name in Germany: once a Luftwaffe test pilot, she began selling sex education pamphlets after the war and now heads a multimillion-euro corporation dedicated to all things sexual. Located on three floors above her sex shop, the museum is really an assemblage rather than an organized exhibition, but it does present a surprisingly extensive collection of prints, paintings and objects – including Japanese silk paintings, Balinese fertility shrines, Indian reliefs in wood and Chinese bordello tokens, to name a few. The assortment of 1920s and 1930s artwork from Europe, including charcoal sketches of cabaret artist Anita Berber, and pieces by George Grosz and local favourite Heinrich Zille, is particularly good, suggesting – albeit faintly – something of the atmosphere of Weimar Berlin.

Breitscheidplatz and Kaiser-Wilhelm-Gedächtniskirche

A short two-block walk east of Bahnhof Zoo, the angular concrete **Breitscheidplatz**, is a magnet for vendors, caricaturists and street musicians alike and often hosts fairs and festivals, including a large Christmas market. On its eastern edge is the rather generic **Europa Center** shopping mall, which was built in the 1960s as a capitalist symbol for West Berlin, topped by a huge, rotating Mercedes-Benz symbol. An intriguing sculpture entitled *Flow of Time*, an alternative clock consisting of an elaborate series of liquid-filled glass pipes, does, however, deserve some attention down in the lobby. The focal point of the square is **Kaiser–Wilhelm–Gedächtniskirche** (Kaiser Wilhelm Memorial Church; Ⓦwww.gedaechtnis kirche-berlin.de), one of Berlin's great landmarks and a postcard favourite. Built at the end of the nineteenth century, it was destroyed by British bombing in November 1943. Left as a reminder, it's a strangely effective memorial, the crumbling tower providing a hint of the old city. It's possible to go inside what remains of the nave (Mon–Sat 10am–4pm): there's a small exhibit showing wartime destruction and a "before and after" model of the city centre. Adjacent, a modern **chapel** (daily 9am–7pm) contains a sad charcoal sketch by Kurt Reubers, *Stalingrad Madonna*, dedicated to those that died – on both sides – during the battle of Stalingrad. The blue-glass campanile on the opposite side of the ruined church to the side of the chapel has gained the nicknames the "Lipstick" or the "Soul-Silo" because of its tubular shape; its base contains a shop selling Third World gifts.

Tauentzienstrasse

East of the Kaiser-Wilhelm-Gedächtniskirche, the Ku'damm becomes the rather bland chain-store shopping street **Tauentzienstrasse**, which is also arranged around a wide boulevard. At its eastern end is the largest department store in Europe, **KaDeWe**. An abbreviation of Kaufhaus Des Westens ("the Department Store of the West"), it opened in 1907 and quickly became a temple of luxury in a rapidly modernizing city. Decades later the Nazis seized it from its Jewish owners, and in 1943 an American fighter plane crashed into it, igniting a fire that gutted the building. Almost 180,000 Berliners attended its reopening in 1950, and

▲ Sculpture on Tauentzienstrasse

during the Cold War it became a symbol of West Berlin's capitalist prosperity. Some days it averages 50,000 visitors, many of whom head to the superb sixth-floor food hall with its many mouth-watering snacks.

Outside KaDeWe, **Wittenbergplatz U-Bahn station** has been likeably restored to its prewar condition both inside (1920s kitsch) and out (Neoclassical pavilion). Near the entrance, a tall sign reminds passers-by of the wartime concentration camps: it states that the German people must never be allowed to forget the atrocities that were carried out there, and lists the names of some of the camps. It's an odd memorial, neither terribly poignant nor at a significant site, and one that goes largely unnoticed by shoppers.

Käthe-Kollwitz-Museum

West along the Ku'damm, just before Uhlandstrasse U-Bahn station, Fasanenstrasse crosses it; the **Käthe-Kollwitz-Museum** is at no. 24 (daily 11am–6pm; €6; ☎030/882 52 10, ⓦwww.kaethe-kollwitz.de; U-Bahn Uhlandstrasse). The drawings and prints of Käthe Kollwitz are among the most moving works from the first half of the twentieth century. Born in 1867, she lived for almost all her life in Prenzlauer Berg in the eastern part of the city (see Chapter 8), where her work developed a radical left-wing perspective. Following the death of her son in World War I, her woodcuts, lithographs and prints became explicitly pacifist, often dwelling on the theme of mother and child – her most famous print, *No More War*, a stark, furious work depicting a protesting mother, is a perfect example. Her sculptures, too, often deal with this subject: two of her bronzes, *Tower of Women* and the pietà *Mother with Dead Son*, can be seen here. When her grandson was killed in World War II her work became even sadder and more poignant. A staunch pacifist and committed socialist, the Nazis kept a careful watch over her and forced her resignation from a prestigious post at the Faculty of Arts, while at the same time using some of her work for their own propaganda purposes. She died in 1945, shortly before the end of the war. The museum's comprehensive collection of her work makes it possible to trace its development, culminating in the tragic sculptures on the top floor.

The Story of Berlin

Just west of the Uhlandstrasse U-Bahn on Ku'damm lies **The Story of Berlin**, at no. 207–208 (daily 10am–8pm, last admission 6pm; €10; ☎030/88 72 01 00, ⓦwww.story-of-berlin.de), an excellent multimedia exhibition and an ideal first step in unravelling Berlin's history. Tucked away in the back of a mall, the museum uses its odd layout to its advantage, with each subsection extensively labelled in English. On the way round you'll be confronted with life-size dioramas, film clips, noises, flashing lights, smoke and smells, which illustrate the trawl through the highs and lows of the city's turbulent past. The end result will entertain all ages and will take at least two hours to complete, not including the additional bonus: a taste of the Cold War given on the frequent guided tours of the 1970s Allied-built nuclear bunker below the mall. It's still functional and designed for around 3500 people to shelter in the first few weeks after a nuclear attack. If you've run out of time or energy having visited the museum, it's possible to use your ticket to come back another day to view the bunker.

Schloss Charlottenburg

Schloss Charlottenburg (ⓦwww.spsg.de) comes as a surprise after the unrelieved modernity of the city streets. Commissioned as a country house by the future Queen Sophie Charlotte in 1695 (she also gave her name to the district), the

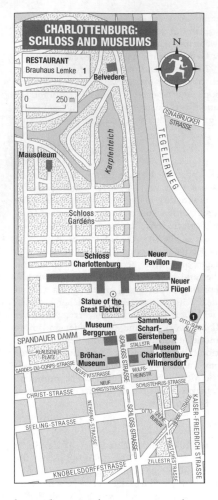

CHARLOTTENBURG:
SCHLOSS AND MUSEUMS   N

RESTAURANT
Brauhaus Lemke 1

Belvedere

0   250 m

OSNABRÜCKER STRASSE

Karpfenteich

TEGELERWEG

Mausoleum

Schloss
Gardens

Schloss
Charlottenburg

Neuer
Pavillon

Neuer
Flügel

Statue of the
Great Elector

OTTO-SUHR-ALLEE

Museum
Berggruen

Sammlung
Scharf-
Gerstenberg

SPANDAUER DAMM

STALLSTR.

Museum
Charlottenburg-
Wilmersdorf

KLAUSENER
PLATZ

Bröhan-
Museum

SCHLOSS STRASSE

WULFS-
HEINSTR.

GARDES-DU-CORPS-STRASSE

NEUFERTSTRASSE

NEUF.-
CHRISTSTRASSE

SCHUSTEHRUS-STRASSE

CHRIST-STRASSE

NEHRING-STRASSE

KAISER-FRIEDRICH STRASSE

SEELING-STRASSE

SCHLOSS STRASSE

OTTO-GRÜNEBURGW.

FRISCHEN STRASSE

SYBEL-STRASSE

KNOBELSDORFFSTRASSE

ZILLESTR.

FRITSCHESTRASSE

Schloss was expanded and added to throughout the eighteenth and early nineteenth centuries to provide a summer residence for the Prussian kings; master builder Karl Friedrich Schinkel (see p.58) provided the final touches. Approaching the sandy elaborateness of the Schloss through the main courtyard, you're confronted with Andreas Schlüter's **statue** of Friedrich Wilhelm, the Great Elector, cast as a single piece in 1700. It's in superb condition, despite (or perhaps because of) spending the war years sunk at the bottom of the Tegeler See for safekeeping.

Allow at least a day to cover **Schloss Charlottenburg** and the clutch of excellent **museums** opposite the palace. The various parts of the Schloss can be visited and paid for separately, but **combined day tickets** are the best value (€14), if you wish to see all of it. The area is best reached using bus #M45 from Bahnhof Zoo, since the nearest train stations are a ten-minute walk away.

The Altes Schloss

Immediately behind the statue of Friedrich Wilhelm is the entrance to the **Altes Schloss** (Old Palace; April–Oct Tues–Sun 10am–6pm; Nov–March Tues–Sun 10am–5pm; last tour 1hr before close; tour of lower-floor royal apartments and upper floors €10), which includes the apartment of Friedrich Wilhelm IV and the Baroque rooms of Friedrich I and Sophie Charlotte. To see these you're obliged to go on the conducted **tour** in German – though free English audio-guides are available. The tour is a traipse through increasingly sumptuous chambers and bedrooms, filled with gilt and carvings. Look out for the **porcelain room**, packed to the ceiling with china, and the **chapel**, which includes a portrait of Sophie Charlotte as the Virgin ascending to heaven.

The Neuer Flügel

It's just as well to remember that much of the Schloss is in fact a fake, a reconstruction of the buildings following wartime damage. This is most apparent in the Knobelsdorff-designed **Neuer Flügel** (New Wing; April–Oct Wed–Mon 10am–6pm; Nov–March Wed–Mon 10am–5pm; €6 including audio-guide) to the right of the Schloss entrance as you face it; the upper rooms, such as the elegantly designed Golden Gallery, are too breathlessly perfect, the result of intensive restoration. Better is the adjacent White Hall, whose eighteenth-century ceiling, made grungy by regular clouds of candle soot during festivities, was replaced at the end of the nineteenth century by a marble and gold confection with full electric illumination. Next door, the Concert Room contains a superb collection of works by **Watteau**, including one of his greatest paintings, *The Embarcation for Cythera*, a delicate Rococo frippery tinged with sympathy and sadness. Also here is his *The Shop Sign*, painted for an art dealer in 1720.

The Schloss Gardens

Laid out in the French style in 1697, the **Schloss Gardens** (daily 9am–dusk; free) were transformed into an English-style landscaped park in the early nineteenth century; after severe damage in the war, they were mostly restored to their Baroque form. Though it's possible to buy a map in the Schloss, it's easy enough to wander through the garden to the lake and on to the grounds behind, which do indeed have the feel of an English park.

The first place to head for, before hitting the gardens proper, is the **Neuer Pavillon** (also called the Schinkel Pavillon; April–Oct Tues–Sun 10am–6pm, Nov–March Tues–Sun noon–4pm; €3), just to the east of the Schloss, which was designed by Schinkel (see p.58) for Friedrich Wilhelm III, and where the king preferred to live, away from the excesses of the main building. Inside, furniture, various decorative arts and paintings from the Romantic and Biedermeier periods are on display, including works by Carl Blechen, Schinkel and Eduard Gaertner.

Deeper into the gardens, on the north side of the lake, is the **Belvedere** (April–Oct Tues–Sun 10am–6pm; Nov–March Tues–Sun noon–4pm; €3), built as a teahouse in 1788 and today housing an unexciting collection of Berlin porcelain.

On the western side of the gardens a long, tree-lined avenue leads to the hushed and shadowy **Mausoleum** (March–Oct Tues–Sun 10am–6pm; Nov–Feb Tues–Sun noon–4pm; €2), where Friedrich Wilhelm III is buried: his sarcophagus, carved with his image, makes him seem a good deal younger than his seventy years. Friedrich Wilhelm had commissioned the mausoleum to be built thirty years earlier for his wife, Queen Luise, whose own delicate sarcophagus apparently depicts her not dead but sleeping, though it's hard to tell. Later burials here include Kaiser Wilhelm I, looking every inch a Prussian king.

Museums opposite the Schloss

Though you could happily spend a whole day wandering around the Schloss and its gardens, just across the way another group of excellent **museums** beckons. These in themselves could easily take an afternoon of your time.

Sammlung Scharf-Gerstenberg

The two buildings at the head of Schlossstrasse together served the palace's Garde du Corps-Regiments in the late nineteenth-century. The building to the east, the former stables, has been revamped successfully and at great expense to house the

---

Entrance to Charlottenburg's state museums

The entrance ticket (€8) sold at the state museums in this chapter (Sammlung Scharf-Gerstenberg, Museum Berggruen and Museum für Fotografie) is valid for same-day entry into all on this list. For information on day tickets valid in all of Berlin's state museums, see p.65.

Sammlung Scharf-Gerstenberg (Scharf-Gerstenberg Collection; Tues–Sun 10am–6pm; €8, free Thurs 2–6pm; audio-guide included; ⓦ www.smb.museum), the personal collection of Otto Gerstenberg who made his fortunes in the insurance industry of the early twentieth century. His interest in art was that he simply "liked looking at pictures" in the words of his grandson Dieter Scharf who expanded the collection (which was prodigious despite extensive losses in the war and its ransacking by Russians looking for war booty) and put it at Berlin's disposal. The collection suggests Gerstenberg had a penchant for the graphic arts and sculptures, particularly from the French Romantic and Surrealist schools, but there's no doubting the pictures Gerstenberg liked to look at tended to be weird.

On show are the massive structures by Giovanni Battista Piranesi, some odd island-like forms by Victor Hugo and a woman copulating with a beast in Henri Rousseau's *Beauty and Beast* – who apparently uses the depiction to play with notions of the active and the passive. Other oddities include Max Klinger's local roller-skating works, which were based on his dreams, and some experimental use of materials Wolfgang Paalen painted with candle soot; Jean Dubuffet used coal, cement and butterfly wings. Other works in the collection are perhaps more mainstream by surrealist standards, but include impressive pieces by some of the greats, including Max Ernst, René Magritte, Salvador Dali and Paul Klee who contributed a bit of orderly Bauhaus structure – and many more of his works can be enjoyed over the road at the Museum Berggruen (see below).

Perhaps strangest of all, maybe because they seem to fit in, is the presence of two real ancient Egyptian gems: the Kalabsha Gate from around 20 BC and the Pillar of the Sahuré temple from around 2000 BC. Both are guests here until they're united with their peers in the new wing of the Pergammon museum (see p.68).

Museum Charlottenburg-Wilmersdorf

Next door to the Scharf-Gerstenberg collection and completely overshadowed by its neighbour, is the **Museum Charlottenburg-Wilmersdorf**, Schlossstrasse 69 (Tues–Fri 10am–5pm, Sun 11am–5pm; free; ⓦ www.heimatmuseum -charlottenburg.de). Though nothing special, this district museum can be worth ducking into for a quick look at a few evocative photos of Weimar and wartime Charlottenburg, and the occasional interesting temporary exhibition on the neighbourhood.

Museum Berggruen

On the other side of Schlossstrasse the wonderful **Museum Berggruen** (Tues–Sun 10am–6pm; €8, free Thurs 2–6pm; ⓦ www.smb.museum), houses the collection of Heinz Berggruen, a young Jew forced to flee Berlin in 1936, who wound up as an art dealer in Paris – where he got to know Picasso and his circle – and assembled a collection of personal favourites. In 1996 Berlin gave him this building to show off his revered compilation – which includes a dozen or so Picassos – in a comfortable and uncrowded setting. Most of these have rarely been seen before – highlights include the richly textured Cubist work *The Yellow Sweater* and large-scale *Reclining Nude* – but there are also a handful of Cézannes and Giacomettis and a pair of van Goghs. The top floor is very strong on Paul Klee, with works spanning the entire interwar period. Be sure to pick up the audio tour, which is in English and included in the price of entry.

The Bröhan-Museum

Just south of the Berggruen Collection, the compact and easily enjoyed **Bröhan-Museum**, at Schlossstrasse 1a (Tues–Sun 10am–6pm; €6;

@www.broehan-museum.de), houses a fine collection of Art Deco and Jugendstil ceramics and furniture. Their assembly was the passion of Karl Bröhan (1921–2000), who donated all the pieces he had amassed to the city to commemorate his sixtieth birthday. Each of the museum's period rooms is dedicated to a particular designer and hung with contemporary paintings – the best of which are the pastels of Willy Jaeckel and the resolutely modern works of Jean Lambert-Rucki.

The Westend

In the late nineteenth century, mansions and villas belonging to Berlin's wealthy bourgeoisie sprung up in northwestern Charlottenburg-Wilmersdorf, in an area that became known as the **Westend**, inspired by London's West End. Though the Westend is well served by trains, buses rival them for speed and reveal a lot more of the city on the way. From Bahnhof Zoo #M49 heads to the Funkturm, then on to **Theodor-Heuss-Platz**, a huge square formerly known as Adolf-Hitler-Platz. In its centre flickers an eternal flame originally dedicated to the reunification of East and West Germany – with that done, it's now been assigned the task of remembering victims of persecution. Bus #M49 then heads along the broad avenue of Heerstrasse to S-Bahn Heerstrasse for the Georg-Kolbe-Museum, then on to the Flatowallee stop for the Olympic stadium, from which you have a choice of U- and S-Bahn stations to whizz you back into the centre.

The Georg-Kolbe-Museum and the Le Corbusier house

Occupying his former villa, the **Georg-Kolbe-Museum**, Sensburger Allee 25 (Tues–Sun 10am–5pm; €5; @www.georg-kolbe-museum.de; S-Bahn Heerstr.), displays numerous drawings and bronzes by the artist who died in 1947, and is rewarding even if Kolbe never achieved quite the eminence of his contemporary Ernst Barlach. Nevertheless his vigorous, modern, simplified classical style had broad appeal: it was particularly prized by the Nazis, who provided many major commissions, as well as by Mies van der Rohe, who used a Kolbe sculpture for his Barcelona Pavillion.

There's more world-class design at the other end of Sensburger Allee where the blocky **Le Corbusier** house comes into view. Built by French architect Le Corbusier for the 1957 International Building exhibition, it contains over five hundred apartments and was heralded a modernist ideal living environment. A German-language exhibition (always open) on the ground floor tells its story and you are free to ride the lifts up to the shiny corridors on the top floor for views from the fire escapes over this part of Berlin.

The Funkturm

The **Funkturm** (Mon 10am–8pm, Tues–Sun 10am–11pm; €4; S-Bahn Messe Nord ICC) was built in 1928 as a radio and, eventually, a TV transmitter. One of Dr Goebbels's lesser-known achievements was to create the world's first regular TV service in 1941. Transmitted from the Funkturm, the weekly programme could only be received in Berlin; the service continued until just a few months before the end of the war. Today the Funkturm only serves police and taxi frequencies, but the mast remains popular with Berliners for the toe-curling views from its 126-metre-high **observation platform**. With the aluminium-clad monolith of the **International Congress Centre** (ICC) immediately below, it's possible to look out across deserted, overgrown S-Bahn tracks to the gleaming city in the distance – a mesmerizing sight at night.

The Olympic Stadium

Built for the 1936 Games, the **Olympic Stadium** (daily: April–Oct 10am–7pm; Nov–March 10am–4pm; exhibition €4; ☎030/25 00 23 22, ⓦwww .olympiastadion-berlin.de; U- & S-Bahn Olympiastadion) is one of Berlin's few remaining fascist-era buildings, and remains very much in use, and even well looked after thanks to a major renovation for the 2006 football World Cup. Whatever your feelings about its history, the building is impressive, the huge Neoclassical space a deliberate rejection of the modernist architecture that began to be in vogue in the 1930s.

Inside the stadium its sheer size comes as a surprise, since the seating falls away below ground level to reveal a much deeper auditorium than you'd imagine. On the western side, where the Olympic flame was kept and where medal winners are listed on the walls, it's easy to see how this monumental architecture, and the massive sculptures dotting the grounds outside, some of which are still extant, could inspire the crowds. During the Olympics, Berliners were kept up to date with commentary on the games, interspersed with stirring music, from hundreds of loudspeakers that ran all the way from the Museum Island via Unter den Linden and the Brandenburg Gate, through the Tiergarten and out to the stadium. Standing here, looking back out to the city, you realize what an achievement this was.

As the home ground of Hertha BSC, Berlin's best football team, the stadium is regularly closed for sporting events, so it's best to check online before trudging out. The website will also tell you times of English-language tours (1hr; €8), which vary tremendously throughout the year: there's usually one at 11am every day all year, but as many as four daily tours in summer. The tours take you behind the scenes, to the VIP areas, locker rooms and so on, which are remarkable mostly for their great cost and understated decor, in keeping with the stadiums Neoclassical clean lines. The knowledgeable guides provide plenty of interesting anecdotes along the way and after the tour you are free to wander around the stadium and its grounds marvelling at the structure, imagining the atmosphere and excitement in 1936 and reading the many interesting signs relating historical details. To do the wandering without the tour costs €4.

Around the Olympic Stadium

If you leave the stadium area beside the visitor centre towards the S-Bahn station, then right down the road named after Jesse Owens, and right again onto Passenheimer Strasse, you reach the **Glockenturm** (bell tower; daily 9am–6pm; €3.50), above the spot where Hitler would enter the stadium each morning, state business permitting. Rebuilt after wartime damage, the building includes a first-rate exhibition about the history of the Olympic grounds here, while its tower offers stupendous views not only over the stadium but also north to the natural amphitheatre that forms the **Waldbühne**, an open-air concert site, and across the beginnings of the Grunewald to the south. Also easy to spot is the **Teufelsberg** (Devil's Mountain), a massive mound topped with a faintly terrifying fairytale castle that used to be a US signals and radar base, built to listen in to eastern bloc radio signals; no longer needed, it's scheduled to be dismantled – though no one seems in a hurry. The mountain itself is artificial: at the end of the war, the mass of debris that was once Berlin was carted to several sites around the city, most of the work being carried out by women known as *Trümmerfrauen* – "rubble women". Beneath the poplars, maples and ski runs lies the old Berlin, about 25 million cubic metres of it, perhaps awaiting the attention of some future archeologist. In the meantime, it's popular as a place for weekend kite flying, and skiing and tobogganing in winter.

The Plötzensee Prison Memorial

Another of Berlin's handful of Third Reich buildings survives in the northwest of the city centre, on the border of Charlottenburg and Wedding as the **Plötzensee Prison Memorial** (Gedenkstätte Plötzensee; daily: March–Oct 9am–5pm; Nov–Feb 9am–4pm; free; ⓦ www.gedenkstaette-ploetzensee.de; stop "Gedenkstätte Plötzensee" on bus #123 from Hauptbahnhof then walk back along the route and turn right on Hüttigpfad for entrance). These buildings were where the Nazis brought many dissidents and political opponents for imprisonment and execution. Many of the former prison buildings have been refurbished to provide a juvenile detention centre, so the memorial consists of only those buildings where executions took place. Between 1933 and 1945 over 2500 people were hanged or guillotined here; their relatives sent a bill for the execution afterwards.

Following the July Bomb Plot (see p.106), 89 of the 200 people condemned were executed here in a few days. The hangings were carried out with piano wire, so that victims would slowly choke rather than die from broken necks. Today, the execution chamber has been restored to its wartime condition: on occasion, victims were hanged eight at a time, and the hanging beam, complete with hooks, still stands. Though decked with wreaths and flowers, the atmosphere in the chamber is chilling, and in a further reminder of Nazi atrocities an urn in the courtyard contains soil from each of the concentration camps. Perhaps more than at any other wartime site in Berlin, it is at Plötzensee that the horror of senseless, brutal murder is most palpably felt.

The Maria Regina Martyrum church

From the memorial hop back on the #123 bus for four more stops and you'll arrive a short walk from the **Maria Regina Martyrum** at Heckerdamm 230, a purposefully sombre memorial church dedicated to those who died under the Nazis. Completed in 1963, the church's brutally plain exterior is surrounded by a wide courtyard whose walls are flanked by abstract *Stations of the Cross* modelled in bronze. The interior is a plain concrete shoebox, adorned only with an abstract altarpiece that fills the entire eastern wall. It's a strikingly unusual design, and one that successfully avoids looking dated.

Schöneberg

Once a separate entity, **Schöneberg** was swallowed up by Greater Berlin as the city expanded in the late eighteenth and nineteenth centuries. Blown to pieces during the war, it's now a mostly middle-class residential area. There aren't many things to see but all are scant reminders of a fascinating and moving past. The obvious gateway to the district is **Nollendorfplatz**, a long-standing centre in the city's gay and lesbian community. Schöneberg's main drag, Potsdamer Strasse, runs a block or so east of here and was once lined by the **Sportpalast** and **Kammergericht**, the scenes of several important chapters in city history. A short bus ride from there on #106 brings you to **Rathaus Schöneberg** where John F. Kennedy made his "Berliner" speech.

Nollendorfplatz

Long a key place for Berlin's large **gay and lesbian community** the busy road and rail intersection of **Nollendorfplatz** throbs by night as western Berlin's main gay hub, but by day holds few specific attractions. Even so, it's worth doing a lap of the block on the south side of the square, east of the proto-Deco **Metropol Theater**, and down Massenstrasse and on to Nollendorfstrasse, where at no. 17 stands the

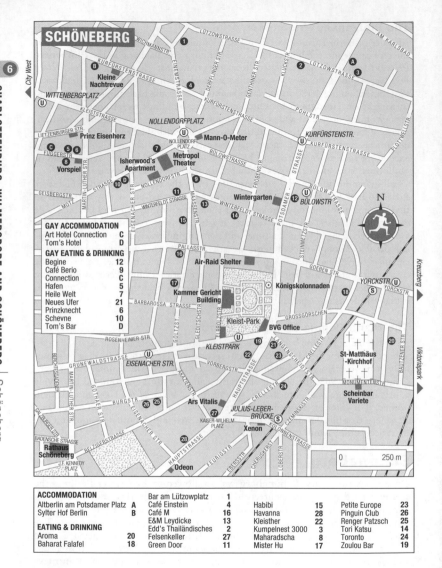

SCHÖNEBERG

GAY ACCOMMODATION

| Art Hotel Connection | C |
| Tom's Hotel | D |

GAY EATING & DRINKING

Begine	12
Café Berio	9
Connection	C
Hafen	5
Heile Welt	7
Neues Ufer	21
Prinzknecht	6
Schevne	10
Tom's Bar	D

0   250 m

ACCOMMODATION						
Altberlin am Potsdamer Platz	A	Bar am Lützowplatz	1			
Sylter Hof Berlin	B	Café Einstein	4	Habibi	15	Petite Europe	23
		Café M	16	Havanna	28	Pinguin Club	26
EATING & DRINKING		E&M Leydicke	13	Kleisther	22	Renger Patzsch	25
Aroma	20	Edd's Thailändisches	2	Kumpelnest 3000	3	Tori Katsu	14
Baharat Falafel	18	Felsenkeller	27	Maharadscha	8	Toronto	24
		Green Door	11	Mister Hu	17	Zoulou Bar	19

building in which **Christopher Isherwood** lived during his years in prewar Berlin, a time elegantly recounted in his famous collection of stories about the city – *Goodbye to Berlin*:

From my window, the deep solemn massive street. Cellar shops where lamps burn all day, under the shadow of top-heavy balconied facades, dirty plaster frontages embossed with scroll work and heraldic devices. The whole district is like this: street leading into street of houses like shabby monumental safes crammed with the tarnished valuables and secondhand furniture of a bankrupt middle class.

Schöneberg has since been reborn as a fancy, even chic, neighbourhood; the would-be Isherwoods of the moment hang out in Eastern Kreuzberg, or Friedrichshain.

Kleistpark and around

A ten-minute walk further down Massenstrasse – which becomes Gleditschstrasse – from Nollendorfstrasse, brings you to Pallasstrasse. Heading east along it, you'll soon spot a huge and undistinguished apartment building straddling the road and backing onto the northern edge of the **Kleistpark**. On the south side of the street a huge concrete cube forms the base of the structure; this began life as one of Berlin's **air raid shelters** in case of Allied raids. After the war the tower proved impervious to demolition attempts, and the lower levels were used by NATO troops to store food and provisions in case of a Soviet invasion. Ironically, in the post Cold War years, supplies reaching the end of their shelf life were sold off – usually on the cheap to Russia. On the northern side of the street the apartment building rests on land that once accommodated the **Sportpalast**, a sports centre that became the main venue for Nazi rallies in the 1930s. Hitler delivered some of his most famous speeches here and many of the old newsreels showing the Führer working himself up into an oratorical fever were filmed here. It was also here that Goebbels asked the German people if they wanted "total war" – which they jubilantly applauded. The Sportpalast was demolished in 1974 to make way for the apartment building.

At its eastern end, Pallasstrasse finishes at Potsdamer Strasse, Schöneberg's main drag. A couple of minutes' walk south down it brings you to the **Königskolonnaden** – a colonnade from 1780 that originally stood on Alexanderplatz – which on a misty morning makes this stretch of road look a little Parisian. On the opposite side of the Kleistpark looms the sturdy **Kammergericht building**, once the Supreme Court of Justice. Here Nazi show trials took place, as did the "People's Court" under the infamous Judge Freisler following the July Bomb Plot (see p.106), both preludes to the inevitable executions, which often took place in Plötzensee Prison (see p.127). Freisler met his unlamented end here in the final

Gay Berlin in the Weimar and Nazi years

Even by contemporary standards, Weimar Berlin's gay scene in the 1920s and early 1930s was prodigious: there were around forty gay bars on and near **Nollendorfplatz** alone, and gay life in the city was open, fashionable and well organized, with its own newspapers, community associations and art. The city's theatres were filled with plays exploring gay themes, homosexuality in the Prussian army was little short of institutionalized, and gay bars, nightclubs and brothels proudly advertised their attractions – there were even gay working men's clubs. All this happened at a time when the rest of Europe was smothered under a welter of homophobia and repression, when to be "discovered" as a homosexual or lesbian meant total social ostracism.

Under the Third Reich, however, homosexuality was quickly and brutally outlawed: gays and lesbians were rounded up and taken to concentration camps, branded for their "perversion" by being forced to wear pink or black triangles. (The black triangle represented "antisocial" offenders: in an attempt to ignore the existence of lesbianism, lesbians were arrested on pretexts such as swearing at the Führer's name.) As homosexuality was, at the time, still illegal in Allied countries, no Nazis were tried for crimes against gays or lesbians at Nürnberg. A red granite plaque in the shape of a triangle at Nollendorfplatz U-Bahn station commemorates the gay men and women who were murdered for their sexuality.

weeks of the war: on his way from the courtroom a bomb from an American aircraft fell on the building, dislodging a beam that crushed his skull. Later it was a meeting place of the Allied Air Control, which oversaw safety in the air corridors leading to the city, until the meetings came to an end with unification; a place was always set for a Soviet representative – even though they ceased to attend meetings in 1948. The building is now used by NATO.

Over Potsdamer Strasse from the Kleistpark, at the end of Grossgörschenstrasse, lies the **Sankt-Matthäus-Kirchhof**, a graveyard that contains the bodies of the Brothers Grimm, united in death as they were in copyright. The bodies of Stauffenberg and his co-conspirators were also buried here following the July Bomb Plot, only to be exhumed a few days later and burned by Nazi thugs.

Rathaus Schöneberg

Schöneberg's most famous attraction actually offers very little to see: **Rathaus Schöneberg** on Martin-Luther-Strasse, the penultimate stop on U-Bahn line #4. Built just before World War I, the Rathaus became the seat of the West Berlin parliament and senate after the last war, and it was outside here in 1963 that **John F. Kennedy** made his celebrated speech on the Cold War, just a few months after the Cuban missile crisis:

There are many people in the world who really don't understand, or say they don't, what is the great issue between the free world and the Communist world. Let them come to Berlin. There are some who say that Communism is the wave of the future. Let them come to Berlin. And there are some who say in Europe and elsewhere we can work with the Communists. Let them come to Berlin. And there are even a few who say it is true that Communism is an evil system, but it permits us to make economic progress. Lässt sie nach Berlin kommen. Let them come to Berlin...All free men, wherever they may live, are citizens of Berlin, and, therefore, as a free man, I take pride in the words "Ich bin ein Berliner".

Rousing stuff. But what the president hadn't realized as he read from his phonetically written text was that what he had said could also mean "I am a doughnut", since *Berliner* is a name for jam doughnuts – though not in Berlin, where it is usually known as a *Pfannkuchen*. The urban myth that peals of laughter greeted this embarrassing error only developed years later. People did laugh at the time, after applauding, but because the president thanked his interpreter, who had simply repeated his quote, for translating his German. The notion that he been laughed at for erroneously calling himself a jam doughnut was largely the work of pedants long after the event. The day after Kennedy was assassinated, the square in front of the Rathaus was given his name – a move apparently instigated by the city's students, among whom the president was highly popular.

You can climb the Rathaus tower (April–Oct daily 10am–5pm; free) and see the replica **liberty bell** donated to the city by the US in 1950.

Kreuzberg-Friedrichshain and around

Just southwest of Mitte lies the mainly residential borough of **Kreuzberg-Friedrichshain**, which divides into the more middle class and less ethnically mixed **western Kreuzberg**, unkempt **eastern Kreuzberg** with its large, mainly Turkish, immigrant community and many bohemians (a mix of punks, old hippies and students), and Friedrichshain, an old East Berlin neighbourhood that's now another rather gritty inner-city district and the city's hippest night-time hangout.

By day the borough has its share of attractions. The well-visited **Jüdisches Museum** (Jewish Museum) and the **Berlinische Galerie** are just a couple of the many respectable museums in northwest Kreuzberg, while also here is the world's most famous Cold War border crossing, **Checkpoint Charlie**. Just south of Kreuzberg, the adjacent districts of **Tempelhof** and **Treptow** are interesting for two huge and impressive monuments to crumbled regimes: the Nazi **Tempelhof Airport** and **Soviet Memorial** respectively.

Western Kreuzberg's main sights are all within walking distance of the **U6 U-Bahn** line, which runs south from Friedrichstrasse in Mitte. If you're feeling energetic, you could easily walk between all of them in a day, in which case you might like to start by taking bus #248 from Alexanderplatz to the Jewish Museum, then follow the order below. In eastern Kreuzberg the U-Bahn stations **Kottbusser Tor** or **Schlesisches Tor** are the best way in, after which it's mostly a matter of walking around – though the Treptower Park's Soviet Memorial is a bus ride from the latter.

Western Kreuzberg

When in the 1830s, Berlin's industries started recruiting peasants from the outlying countryside to work in their factories and machine shops, it was to the small village of **Kreuzberg** that many came. They ended up living in buildings thrown up by speculators as low-rent accommodation. Kreuzberg thus became a solidly working-class area and, in time, a suburb of Greater Berlin. Siemens, the

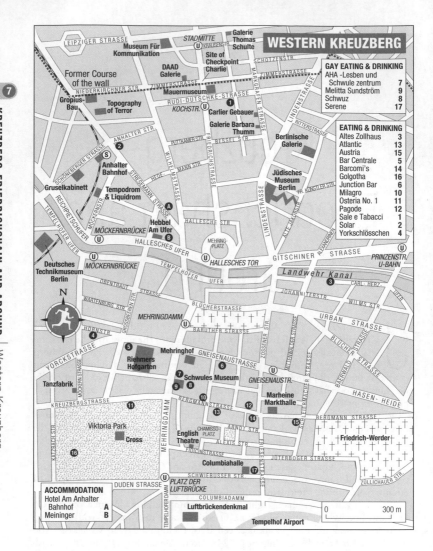

electrical engineering giant, began life in a Kreuzberg courtyard. In the 1930s local trade unionists and workers fought street battles with the Nazis, and during the war it was one of the very few areas to avoid total destruction, and among the quickest to revive in the 1950s.

The rather nondescript modern city blocks just south of Mitte are only part of Kreuzberg on paper. Here you'll find almost no evidence of its counter-cultural roots or the preserved nineteenth-century past that typifies much of the rest of Western Kreuzberg. Nonetheless, this part of the district is worth investigating for its many good museums as well as its most famous sight, the old site of **Checkpoint Charlie** at the southern end of Friedrichstrasse.

The Jüdisches Museum Berlin

A phenomenal silver fortress in the midst of residential streets once levelled by wartime bombing, the **Jüdisches Museum Berlin**, Lindenstrasse 9–14 (Jewish Museum Berlin; Mon 10am–10pm, Tues–Sun 10am–8pm; ☏030/25 99 33 00; €5; ⓦwww.jmberlin.de; U-Bahn Hallesches Tor or bus #248 from Alexanderplatz), is one of Berlin's most exciting pieces of architecture. The building's uncomfortable angles and severe lines create a disturbed and uneasy space to mirror the difficult story portrayed inside: that of the history and culture of German Jewry.

The extraordinary museum **building** is by Daniel Libeskind. The ground plan is in the form of a compressed lightning bolt (intended as a deconstructed Star of David), while the structure itself is sheathed in polished metallic facing, with windows – or, rather, thin angular slits – that trace geometric patterns on the exterior. There's no front door and entry is through an underground tunnel connected to the **Kollegienhaus** – the Baroque building next door that serves as an annexe to the museum and is used for temporary exhibitions.

The museum **interior** is just as unusual, manifesting Libeskind's ideas about symbolic architecture, whilst retaining a sculptural symmetry: a "void" – an empty and inaccessible diagonal shaft – cuts through the structure, while three long intersecting corridors, each representing an element of Jewish experience, divide the space at **basement** level. At the foot of the basement stairs the "axis of exile" leads outside to a garden of pillars; the "axis of the Holocaust" crosses it, connecting with the Holocaust Tower, dimly lit and, again, completely empty; and the "axis of continuity" follows, leading to a trudge up several flights of stairs to the permanent exhibition space. Part way up the stairs, the first floor contains the **Memory Void**, an eerie space filled with the sounds of clanking as visitors walk across a space scattered with piles of thousands of grimacing iron masks; a powerful reminder of the Holocaust.

The **permanent exhibition** begins on the top floor of the museum and focuses, in a broadly chronological way, on pre-1900 German-Jewish history before moving to the second floor to deal with the painful twentieth century, and ending with the present day.

Berlinische Galerie

Behind the **Jüdisches Museum** at Alte Jakobstrasse 124–128, lie the vast airy halls of a former warehouse that have been clinically renovated to house the **Berlinische Galerie** (Wed–Mon 10am–6pm; €6, €2 on 1st Mon of the month; ☏030/78 90 26 00, ⓦwww.berlinischegalerie.de; U-Bahn Hallesches Tor). Some of Berlin's darkest and most tortured pieces of art are displayed here as part of a permanent collection, which is mostly twentieth century, when movements such as Secessionism, Dadaism and the New Objectivity called Berlin home. All challenged the accepted art world and the establishment, reflecting Europe's troubled times, so the collection is anything but light-hearted and much of it unsettling – difficulties compounded for non-German speakers using the German-only audio guide.

Pieces to look for include the beautifully crafted *Berlin Street Scene* (1889) by Lesser Ury, which evokes a moody Prussian majesty in the driving night rain. Disharmony is even more central to George Grosz's *Da um* (1920) which depicts the clash between soft tradition and harsh modernity using his own union with his (much younger) wife as the metaphor. Awkward contrasts are also the subject of Otto Dix's *Kartenspieler* (Card Players, 1920). Traumatized by World War I, Dix used dry-point technique to produce ghastly caricatures of mutilated war veterans playing cards. His portrait of *Der Dichter Iwar von Lücken* (1920), showing a

▲ Berlinische Galerie

bedraggled poet looking unsure and lost, is equally celebrated and often seen as a social comment on the state of post-World War I Germany. A very different side to 1920s Berlin is depicted in a score of portraits by local photographers, in which emasculated women with short hair puff on cigarettes and evoke the milieu from which Marlene Dietrich rose to fame.

The 1930s also take their share of the exhibition hall, with Werner Heldt's *Parade of the Zeros* (1935) perhaps best summing up the times. Here an immense crowd of zeros are squeezed between the buildings of a big city, threatening to become a destructive and unstoppable flood.

The Berlinische collection also gives fleeting insights into postwar Berlin, though its art becomes increasingly symbolic and impenetrable. The seven gigantic avant-garde structures of Emilio Vedova's *Absurd Berlin Diary '64* recall something of West Berlin's tensions, but by the time you've moved on in time to the vivid oil-paint-smeared canvases by artists like Hartwig Ebersbach, the work's message becomes unclear.

Checkpoint Charlie

From the Jüdisches Museum and Berlinische Galerie it's a short walk across Lindenstrasse and up Markengrafenstrasse – where several of Berlin's best contemporary art galleries (see p.232) have settled – to Kochstrasse on which a left turn takes you to Friedrichstrasse and the site of **Checkpoint Charlie**. One of the most famous names associated with the Wall and Cold War-era Berlin, this Allied military post marked the border between East and West Berlin and was the main gateway between the two Berlins for most non-Germans. And with its dramatic "YOU ARE NOW LEAVING THE AMERICAN SECTOR" signs and unsmiling border guards, it became the archetypal movie-style Iron Curtain crossing. In the Cold War years it was the scene of repeated border incidents, including a standoff between American and Soviet forces in October 1961, which culminated in tanks from both sides growling at each other for a few days.

The site of the border crossing itself is barely recognizable now. Removed in July 1990, the original border post is in the Allied Museum (see p.173), and a **replica** now marks the original site. Around it modern offices and retail complexes have sprung up, and the derelict plots of land that surrounded the site – peopled for years by hawkers of GDR-era merchandise and souvenir bits of Wall – have been encircled by barriers, awaiting construction projects. One barrier on Zimmerstrasse, diagonally across from the Mauermuseum, has on it an interesting exhibition on the Berlin Wall.

Mauermuseum

For tangible evidence of the trauma of the Wall, head for the **Mauermuseum** at Friedrichstrasse 43-45 (Wall Museum; daily 9am–10pm; €12.50; ⓦwww .mauermuseum.de; U-Bahn Kochstrasse). Here the history of the Wall is told in photos of escape tunnels and with the home-made aircraft and converted cars by which people attempted, succeeded, and sometimes tragically failed, to break through the border. Films document the stories of some of the 230-odd people murdered by the East German border guards, and there's a section on human rights behind the Iron Curtain, but it's a jumbled, huge and rambling collection, and not quite the harrowing experience that some visitors expect. For more details, pick up a copy of *It Happened at the Wall* or *The Wall Speaks*, both on sale here.

Museum für Kommunikation

A block west along the high-rise-lined arterial road of Leipziger Strasse, from its junction with Friedrichstrasse, lies the former Imperial postal ministry, now home to the **Museum für Kommunikation** (Tues 9am–8pm, Wed–Fri 9am–5pm, Sat & Sun 10am–6pm; €3; ⓦwww.museumsstiftung.de; U-Bahn Mohrenstrasse). The museum traces its roots back to the world's first postal museum, which opened in Berlin in 1872 and moved into this Baroque palace to share space with the postal ministry in 1898. When the building was damaged in the war the collection was dispersed, and only after reunification and several years of renovation did it reopen in its historic home in March 2000. There's a lot more here than just stamps, and if you have a keen interest in the gadgets and devices that led us to the world of the internet, you should have a look. The interior itself, ornate Wilhelmine detailing around a wonderful, light-filled central court, is worth checking out too.

The Luftfahrtministerium

The city block west of the Museum für Kommunikation is marked out by Hermann Göring's fortress-like **Luftfahrtministerium** (air ministry), a rare relic of the Nazi past that has survived very much intact and once formed the southern end of the former Third Reich government quarter along Wilhelmstrasse (see p.51). Göring promised Berliners that not a single bomb would fall on the city during the war; if this were to happen, the Reichsmarschal said, he would change his name to Meyer – a common Jewish surname. Ironically, the air ministry was one of the few buildings to emerge more or less unscathed from the bombing and

The Berlin Wall

After the war, Berlin was split among Britain, France, the US and USSR, as Stalin, Roosevelt and Churchill had agreed at Yalta. Each sector was administered by the relevant country, and was supposed to exist peacefully with its neighbours under a unified city council. But, almost from the outset, antagonism between the Soviet and other sectors was high. Only three years after the war ended, the Soviet forces closed down the land access corridors to the city from the Western zones in what became known as the **Berlin Blockade**: it was successfully overcome by a massive **airlift** of food and supplies that lasted nearly a year (see p.141). This, followed by the 1953 uprising (see p.138), large-scale cross-border emigration (between 1949 and 1961, the year the Wall was built, over three million East Germans – almost a fifth of the population – fled to the Federal Republic) and innumerable "incidents", led to the building of what the GDR called an "an antifascist protection barrier".

The Wall was erected overnight on **August 13, 1961** when, at 2am, forty thousand East German soldiers, policemen and Workers' Militia went into action closing U- and S-Bahn lines and stringing barbed wire across streets leading into West Berlin to cordon off the Soviet sector. The Wall followed its boundaries implacably, cutting through houses, across squares and rivers with its own cool illogicality. Many Berliners were rudely evicted from their homes, while others had their doors and windows blocked by bales of barbed wire. Suddenly the British, American and French sectors of the city were corralled some 200km inside the GDR, yet though they reinforced patrols, the Allies did nothing to prevent the sealing of the border.

Despite earlier rumours, most people in West and East Berlin were taken by surprise. Those who lived far from the border area only learned of its closure when they found all routes to West Berlin blocked. Crowds gathered and extra border guards sent to prevent trouble. There was little most people could do other than accept this latest development, though some – including a few border guards – managed to find loopholes in the new barrier and flee west. But within a few days, building workers were reinforcing the barbed wire and makeshift barricades with bricks and mortar. As an additional measure, West Berliners were no longer allowed to cross the border into East Berlin. From 1961 onwards the GDR strengthened the Wall making it an almost impenetrable barrier – in effect two walls separated by a *Sperrgebiet* (forbidden zone), dotted with watchtowers and patrolled by soldiers and dogs. It was also known as the *Todesstreifen* (death strip) as border troops, known as Grepos, were under instructions to shoot anyone attempting to scale the Wall, and to shoot accurately: any guard suspected of deliberately missing was court-martialled, and his family could expect severe harassment from the authorities. Over the years, over two hundred people were **killed** endeavouring to cross the Wall.

Red Army shelling. After the establishment of the GDR it became the SED regime's **Haus der Ministerien** (House of Ministries), and was the target of a mass demonstration on June 16, 1953 (see box, p.138), which was to be a prelude for a general but short-lived uprising against the communist government the next day. There's a historical irony of sorts in the fact that the building became, for a number of years after reunification, the headquarters of the Treuhandanstalt, the agency responsible for the privatization of the former GDR's economy. It has again been tidied up and now houses the Federal Finance Ministry.

The Topography of Terror

In Nazi times the Luftfahrtministerium's southern neighbour, across Nieder-kirchnerstrasse, was the Reich Security office, which included the headquarters of the Gestapo and SS. Little has been done with the plot since the destruction

Initial escape attempts were straightforward, and often successful – hollowing out furniture, ramming checkpoint barriers and simple disguise brought many people over. However, the authorities quickly rose to the challenge, and would-be escapees were forced to become more resourceful, digging tunnels and constructing gliders, one-man submarines and hot-air balloons. By the time the Wall came down, every escape method conceivable seemed to have been used – even down to passing through Checkpoint Charlie in the stomach of a pantomime cow – and those desperate to get out of the GDR preferred the long wait and complications of applying to leave officially to the risk of being gunned down by a border guard.

An oddity of the Wall was that it was built a few metres inside GDR territory; the West Berlin authorities therefore had little control over the **graffiti** that covered it. The Wall was an ever-changing mixture of colours and slogans, with occasional bursts of bitterness: "My friends are dying behind you"; humour: "Why not jump over and join the Party?"; and stupidity: "We shoulda nuked 'em in 45".

Late in 1989 the East German government, spurred by Gorbachev's *glasnost* and confronted by a tense domestic climate, realized it could keep the impossible stable no longer. To an initially disbelieving and then jubilant Europe, travel restrictions for GDR citizens were lifted on November 9, 1989 – effectively, the Wall had ceased to matter, and pictures of Berliners, East and West, hacking away at the detested symbol filled newspapers and TV bulletins around the world. Within days, enterprising characters were renting out hammers and chisels so that souvenir hunters could take home their own chip of the Wall.

Today, especially in the city centre, it's barely possible to tell exactly where the Wall ran: odd juxtapositions of dereliction against modernity, an unexpected swathe of erstwhile "Death Strip", are in most cases all that's left of one of the most hated borders the world has ever known. The simple row of cobbles that has been placed along much of the former course of the Wall acts as a necessary reminder. Few significant stretches remain; the sections devoted to the East Side Gallery (see p.147) and the Berlin Wall Memorial (see p.95) being the most notable exceptions.

One sad postscript to the story of the Wall hit the headlines in spring 1992. Two former **border guards** were tried for the murder of Chris Gueffroy, shot dead while illegally trying to cross the border at Neukölln in February 1989. Under the GDR government the guards had been treated to a meal by their superiors and given extra holiday for their patriotic actions; under the new regime, they received sentences for murder – while those ultimately responsible, the former leaders of the GDR, largely evaded punishment.

of the offices at the end of the war, partly because it sat immediately beside the Berlin Wall, a tatty remnant of which still runs along the road. A museum of Nazi history has been on the drawing board for the site since 1993 but until work finally starts on it the outdoor exhibition, **The Topography of Terror** (daily: May–Sept 10am–8pm; Oct–April 10am–6pm or dusk; free; ⓦ www .topographie.de; S- & U-Bahn Potsdamer Platz), is well-worth investigating. Here a numbered series of noticeboards with photographs and German texts (audio-guides in English are free but require ID as a deposit) indicate the sites of the most important buildings and reveal just how massive a machine the Nazi organization became: it was here that Himmler organized the Final Solution – the deportation and genocide of European Jews – and organized the Gestapo, the feared secret police. The ground underneath the exhibition once held the cellars of the Gestapo headquarters, then Prinz-Albrecht-Strasse 8 (now

The uprising of June 1953

On June 16 and 17, 1953, Leipziger Strasse was the focal point of a **nationwide uprising** against the GDR's communist government. General dissatisfaction with economic and political conditions in the eastern half of the city came to a head when building workers (the traditional proletarian heroes of GDR mythology) went on strike, protesting at having to work longer hours for the same pay. The first to protest were workers on block 40 of the prestigious Stalinallee construction project, who downed tools on June 16 to march on the city centre, joined by other workers and passers-by. At Strausberger Platz they swept aside Volkspolizei units who tried to stop them and headed, via Alexanderplatz, for Unter den Linden. From here, the now roughly eight thousand-strong **demonstration** marched to the Haus der Ministerien – then the seat of the GDR government. Here they demanded to speak to GDR President Otto Grotewohl and SED General Secretary Walter Ulbricht. Eventually three lesser ministers were sent out to speak to the demonstrators. Clearly alarmed at the scale of the demonstration, they promised to try and get the work norms lowered. But by now the crowd wanted more, and began calling for political freedom. After declaring a **general strike** for the next day, the protesters returned to Stalinallee, tearing down SED placards on the way. Grotewohl's announcement rescinding the new work norms later that day failed to halt the strike, news of which had been broadcast across the GDR by western radio stations. About 300,000 workers in 250 towns joined in, and by 7am traffic in East Berlin came to a standstill as a crowd of 100,000 people marched towards the House of Ministries once again. Clashes with the police followed as demonstrators attacked SED party offices and state food stores. The GDR authorities proved unequal to the situation, and at 1pm the Soviet military commandant of the city declared a state of emergency. When **Soviet tanks** appeared in Leipziger Strasse before noon, they found their route blocked by a vast crowd that refused to budge. The Soviet commandant, General Pavel Dibrova, warned by loudspeaker that martial law had been declared, and all violators would face summary punishment – but with little effect. Dibrova ordered his troops to move forward with the tanks following in close support, and it was at this point that the shooting started. The crowd scattered as the first shots rang out, leaving youths to confront the T-34s with bricks and bottles. **Street fighting** raged throughout East Berlin for the rest of the day, and it wasn't until nightfall that the Soviets reasserted communist control. At least 267 demonstrators, 116 policemen and 18 Soviet soldiers were killed during the fighting, and it's estimated that 92 civilians (including a West Berliner just passing through) were summarily shot after the **suppression of the uprising**. The western Allies did nothing to prevent this, nor the subsequent trials of "counter-revolutionaries" at which fourteen death sentences and innumerable prison terms were meted out – final confirmation that Berlin was divided. Additionally eighteen Soviet soldiers were executed for "moral capitulation to the demonstrators".

Niederkirchnerstrasse), where important prisoners were interrogated and tortured. The staff of the SS were based in the former *Hotel Prinz Albrecht* next door, and just around the corner in the Prinz-Albrecht-Palais (opposite the entrance to Kochstrasse) was the SS security service headquarters, where extensive records of all "enemies of the state", a category that included Jews and homosexuals, were kept.

The Martin-Gropius-Bau

The magnificently restored building beside the Topography of Terror on Niederkirchnerstrasse is the **Martin-Gropius-Bau** (Wed–Mon 10am–8pm;

prices vary around €10 ; ☎030/25 48 60, ⓦwww.gropiusbau.de; S- & U-Bahn Potsdamer Platz), designed in 1877 by Martin Gropius, a pupil of Schinkel and the uncle of Bauhaus guru Walter (see p.109). Until its destruction in the war the Gropius-Bau was home of a museum of applied art, but rebuilt and refurbished, it now houses changing exhibitions of art, photography and architecture. The *Gropius Restaurant* serves snacks and meals, making it a useful, and possibly necessary, pick-me-up after tackling the adjacent Topography of Terror exhibition.

Anhalter Bahnhof

Situated on Stresemannstrasse is the **Anhalter Bahnhof**, a sad reminder of a misguided civic act that some would term vandalism. This train station was once one of Europe's great rail termini, forming Berlin's gateway to the south. Completed in 1870, it received only mild damage during World War II, which left it roofless but otherwise mostly intact. Despite attempts to preserve it, it was blown up in 1952 – essentially because someone had put in a good offer for the bricks. Now only a fragment of the facade stands, giving a hint at past glories. The patch of land that the station once covered is today devoted to a park – the rear portion of which sports the **Tempodrom**, a tent-shaped arts venue.

The Gruselkabinett

The blunt and featureless building just southwest of the old Anhalter Bahnhof is a former bunker built during the war by the *Reichsbahn* for travellers using Anhalter Bahnhof, and another of a handful of Nazi buildings left in the city. Now it contains the **Gruselkabinett** (Mon 10am–3pm, Tues, Thurs, Fri & Sun 10am–7pm, Sat noon–8pm; €8.50; ⓦwww.gruselkabinett-berlin.de; S-Bahn Anhalter Bahnhof), Schöneberger Strasse 23a, an amateurish "chamber of horrors", the most interesting part of which is the section given over to the bunker itself, with a few odd artefacts found here and in Hitler's bunker (see p.50).

The Deutsches Technikmuseum Berlin

Deutsches Technikmuseum Berlin (German Technology Museum of Berlin; Tues–Fri 9am–5.30pm, Sat & Sun 10am–6pm; €4.50; ⓦwww.dtmb.de; U-Bahn Möckernbrücke) at Trebbiner Strasse 9 is one of the city's most interactive museums – a children's and button-pushers' delight. The technology section has plenty of experiments, antiquated machinery and computers to play with, alongside some elegant old cars and planes. The museum's collection of ancient steam trains and carriages is even more impressive; the polished behemoths have been brought to rest in what was once a workshop of the old Anhalter Bahnhof.

Bergmannstrasse and around

From U-Bahn Möckernbrücke it's a single stop on U7 to U-Bahn Gneisenaustrasse, the nearest stop to western Kreuzberg's vague centre, along Bergmannstrasse, a city block to the south. Many buildings around here housed working-class families at the end of the nineteenth century and survived the war to be painstakingly restored in what was West Berlin. The area is now thoroughly gentrified, though with a laid-back bohemian feel, and there's no denying that it's a pleasant place to live. Bergmannstrasse itself is lined with cafés, bistros and *Trödelläden* (junk and occasionally antique shops), as well as the **Marheineke Markthalle**, a good indoor grocery market.

Along the eastern stretches of Bergmannstrasse lie several large eighteenth- and nineteenth-century **cemeteries**. They're full of forgotten Berlin worthies, the only name of any real note being Gustav Stresemann, chancellor and foreign minister in the Weimar years – he's in Luisenstädtischen Kirchhof, the most southeasterly of the four cemeteries.

Also worth a look is **Chamissoplatz**, just south of Bergmannstrasse, for its well-preserved, balconied nineteenth-century houses and, a block south, water tower. The square also boasts one of Berlin's few remaining Wilhelmine *pissoirs* – ornate public toilets, characteristically dark green in colour, erected in an early attempt at sanitation. This one has been recently renovated, and is open to the public (men only), for a Bismarkian moment of relief.

Viktoriapark

At its western end Bergmannstrasse meets the broad thoroughfare of Mehringdamm, location of the **Schwules Museum** (Gay Museum) at no. 61 (see p.254), which offers thoroughly researched temporary exhibits on a huge variety of gay issues and history. Beyond Mehringdamm Bergmannstrasse becomes Kreuzebergstrasse, a short walk along which leads to **Viktoriapark** (the "Kreuzberg", as it's popularly known). Draped across the slopes of a hill, the park is one of the city's most likeable, a relaxed ramble of trees and green space with a pretty brook running down the middle. To one side is the *Golgotha Café* and disco (see p.214), packed on summer evenings; on another side is what claims to be Germany's northernmost vineyard; and atop the hill is the **Cross** (more a Neoclassical spire) from which Kreuzberg gets its name, designed by Schinkel to commemorate the Napoleonic Wars. The view is a good one, too.

Tempelhof airport

A five-minute walk south along Mehringham from its intersection with Bergmannstrasse, housing fades away to the flatlands of **Tempelhof Airport** (U-Bahn Platz der Luftbrücke). The airport was opened in 1923 and was once Germany's largest; the present complex was built in 1936–41 and is one of the best surviving examples of Nazi architecture. A huge bronze eagle that surmounted the building was removed in the 1960s, ostensibly to make way for a radar installation (the eagle's head can still be seen at the entrance to the airport), but you can't help thinking that its removal probably had more to do with it being an ugly reminder of the Nazi past. After the war the airport was used for visiting dignitaries and the military and a light load of small carrier flights, until it finally closed on the 30th October 2008, as part of a plan to centralise all of Berlin's air traffic using the new Berlin-Brandenburg Airport at Schönefeld. The site's future use has been opened up to a Europe-wide competition, and thankfully only plans to preserve the terminal buildings are being considered. One strong possibility is that the Allied Museum (see p.173) will move here.

Platz der Luftbrücke

It was to Tempelhof that the Allies flew in supplies to beat the **Berlin Blockade** of 1948–49 (see box opposite) and the **Luftbrückendenkmal**, a memorial in the centre of the **Platz der Luftbrücke** that forms the entrance to the airport, commemorates the airmen and crew who died in crashes. The memorial represents the three air corridors used, and forms half of a bridge: the other half, "joined by air", is in Frankfurt. Inside the airport a small exhibition shows photographs of its building and the Blockade – mostly publicity shots of gleaming USAF pilots and scruffy kids, with little on the role of Tempelhof in the war years.

The Berlin Blockade (1948–49)

The **Berlin Blockade** was the result of an escalation in tensions between East and West in the late 1940s. These came to a head when the Western zone introduced the Deutschmark as currency in June 1948; the Soviets demanded that their own Ostmark be accepted as Berlin's currency, a move that was rejected by the city's parliament. Moscow's answer to this was an attempt to bring West Berlin to its knees by severing all road and rail links to the Western zones and cutting off the power provided by plants on the Eastern side. There was now only one month's food and ten days' coal supply left in the city.

The British and Americans realized that they had to support West Berlin, but were unwilling to use military force to push their way in overland. After some consideration it was decided to try and supply the city by air: the Soviets, it was gambled, would not dare risk an international incident – possibly even war – by shooting down Western aircraft. However, there were serious doubts as to whether it was possible to sustain two million people by an airlift. The only previous attempt on a comparable scale – maintaining the German Sixth Army at Stalingrad – had been an utter failure. Berlin's needs were calculated at 4000 tons of supplies per day, yet the available aircraft could carry fewer than 500 tons.

Nevertheless the airlift began on June 26, 1948 and at its height nine months later, it had become an around-the-clock precision operation with planes landing or taking off every thirty seconds, bringing 8000 tons of supplies to the city each day. Winter was exceptionally tough. Power cuts and severe food rationing reduced living standards to the level of the immediate postwar period. The Russians made supplies available in the eastern half of the city, but relatively few West Berliners – in a spirited show of defiance – chose to take advantage of them.

The Soviets called off the Blockade in May 1949, but they had been defeated in more ways than one. Though it cost the lives of 78 airmen and crew and millions of dollars, the airlift thwarted Stalin's attempt to expel the Allies from West Berlin. Moreover for the occupying British and Americans the propaganda value was enormous: aircrews who a few years previously had been dropping bombs on the city now provided its lifeline. Photographs of the "candy bomber" – a USAF captain who dropped chocolate bars and sweets from his plane on small parachutes for the city's children – went around the world. No longer were the occupiers seen as enemies, but rather as allies against the Soviet threat.

Having seen the airport you might want to have a quick look at the **Polizeihistorische Sammlung** (Police History Collection; Mon–Wed 9am–3pm; €2; ☎030/46 64 99 47 62; U-Bahn Platz der Luftbrücke), next door at Platz der Luftbrücke 6, worth dipping into for its nineteenth-century uniforms and illustrations intended to help police determine "typical criminal types".

Eastern Kreuzberg

During the war **eastern Kreuzberg** was one of the very few areas to avoid total destruction, and among the quickest to revive in the 1950s. When the Wall was built in 1961, things changed: with the neighbourhood severed from its natural hinterland in the East, families moved out, houses were boarded up and it started dying. But at the same time, by providing Berlin's cheapest rentable property it attracted waves of **immigrant workers** from southern Europe – particularly Turkey – who brought their families and customs. Here too, came the radicals, students and dropouts of the 1968-generation – coming to Berlin because of its national service loophole, and to Kreuzberg for its vast **squatting** potential (see box, p.145). Since then the squatter movement has

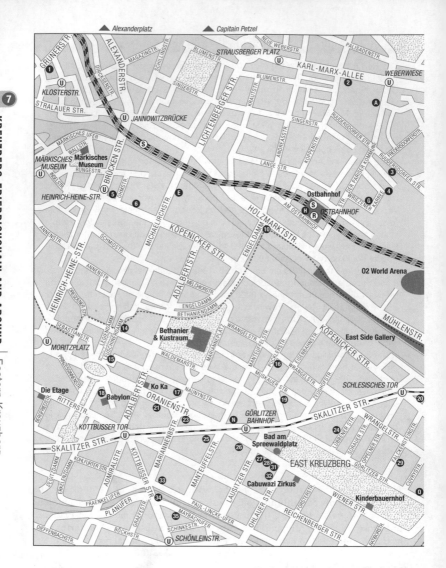

gradually all but died out but Turks and other immigrants still thrive, and the first signs of gentrification have begun to appear, stimulated in part by a vibrant café and **nightlife** scene. Nonetheless the neighbourhood remains extremely gritty and doesn't generally invite relaxed exploration – **Görlitzer Park** at its centre remains the stomping ground of itinerant punks and drug pushers, and the vending machine dispensing syringe needles at **Kottbusser Tor** attracts over a hundred users a day.

At the eastern edge of the district, and hard on the former East Berlin border, is **Schlesisches Tor**, a practical gateway for the short bus ride to the **Soviet Memorial** in **Treptower Park**, or a one-stop ride over the river Spree on the U-Bahn from Friedrichshain.

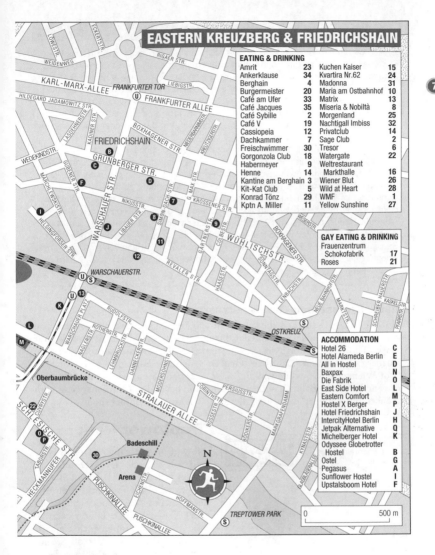

EATING & DRINKING

Amrit	23	Kuchen Kaiser	15
Ankerklause	34	Kvartira Nr.62	24
Berghain	4	Madonna	31
Burgermeister	20	Maria am Ostbahnhof	10
Café am Ufer	33	Matrix	13
Café Jacques	35	Miseria & Nobiltà	8
Café Sybille	2	Morgenland	25
Café V	19	Nachtigall Imbiss	32
Cassiopeia	12	Privatclub	14
Dachkammer	7	Sage Club	2
Freischwimmer	30	Tresor	6
Gorgonzola Club	18	Watergate	22
Habermeyer	9	Weltrestaurant	
Henne	14	Markthalle	16
Kantine am Berghain	3	Wiener Blut	26
Kit-Kat Club	5	Wild at Heart	28
Konrad Tönz	29	WMF	1
Kptn A. Miller	11	Yellow Sunshine	27

GAY EATING & DRINKING

Frauenzentrum	
Schokofabrik	17
Roses	21

ACCOMMODATION

Hotel 26	C
Hotel Alameda Berlin	E
All in Hostel	D
Baxpax	N
Die Fabrik	O
East Side Hotel	L
Eastern Comfort	M
Hostel X Berger	P
Hotel Friedrichshain	J
IntercityHotel Berlin	H
Jetpak Alternative	Q
Michelberger Hotel	K
Odyssee Globetrotter	
Hostel	B
Ostel	G
Pegasus	A
Sunflower Hostel	I
Upstalsboom Hotel	F

Kottbusser Tor

Catching U-Bahn line #1 (unkindly named the "Istanbul Express" along this stretch) to **Kottbusser Tor** is a good introduction to eastern Kreuzberg. The intersection around the U-Bahn has its own special feel – think Istanbul market in an eastern-bloc housing development – and the area around the station is a scruffy, earthy shambles of Turkish street vendors and cafés, the air filled with the aromas of southeast European cooking. Things are at their liveliest on Tuesday and Friday afternoons at the colourful oriental **food market**, a ten-minute walk south along Kottbusser Strasse – over the **Landwehrkanal** and left down Maybachufer. From here, the walk east along the leafy canal at the southern edge of the district passes along Berlin's most attractive stretches of water through a residential district: more reminiscent of Amsterdam than Berlin.

Berlin's blight or bounty?

Ever since the Wall provided the world's most famous canvas for **graffiti**, this form of self-expression has thrived in Berlin, with artists from all over Europe and North America joining the hundreds of local sprayers. It's everywhere – as the S-Bahn ride through central Berlin reveals – but the greatest concentrations are in central, lower rent neighborhoods where older tenements have survived. Kreuzberg is particularly well-smothered, with thousands of tags and the occasional more complex piece on every accessible piece of wall – and a few near-inaccessible spots too.

A form of art and a sign of a vibrant youth culture, perhaps, but certainly all this daubing costs Berlin around €8m per year to fix, triggering numerous campaigns against it, with some even involving nocturnal helicopter missions with infra-red cameras. Polls suggest at least two-thirds of Berliners hate graffiti, but there are signs too that it's becoming part of the city's identity. Tours of the more worthwhile pieces in the Spandauer Vorstadt and Kreuzberg are offered by companies such as Alternative Berlin tours (see p.28) who even offer workshops, where you can learn the ropes and get directions to free legal walls. For supplies try Overkill, Köpenicker Strasse 195 (⊕030/69 50 61 26; ⊛www.overkillshop.com; U-Bahn Schlesisches Tor), whose sheer professionalism and impressive battery of spray cans makes it hard to believe the activity is mostly illegal.

Wiener Strasse and Oranienstrasse

Following Maybachufer and the canal east and crossing the first bridge takes you down the unremarkable residential Ohlauer Strasse, two blocks from **Weiner Strasse**. This, and its northwestern continuation, Oranienstrasse, forms eastern Kreuzberg's **bohemian** main drag. Grubby **Görlitzer Park** flanks the northern side of Wiener Strasse, while walking west takes you past a series of eateries, bike shops and bars to U-Bahn Görlitzer Bahnhof and beyond to **Oranienstrasse** with its concentration of café-bars, art galleries and alternative clothes shops.

Treptower Park

Now of principle interest for its large and sobering **Soviet Memorial** to troops killed in the Battle of Berlin, Treptower Park (S-Bahn Treptower Park; or bus #265 from Schlesisches Tor), was originally built as a park for Berlin's nineteenth-century tenement-dwellers to let off steam. By 1908 it had over thirty dance halls and restaurants. Later, during the interwar years, the park became a well-known assembly point for revolutionary workers about to embark on demonstrations or go off to do battle with the Brownshirts.

Until the *Wende* most park visitors were either East Berliners out for a day at **Spreepark**, a GDR-era amusement park, or Soviet citizens arriving by the busload to pay their

Squatting in Kreuzberg

With cheap rents and abundant squatting opportunities throughout the 1970s and 1980s, Kreuzberg became West Berlin's hive for squatters, radicals and non-conformists. It was here that the youth of the Federal Republic came to get involved in alternative politics, making it West Berlin's "hip" quarter, and the place to hang out and hit raucous and avant-garde nightspots.

Until the Wall came down, to say you lived in Kreuzberg was something of a left-wing and anti-establishment political statement. At that time, happenings on streets here were the easiest gauge of West Berlin's political temperature. Even as late as 1988, Kreuzberg constituted enough of a threat for the authorities to seal the area off during an IMF conference.

One reason for the presence of so many young alternative types in the city was a national service loophole. Its "occupied" status meant Berlin was the only place in Germany where the eighteen months' **national service**, compulsory for all men between the ages of 18 and 32, could be evaded (an anomaly abolished after reunification). Consequently in the 1960s, 1970s and 1980s, especially when anti-war feelings were running high, the city became a haven for those avoiding service.

Service dodgers were often attracted to Kreuzberg for its **squatting opportunities**, which came as a result of a ruling that pre-1950s apartments were subject to rent restrictions, so that speculators often allowed them to fall into disrepair so that they could erect new buildings and charge whatever rent they pleased; squatters who maintained and developed these old apartments thus saved some of the city's old architecture. In the 1980s the Social Democratic city government adopted a liberal approach to squats, offering subsidies to well-organized squats and giving them some security of tenure.All went well until the Christian Democrats took over the city in 1981. On the back of growing problems of crime and drug dealing in eastern Kreuzberg, the right-wing minister of the interior ordered the riot police to forcibly close down the squats. There were riots in the streets, demonstrations all over the city and intense political protest, which reached its peak with the death of a 15-year-old boy, hit by a bus during a demonstration. Activists called a strike and the city government had to back down. Today, the city government still has to occasionally clear out a building, but generally the squatters themselves have moved on of their own volition and less than a handful of squats remains.

The political climate has also changed with only the occasional uprising occurring, usually on May Day, when an annual demonstration ritually turns into a riot between police and demonstrators: anarchists and far-leftists espousing anti-imperialist, anti-capitalist views. But the atmosphere is nonetheless more subdued and less political than it was pre-*Wende*.

respects at the memorial. But since the beginning of the 1990s increasing numbers of former West Berliners have discovered the place, and the park has become a popular Sunday destination for the space-starved inhabitants of Neukölln and Kreuzberg. The pleasant harbour area close to the Treptower Park S-Bahn station is one attraction, but the main hub of activity is now on and around the Insel der Jugend, further south along the Spree.

The Soviet Memorial

At the heart of the park, the **Soviet Memorial** (Sowjetisches Ehrenmal) commemorates the Soviet Union's 305,000 estimated casualties during the Battle of Berlin in April and May 1945 and is the burial place of 5000 of them. It's best approached from the arched entrance on the south side of Puschkinallee. A little way to the south of here is a sculpture of a grieving woman representing the Motherland, to the left of which a broad concourse slopes up towards a viewing point flanked by two vast triangles of red granite, fashioned from stone bought from Sweden by the Nazis to furnish Berlin with projected victory monuments. From the viewing point, a long sunken park of mass graves of the Red Army troops is lined by sculpted frescoes of stylized scenes from the Great Patriotic War and quotes from Stalin with German translations. These lead the way to the centrepiece: a vast symbolic statue and typical piece of Soviet gigantism, built using marble from Hitler's Chancellery. Over 11m high, and set on top of a hill modelled on a *kurgan* or traditional warriors' grave of the Don region, it shows an idealized Russian soldier clutching a saved child and resting his sword on a shattered swastika.

Inside the plinth is a memorial crypt with a mosaic in true Socialist Realist style, showing Soviet citizens (soldiers, mother, worker, peasant and what looks like an old-age pensioner) honouring the dead. One significant aspect of the crypt and memorial generally is the lack of religious iconography – eschewed by the Soviet state – showing that grandiose memorials needn't depend on pious objects for their spiritual power.

The rest of the park

The rest of the park conceals a couple of low-key attractions, including the **Karpfenteich**, a large carp pool just south of the memorial, and, a little to the east of here, the **Archenhold Sternwarte** (Wed–Sun 2–4.30pm; tours Thurs 8pm, Sat & Sun 3pm; museum €2.50, tours €4; ☏030/536 06 37 19, Ⓦwww.sdtb.de), Alt-Treptow 1an, an observatory with the longest refracting telescope in the world. Check the website for night-time planetary viewings.

The park continues north of Puschkinallee, where you'll also find *Haus Zenner* (see p.215), a riverside *Gaststätte* whose origins go back to the eighteenth century. Just to the east is the **Insel der Jugend**, a small island in the Spree reached via the **Abteibrücke**, an ornamental footbridge built by French prisoners of war in 1916 to link the island to the mainland. The end of Treptow's summer festival is marked by a firework display from this bridge, an event known as *Treptow in Flammen* or "Treptow in Flames". The island was originally the location of an abbey, but now the main attraction is *Die Insel*, a tower-like clubhouse that houses a café, cinema and gallery and is a regular venue for club nights and gigs, with occasional outdoor raves in summer. Returning across the bridge, walk northwest back to the S-Bahn station via a grass-lined boardwalk, which is good for picnicking or just relaxing by the water – there's boat rental nearby, providing rowing boats and paddle boats (from €12 per hour). At the beginning of the boardwalk, you'll find a very tasty *Imbiss* stand serving fresh smoked fish.

Southeast from the bridge lies **Spreepark**, a popular amusement park in the GDR days which has since been closed down awaiting reinvestment and reopening. Until then the surrounding **Plänterwald** woods, which cover a couple of square kilometres, are the main draw, for gentle strolling. Just to the southwest of Neue Krug is the *Plänterwald*, a largish *Gaststätte* that makes a good place to interrupt your wanderings. You can also take a cruise around the surrounding waterways (see p.28).

Friedrichshain

East of the Spree from Kreuzberg, the former East Berlin borough of **Friedrichshain** is also overwhelmingly residential, but was in contrast comprehensively destroyed during the war. It lost over two thirds of its buildings – as much as any Berlin district – and so today is virtually all of GDR vintage and contains very little real sightseeing. Yet the neighbourhood has become a real nightlife hotspot, with dozens of bars clustered on **Simon-Dach-Strasse** and various clubs inhabiting old industrial buildings on its fringes.

The district gathers around two major arterial roads: Warschauer Strasse, which forms the link to Kreuzberg and East Side Gallery, Berlin's longest surviving stretch of Wall; and the grand **Karl-Marx-Allee**, connecting to Alexanderplatz and Mitte. Forming Friedrichshain's northwestern boundary is **Volkspark Friedrichshain**, one of the eastern city's oldest and best parks; it's best accessed from Prenzlauer Berg, and so dealt with in that chapter (see p.149).

Friedrichshain is well-connected to the centre: a rapid U-Bahn line travels beneath the Karl-Marx-Allee from Alexanderplatz, from which the S-Bahn also leaves for the Ostbahnhof and Warschauer Strasse – the stations at either end of the East Side Gallery.

East Side Gallery

Trailing the banks of the River Spree on the southern edge of Friedrichshain, a 1.3-kilometre surviving stretch of Berlin Wall is known as the **East Side Gallery** for its collection of political and satirical murals. Originally painted just after the Wall fell they resonate with the attitude and aesthetics of the time: some are imaginative, some trite and some impenetrable, but one of the most telling shows Brezhnev and Honecker locked in a passionate kiss, with the inscription, "God, help me survive this deadly love". Given their outdoor and exposed nature, all the paintings are steadily decaying, so that original artists have been invited back to repaint their works a couple of times, most recently to mark the twentieth anniversary of the fall of the Wall in 2009. Behind the gallery, look out for the landmark **Oberbaumbrücke**, a neo-Gothic double-decker bridge that dates back to 1896 and leads over to Kreuzberg.

Warschauer Strasse and around

At the southeastern end of the East Side Gallery **Warschauer Strasse** climbs up to cross railway tracks and become Friedrichshain's main cross street. It's fairly dull and functional and tram #M10 is a welcome way to speed your journey, but it's better still to peel off at the first opportunity with a right turn down Revaler Strasse where graffiti paves the way to **Cassiopeia**, a medley of skate park, climbing wall, cinema, beer garden and club that started as a squat. Opposite lies the **Simon-Dach-Strasse**, at first glance an ordinary tree-lined residential street, but also the hub of the local nightlife scene and good cafés, restaurants and bars, many with outdoor seating. At its northern end Simon-Dach-Strasse joins Boxhagener Strasse: a block to the right lies the leafy Boxhagener Platz which bustles with a fleamarket on Sundays.

Karl-Marx-Allee

A vast boulevard lined with 1.5km of model 1950s and 1960s communist housing developments, **Karl-Marx-Allee** (or Stalinallee, as it was known in the 1950s) is a mixed bag. On the onehand its inhuman scale makes it hard to explore on foot and no buses or trams run along the road so businesses struggle, giving the place a bit of an eerie and empty feel – despite the traffic thundering up and down the road. Nevertheless the monumentalist *Zuckerbäckerstil* (wedding-cake style) buildings are architecturally impressive, their construction standards commendably high, and their apartments among the Eastern Bloc's finest. The best way to explore is to walk (or bike) the kilometre from U-Bahn Frankfurter Tor to Strausberger Platz with a break at **Café Sybille** (daily 10am–8pm; free; ☎030/29 35 22 03; U-Bahn Weberwiese) at Karl-Marx-Allee 72. This stylish, minimalist café has a great exhibition, which charts the history of the Stalinallee.

8

Prenzlauer Berg and around

Fanning out immediately northeast of Mitte, the former East Berlin borough of **Prenzlauer Berg** was a densely populated old working-class residential district. It was fought over street-by-street during the war, which has meant that many of its hallmark turn-of-the-twentieth-century tenement blocks survived fairly well, leaving some tight networks of leafy cobbled streets. In the GDR days, the district was a uniquely vibrant and exciting corner of East Berlin, home to artists and young people seeking an alternative lifestyle, who chose to live here on the edge of established East German society (literally as well as figuratively – the district's western boundary was marked by the Berlin Wall). After the *Wende*, the district's venerable atmosphere, central location and low rents quickly made it a lively and fashionable district, with some of the best cafés, bars and nightlife in the city. This has died down a little since and aged along with the first wave of migrants who have become typified as bohemian yuppies. And so health-food stores proliferate here, including Europe's largest organic supermarket, and, with one of Germany's highest birth rates, so do many children, equipped with their fair-trade garments and wooden toys.

Prenzlauer Berg is strung out along several arterial roads that are well served by public transport from Alexanderplatz or Hackescher Markt. From Alexanderplatz, **Greifswalder Strasse** heads northeast, passing close to **Volkspark Friedrichshain**, one of the city's best parks and final resting place for victims of the 1848 revolution. From here you pass the bland, GDR-era **Ernst-Thälmann-Park**, behind which lurks the **Zeiss Planetarium** and the modest late-1920s model housing development, **Flamensiedlung**, before reaching the tidy middle-class district of **Weissensee**, where you'll find the city's largest **Jewish cemetery**. Another arterial road to the west, **Schönhauser Allee**, runs close to the former East–West border and is the main route to all the trendiest parts of Prenzlauer Berg. This is the place to explore on foot, taking in sights such as the **Kulturbraueri** and **Kollwitzplatz**, which was once another important area for Jews, as a large nearby **cemetery** and still-functioning **synagogue** attest.

North of Prenzlauer Berg lies the tidy bourgeois district of **Pankow**, once home to much of the GDR's elite, which has some pleasant parks but few really worthwhile sights. But as Berlin's northeastern-most borough before the city gives way to countryside, it has a sedate, almost village-like atmosphere and so makes for an hour or two's pleasant strolling.

The quickest way to explore areas covered in this chapter is by **public transport** from Alexanderplatz. Tram #M4 travels up Greifswalder Strasse to Weissensee; while U-Bahn #2 heads to Senefelder Platz, which offers an ideal place to start a **walking tour** of Prenzlauer Berg. The same line continues up to U-Bahn Pankow, which lies a short walk from its main drag, Breite Strasse. A good way to return from explorations is by tram #M1, which stops at U-Bahn Eberswalder Strasse, the district's central hub, en route to Hackescher Markt via some of eastern Berlin's lesser-known backstreets.

Greifswalder Strasse and around

Greifswalder Strasse more-or-less forms the dividing line between Prenzlauer Berg and Friedrichshain. It still looks very neat with its freshly painted facades, and in pre-*Wende* days traffic came to a standstill along the side streets a couple of times a day as a convoy of black Citroëns and Volvos sped by, whisking high-ranking government members (notably Erich Honecker himself) from the Palast der Republik (see p.63) to their homes in the lakeside town of Wandlitz to the north of Berlin. But behind the immaculate facades, the *Hinterhöfe* of Greifswalder Strasse were just as run-down as those in the backstreets.

Volkspark Friedrichshain

By the start of Greifswalder Strasse, where Friedenstrasse and Am Friedrichshain meet, is **Volkspark Friedrichshain**. Just within the limits of the Friedrichshain district, it's one of the city's oldest and largest parks (and a well-known gay cruising area). At the western entrance to the park is the **Märchenbrunnen** (Fairytale Fountain), a neo-Baroque arcade and fountain with statues of characters from Brothers Grimm stories. Intended as a gift to tenement-dwelling workers, it was put up in 1913 at the instigation of Social Democratic members of the city council, in direct contravention of the Kaiser's wishes.

A few hundred metres to the southeast of the Märchenbrunnen stands the **Gedenkstätte für die Deutschen Interbrigadisten**, a monument to the German members of the International Brigades who fought against the fascists in Spain in the Spanish Civil War. Of the five thousand Germans (including many leading communists) who went to Spain, only two thousand returned. There's another monument to the east of here (just off Landsberger Allee), this time to victims of an upheaval closer to home. The **Friedhof der Märzgefallenen** is where many of the 183 Berliners killed by the soldiers of King Friedrich Wilhelm IV during the revolution of March 1848 were buried, their interment attended by 80,000 of their fellow citizens. Only a few of the original gravestones survive, but the dead of 1848 have been joined by 33 of those killed in the November Revolution of 1918, commemorated by a statue of a *Rote Matrose* or "Red Sailor" at the cemetery entrance, reflecting the role played in the revolution by Imperial navy sailors.

The Bunkerbergs

The final resting place of the revolutionaries is overshadowed by the **Grosser Bunkerberg** and **Kleiner Bunkerberg**, two artificial hills created when a million cubic metres of rubble from bombed-out Berlin were dumped over the ruins of a flak gun and control tower respectively. In between the two is a small, tree-shaded lake, and nearby you'll find the kind of worthy sporting amenities (*Sport und Erholungszentrum* or sports centre), and giant outdoor chess sets that keep many Germans amused in their free time. Set on a grassy slope a little to the east is a

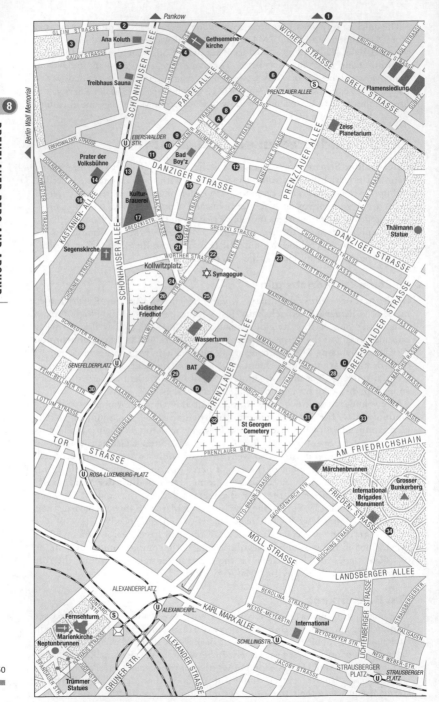

▲ Pankow

WICHERT STRASSE

GLEIM STRASSE

GAUDY STRASSE

Ana Koluth

Gethsemene-
kirche

Berlin Wall Memorial

Treibhaus Sauna

SCHÖNHAUSER ALLEE

PAPPELALLEE

STARGARDER STRASSE

GREIFSWALDER STRASSE

PRENZLAUER ALLEE

Flamensiedlung

GRELL STRASSE

Zeiss
Planetarium

EBERSWALDER STRASSE

Prater der
Volksbühne

EBERSWALDER
STR.

Bad
Boy'z

DANZIGER STRASSE

Kultur-
Brauerei

KNAACKSTRASSE

SREDZKISTRASSE

SREDZKI STRASSE

DANZIGER STRASSE

Thälmann
Statue

KASTANIEN-ALLEE

Segenskirche

OERBERGER STRASSE

SCHWEDTER
STRASSE

HUSEMANN STRASSE

WÖRTHER STRASSE

Kollwitzplatz

Synagogue

CHODOWIECKIS TRASSE

JABLONSKIS TRASSE

CHRISTBURGER STRASSE

Jüdischer
Friedhof

MARIENBURGER STRASSE

Wasserturm

BELFORTER STRASSE

IMMANUELKIRCH-STRASSE

GREIFSWALDER STRASSE

PASTEUR

HUFELAND

SENEFELDERPLATZ

METZER STRASSE

BAT

SAARBRÜCKER STRASSE

HEINRICH-ROLLER-STRASSE

WINS STRASSE

NIEDERKIRCHNER STRASSE

E. M. KARSTRASSE

FEHR-BELLINER STR.

LOTTUM STRASSE

STRASSBURGER STRASSE

St Georgen
Cemetery

PRENZLAUER BERG

TOR STRASSE

AM FRIEDRICHSHAIN

ROSA-LUXEMBURG-PLATZ

Märchenbrunnen

Grosser
Bunkerberg

OTTO-BRAUN-STRASSE

GEORGENKIRCH STR.

FRIEDEN-STRASSE

International
Brigades
Monument

BÜSCHING STRASSE

MOLL STRASSE

LANDSBERGER ALLEE

ALEXANDERPLATZ

BEROLINA STRASSE

WEYDE-MEYERSTR

LICHTENBERGER STRASSE

STRAUSBERGER STR.

PALISADEN

Fernsehturm

Marienkirche

Neptunbrunnen

ALEXANDERPL.

KARL MARX ALLEE

International

SCHILLINGSTR.

WEYDEMEYER STR.

NEUE WEBER-STR.

GRUNER STR.

ALEXANDERSTRASSE

JACOBY STRASSE

STRAUSBERGER
PLATZ

Trümmer
Statues

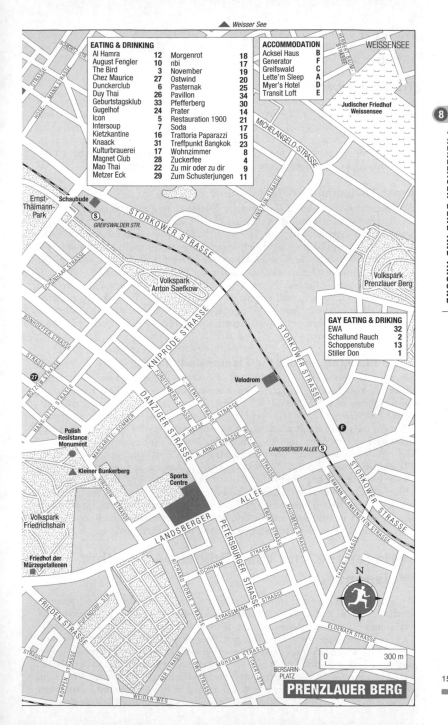

Weisser See

WEISSENSEE

EATING & DRINKING

Al Hamra	12
August Fengler	10
The Bird	3
Chez Maurice	27
Dunckerclub	6
Duy Thai	26
Geburtstagsklub	33
Gugelhof	24
Icon	5
Intersoup	7
Kietzkantine	16
Knaack	31
Kulturbrauerei	17
Magnet Club	28
Mao Thai	22
Metzer Eck	29

Morgenrot	18
nbi	17
November	19
Ostwind	20
Pasternak	25
Pavillon	34
Pfefferberg	30
Prater	14
Restauration 1900	21
Soda	17
Trattoria Paparazzi	15
Treffpunkt Bangkok	23
Wohnzimmer	8
Zuckerfee	4
Zu mir oder zu dir	9
Zum Schusterjungen	11

ACCOMMODATION

Acksel Haus	B
Generator	F
Greifswald	C
Lette'm Sleep	A
Myer's Hotel	D
Transit Loft	E

Jüdischer Friedhof
Weissensee

MICHELANGELO-STRASSE

Ernst-
Thälmann-
Park

Schaubude

GREIFSWALDER STR.

STORKOWER STRASSE

Volkspark
Anton Saefkow

Volkspark
Prenzlauer Berg

GAY EATING & DRIKING

EWA	32
Schallund Rauch	2
Schoppenstube	13
Stiller Don	1

KNIPRODE STRASSE

STORKOWER STRASSE

Velodrom

DANZIGER STRASSE

Polish
Resistance
Monument

LANDSBERGER ALLEE

Kleiner Bunkerberg

Sports
Centre

Volkspark
Friedrichshain

LANDSBERGER   ALLEE

PETERSBURGER STRASSE

HERMANN BLANKENSTEIN STRASSE

STORKOWER STRASSE

Friedhof der
Märzegefallenen

N

FRIEDEN STRASSE

ELDENAER STRASSE

0   300 m

BERSARIN-
PLATZ

PRENZLAUER BERG

monument commemorating the joint fight of the Polish army and German resistance against the Nazis. Given the feelings most Germans and Poles had for each other, the sentiments expressed seem rather unconvincing.

The St Georgen cemetery

Opposite the westernmost corner of Volkspark Friedrichshain and on the other side of Greifswalder Strasse lies the **St Georgen cemetery**, a venerable and overgrown affair dating back to the early nineteenth century, with some elaborate tombstones and vaults. Many of the memorials bear shrapnel and bullet scars, an indication of just how intense the fighting during the Battle for Berlin must have been; even the city's graveyards were fought for inch by inch.

Ernst-Thälmann-Park and around

At the northeastern end of Greifswalder Strasse is another example of former-GDR civic window-dressing in the shape of the **Ernst-Thälmann-Park** (a 1km walk along Greifswalder Strasse from the St Georgen cemetery, or take tram #M4). Here a model housing development is set in a small park fronted by a gigantic marble sculpture of the head and clenched fist of Ernst Thälmann, the pre-1933 communist leader who was imprisoned and later murdered by the Nazis. Floodlit and guarded round the clock by police in pre-*Wende* days, his likeness is now daubed with graffiti, and the concrete terrace on which it stands is favoured by local skateboarders. About 4000 people, mostly from the ex-GDR elite, live here in high-rise buildings with restaurants, shops, nurseries and a swimming pool all immediately at hand.

Zeiss Planetarium and the Flamensiedlung

On foot it's possible to cut through the Ernst-Thälmann-Park past several miserable high-rises to the silver-domed **Zeiss Planetarium** (show times vary – call or check web; €5; ☎030/421 84 50, ⓦwww.sdtb.de; S-Bahn Prenzlauer Allee), Prenzlauer Allee 80, with its imaginative assortment of narrated (German-only) and children's shows on the universe. Nearby is Prenzlauer Allee's distinctive, yellow-brick 1890s S-Bahn station, one of the best-looking in the city, and just northeast of here, between Sültstrasse and Sodtkestrasse, is the so-called **Flamensiedlung** (Flemish Colony), a model housing development built in 1929–30 according to plans by the architect Bruno Taut. With his associate Franz Hillinger, Taut wanted to create mass housing that broke away from the tenement-house concept. Basing their design on work already done in Holland, they diffused the angularity of their apartment blocks with corner windows and balconies, and left open areas between them to create cheerful bright back yards.

Weissensee and the Jüdischer Friedhof Weissensee

As it travels northeast and leaves Prenzlauer Berg, Greifswalder Strasse becomes **Berliner Allee** in the predominantly middle-class neighbouring borough of **Weissensee**. Its main attraction is the **Jüdischer Friedhof Weissensee** (April–Oct Sun–Thurs 8am–5pm, Fri 8am–3pm; Nov–March Sun–Thurs 8am–4pm, Fri 8am–3pm), which lies at the end of Herbert-Baum-Strasse (named after the Jewish resistance hero executed for his part in an attack on a Nazi propaganda exhibition in the Lustgarten in 1942), ten minutes south of Berliner Allee and the #M4 tram Albertinenstrasse stop. The cemetery was opened in 1880, when the Schönhauser Allee cemetery had finally been filled and it became Europe's largest Jewish

▲ Jüdischer Friedhof Weissensee

cemetery – its 115,600 graves spreading over the equivalent of 86 football pitches. At its entrance a sign requests male visitors to cover their heads before entering; you can borrow a skullcap from the cemetery office to the right.

Immediately in front of the entrance is a memorial "to our murdered brothers and sisters 1933–45" from Berlin's Jewish community. It takes the form of a circle of tablets bearing the names of all the large concentration camps. Like many memorials to the war years in the city, it's a poignant monument to the horrors that occurred, and succeeds in being less inflated and militaristic than many others.

Beyond here are the cemetery administration buildings (where information about the cemetery is available), with the cemetery itself stretching back from the entrance for about 1km: row upon row of headstones, with the occasional extravagant family monument including some Art Nouveau graves and mausoleums designed by Ludwig Mies van der Rohe and Walter Gropius (the grave of Albert Mendel). But more moving are the 400 urns containing the ashes of concentration-camp victims (Lot G7), and the headstones on the hollow graves of those whose remains were never found or identified.

A handful of well-tended postwar graves near the administration buildings are, paradoxically, symbols of survival – witness to the fact that a few thousand Berlin Jews did escape the Holocaust and that the city still has a small Jewish community (see p.88).

Schönhauser Allee and around

The quickest way into Prenzlauer Berg by public transport is by U-Bahn from Alexanderplatz to Senefelderplatz. From here the uphill walk along **Schönhauser Allee** soon arrives at **Senefelderplatz**, previously known as Pfefferberg (Pepper Hill), but later renamed after the inventor of the lithographic process (printing from engraved stone), Alois Senefelder. A statue of Senefelder stands on the square, with his name appearing on the base in mirror script, as on a lithographic block. The name **Pfefferberg**, incidentally, is still in use, and applies to a former factory complex just below Senefelderplatz that features an arts centre and *Biergarten* (see p.230).

Jüdischer Friedhof

Just past the police station on Schönhauser Allee is the **Jüdischer Friedhof** (Mon–Thurs 8am–4pm, Fri 8am–1pm; male visitors should keep their heads covered, skullcaps loaned free at the entrance), Schönhauser Allee 23–25, Prenzlauer Berg's Jewish cemetery, which opened when space ran out at the Grosse Hamburger Strasse cemetery. Over 20,000 people are buried here, but for most, this last resting place is an anonymous one: in 1943 many of the gravestones were smashed and a couple of years later the trees under which they had stood were used by the SS to hang deserters found hiding in the cemetery during the final days of the war. Today many of the stones have been restored and repositioned, and a memorial stone near the cemetery entrance entreats visitors: "You stand here in silence, but when you turn away do not remain silent."

The Wasserturm and Synagogue Rykestrasse

From Senefelder Platz, Kollwitzstrasse runs north, roughly parallel to Schönhauser Allee, through a quiet and almost bucolic residential streets. Adding to the relaxed atmosphere is a small urban park, a block to the east, around the huge red-brick **Wasserturm** (water tower). Built in 1875 on the site of a pre-industrial windmill, the tower has converted into apartments with quirky room plans that follow the building's circular shape. Sadly these rest atop another location of Nazi atrocities: once the party came to power the SA turned the basement into a torture chamber and the bodies of 28 of their victims were later found in the underground pipe network. A memorial stone on Knaackstrasse commemorates them: "On this spot in 1933 decent German resistance fighters became the victims of fascist murderers. Honour the dead by striving for a peaceful world." Before the construction of the Wasserturm, Prenzlauer Berg's water requirements had been provided by the slim tower at the southern end of the square. Before that, people had to lug their water up from wells, and open sewers took their waste back downhill to the Spree, with the unsurprising result that disease was rife.

Just north of the Wasserturm and its attendant park, Rykestrasse leads north past a functioning **synagogue**, marked out by the ornate edifice in the courtyard of house no. 53. Built in 1904–5, it survived both *Kristallnacht* and use as a stables by the SA, to be designated a "Temple of Peace" in 1953, then transformed back into a working synagogue in 2007. Poignantly though, its capacity continues to far-exceed the local Jewish population.

Kollwitzplatz

One block behind the Rykestrasse synagogue lies **Kollwitzplatz**, a Prenzlauer Berg focal point and home to the well-known and well-regarded *Restauration 1900*, a restaurant established long before the Wall came down (see p.221). The square is named after artist **Käthe Kollwitz**, of whom there's an unflattering statue in the little park on the square. From 1891 to 1943 she lived on nearby Kollwitzstrasse (then Weissenburgerstrasse) and engaged in political and pacifist art that's best appreciated in the Käthe Kollwitz Museum (see p.121).

The street running north from Kollwitzplatz is **Husemannstrasse**, a nineteenth-century tenement street that was restored to its former glory in late-GDR days and turned into a kind of living museum in an attempt to recall the grandeur of old Berlin. Since the *Wende*, restoration projects have transformed neighbouring streets too, covering raddled facades with fresh stucco and installing new wrought-iron balconies.

U-Bahn Eberswalder Strasse and the Kulturbrauerei

A quiet stroll north on Husemannstrasse finds its abrupt end at the busy Danziger Strasse, where trams and traffic and shop fronts fight for space and attention. It leads west to **U-Bahn Eberswalder Strasse**, Prenzlauer Berg's busiest hub. Under the station and the elevated railway tracks along Schönhauser Allee lies *Konnopke's*, Berlin's oldest and most famous **sausage kiosk**, which opened in 1930 and is a rare family business to have survived both fascism and communism. The kiosk has a reputation for serving the best *Currywurst* (see p.208) in Berlin.

North of the U-Bahn station, Schönhauser Allee assumes its true identity as Prenzlauer Berg's main drag, an old-fashioned shopping street that, thanks to its cobbled streets and narrow shop facades, still retains a vaguely prewar feel. This feel is accentuated by the **Kulturbrauerei**, an events centre that all but fills the city block south east of the U-Bahn station. Originally built as a complex for major local brewer Schultheiss in the 1890s, it was given the pseudo-Byzantine style that was fashionable at the time and is entered by a narrow gateway on Danziger Strasse. This quickly widens to reveal a spacious inner courtyard which often serves as a live-music venue, and is flanked by old workshops which now house a theatre, various exhibition spaces, a couple of clubs and bars and a cinema. All tend to have a somewhat alternative slant and there's almost always something – cultural, political or just entertaining – going on (see p.229). The southern gateway leaves the complex on Sredzkistrasse, near the bustle of Schönhauser Allee. Crossing the main road here leads to a couple of streets: **Oderberger Strasse** and **Kastanienalle**, which have some of the best **cafés**, **bars** and **restaurants** in the eastern part of Berlin. Around here a few buildings have survived whose facades have not been touched since the *Wende* and continue to preserve evidence of the damage inflicted during the Battle of Berlin in the form of scores of bullet and shell marks.

Pankow

From Prenzlauer Berg, Schönhauser Allee leads north to the district of **Pankow**, which during the GDR days was always much more than just another East Berlin suburb. For years its villas and well-maintained flats were home mainly to members of the upper reaches of East Berlin society: state-approved artists and writers, scientists, East Berlin resident diplomats and the *Parteibonzen* (party bigwigs) of the old regime. Up until the 1960s the area was perceived in the West as being the real centre of power in the old GDR: Schloss Niederschönhausen, an eighteenth-century palace on the edge of the *Bezirk* (district), was the official

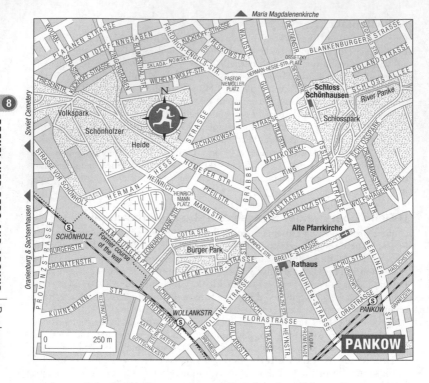

residence of the GDR's first president, Wilhelm Pieck, and later of SED General Secretary Walter Ulbricht, the man who took the decision to build the Wall. The name of the suburb was also appropriated by one of the ex-GDR's best-known rock bands, in a satirical dig at the social hierarchy of the workers' and peasants' state. Today, it's a pleasant, very middle-class borough, focused on the large shopping street **Breite Strasse**, and is most attractive for the belt of parks – the **Schlosspark**, **Bürgerpark** and **Volkspark Schönholzer Heide** – that lies a block or so to the north.

Breite Strasse

At the junction of Berliner Strasse and Breite Strasse, on a mid-road island that used to be the village green, is the **Alte Pfarrkirche**, Pankow's parish church and oldest building. It dates back to the fifteenth century but was extensively restored in 1832, a project in which Schinkel had a hand, resulting in an unusual-looking neo-Gothic jumble. At the western end of Breite Strasse, at the end of the main strip of chain stores and boutiques, is the turn-of-the-twentieth-century neo-Baroque **Rathaus**, a red-brick affair of fanciful gables, towers and cupolas, with a good *Ratskeller* in its basement.

The Schlosspark

North of Breite Strasse is the **Schlosspark**, in whose leafy grounds lurks **Schloss Schönhausen** (April–Oct Tues–Sun 10am–6pm; Nov–March Tues–Sun 10am–5pm; €6; ⓦwww.spsg.de; S- & U-Bahn Pankow), former home of Elisabeth Christine, the estranged wife of Frederick the Great. The Schloss was built at the beginning of the eighteenth century and given an extensive but run-of-the-mill face-lift in 1764. During GDR days it could only be admired from a distance, as it served first as official residence of GDR president Wilhelm Pieck, from 1949 to 1960, and then as the old regime's most prestigious state guesthouse. Since then it has been revamped and reopened to visitors who can admire some of the original royal residence interiors; the offices of the GDR's president; and the suites of its most honoured guests. The palace is also surrounded by a slightly dreary 1950s-era garden that you're free to wander round (daily 8am–sunset). A few streets to the north of the park on Platanenstrasse is Pankow's most unusual building, the **Maria-Magdalenenkirche**, an Expressionist church from 1930, with a bizarre slab of a tower topped by three giant crucifixes.

Volkspark Schönholzer Heide

Northwest of the Bürgerpark, the heath-like **Volkspark Schönholzer Heide** is Pankow's most impressively wild park. In its southwest corner lies a small humble cemetery, a burial ground for civilians who died in the final days of the Battle of Berlin. Most are women or children and for many the dates of birth and death, and in some cases even names, are unknown, a stark reminder of the many untold stories that are lost in the dehumanizing chaos of war. In stark contrast is the grandeur of the huge **Soviet cemetery**, at the northwestern edge of the park. Here dozens of communal graves contain the remains of 13,200 soldiers killed during the same battle and military hierarchy is observed in death as in life, with officers occupying the central lower tiers and privates around the fringes of the grounds.

9

The eastern suburbs

I f you have enough time, head out to Berlin's **eastern suburbs** – which have changed significantly since reunification. Projects designed to iron out the differences between the two sides of the city have resulted in a strange mixture of past and present: old GDR-style socialist architecture sits alongside the clean-cut lines and flashy design of new buildings, and they don't quite gel. Visiting these primarily residential areas moulded by almost fifty years of communist rule, unpleasant as this sometimes is, is an important part of getting a complete picture of Berlin – and on their southern fringes some genuine rural breathers offer a break from the city.

The most important sights in this part of town relate to the GDR secret police, or Stasi, particularly the **Stasi Prison Hohenschönhausen** and **Stasi headquarters** in the borough of **Lichtenberg**. Both are sombre places, while the rewarding **Deutsch-Russisches Museum** in the same borough, concerns itself with twentieth-century German-Russian relations so is hardly uplifting either. Thankfully in the midst of them, lies the more cheerful **Tierpark Friedrichsfelde**, eastern Berlin's sprawling zoo with its pleasant wooded grounds. East of Lichtenberg is **Marzahn-Hellersdorf**, a late-1970s satellite town and perhaps Berlin's least obvious sightseeing destination. Silo-like apartment blocks and soulless shopping precincts stretch for miles out towards the edge of the city in what has to be one of the most desolate of the city's boroughs. However, this *is* Berlin for tens of thousands of Berliners, and worth a look for this reason alone. But probably the most pleasant day out in the eastern suburbs is **Köpenick**, in the far southeast, with its attractive small-town feel and surprisingly unspoiled **lakes**, particularly the Grosser Müggelsee with its thick belt of surrounding woods.

All of the places described in this chapter are easily reached on **public transport** by S- or U-Bahn, though a slower tram or bus journey will allow you to see a bit more of the city; links are suggested throughout the chapter.

Lichtenberg

East of Friedrichshain lies the sprawling working-class district of **Lichtenberg**, part prefabricated postwar mass dwellings and part traditional tenement blocks, with heavy concentrations of industry in the north and south. Until the mid-nineteenth century Lichtenberg was little more than a country town and popular Sunday outing destination for Berliners. With industrialization, however, the familiar Berlin tenements sprang up and the area's rustic past was soon forgotten. Unfortunately, in these post-unification days Lichtenberg has been hard hit by the collapse of the old order, with unemployment running high.

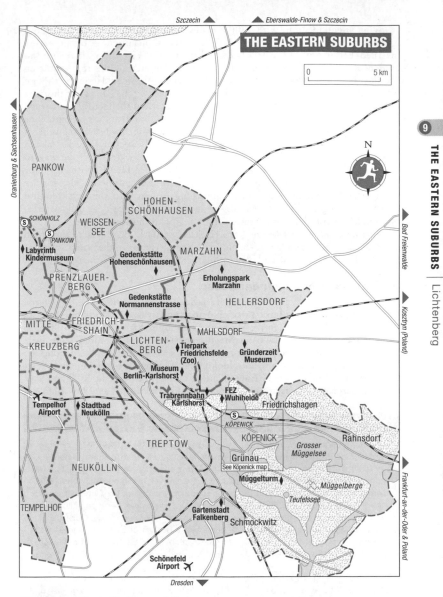

THE EASTERN SUBURBS

0   5 km

Szczecin ▲   ▲ Eberswalde-Finow & Szczecin

N

PANKOW

HOHEN-
SCHÖNHAUSEN

SCHÖNHOLZ

WEISSEN-
SEE

PANKOW

MARZAHN

Labyrinth
Kindermuseum

Gedenkstätte
Hohenschönhausen

PRENZLAUER-
BERG

Erholungspark
Marzahn

Gedenkstätte
Normannenstrasse

HELLERSDORF

MITTE   FRIEDRICH-
SHAIN

MAHLSDORF

KREUZBERG

LICHTEN-
BERG

Tierpark
Friedrichsfelde
(Zoo)

Gründerzeit
Museum

Museum
Berlin-Karlshorst

Tempelhof
Airport

Stadtbad
Neukölln

Trabrennbahn
Karlshorst

FEZ
Wuhiheide

Friedrichshagen

KÖPENICK

KÖPENICK

Grosser
Müggelsee

Rahnsdorf

TREPTOW

Grünau
See Köpenick map

NEUKÖLLN

Müggelturm

Müggelberge

Teufelssee

TEMPELHOF

Gartenstadt
Falkenberg

Schmockwitz

Schönefeld
Airport

Dresden ▼

Oranienburg & Sachsenhausen ◄

Bad Freienwalde ►

Kosztyn (Poland) ►

Frankfurt-an-der-Oder & Poland ►

THE EASTERN SUBURBS | Lichtenberg

Gedenkstätte Hohenschönhausen

A potent antidote to *Ostalgie* – nostalgia for the GDR – is a visit to the grim former Stasi prison at **Gedenkstätte Hohenschönhausen**, Genslerstrasse 66 (Memorial Hohenschönhausen; daily 9am–4pm, tours in German Mon, Wed & Fri 11am & 1pm, Tues & Thurs 11am, 1pm & 3pm, Sat & Sun hourly until 4pm, tours in English by arrangement; €3, Mon free; ☎030/98 60 82 34, ⓦwww.stiftung-hsh.de), which offers an insight into the fear and oppression upon which the regime was founded. Hohenschönhausen began life in 1945 as

159

a **Soviet Special Camp**, with 4200 inmates penned in together in horrendous living conditions. By 1946 around 3000 had died. Officially most of these were interned because of suspected Nazi links, but in most cases there was no evidence. This made underground torture chambers vital for acquiring "confessions" that would usually led to decades of forced labour – though ultimately almost all prisoners were declared innocent by the Russian authorities in the 1990s. In 1951 the Stasi (see box below) inherited the facility and turned it into a **remand prison** which was quickly blotted from city maps. The smallest sign of resistance or opposition to the state, including comments written in personal letters – which were all routinely steamed open – would earn you a spell here. Typically, you'd be caught unawares on your way to work, bundled into a van marked with something like H&O Lebensmittel or Frischfisch (groceries or fresh fish) – and then brought here. The former prisoners who lead tours deliver an absorbing insight into the psychological rather than physical abuse that followed in the solitary world of padded cells, tiny exercise yards, endless corridors and interrogation rooms.

To get here take tram #M5 or from Hackescher Markt or, if you're already in Lichtenberg, bus #256 from U-Bahn Lichtenberg. Get off either tram or bus at Freienwalder Strasse at the end of which is the entrance to the former jail.

Gedenkstätte Normannenstrasse

One building in the huge former **Stasi headquarters** complex is now the **Forschungs- und Gedenkstätte Normannenstrasse**, (Normannenstrasse Research and Memorial Centre; Mon–Fri 11am–6pm, Sat & Sun 2–6pm; €3.50; Ⓦ www.stasimuseum.de; U-Bahn Magdalenenstrasse). This museum uncovers the massive surveillance apparatus of the GDR's secret police. Walking along the bare, red-carpeted corridors and looking at the busts of Lenin and Felix Dzerzhinsky – founder of the Soviet Cheka, models for both the KGB and Stasi – it all seems part of a distant past, not an era that ended only in 1990. But then

The Stasi

East Germany's infamous Staatssicherheitsdienst (State Security Service), or Stasi, kept tabs on everything in the GDR. It ensured the security of the country's borders, carried out surveillance on foreign diplomats, business people and journalists, and monitored domestic and foreign media. It was, however, in the surveillance of East Germany's own population that the organization truly excelled. Very little happened in the GDR without the Stasi knowing about it: files were kept on millions of innocent citizens and insidious operations were orchestrated against dissidents, real and imagined. By the *Wende* the Stasi had a budget of £1 billion and 91,000 full-time employees and 180,000 informers within the East German population; figures brought into context by the more puny, albeit more ruthless, 7000-strong Nazi Gestapo.

At the beginning of 1991 former citizens of the GDR were given the right to see their Stasi files. Tens of thousands took the opportunity to find out what the organization had recorded about them, and, more importantly, who had provided the information; many a friendship and not a few marriages came to an end as a result. The process of unravelling truths from the archives also provided material for many a story, including Timothy Garton Ash's **book** *The File: A Personal History* (see p.294) and the **film** *Das Leben der Anderen* (Lives of Others; see p.302). Not all documents survived though, many were briskly shredded as the GDR regime collapsed, resulting in an unenviable task for one government organization who spent literally years piecing them together to bring people to justice, thankfully with some success.

▲ Bugging device, Stasi headquarters

the obsessively neat office and apartment of **Erich Mielke**, the Stasi head from 1957 to October 1989, makes it all the more immediate. Everything is just as he left it: white and black telephones stand on the varnished wooden desk as though awaiting calls, and Mielke's white dress uniform hangs in a wardrobe. Other rooms have displays of Stasi surveillance apparatus described in German (the accompanying English-language booklet costs €3), but which mostly speak for themselves. The many bugging devices and cameras – some concealed in watering cans and plant pots – reveal the absurd lengths the GDR went to in order to keep tabs on its citizens. You'll also find a couple of rooms stuffed with medals, badges, flags and other GDR kitsch. Sections on political terror during the Stalin years and forced resettlement from border zones throw light on otherwise little-known aspects of GDR history.

Dorfkirche and Gedenkstätte der Sozialisten

Just north of the rather sinister-looking Rathaus Lichtenberg, at the junction of Normannenstrasse and Möllendorffstrasse, is an improbably rustic **Dorfkirche**, a church dating back to Lichtenberg's village origins. The stone walls date from the original thirteenth-century structure, but the rest is more modern, with the spire tacked on as recently as 1965. The **Gedenkstätte der Sozialisten** or "Memorial to the Socialists", is a kilometre or so northeast of Lichtenberg U- and S-Bahn station, at the end of Gudrunstrasse, and perhaps only for die-hard fans of GDR relics. Its centrepiece is a four-metre chunk of red porphyry bearing the inscription *Die Toten mahnen uns* – "The dead remind us" – commemorating the GDR's socialist hall of fame from Karl Liebknecht and Rosa Luxemburg onwards. A tablet bears a list of names that reads like the street directory of virtually any town in pre-*Wende* East Germany, recording the esoteric cult figures of the workers' and peasants' state in alphabetical order;

until 1989 the East Berlin public were cajoled and coerced into attending hundred-thousand-strong mass demonstrations here. The whole thing actually replaced a much more interesting Mies van der Rohe-designed memorial that stood here from 1926 until the Nazis destroyed it in 1935. Altogether more uncompromising, featuring a huge star and hammer and sickle, the original memorial caused problems for van der Rohe when he came before Joseph McCarthy's Un-American Activities Committee in 1951. The Gedenkstätte is also the burial place of Walter Ulbricht, the man who decided to build the Berlin Wall, and Wilhelm Pieck, the first president of the GDR.

Tierpark and Schloss Friedrichsfelde

Lichtenberg's sprawling zoo, **Tierpark Friedrichsfelde** (daily 9am–sunset or 6pm; €11; Ⓦwww.tierpark-berlin.de; U-Bahn Tierpark), ranks as one of the largest zoos in Europe and a thorough exploration of its wooded grounds could easily absorb the better part of a day. The entrances are on the eastern side of Am Tierpark, and it's an ideal family destination, though some visitors may balk at the traditional nature of the place and the fact that some of the animals are kept in very small cages. However, others have much more space to roam around and virtually every species imaginable, from alpaca to wisent, can be found here, including rare Przewalski horses, which have been bred in the zoo in great numbers over the years, bringing the breed back from the edge of extinction.

Hidden away in the grounds of the zoo, just beyond an enclosure of lumbering pelicans, is **Schloss Friedrichsfelde** (tours on the hour: Tues–Sun 11am–2pm; €2 on top of zoo entrance; Ⓦwww.stadtmuseum.de), a Baroque palace housing an exhibition of eighteenth- and nineteenth-century interior decor. Theodor Fontane described it as the Schloss Charlottenburg of the East, but he was exaggerating – the best thing about it is its pretty, ornamental grounds; to see the inside you need to take a German-only tour.

Karlshorst and the Deutsch-Russisches Museum

From the Tierpark, a stroll south down Am Tierpark, bearing left along Treskowerallee for about 1km, will bring you to the sub-district of **Karlshorst**. For many years you were more likely to hear Russian than German spoken here, as the area was effectively a Russian quarter, thanks to the presence of large numbers of Soviet soldiers and their dependants. The Russians accepted the unconditional surrender of the German armed forces in a Wehrmacht engineers' school here on May 8, 1945, and went on to establish their Berlin headquarters nearby. For many years after, Karlshorst was a closed area, fenced off and under armed guard, out of bounds to ordinary East Germans. Later, they were allowed back in part, but Karlshorst retained an exclusive cachet, its villas housed the GDR elite – scientists and writers – or used as foreign embassy residences.

The Russians finally left in the summer of 1994, but a reminder of their presence endures as the **Deutsch-Russisches Museum**, Zwieseler Strasse 4 (Tues–Sun 10am–6pm; free; ☏030/50 15 08 10, Ⓦwww.museum-karlshorst.de; S-Bahn Karlshorst), in the building where the German surrender was signed. When the GDR still existed, this museum was officially known as the "Museum of the Unconditional Surrender of Fascist Germany in the Great Patriotic War 1941–45". Since then it has been renamed and rearranged to convey a self-consciously balanced view of the tumultuous German-Russian relations in the twentieth century. Its hundreds of photos and video footage make the exhibition worthwhile, but if you can't read German be sure to borrow an English language folder with translations.

Marzahn-Hellersdorf

To see the most enduring legacy of East Berlin – **Marzahn-Hellersdorf** – it's probably best to go by day and not look too much like a tourist, as the area has a reputation for violence. It's in places like this, all across the former GDR, that people are bearing the economic brunt of reunification's downside – unemployment – and where you'll see the worst effects caused by the collapse of a state that, for all its faults, ensured a certain level of social security for its citizens. Ironically, Marzahn was one of the GDR's model new towns of the late-1970s – part of Honecker's efforts to solve his country's endemic housing shortage by providing modern apartments in purpose-built blocks with shopping facilities and social amenities to hand. The result here was several kilometres of high-rise developments housing 250,000 people, where, like similar developments in the West, things never quite worked according to plan, with the usual crime and drugs surfacing.

Most people will see enough of the area by travelling to S-Bahn Springfuhl and then taking tram #M8 past endless high-rises to **Alt-Marzahn**, the original, slightly quaint and now hugely incongruous district centre. Complete with a green, pub, cobbled streets, war memorial and parish church, something of a village past survives. Admittedly it's not a very pleasant past: from 1866 the fields of the area were used as *Rieselfelder*, designated for the disposal of Berlin's sewage. Despite this malodorous development, Marzahn acquired a Dorfkirche in neo-Gothic style a few years later, built by Schinkel's pupil Friedrich August Stüler.

From here you can wander to other arterial roads beside Alt-Marzahn: Landsberger Allee, to take in the immensity of all the high-rises and bus #195 to the **Erholungspark Marzahn**, a large park with a collection of exotic ornamental gardens. This bus goes on, though very indirectly, to the **Gründerzeitmuseum Mahlsdorf**, a museum that brings together a fine collection of late nineteenth-century furnishings from the beginning of the German Empire.

Erholungspark Marzahn

Opened in 1987 as part of the city's 750th birthday celebrations, **Erholungspark Marzahn** (daily: March & Oct 9am–6pm; April–Sept 9am–8pm; Nov–Feb 9am–4pm; €3; Ⓦwww.erholungspark-marzahn.de), a large tidy park, forms an attractive oasis amid Marzahn's high-rises. The park is dotted with decorative features, pleasant nooks and playgrounds, but its star turns are the trio of exotic gardens, of which two are largely the result of Berlin's twinning with Beijing and Tokyo. The sprawling and ornate **Chinese Garden** is perhaps the best known in the park, being the biggest in Europe, and has a restaurant, snack bar and a teahouse (April–Oct daily 10.30am–6pm & winter weekends with fine weather) where you can take part in a traditional tea ceremony (reservations necessary and six person minimum; €6; Ⓣ0179/394 55 64, Ⓦwww.china-teehaus.de).

Smaller and much more regimented is the **Japanese Garden** (April–Sept Mon–Fri noon–8pm, Sat & Sun 9am–8pm, Oct Mon–Fri noon–6pm, Sat & Sun 9am–6pm), where water and rock features compete for space with the shrubs and bonsai trees, and tidy attention to detail is evident throughout. The park also boasts several other themed gardens, including a **Balinese Garden** in a warm damp greenhouse where you'll find a traditional rural family home amid the ferns and orchids.

The Gründerzeitmuseum Mahlsdorf

The suburb of **Mahlsdorf**, about 5km southeast of Alt-Marzahn, is no cultural centre, but it does boast one of the city's most notable museums, the excellent **Gründerzeitmuseum Mahlsdorf** (Wed & Sun 10am–6pm; €4.50;

☎ 030/567 83 29, ⓦ www.gruenderzeitmuseum.de; tram #62 to Alt-Mahlsdorf from S-Bahn Mahlsdorf), Hultschiner Damm 333, a collection of furniture and household gear from 1880–1900, the period known as the *Gründerzeit* or "foundation time" when the newly united Germany was at its imperial peak. The house can only be visited as part of a guided tour and if you need one in English you'll need to call ahead.

The founder of the museum, Lothar Berfelde (better known as a writer under the pseudonym, **Charlotte von Mahlsdorf**), put the collection together during GDR days when such an undertaking was by no means an easy task, creating a representative *Gründerzeit* apartment by taking the complete contents of rooms and relocating them in this eighteenth-century manor house. Depending on your tastes the result is either exquisite or over the top, but either way the museum is fascinating and certainly worth the long haul out to the suburbs.

In the basement are furnishings from the *Mulack-Ritze*, a famous turn-of-the-twentieth-century Berlin *Kneipe* (pub) that originally stood on Mulackstrasse in the Scheunenviertel. Lothar Berfelde, one of Berlin's better-known transvestites, was awarded the Bundesverdienstkreuz, Germany's equivalent of the OBE, in the summer of 1992 for his services to the preservation of the city's cultural and social heritage. He died in 2002, and the following year, his life became the subject of the Pulitzer Prize-winning Broadway theatre piece, *I am my own wife* by playright Doug Wright.

Köpenick

A slow-moving little place on the banks of the River Spree near the southeast edge of Berlin, **Köpenick** is one of the more pleasant of the city's eastern districts, and easily reached by S-Bahn from Alexanderplatz. Köpenick is both an ideal escape from the city centre and a convenient base for exploring Berlin's southeastern lakes, in particular the **Müggelsee**, with its appealing shoreline towns of Friedrichshagen and Rahnsdorf. Also easily accessible are the **Müggelberge**, Berlin's 150-metre-high "mountains", and the towns of **Grünau** and **Schmöckwitz** on the banks of the Langer See, which give access to the Zeuthener See and Krossinsee.

Köpenick was a town in its own right during medieval times, and though it has since been swallowed up by Greater Berlin, it still retains a distinct identity. The presence of a number of major factories meant that Köpenick always had a reputation as a "red" town. In March 1920, during the Kapp putsch attempt, workers from Köpenick took on and temporarily drove back army units who were marching on Berlin to support the coup. The army later returned, but its success was short-lived as the putsch foundered – thanks mainly to a highly effective general strike. This militancy continued into the Nazi era: on January 30, 1933, the day Hitler came to power, a red flag flew from the chimney of the brewery in the suburb of Friedrichshagen. This defiance was punished during the *Köpenicker Blutwoche* ("Köpenick Week of Blood") in June, during which the SA swooped on Social Democrats and communists. Five hundred people were imprisoned and 91 murdered.

The Altstadt

To walk to Köpenick's Altstadt, or old town, from the S-Bahn station, follow Borgamannstrasse to Mandrellaplatz, location of Köpenick's **Amtsgericht** (district court), where victims of the *Köpenicker Blutwoche* were executed. From Mandrellaplatz, Puchanstrasse leads to Am Generalshof and the **Platz des 23 April**, which commemorates the arrival in Köpenick of the Soviet army – liberators or conquerors, depending on your point of view. On the platz a sculpted clenched fist on top of a stone tablet honours those killed by the Nazis in 1933.

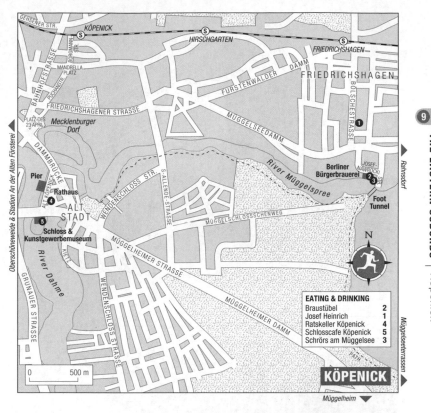

EATING & DRINKING

Braustübel	2
Josef Heinrich	1
Ratskeller Köpenick	4
Schlosscafe Köpenick	5
Schrörs am Müggelsee	3

KÖPENICK

From the platz, the Dammbrücke (boats can be rented at the foot of the bridge for €5 per hour) leads across the Spree into Köpenick's **Altstadt** (linked to the S-Bahn station by tram #60 and #68). Situated on an island between the Spree and Dahme rivers, the Altstadt's streets run more or less true to the medieval town plan and remain slightly down-at-heel so it's not hard to picture this area as it must have been a century or so ago. A number of typical nineteenth-century *Bürgerhäuser* with restored facades on **Grünstrasse** and **Böttcherstrasse** are worth a look, but the most prominent building is the early twentieth-century neo-Gothic **Rathaus** on Alt Köpenick, a typically over-the-top gabled affair with an imposing clock tower. A statue of one **Wilhelm Voigt** at the entrance to the buildings commemorates the town's most famous incident, when on October 16, 1906, unemployed shoemaker Voigt, disguised himself as an army officer, commandeered a troop of soldiers, marched them to Köpenick's Rathaus and requisitioned the contents of its safe. Having ordered his detachment to take Köpenick's mayor and book-keeper to the guardhouse in the city centre, he disappeared. Voigt was soon caught, but the story became an example of the Prussian propensity to blindly follow anyone wearing uniform. Later, playwright Carl Zuckmeyer turned the incident into a play, *Der Hauptmann von Köpenick* ("The Captain of Köpenick") and the robbery is now re-enacted every summer in the second half of June during the Köpenick summer festival.

▲ Clock tower, Rathaus

Schloss Köpenick

At the southern end of the Altstadt a footbridge leads to the Schlossinsel, the island home of **Schloss Köpenick**, the seventeenth-century fortified Baroque manor which houses the **Kunstgewerbemuseum** (Museum of Decorative Art; Tues–Sun 10am–6pm; €4, free Thurs 2–6pm; ☎030/226 29 02, ⓦwww.smb .museum), another of Berlin's fine state museums. Showcasing a collection of

Renaissance, Baroque and Rococo furnishings from the sixteenth to eighteenth century, it's perhaps less impressive than the Kulturforum's Kunstgewerbemuseum (day tickets to both cost €8), but Schloss has the advantage being able to display many pieces in situ. A first-class audio tour, included in the admission price, greatly enhances a visit.

The exhibition begins with the Italian Renaissance, which sparked Europe-wide stylistic change and was quickly bolstered by the French, whose grand pieces of furniture inhabit the next room. These form a preamble to the German Renaissance, the museum's strong point, and on the first floor themes of love, marriage and fertility are duly explored by sturdy Teutonic furniture, and a series of ornate sixteenth-century backgammon boards. After a brief foray into Dutch Baroque, the self-guided tour leads to a group of gigantic beer mugs, strongly underlining the Germanic nature of the collection and then a few Polish Renaissance pieces, which offer a distraction en route to the museum's most famous exhibit: the silver buffet from the Berliner Schloss – one of its few treasures to survive intact.

The second floor is replete with Chinese vases and commodes that seventeenth-century Dutch and British traders brought back from the Orient, which helped inspire the Rococo movement. Much of the sizeable collection was once that of Frederick II, who was clearly a big fan of the style. The *pièce de résistance*– a gaudy and excessively flamboyant porcelain lampshade – was one of a series that Frederick liked to give as presents in an era when gifts like these would win friends and influence people.

Frauentog and the Kietz

Just beside the Schloss Köpenick and its attendant Schlossplatz are views out over the **Frauentog**, a small bay where Köpenick's fishermen used to cast their nets, which becomes the Langer See further south. This sheltered bay is now home to the Solarbootpavillon (Mon–Fri noon–8pm, Sat & Sun 10am–8pm; ℡060/630 99 97), a boat-rental company that offers the novelty of hiring out **solar-powered craft** from €10 per hour.

On the east side of this small bay and just to the southeast of the Altstadt is the **Kietz**, a cobbled street of fishing cottages whose origins go back to the early thirteenth century. Recent renovation has brightened up the shutters and white-washed facades of most of these cottages, making it a pleasant street for a stroll.

The Grosser Müggelsee and around

Sitting just a few kilometres east of Köpenick, the **Grosser Müggelsee** is one of Berlin's main lakes. The lake has a couple of suburbs – **Friedrichshagen** and **Rahnsdorf** – with lovely, small-town atmospheres. Wandering these suburbs, the shores of the lake and the surrounding woods are welcome relief from pounding Berlin's relentless urban streets, but beware – the Müggelsee area can get crowded at any time of year – in summer, people swarm here for sun and sailing, and in winter to ice-skate.

You can get there by boat with Stern und Kreisschiffahrt (see p.29) from the quay opposite the Rathaus in Köpenick; or take tram #60 from Köpenick's Schlossplatz or the S-Bahn to Friedrichshagen.

Friedrichshagen

Friedrichshagen is a small town founded in 1753 as a settlement for Bohemian cotton spinners who, as a condition of their being allowed to live here, were legally required to plant mulberry trees to rear silkworms. Both tram and train stop beside Friedrichshagen's main drag, **Bölschestrasse**, where a number of single-storey houses survive from the original eighteenth-century settlement, dwarfed by later nineteenth-century blocks, and a few vestigial mulberry trees still cling to life at the roadside. About halfway down this otherwise attractive street the **Christophoruskirche**, a gloomy neo-Gothic church in red brick, puts a Lutheran damper on things.

To get away from it, make for the lake, along Josef-Nawrocki-Strasse, passing the extensive **Berliner Bürgerbrauerei**, the brewery from whose chimney the red flag flew provocatively the day Hitler was sworn in as chancellor. Following the road around leads to a small park at the point where the Spree flows into the Grosser Müggelsee. Here there's a cruise-ship pier and a foot tunnel that takes you under the river. At the other side a path through the woods follows the lakeshore that's perfect for strolling and leads to the Müggelberge 2km away (see below).

Rahnsdorf

Reached by S-Bahn or tram #61 from Friedrichshagen, the little town of **Rahnsdorf** is one of eastern Berlin's more delightful hidden corners, a sprawl of tree-shaded lakeside houses with an old fishing village at its core. Head for **Dorfstrasse**, a cobbled street at the southern end of the village (bus #161 from the S-Bahn to "Grünheider Weg", then follow the signs for Altes Fischerdorf), lined by fishermen's cottages and centred around a small parish church. The best way to explore Rahnsdorf is to simply wander the lakeside and soak up the atmosphere. Just off Fürstenwalder Damm, on the western edge of town, there's an FKK (*Freikörperkultur*) **nudist beach** for hardy souls.

The Müggelberge

Accessed via a two-kilometre lakeshore path from Friedrichshagen (see p.167) or bus #X69 from Köpenick S-Bahn, the **Müggelberge** are a series of rolling forested hills overlooking the Grosser Müggelsee. From bus stop Rübezahl, a path leads south through the woods up to the summit of the hills. Around about the halfway mark is the **Teufelssee** (Devil's Lake), a small pool with a glass-smooth surface, from which various nature trails start. More information on these, and on the flora and fauna of the area, can be obtained at the nearby **Lehrkabinett** information centre (May–Sept Wed–Fri 10am–4pm, Sat & Sun 10am–5pm; Oct–April Wed, Thurs, Sat & Sun 10am–4pm). Pushing on and up through the woods leads to the **Müggelturm** (closed for renovations), a functional-looking observation tower offering great views of the lake and woods, plus a café, bar and restaurant (also closed for renovations). Both the Teufelssee and Müggelturm are accessible by car and bike along reasonably well-surfaced tracks from the main road.

The western suburbs

t's worth heading to the laid-back **western suburbs** for a disparate group of attractions of considerable cultural and historical interest, as well as the woodlands and lakes beyond them that feel a world away – not just a half-dozen S-Bahn stops – from the centre of town. Few people associate Berlin with hikes through dense woodland or swimming off sandy beaches, but that's just what the **Grunewald** forest and the adjacent **Havel** lake offer.

Culturally speaking, the important targets in the west are the **Dahlem museums**, in the suburb of the same name, which contains a world-class ethnological museum as well as museums of Asian art and European cultures. A short bus ride west lie other interesting museums, particularly the **Allied Museum**, where the original Checkpoint Charlie booth is kept.

Beyond here the lakes and verdant woodlands of the **Grunewald** begin in earnest and is flanked by the huge Havel lake, where one bay, the **Wannsee**, is famed for its large sand beach as well as being the location of the **Wannsee villa**, where a Nazi conference sealed the fate of millions of Jews. At the northern end of the Havel, where it joins the Spree, lies **Spandau**, which has a small-town feel far removed from Berlin, a sense enhanced by the presence of its **Zitadelle**, one of the world's best preserved Renaissance forts.

Thanks to the efficient **U- and S-Bahn** systems, it's possible to reach Berlin's western edges in 45 minutes, but once there the only form of public transport is often **bus** – the double-deckers great for sightseeing. Also part of the BVG public transport system and in the price of a day ticket is the hourly **ferry** across the Havel. This, linked with bus #X34 or #134 from Alt-Kladow on the opposite side of the lake, is a picturesque way of getting to Spandau. Given these transport links it's possible to have a good day out visiting a Dahlem museum, going for a short hike in the Grunewald, then rounding the day off with a visit to Spandau's Zitadelle. Alternatively, you can try a programme offered by the private boat trips on the Havel, summarized on pp.28–29.

Dahlem and around

The mostly residential suburb of **Dahlem** lies to the southwest of central Berlin and has the feel of a neat village-like enclave a world away from the city centre. It's home to the better-off bourgeoisie and the Free University. The main draw is the excellent **Museen Dahlem** at Lansstrasse 8 (Dahlem Museums; Tues–Fri 10am–6pm, Sat & Sun 11am–6pm; €6, free Thurs 2–6pm; ⓦwww.smb.museum), a complex clearly signposted from U-Bahn Dahlem-Dorf. Here you'll find the **Museum of Ethnology** and the **Asian Art Museum**. A block in the opposite direction from the underground station at Im Winkel 6/8 is the **Museum of European Cultures**. For information on tickets that cover all of Berlin's state museums see p.65.

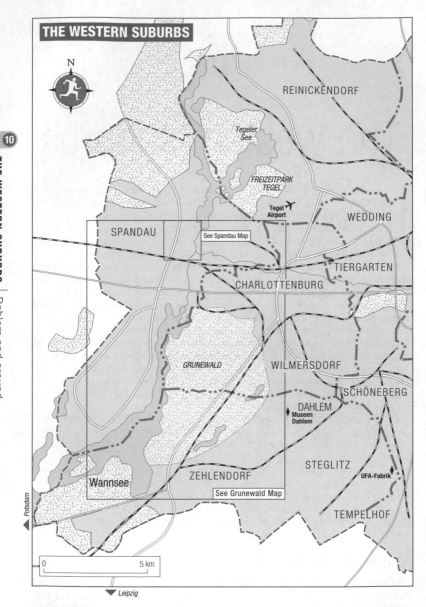

While you're in the vicinity you might like to visit the **Domäne Dahlem**, a working pre-industrial farm-cum-museum, the local parish church **Dorfkirche St Annen** and the city's impressive **Botanical Gardens**. When you've begun to feel heavy on your feet, you should investigate the good **beer gardens** of the area (see p.215) – popular thanks to the local presence of a student population.

The Museum of Ethnology

On display at the **Museum of Ethnology** (Ethnologisches Museum; ☏030/830 14 38) is a small portion – imaginatively and strikingly laid out – of one of the world's most extensive ethnological collections. Covering Asia, Africa, the Americas and the Pacific and South Sea islands – the museum details the varying cultures of dozens of civilizations and ethnic groups, each with their own traditions, religious beliefs and artistic forms. In particular, look out for the dramatically lit group of sailing boats from the South Seas; the huge and macabre engraved stone stele from Guatemala; and the thoughtful exhibition on North American Indians, which not only contains artefacts such as clothing and weapons, but also examples of the non-Indian literature and ephemera – dime novels, advertising signs, rodeo posters and the like – that created many of our perceptions of indigenous American life. Equally imposing is a wall of painted ceremonial masks from South Asia and an exhibit of huts from Polynesia, Micronesia, New Guinea and New Zealand. But many of the smaller pieces, such as bronzes from Benin and carved figures from Central America, are also captivating.

The Asian Art Museum

The exceptional **Asian Art Museum** (Museum für Asiatische Kunst; ☏030/83 01 43 82) is split into two sections – one dealing with the Indian subcontinent and one devoted to the Far East. The former includes an assortment of intricate bronze, wood or jade religious sculptures, many of which come from the Buddhist temples and monasteries along the northern Silk Route, and indeed religious art naturally comprises the great bulk of the collection. There is, however, an intriguing series of miniature paintings on display, in which the artists were clearly free to explore more secular themes; with subjects such as court scenes and nature studies, the works are characterized by a certain informality and playfulness. The Far East section includes an impressive Chinese calligraphy collection but many of the best exhibits are Japanese, and include woodcuts; a stunning seventeenth-century gold and lacquer throne inlaid with mother-of-pearl; and a tearoom.

The Museum of European Cultures

A short signposted walk down Archivstrasse directly opposite U-Bahn Dahlem-Dorf brings you to the modest **Museum of European Cultures**, Im Winkel 6 (Museum Europäischer Kulturen; ☏030/266 42 68 02), which is closed for renovation until the summer of 2011. When it reopens, it will use its collection of handicrafts, paintings, prints and the like to put together changing exhibitions on subjects such as religious practices, handicrafts, modernization and commerce, of the regional and national cultures of the continent. It's strong on German culture, though exhibitions often include plenty of French and Russian artefacts.

Domäne Dahlem and Dorfkirche St Annen

Just west of and over the road from U-Bahn Dahlem-Dorf, the working farm and handicrafts centre **Domäne Dahlem**, Königin-Luise-Strasse 49 (Wed–Mon 10am–6pm; €3; ☏030/666 30 00, ⊛www.domaene-dahlem.de), attempts to show the skills and crafts of the pre-industrial age. The old estate house has a few odds and ends, most intriguing of which are the thirteenth-century swastikas, but the collection of agricultural instruments in an outbuilding is better, with some good early twentieth-century inducements to farmers from grain manufacturers. Elsewhere are woodcarving demonstrations, wool and cotton spinning and various other farm crafts, and at weekends some of the old agricultural machinery is fired up and the animals are paraded.

A little further down Königin-Luise-Strasse, at no. 55, is the **Dorfkirche St Annen**, a pretty little brick church that dates back to 1220. If it's open (officially but unreliably: Mon, Wed & Sat 2–5pm), pop in for a glimpse of the Baroque pulpit and gallery, and carved wooden altar.

The Botanical Gardens

Another way to escape cultural overload in Dahlem is to catch the #X83 bus heading east to the **Botanical Gardens**, Königin-Luise-Strasse 6–8 (daily 9am–dusk, greenhouse closes 30min before garden; €5; ⓦ www.bgbm.org; S-Bahn Botanischer Garten), where you'll find palatial, sticky hothouses sprouting every plant imaginable (some 18,000 species, including several gruesome fly-eating plants, lots of vicious-looking cacti, and a huge variety of tulips), enticingly laid-out gardens and an uninspiring **Botanical Museum** (daily 10am–6pm; included in Botanical Gardens entry or €2).

The Grunewald

The **Grunewald** makes up around 32 square kilometres of mixed woodland and though more than two thirds were cut down in the postwar years for badly needed fuel, subsequent replanting has replaced pine and birch with oak and made it more attractive and popular with Berliners for its clean air and walks.

The eastern edge of the Grunewald, where the wealthy suburb of Zehlendorf begins, is dotted with a series of modest but unusual **museums** that can be combined with time spent hiking in the forest to make a well-rounded day out. The museums include the **Brücke Museum**, which showcases German Expressionism, the **Jagdschloss Grunewald** with its small collection of old masters, the **Allied Museum**, which has important relics of Cold War Berlin, and the **Museumsdorf Düppel**, which re-creates medieval village life. All these museums are connected with the city centre by bus #115 from U-Bahn Fehrberliner Platz and S-Bahn Hohenzollern.

The Brücke Museum

Bus #115 stops at Pücklerstrasse, just outside the **Brücke Museum**, Bussardsteig 9 (Wed–Mon 11am–5pm; €4; ⓦ www.bruecke-museum.de), which displays German Expressionist works by the group known as Die Brücke ("The Bridge"). The group worked in Dresden and Berlin from 1905 to 1913, and their work was banned by the Nazis. The big names are Kirchner, Heckel and Schmidt-Rottluff, who painted Expressionist cityscapes – using rich colours and playful perspectives – and who had a great influence on later artists. Many of their works were destroyed during the war, making this collection all the more interesting. Museum exhibitions change regularly, but always try to include early and later works from the movement.

Jagdschloss Grunewald and Grunewald hikes

From the Brücke Museum it's a ten-minute walk west along Pücklerstrasse into the depths of the Grunewald and **Jagdschloss Grunewald**, Hüttenweg 10 (April–Oct Tues–Sun 10am–6pm; Nov–March Sat & Sun tours at 11am, 1pm & 3pm; April–Oct €4, Nov–March €5; ⓣ030/813 35 97), a royal hunting lodge built in the sixteenth century and enlarged by Friedrichs I and II. Today it's a museum housing old furniture and Dutch and German paintings, including works by Cranach the Elder and Rubens. There's also a small hunting museum in the outbuildings. However, walking around the adjacent lake, the **Grunewaldsee** may prove more stimulating than the collections. The Jagdschloss is also a good

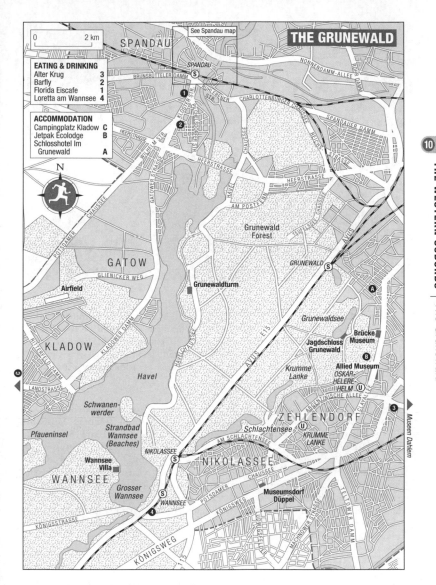

starting point for longer **hikes** into the Grunewald: a 45-minute ramble along the eastern side of the Grunewaldsee brings you to S-Bahn Grunewald; or you can walk south to U-Bahn Krumme Lanke in about an hour, crossing Hutten Weg and then Onkel-Tom-Strasse to then walk around the shores of Krumme Lanke lake.

The Allied Museum

If you have an interest in Cold War Berlin, you should walk fifteen minutes southeast of the Jadgschloss Grunewald along Im Jagen to the **Allied Museum**,

▲ A display in the Allied Museum

Clayallee 135 (Thurs–Tues 10am–6pm; free; Ⓦ www.alliiertenmuseum.de; U-Bahn Oskar-Helene-Helm). The highlights here are a segment of the Wall, a guardtower, and, most impressively, the original Checkpoint Charlie guardpost. The rest of the museum delivers a well-presented, but nevertheless somewhat turgid exhibition on Cold War Berlin, enlivened only occasionally by a spy story.

Museumsdorf Düppel

You can see a Berlin of a very different sort at the reconstructed medieval country village **Museumsdorf Düppel**, Clauertstrasse 11 (Düppel Museum Village; Easter–Oct Thurs 3–7pm, Sun & holidays Sun 10am–5pm; €2; ☏030/802 66 71; Ⓦ www.dueppel.de; bus #115 to Ludwigsfelderstrasse), in the far southwest edge of the city. The open-air museum gives an impression of what things might have looked like hereabouts 800 years ago with its dozen thatched buildings built on the actual site of a twelfth-century settlement. Here traditional local breeds of sheep are reared and old strains of rye grown, and demonstrations of handicrafts and farming techniques from the Middle Ages take place. If you've still time and energy afterwards, explore the lovely surrounding Düppel Forest.

The Wannsee

Of the many lakes that dot the Grunewald, the best known is the **Wannsee**. The main attraction here is the **Strandbad Wannsee**, a kilometre-long strip of pale sand that's the largest inland beach in Europe, and one that's packed as soon as the sun comes out. From here it's easy to wander into the forests and to smaller, less-populated beaches along the lakeside road **Havelchaussee**. The main tourist destination around the Wannsee is, however, the **Wannsee villa** (see box, p.176). A useful nearby pick-me-up comes in the form of the infinitely more pleasant **Pfaueninsel**, once a royal island playground that's now a bucolic park in which peacocks roam.

Most destinations around the Wannsee are best reached by **public transport** from S-Bahn Wannsee, from where various buses radiate. The only exception to this is the Strandbad Wannsee which is a ten-minute walk from S-Bahn Nikolassee, one stop earlier on the line from central Berlin. Cross the main road outside S-Bahn Wannsee and you're a couple of minutes' walk through a park away from regular ferries to Alt-Kladow (and included in the price of a BVG day-ticket).

Strandbad Wannsee and the Havelchaussee

In essence Berlin's seaside, the **Strandbad Wannsee** has changed little in character since Heinrich Zille sketched the working classes at play here in the late nineteenth century. It's a busy commercial beach scene, but if you are looking for a quieter sandy spot by the water, you should head north along the shore, following the **Havelchaussee**. Usefully, bus #218 from S-Bahn Wannsee and Nikolassee goes this way and runs along 6km of sandy coves where there are few facilities. This area is also good for a spot of hiking – both along the lakeshore and inland into the forest.

One possible start or terminus of a hike is the **Grunewaldturm** (daily 10am–6pm; €1), an observation tower around 4km north of the Strandbad and right next to the Havel. Built at the end of the nineteenth century as a memorial to Kaiser Wilhelm I, this 55-metre-high tower has a smart restaurant and fine views out across the lakes.

The Wannsee villa

While not the most enjoyable of sights, one place that should on no account be missed on a trip to the Wannsee is the house overlooking the lake, where, on January 20, 1942, the fate of European Jewry was determined: the **Wannsee villa**, Am Grossen Wannsee 56–58 (Haus der Wannsee Konferenze; daily 10am–6pm; free; ⓦ www.ghwk.de). To get here, catch a #114 bus from S-Bahn Wannsee to stop "Haus der Wannsee-Konferenz".

The villa exhibition shows the entire process of the Holocaust, from segregation and persecution to the deportation and eventual murder of the Jews from Germany, its allies and all the lands the Third Reich conquered. It is deeply moving: many of the photographs and accounts are horrific, and the events they describe seem part of a world far removed from this quiet locale – which, in many ways, underlines the tragedy. Particularly disturbing is the photograph of four generations of women – babe-in-arms, young mother, grandmother and ancient great-grandmother – moments before their execution on a sand dune in Latvia.

The room where the conference took place remains as it was, with documents from the meeting on the table and photographs of participants ranged around the walls, their biographies showing many lived to a comfortable old age. Even fifty years after the event, to stand in the room where a decision was formalized to coldly and systematically annihilate a race of people brings a shiver of fear and rage.

Pfaueninsel

Designed as a royal fantasy getaway on one of the largest of the Havel islands, the **Pfaueninsel** (Peacock Island; ⓦ www.spsg.de) is now a conservation zone with a flock of peacocks stalking around its landscaped park. No cars are allowed on the island (nor are dogs, ghetto-blasters or smoking), which is accessed by a regular passenger ferry (daily: March–April & Sept–Oct 9am–6pm; May–Aug 8am–9pm;

The Wannsee conference

The conference at the **Wannsee villa** on January 20, 1942, was held at the instigation of Reinhard Heydrich, Chief of Reich Security Head Office, who had been ordered by Göring to submit plans for rounding up, deporting and destroying all Jews in Reich territory. Heydrich summoned SS and government officials, including Adolf Eichmann and Roland Freisler, who later gained infamy as the judge at the Volksgerichtshof (see Kammergericht, p.129). Eichmann kept a complete set of minutes of the meeting, and these documents, discovered after the war – despite the fact that all recipients had been requested to destroy their copies – played an important part in the Nürnberg trials of war criminals.

The problem Heydrich delineated was that Europe contained eleven million Jews: the "Final Solution" to the "Jewish Question" was that these people should be taken to camps and worked to death, if they were able-bodied, murdered on arrival if not. Those who survived would eventually be executed, since, under Nazi principles of natural selection, they would be the toughest, and in Heydrich's words could be "the germ cell of a new Jewish development". In these early stages systematic killing machines like Auschwitz and Treblinka were not yet fully operational. More discussion was spent on how the Jews should be rounded up: great deception would prevent panic and revolt, and the pretence that Jews were being moved for "resettlement" was extremely important. Heydrich charged Eichmann with this task, which eventually cost him his life when he was sentenced to death for war crimes in Israel in 1960.

At no time during the conference were the words "murder" or "killing" written down, only careful euphemisms to shield the enormity of what was being planned. Reading through the minutes (copies are kept in the villa's library), it's difficult not to be shocked by the matter-of-fact manner in which the business was discussed, and the way in which politeness and efficiency absorb and absolve all concerned. When sterilization was suggested as one "solution" it was rejected as "unethical" by a doctor present, and there was much self-congratulation as various officials described their areas as "Judenfrei" (free of Jews).

Heydrich died following an assassination attempt in Prague a few months later; some of the others present did not survive the war either, but, in contrast to the millions who were destroyed by their organizational ability, many of the Wannsee delegation lived on to gain a pension from the postwar German state.

Nov–Feb 10am–4pm; €2) from the terminus of bus #218 from S-Bahn Wannsee. The island's attractions include a mini-Schloss, built by Friedrich Wilhelm II for his mistress and today containing a small **museum** (April–Oct daily 10am–5pm; Nov–March Sat & Sun 11am–3.30pm; €3). Most enjoyable, though, are the gardens, landscaped by Peter Lenné, the original designer of the Tiergarten. The Pfaueninsel was a favourite party venue for the Nazis: on August 15, 1936, to mark the end of the Olympic Games, Joseph Goebbels, minister of propaganda, hosted a massive "Italian evening" here for over a thousand guests, including many famous German film stars and celebrities of the day and hundreds of foreign visitors including British MPs.

Spandau

SPANDAU, situated on the confluence of the Spree and Havel rivers, about 10km northwest of its centre, is Berlin's oldest suburb. Granted a town charter in 1232, it managed to escape the worst of the wartime bombing, preserving a couple of old village-like streets – at their best during the Christmas market – and an ancient moated fort, the **Zitadelle**. But the word Spandau immediately brings to mind the

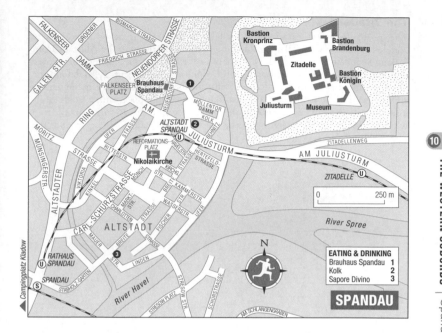

name of its jail's most famous – indeed in later years only – prisoner, **Rudolf Hess**. However, there's little connection between Hess and Spandau itself. The jail, 4km away from the centre on Wilhelmstrasse, was demolished after his death to make way for a supermarket for the British armed forces.

The Altstadt

In comparison to its Zitadelle, Spandau's **Altstadt** or old town is of minor interest. It begins just to the northeast of the Rathaus and is at its best around the Medieval **Nikolaikirche**; the **Reformationsplatz** (with a good *Konditorei*), where playful sculptures adorn the modern marketplace; and in the restored street called **Kolk**. Also here is the **Brauhaus Spandau**, a nineteenth-century brewery that produces beer to a medieval recipe, and has tours explaining the brewing process.

Rudolf Hess (1894–1987)

Rudolf Hess marched in the Munich Beer Hall *Putsch* of 1923 and was subsequently imprisoned with Hitler in Landsberg jail, where he took the dictation of *Mein Kampf*. For a time he was the **deputy leader** of the Nazi party, second only to the Führer himself. An experienced World War I airman, he flew himself to Scotland in 1941, ostensibly in an attempt to sue for peace with King George VI and ally Great Britain with Germany against the Soviet Union. It remains unclear whether he did this with Hitler's blessing, but there is evidence to suggest that the Führer knew of Hess's plans. Either way, he was immediately arrested and Churchill refused to meet him; he was held until sentenced to life imprisonment at the Nürnberg trials. He finally committed suicide in 1987 in his Spandau jail – the only inmate in a jail designed for six hundred – hanging himself on a short piece of lamp flex, aged 93.

The Zitadelle

The postcard-pretty **Zitadelle** (Citadel; daily 10am–5pm; €4.50; Ⓦwww
.zitadelle-spandau.de; U-Bahn Zitadelle; 10min walk through the Aldstadt from
S-Bahn Spandau from where the #134 from Alt Kladow stops), just northeast over
the Havel from the Altstadt, was established in the twelfth century to defend the
town. Its moat and russet walls were built during the Renaissance by an Italian
architect and it's an explorable, if not totally engrossing, place with a small local-
history museum, a pricey restaurant and the thirteenth-century **Juliusturm**, from
which there's a good view over the ramshackle Zitadelle interior and the
surrounding countryside.

Day-trips

W hen Berlin's city fringes don't seem like breather enough from its bustle, a day-trip into its sleepy Brandenburg hinterland might be just the thing. This federal state is replete with gentle scenery, a patchwork of beech forests, fields of dazzling rapeseed and sunflowers and heaths, all sewn together by a multitude of rivers, lakes and waterways. And thanks to Berlin's superb transport network, all are easy and economical day-trips. But should you wish to strike out by car or bike, you're sure to find cruising the flat tree-lined avenues that typify Brandenburg's minor roads a pleasure.

Almost all the state's headline attractions are southwest of Berlin in **Potsdam**, a town whose size is effectively doubled by surrounding landscaped gardens dotted with royal piles and follies, which include Frederick the Great's famous Schloss Sanssouci. Meanwhile, just north beyond Berlin's fringes, the town of Oranienburg is far less attractive, but equally absorbing as the site of former concentration camp **Sachsenhausen**. East of Oranienburg the giant heaths of the Schorfheide begin to take hold and are the home to a dignified ruined monastery at **Chorin** and an impressive ship hoist at **Niederfinow**.

Worth investigating before you travel is the website of the regional tourism authority Tourismus Marketing Brandenburg (ⓣ0331/200 47 47, ⓦwww .brandenburg-tourism.com), and the Brandenburg-Berlin Ticket which allows up to five people to travel together anywhere within Brandenburg for one day (9am–3am) on all regional trains (RE, IRE, RB) as well as on the entire Berlin BVG network. The ticket costs €27 online at ⓦwww.bahn.de, or €29 from train stations; for timetables see ⓦwww.vbb-online.de.

Potsdam

For most visitors **POTSDAM** means **Sanssouci**, Frederick the Great's splendid landscaped park of architectural treasures which once completed Berlin as the grand Prussian capital. However, Potsdam's origins date back to the tenth-century Slavonic settlement Poztupimi, and predate Berlin by a couple of hundred years. The castle built here in 1160 marked the first step in the town's gradual transformation from sleepy fishing backwater to **royal residence** and **garrison town**, a role it enjoyed under the Hohenzollerns until the abdication of Kaiser Wilhelm II in 1918. World War II left Potsdam badly damaged: on April 14, 1945, a bombing raid killed four thousand people, destroyed many fine Baroque buildings and reduced its centre to ruins. Less than four months later – on August 2 – the victorious Allies converged on Potsdam's **Schloss Cecilienhof** to hammer out the details of a division of Germany and Europe. Potsdam itself ended up in the Soviet zone, where modern "socialist" building programmes steadily erased many architectural memories of the town's uncomfortably prosperous imperial past. Yet it's this past that has given us its most popular sights, apart from those at Park Sanssouci; there are more across the Havel in **Babelsberg**, which is best known as the site of the most important film studio in German film history.

Arrival, town transport and information

All trains, including the S-Bahn from Berlin (around 30min) arrive in Potsdam's Hauptbahnhof, which incorporates a small shopping mall. The southern entrance delivers you to the city's main **bus station**, where you should pick up **bus** #695 or #X15 run by the Verkehrsbetrieb Potsdam (ViP; Ⓦ www.vip-potsdam.de) if you wish to hightail it straight to Schloss Sanssouci. Alternatively take #695, #X5, #650 or #606 to stop "Neues Palais" if you'd like to wander through the entire Sanssouci Park and back to the train station via the Altstadt. If you're bound for the town centre, you could take **tram** #92 from the Hauptbahnhof's west entrance, though it might be quicker and more interesting to simply head north for ten minutes' **walk** across the Lange Brücke into the centre. Use of Potsdam's local bus and tram services is covered by a zone C BVG ticket, so if you're coming from Berlin, buying an ABC day ticket is the most economical way to get here and around.

However, the most rewarding and practical way to explore Potsdam is to **rent a bike**, particularly for reaching the northern part of town as well as the area around **Babelsberg**. Rebhah Rent-a-Bike (daily Mon–Fri 9am–7pm, Sat & Sun 9am–8pm; €11/day; Ⓣ 0331/270 62 10) operates out of a container in a park outside the Hauptbahnhof's northern entrance. They provide a free map of a seventeen-kilometre route that takes in all the main sites in a day.

Potsdam's well-equipped **tourist office** is at Brandenburger Strasse 3 (April–Oct Mon–Fri 9.30am–6pm, Sat & Sun 9.30am–4pm; Nov–March Mon–Fri 10am–6pm, Sat & Sun 9.30am–2pm; Ⓣ 0331/27 55 80, Ⓦ www.potsdam -tourism.com), by the Brandenburg Gate.

The Town

North from the train station beyond Lange Brücke is the **Alter Markt**, the fringe of Potsdam's town centre. From here the northbound and arterial **Friedrich-Ebert-Strasse** leads to its pedestrianized main shopping street **Brandenburger Strasse**. Part of a Baroque quarter, it's best appreciated off the main drag, but in truth the town's attractions are scant in comparison with what awaits in Park Sanssouci.

The Alter Markt

The arresting outlines of the unmistakably GDR-era *Hotel Mercure* and the stately domed **Nikolaikirche** frame the **Alter Markt**, the triangular plaza between. Its surging traffic and extensive building work make it an unprepossessing city gateway, but for most of its life it harboured bustling squares and streets. It was here that the town's earliest fortifications were built and where the medieval town flourished, a past that the highly visible excavations here continually unravel, as remnants of various crafts and the occasional buried treasure are found. But the Alter Markt is best known as the former site of the **Stadtschloss**, a Baroque residence built by the Great Elector between 1662 and 1669. World War II – specifically April 14 and 15, 1945 – reduced it to a bare, roofless shell, and the

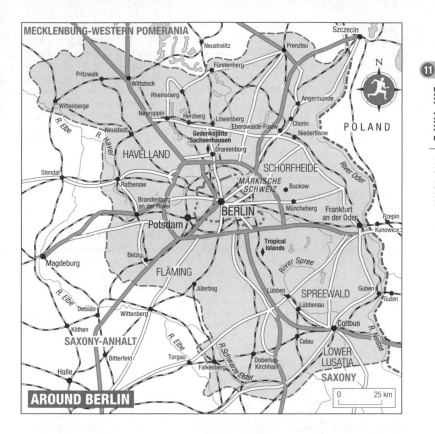

AROUND BERLIN

GDR demolished what remained in 1960 – around eighty percent of the building – to remove the last vestiges of Potsdam's grandest imperial buildings.

A parliament building (**Landtag**) for Brandenburg is planned on the site copying the footprint of the old Schloss; though it may end up a modern building, the gate to the palace forecourt, the domed **Fortunaportal**, has been reconstructed, completing the re-creation of three domed structures that traditionally dominated the Alter Markt. The most significant of these is the elegant, Schinkel-designed Neoclassical **Nikolaikirche** (Mon 2–5pm, Tues–Sat 10am–5pm, Sun 11.30am–5pm), while the third dome belongs to Potsdam's former **Rathaus** (daily Tues–Sun 10am–6pm; free), built during the mid-eighteenth century in Palladian Classical style. Under the GDR the building became an arts centre, a role it retains to this day. The **obelisk** in front of the Rathaus was designed by Knobelsdorff and originally bore four reliefs depicting the Great Elector and his successors. When re-erected during the 1970s these were replaced with reliefs of the architects who shaped much of Potsdam: Schinkel, Knobelsdorff, Gontard and Persius.

The Marstall, Filmmuseum and Am Neuen Markt

Across the main road, Friedrich-Ebert-Strasse, from the Nikolaikirche, lies the squat but elegant **Marstall**, the oldest town-centre survivor. Built as an orangerie towards the end of the eighteenth century and converted into stables by that scourge of frivolity, Friedrich Wilhelm I, the building owes its current appearance to Knobelsdorff, who extended and prettified it during the eighteenth century. Today it houses Potsdam's **Filmmuseum**, Breite Strasse 1a (daily 10am–6pm; €3.50; ☎0331/271 81 12, ⓦwww.filmmuseum-potsdam.de), which draws on material from Babelsberg's UFA studios nearby (see p.189) to present both a technical and artistic history of German film from 1895 to 1980, with some particularly fascinating material concerning the immediate postwar period. There's a vaguely hands-on feel, with a few visitor-operated bioscopes and numerous screens playing clips. The museum **cinema** is the best in Potsdam and there's also a good **café**. Just behind the Marstall, **Am Neuen Markt** leads to a few handsome vestiges of old Potsdam, including some improbably grand eighteenth-century coaching stables with an entrance in the form of a triumphal arch.

The Baroque quarter and around

North beyond Alter Markt you pass through an area once occupied by Potsdam's **Altstadt** before this was comprehensively destroyed in the war. Luckily, the **Baroque quarter** to the north survived the war substantially intact and slowly emerges along the north end of Friedrich-Ebert-Strasse. **Bassinplatz**, though disfigured by a huge modern bus station, offers a good introduction thanks to the nineteenth-century **Peter-Pauls-Kirche**, a replica of the campanile of San Zeno Maggiore in Verona. At the southeastern corner of the square lies the **Französische Kirche**, completed according to plans by Knobelsdorff in 1753, in imitation of the Pantheon in Rome, a recurring theme in German architecture of the period. Just north of Bassinplatz, lies the appealing **Holländisches Viertel** or "Dutch quarter", where 134 gabled, red-brick houses were put up by Dutch builders for immigrants from Holland who were invited to work in Potsdam by Friedrich Wilhelm I. The quarter has seen periods of dereliction since, but recent restoration and gentrification has produced a small colony of trendy shops and cafés.

From the **Holländisches Viertel** the **Baroque quarter** – built between 1732 and 1742 on the orders of Friedrich Wilhelm I – continues west around **Branden-burger Strasse**. The area – some 584 houses – was intended for trades people as the town rapidly expanded. On cross-street Lindenstrasse, the Dutch-style former **Kommandantenhaus**, nos. 54–55, is a building with uncomfortable associations: until the *Wende* it served as a Stasi detention centre known as the "Lindenhotel". It now houses **Gedenkstätte Lindenstrasse** (Tues–Thurs 10am–6pm; €3 with tour, €1.50 without); you can view the chilling cells and an exhibition details the building's use, which included a spell as a Nazi prison and "hereditary-health court", where decisions about compulsory sterilization were made. Further north up Lindenstrasse is the **Jägertor** or "Hunter's Gate", one of Potsdam's three surviving town gates, surmounted by a sculpture of a stag succumbing to a pack of baying hounds. Meanwhile, the triumphal **Brandenburger Tor** marks the western end of Brandenburger Strasse – built by Gontard in 1733 with a playfulness lacking in its Berlin namesake. The **Grünes Gitter** park entrance (see opposite) lies just beyond the northwestern corner of the adjacent **Luisenplatz**.

Park Sanssouci

Stretching west out of Potsdam's town centre, **Park Sanssouci** was built for Frederick the Great as a retreat after he decided in 1744 that he needed a residence where he could live "without cares" – "sans souci" in the French spoken in court. The task was entrusted to architect Georg von Knobelsdorff, who had already proved himself on other projects in Potsdam and Berlin. **Schloss Sanssouci**, on a

Combination tickets for Park Sanssouci buildings

Entrance to Park Sanssouci is free, although a €2 donation is suggested. If you plan to visit several buildings in the Park, consider getting a **combination ticket**. A **Premium-Tageskarte** (€15) allows entry to all Park buildings and is available only at Schloss Sanssouci. The regular **Tageskarte** (€12) is sold at all palaces, and the visitors' centre, and gives access to all buildings in Park Sanssouci except Schloss Sanssouci itself. Despite calling themselves Tageskarten (day tickets), both the above are valid for two consecutive days.

hill overlooking the town, took three years to complete, while the extensive parklands were laid out over the following five years. As a finishing touch Frederick ordered the construction of the **Neues Palais** at the western end of the park, to mark the end of the Seven Years' War. Numerous additions over the following hundred and fifty years or so included the **Orangerie**. The park is most beautiful in spring, when the trees are in leaf and the flowers in bloom, and least crowded on weekdays. The main **visitors' centre** (daily: March–Oct 8.30am–5pm; Nov–Feb 9am–4pm; ☏331/969 42 02, ⊛www.spsg.de) is by the historic windmill (see p.185).

The Grünes Gitter and around

The **Grünes Gitter** provides a southeastern entrance to Park Sanssouci and has an information kiosk. Immediately north of here is the 1850 Italianate **Friedenskirche** (mid-May to Oct daily 10am–6pm; free), designed by Persius for Friedrich Wilhelm IV. With its 39-metre-high campanile and lakeside setting, it conjures up the southern European atmosphere that Friedrich Wilhelm strove for by using the St Clemente Basilica in Rome as a model, and with the design centred on the magnificent Byzantine apse mosaic from Murano. Adjoining the church, the domed Hohenzollern mausoleum contains the tombs of Friedrich Wilhelm IV and his wife Elizabeth, and Friedrich III and his wife Victoria. The garden to the west is the **Marly-Garten**, once the kitchen garden of Friedrich I, who named it, with intentional irony, after Louis XIV's luxurious Marly park.

Schloss Sanssouci

To approach **Schloss Sanssouci** as Frederick the Great might have done, make for the eighteenth-century **obelisk** on Schopenhauerstrasse. Beyond, Hauptallee runs through the ornate Knobelsdorff-designed **Obelisk-Portal** – two clusters of pillars flanked by the goddesses Flora and Pomona – to the **Grosse Fontäne**, the biggest of the park's many fountains, around which stand a host of Classical statues, notably Venus and Mercury. The approach to the Schloss itself leads up through terraced ranks of vines that are among the northernmost in Germany.

Frederick had definite ideas about what he wanted and worked closely with Knobelsdorff on the palace design, which was to be a place where the king, who had no great love for his capital, Berlin, or his wife Elizabeth Christine, could escape both. It's a surprisingly modest one-storey Baroque affair, topped by an oxidized green dome and ornamental statues, looking out over the vine terraces towards the high-rises of central Potsdam.

The **interior** of Schloss Sanssouci (April–Oct Tues–Sun 9am–5pm, €8; Nov–March Tues–Sun 9am–4pm; €12) can only be visited by **guided tour**. These take place every twenty minutes and tickets for the whole day go on sale at 9am – arrive early as demand is high. Once inside, you'll find a frenzy of Rococo in

▲ Detail on an urn at Park Sanssouci

the twelve rooms where Frederick lived and entertained his guests – a process that usually entailed quarrelling with them. The most eye-catching rooms are the opulent **Marmorsaal** (Marble Hall) and the **Konzertzimmer** (Concert Room), where the flute-playing king forced eminent musicians to play his own works on concert evenings. Frederick's favourite haunt was his library where, surrounded by two thousand volumes – mainly French translations of classics and a sprinkling of contemporary French writings – he could oversee work on his tomb. One of Frederick's most celebrated house guests was Voltaire, who lived here from 1750 to 1753, acting as a kind of private tutor to the king, finally leaving when he'd had enough of Frederick's behaviour, damning the king's intellect with faint praise and accusing him of treating "the whole world as slaves". In revenge Frederick had Voltaire's former room decorated with carvings of apes and parrots. The **Damenflügel**, the west wing of the Schloss (mid-May to mid-Oct Sat & Sun 10am–5pm; €2), was added in 1840, and its thirteen rooms housed ladies and gentlemen of the court. Nearby on the terrace is a wrought-iron summerhouse protecting a weather-beaten copy of a Classical statue, while just to the south an eighteenth-century sculpture of Cleopatra looks over the graves of Frederick's horses.

Around Schloss Sanssouci

East of Schloss Sanssouci, overlooking the ornamental **Holländischer Garten**, or Dutch Garden, is the restrained Baroque **Bildergalerie** (mid-May to mid-Oct Tues–Sun 10am–5pm; included in price of guided tour), which, it's claimed, was the first building in Europe built specifically as a museum. Unfortunately, wartime destruction and looting scattered the contents, but the new collection includes Caravaggio's wonderful *Incredulity of St Thomas* and several works by Rubens and Van Dyck.

On the opposite side of the Schloss, from a point near the Cleopatra statue, steps lead down to the **Neue Kammern** (March Sat & Sun 10am–5pm; April–Oct Tues–Sun 10am–5pm; €4 with tour, €3 without), the architectural twin of the Bildergalerie, originally an orangerie and later a guesthouse. Immediately west is the prim **Sizilianischer Garten** or Sicilian Garden, crammed with coniferous trees and subtropical plants, complementing the **Nordischer Garten**, another ornamental garden just to the north, whose most interesting feature is the strange-looking **Felsentor** or Rock Gate, a gateway fashioned out of uncut stones and topped by a lumpen-looking eagle with outstretched wings.

Frederick was prepared to go to some lengths to achieve the desired carefree rural ambience for Sanssouci and retained an old wooden windmill as an ornament just north of the Neue Kammern. Four years after his death, this was replaced by a rustic-looking stone construction, the **Historische Mühle**, now a restaurant.

The Orangerie and around

From the western corner of the Sizilianischer Garten, **Maulbeerallee**, a road open to traffic, cuts through the park past the **Orangerie** (mid-May to mid-Oct Tues–Sun 10am–5pm; €3). This Italianate Renaissance-style structure with its belvedere towers is one of the most visually impressive buildings in the park. A series of terraces with curved retaining walls sporting waterspouts in the shape of lions' heads lead up to the sandy-coloured building, whose slightly down-at-heel appearance adds character.

It was built at the behest of Friedrich IV and, like the Friedenskirche (see p.183), inspired by architecture seen on his Italian travels. The facade is lined with allegorical statues set in niches, such as "Industry" who holds a cog wheel. The western wing of the building is still used as a refuge for tropical plants in winter, and during the summer it's possible to ascend the western tower for views of the Neues Palais and vistas of Potsdam's high-rises. The Orangerie also houses a gallery, the **Raphaelsaal**, with copies of paintings looted by Napoleon.

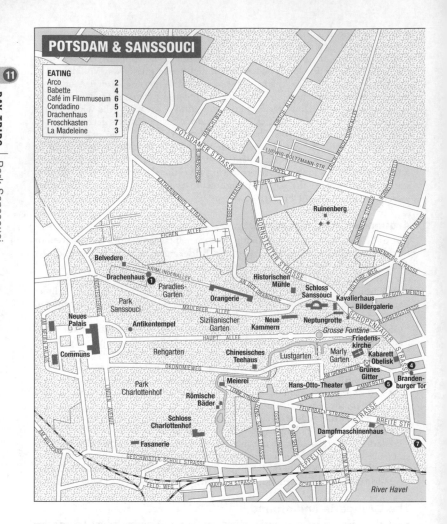

EATING

Arco	2
Babette	4
Café im Filmmuseum	6
Condadino	5
Drachenhaus	1
Froschkasten	7
La Madeleine	3

The Belvedere, Drachenhaus and Antikentempel

From the western wing of the Orangerie, the arrow-straight Krimlindenallee, lined with lime trees, leads towards a Rococo **Belvedere**, the last building to be built under Frederick the Great. It was the only building in the whole park to suffer serious war damage, but has now been restored to its former glory. A couple of hundred metres short of the Belvedere, a path off to the left leads to the **Drachenhaus**, a one-time vintner's house built in the style of a Chinese pagoda for the small vineyard nearby. Today the café inside (see p.190) is an ideal place to interrupt wanderings. Southwest of the Drachenhaus, a pathway leads to the **Antikentempel**, built in 1768 to house part of Frederick the Great's art collection. This domed rotunda is now the last resting place of a number of Hohenzollerns, including the Empress Auguste Victoria, and Hermine, the woman Wilhelm II married in exile, and who became known as the "last Empress".

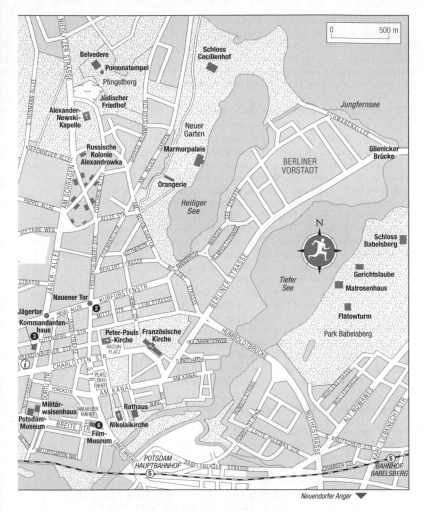

Neuendorfer Anger ▼

The Neues Palais

Rising through the trees at the western end of Park Sansoucci, the **Neues Palais** (April–Oct Mon–Thurs, Sat & Sun 9am–5pm, €6 with tour, €5 without; Nov–March Mon–Thurs, Sat & Sun 9am–4pm, €5 with tour), is another massive Rococo extravaganza from Frederick the Great's time, built between 1763 and 1769 to reaffirm Prussian might after the Seven Years' War. At the centre of the palace is a huge green-weathered dome, topped by a crown, while the edges of the roof around the entire building are adorned by lines of Classical figures, mass-produced by a team of sculptors. The main entrance is in the western facade, and once inside, you'll find the interior predictably opulent, particularly as you enter the vast and startling **Grottensaal** on the ground floor which is decorated entirely with shells and semi-precious stones to form images of lizards and dragons. The equally huge **Marmorsaal** is the other highlight, with its beautiful floor of patterned marble slabs. The southern wing contains Frederick's apartments and theatre where he enjoyed Italian opera and French plays. The last imperial resident of the Neues Palais was Kaiser Wilhelm II, who packed sixty train carriages with the palace contents before fleeing with his family in November 1918, following the revolution and abdication. Facing the Neues Palais entrance are the **Communs,** a couple of Rococo fantasies joined by a curved colonnade. They look grandiose, but their purpose was mundane: they housed the palace serving and maintenance staff.

The Rehgarten and Park Charlottenhof

From the Neues Palais, Ökonomieweg leads east between the **Rehgarten** or Deer Garden, the former court hunting ground (and still home to a few deer) and Park **Charlottenhof**, created by Friedrich Wilhelm III as a Christmas present for his son, and today one of Sanssouci's quieter corners. A path leads over a bridge past a small farm building to the **Römische Bäder** (May–Oct Tues–Sun 10am–5pm; €3), built by Schinkel and Persius in convincing imitation of a Roman villa.

Across the lawns to the south is **Schloss Charlottenhof** (May–Oct Tues–Sun 10am–5pm; €4), another Roman-style building, again designed by Schinkel and Persius for Friedrich IV. Though designated a palace, it is, in reality, little more than a glorified villa, but its interior, unlike most Sanssouci buildings, is original. The effect is impressive: the hallway is bathed in blue light filtered through coloured glass decorated with stars, a prelude to the **Kupferstichzimmer**, or print room, whose walls are now covered in copies of Italian Renaissance paintings. Immediately east of Schloss Charlottenhof is the **Dichterhain** (Poets' Grove), an open space dotted with busts of Goethe, Schiller and Herder, among others. West of here through the woods and across a racetrack-shaped clearing called the **Hippodrom** is the **Fasanerie**, another Italian-style edifice built between 1842 and 1844.

On the Ökonomieweg – en route back to the Grünes Gitter entrance – you'll pass the slightly kitsch **Chinesisches Teehaus** (May–Oct Tues–Sun 10am–5pm; €2), a kind of Rococo pagoda housing a small museum of Chinese and Meissen porcelain and surrounded by eerily lifelike statues of Oriental figures.

The Neuer Garten and Schloss Cecilienhof

Immediately northeast of Potsdam's centre lies another large park complex, the **Neuer Garten,** where the **Marmorpalais** (Marble Palace; March Tues–Fri tours only; April–Oct Tues–Sun 10am–5pm; Nov–March Sat & Sun 10am–4pm; €5 with tour, €4 without; ☎0331/969 42 46), was built for Friedrich Wilhelm II, who died a premature death here in 1797, allegedly a consequence of his dissolute lifestyle. It has now been restored to an approximation of its original royal condition and the sumptuous rooms can be seen once again.

Also in the grounds of the Neuer Garten, but looking like a mock-Elizabethan mansion, is **Schloss Cecilienhof** (April–Oct Tues–Sun 9am–5pm; Nov–March Tues–Sun 9am–4pm; €6 with tour, €5 without; Ⓦwww.spsg.de; tram #92 or #96 to stop "Reiterweg/Alleestrasse" then change to bus #692); the last palace to be commissioned by the Hohenzollerns, it was begun in 1913 and completed in 1917, the war evidently doing nothing to change the architectural style. Cecilienhof would only rate a passing mention, were it not for the fact that the **Potsdam conference** – confirming earlier decisions made at Yalta about the postwar European order – was held here from July 17 to August 2, 1945. The conference was heavily symbolic, providing a chance for Truman, Stalin and Churchill (replaced mid-conference by Clement Attlee) to show the world that they had truly won the war by meeting in the heart of the ruined Reich. As a result, the main attraction inside is the **Konferenzsaal**, or conference chamber, which resembles an assembly hall of a minor British public school, where the Allies worked out details of the division of Europe. Everything has been left pretty much as it was in 1945, with the huge round table specially made in Moscow for the conference still in place. It's also possible to visit the delegates' workrooms, furnished in varying degrees of chintziness. Cecilienhof has been used as an expensive hotel and restaurant since 1960, both for the deep of pocket.

Babelsberg

On the eastern bank of the Havel is **Babelsberg**, once a town but now officially part of Potsdam. Lining the banks of the Tiefer See is **Park Babelsberg**, Potsdam's third great park complex, designed by Lenné, and not as visited. Tracks lead through the hilly, roughly wooded park to **Schloss Babelsberg** (closed for renovation; @www.spsg.de), a neo-Gothic architectural extravaganza, built by Schinkel at the behest of Prince Wilhelm, brother of Friedrich Wilhelm IV, and inspired by England's Windsor Castle.

But Babelsberg's real claim to fame is as the one-time heart of the German film industry. Founded in 1917, it was here that the UFA film studios rivalled Hollywood during the 1920s. Today the huge old studio complex is given over to **Filmpark Babelsberg** (April–Oct daily 10am–6pm; €17; ☎0331/721 27 55, @www.filmpark.de), and served by buses #690 from Babelsberg's S-Bahn station and #601 and #602 from Potsdam's Hauptbahnhof. It's mainly of interest to those with a good knowledge of German film industry, with films produced here during its heyday including *Das Kabinett des Dr Caligari*, *Metropolis* and *Der Blaue Engel*. It's now reinvented itself as a theme park and visitors can wander through costume and props departments and watch technicians going through the motions of shooting film scenes. It's also possible to visit the hangar-like studio where Fritz Lang may have filmed *Metropolis* (no one is quite sure of the exact location) and admire a reproduction of his futuristic set. Aside from the film-related attractions are fairground rides and animal shows.

Eating, drinking and nightlife

Potsdam has an array of pleasant cafés and **restaurants**, with most along Brandenburger Strasse. For **nightlife** the best bet is the *Lindenpark*, Stahnsdorfer Strasse 76–78 (☎0331/74 79 70, @www.lindenpark.de), over in Babelsberg, with regular "alternative" discos and live bands. Also recommended is the Waschhaus, Schiffbauergasse 1 (☎0331/271 56 26, @www.waschhaus.de), just off Berliner Strasse on the way into town from the Glienicker Brücke, a large venue with galleries, open-air cinema and frequent live music. At the same address is Fabrik (☎0331/280 03 14, @www.fabrikpotsdam.de), a theatre for contemporary dance and music.

Restaurants

Arco Friedrich-Ebert-Str. ☎0331/270 16 90. Small, fancy Italian restaurant occupying the east wing of the Nauener Tor, with some outdoor seating in summer. Serves excellent pan-continental food (mains around €9) and a sumptuous Sunday brunch buffet (€7.50). Daily 10am–3pm.

Café im Filmmuseum Breite Str. 1a ☎0331/201 99 96. This atmospheric Lebanese restaurant is good for Lebanese tea or coffee. The small menu of tasty specialities (starters €6, mains €10) is best

explored with several smaller dishes. Tues–Sun noon–midnight.

Condadino Luisenplatz 8 ☎0331/951 09 23. The casual surroundings overlooking a plaza and the Brandenburger Tor make this mid-priced Italian restaurant a perfect place to eat before or after tackling Sanssouci, just up the road. If you don't fancy the pasta and pizza, there's a wealth of perfectly good alternatives: chops, steaks and some pan-fried Iberian and South American food. Daily noon–late.

Cafés and bars

Babette Brandenburger Str. 71 ☎0331/29 16 48. Pleasant café with outdoor seating, in the shadow of the Brandenburger Tor, that's a good place to rest weary feet and have an indulgent Torte after trekking around Park Sanssouci. The large menu is also available in English and has a range of simple snacks (€7) and main meals (€9). Mon–Sat 9am–late, Sun 10am–late.

Drachenhaus Maulbeerallee 4a ☎0331/505 38 08. Genteel little café in the grounds of Schloss Sanssouci, housed in a pagoda-style building once used by royal vintners. You can also eat well here, with a choice of sturdy Brandenburg specialities or just a piece of florid Torte. March–Oct daily 11am–7pm, Nov–Feb Tues–Sun 11am–6pm.

Froschkasten Kiezstr. 4 ☎0331/29 13 15. One of the oldest and most authentic bars in Potsdam, this *Kneipe* also serves good traditional German food, and does a good line in fish dishes too, particularly the grilled salmon fillet (€19). Mon–Sat noon–midnight, Sun noon–10pm.

La Madeleine Lindenstr. 9 ☎0331/270 54 00. A small *creperie* featuring over thirty variations – some decidedly odd (chicken curry) – of the French variety. Prices range from €2.50 to €7.50. Daily noon–10pm.

Gedenkstätte Sachsenhausen

A beastly vehicle for two of the twentieth century's most powerful and oppressive regimes, the former concentration camp of Sachsenhausen has been preserved as the unremittingly miserable **Gedenkstätte Sachsenhausen** (Sachsenhausen Memorial; daily: mid-March to mid-Oct 8.30am–6pm; mid-Oct to mid-March 8.30am–4.30pm; many exhibits close on Mon; free; Ⓦwww.gedenkstaette -sachsenhausen.de). This was one of the Nazis' main camps and a prototype upon which others were based. It was never designed for mass extermination, but all the same around half of the 220,000 prisoners that passed through its gates would never leave, as at the end of the war the camp was systematically used to kill thousands of Soviet POWs and Jewish prisoners on death marches. After the war the Soviets used the infrastructure for similar purposes.

To enter the camp, visitors pass through an **information centre** packed with books, where you can pick up the long-winded audio tour (€3) and a handy little leaflet (€0.50), with a plan of the camp on it, which is all that's really needed since there's plenty in English. At the entrance to the camp, its largest structure, the **New Museum**, charts the camp's origins and though impossibly detailed, is worth skimming. The camp was converted from a defunct brewery to political prison by the SA, who then rounded up locals – often classmates, colleagues or neighbours. The **camp** proper begins under the main **watchtower** and beyond a **gate** adorned with the ominous sign *Arbeit macht frei* ("work frees"). Either side of the **watchtower** is the **death strip**, a piece of land around the entire camp perimeter where prisoners would be shot without warning. The perimeter fence itself was a high-voltage electric one, typical of all the Nazi camps, and site of frequent inmate suicides. Among the few **prison blocks** that remain – though all are largely reconstructions – one on the eastern side houses a thoughtful **museum** that details the fortunes of selected camp prisoners. Beside it, the **camp prison**, from which internees seldom returned, has rudimentary cells used mostly for solitary confinement, where prisoners were fed just enough to keep them alive. One cell, marked with a British flag, housed two captured British officers who were held manacled to a concrete block at the centre of their cell in near darkness for six months before being taken around the back of the prison

Tropical islands

Once home to zeppelins, an old airship hanger 60km south of Berlin has, since 2004, housed **Tropical Islands** (☎0354/7760 50 50, ⓦ www.tropical-islands .de), an indoor landscaped park the size of four football fields and containing all sorts of watery attractions – pools, lagoons, water slides, waterfalls, whirlpools, saunas among them – as well as a clutch of bars, restaurants and shops. The quality of the landscaping is first class, and its tropical shrubbery and tropical birds that flit around its undergrowth luxuriate in the constant 27°C temperature. A Disneyesque quality is added by various interior buildings and monuments – like the Bali, Borneo, Thai and Samoan pavilions – and regular evening dance shows, but what really sets the place apart is its laidback vibe and convenience. A wristband received on entry handles all purchases electronically – to be paid off on exit – but best of all, the place is open all day, every day, allowing you to stay overnight. Tents (€20 per person) can be rented, but most people just crash on the beach with a mat and blanket, which costs an additional €10 per night on top of the one-off complex entry charge of €25. Other one-off additional charges valid for your entire stay include use of waterslides (€3.50) and the immense, nudist sauna area (€8.50). Tropical Islands lies off the A13 motorway from Berlin (exit Staakow), and near Brand (Niederlausitz) train station where free shuttle buses to the complex meet every train.

and summarily shot. The prison yard is also the site of several tall wooden poles to which prisoners would be tied by their hands until their arms separated from their shoulder joints – a routine punishment for minor misdemeanours. Around the main **parade ground**, the two blocks at the heart of the complex were the prison **kitchen** and **laundry**. Inside the latter several films play, one particularly harrowing one showing the camp on liberation. The gap between the two blocks, at the head of the parade, was formerly a public execution site where prisoners would be hung in front of assembled inmates as an example. At Christmas the SS put a decorated tree here.

Until recently, it was thought that the camp was not used for **systematic executions** until the end of the war, but evidence now shows that it was, if not on the scale elsewhere. This is the subject of various information boards close to a large memorial obelisk and at the western perimeter of the camp. These bring the relationship between victim and perpetrator to a more personal level by relating something of the lives of those killed and their murderers. Behind the boards and beyond the camp perimeter lie the pits in which summary executions took place – outfitted so that used bullets could be retrieved and recycled – and a building in which selected prison inmates were sent for what they thought were medicals only to be shot in the nape of the neck while their height was being measured, then incinerated. Finally at the northern tip of the camp an exhibition in a guard tower investigates the question of what the **local populace** knew and thought about the camp, using video interviews. Next door a large modern and visually impressive but rather too jumbled hall examines the **Soviet Special Camp** (1945–50) that existed here after the war. The Russians imprisoned 60,000 people with suspected Nazi links – though it's thought the majority were innocent – of which at least 12,000 died. The exhibition compares the two camps that existed here claiming "neither one nor the other can be trivialized or made light of in comparison", but you can't help feeling this self-conscious comment, and the fact that the Nazis killed twenty times more people here than the Russians, is trying to somehow partially absolve German crimes: in truth any comment or comparison is both distracting and irrelevant.

Practicalities

Tucked away in a northeastern suburb of the small town of Oranienburg, 35km north of Berlin, the former camp can be **reached** by S-Bahn (S1 from Berlin; around 1hr) or regional express train (25min from Hauptbahnhof). From the train station hourly buses (#M804 or #M821; BVG day tickets valid) ply the route to the Gedenkstätte, but the signposted twenty-minute walk may prove quicker: start just north of the square beside the S-Bahn. Near the camp you'll pass a small plaque devoted to the six thousand who died on the *Todesmarch* – the march away from the front line on which the Nazis forced prisoners as the Russians approached. After visiting the camp, there is little else to keep you in Oranienburg, but if you've worked up an appetite, you might try the *Vietnam Bistro*, Stralsunder Strasse 1 (Mon–Fri 10am–10pm; Sat & Sun 11am–10pm), just north of the train station, which serves up tasty Thai and pan-Asian dishes at extraordinarily low prices (mostly around €5 a dish).

Travel details

Trains

Berlin Hauptbahnhof to: Chorin (every 30min; 45min); Niederfinow (7 daily; 1hr via Eberswalde); Oranienburg (every 30min; 25min); Potsdam (every 15min – including S-Bahn; 30min).

Listings

Listings

Accommodation

B erlin has a good selection of **guesthouses, hotels, hostels** and **campsites**, and it's also possible to stay in a **private room** or **rent an apartment**. In typically Berlin fashion there is considerable overlap between all these categories – particularly noteworthy are the large and growing stock of private rooms in the city's many hostels, making our hostel listings worth scanning for budget options even if you don't want to share a room.

Even though the city's accommodation is continually increasing in both quality and quantity, try to book at least a couple of weeks in advance to be assured of getting exactly what you want, or even further ahead during important festivals (see p.31).

If you are stuck for accommodation at short notice or want to cut some of the work involved in hunting it out, try the telephone or online **reservation service** of Berlin Tourist (℡030/25 00 25, ⓦberlin-tourist-information.de). They are great for hotel and pensions bookings, and have a more limited selection of hostel beds and private rooms too. If you're after these, you're better off with the **booking websites** listed on p.201 & p.205 respectively.

Hotels and pensions

A pension is usually smaller and cheaper than a **hotel**, although the categories overlap and there are also "Hotel-Pensions", which may be either or both, so don't take too much notice of the labels. But do look out for the good deals at many of the more upmarket hotels, who slash their rates at the weekend. Note that **single rooms** are usually only a third cheaper than doubles and breakfast is rarely included in the price of a room, particularly at the more expensive places.

Unter den Linden and around

The following places are marked on the map on pp.46–47.

Adlon Unter den Linden 77 ℡030/226 10, ⓦwww.hotel-adlon.de. The jewel of Berlin's prewar luxury hotels has been re-created in all its excessive splendour. Prices are fit for a Kaiser – you'll part with at least €8500 per night for the presidential suite. S-Bahn Unter den Linden. €360

Hilton Mohrenstr. 30 ℡030/202 30, ⓦwww.hilton.com. Luxurious, expensive and not much different from any other *Hilton* hotel in the world, but for its fine view of the Gendarmenmarkt. Facilities include a sauna, swimming pool and squash court. U-Bahn Stadtmitte. €345

Intermezzo Gertrude-Kolmar-Str. 5 ℡030/22 48 90 96, ⓦwww.hotelintermezzo.de. Spartan but not unattractive women-only pension (which accepts children up to age 10) within walking distance of Potsdamer Platz and Unter den Linden. Not all rooms are en suite. U-Bahn Mohrenstr. €75

Westin Grand Friedrichstr. 158–164 ℡030/202 70, ⓦwww.westin.com/berlin. Fully living up to its name, this GDR-era hotel originally

With Berlin a city of distinct districts, deciding **where to stay** may be your most important choice. Even though public transport is excellent, staying in the area of town that suits you best will make your visit easier. **Mitte** – covered in chapters 1 to 5 – is the most obvious area to stay, particularly if you want a room in a major hotel. Within this area, the **Spandauer Vorstadt** around Oranienburger Strasse (see Chapter 4) is best for smaller-scale or budget accommodation with several hostels and little boutique hotels. As well as being within walking distance of many city-centre attractions, they are also in a popular restaurant and nightlife district. If you are going to be in Berlin a little longer than a weekend or prefer a quieter, less touristy but equally happening residential neighbourhood, **Prenzlauer Berg** is a good choice, as is **Schöneberg** – the latter particularly if you are gay (see p.252). If you're hell-bent on clubbing, try to lay your head in **Friedrichshain** or **Kreuzeberg**, where you'll find the most cutting-edge nightlife. The other major concentration of accommodation in the city is in **City West** and central **Charlottenburg** – the old centre of West Berlin – where you'll find plenty of accommodation of every standard, particularly more moderate guesthouses, even if recent changes in the city's dynamic have left them stranded a bit away from many of Berlin's brightest lights.

served party bigwigs but has since been overhauled to provide oodles of traditional upmarket luxury, and is a little more atmospheric than some of its rivals. U-Bahn Friedrichstr. €375

Alexanderplatz and around

The following places are marked on the map on p.71.

Alexander Plaza Rosenstr. 1 ☎030/24 00 10, ⓦwww.alexander-plaza.com. Once housing a fur atelier, this building survived the war and the GDR, and has been beautifully renovated to become a sleek, bright, dynamic hotel. Some rooms have kitchenettes and all are decorated with modern art. S-Bahn Hackescher Markt. €125

art'otel Berlin Mitte Wallstr. 70–73 ☎030/24 06 20, ⓦwww.artotel.de. Smart, lively hotel with quirky decor – lots of contemporary and modern art – in a quiet corner of Berlin, close to the U-Bahn. When reserving, you can pick the colour of your room: green, blue, red or aubergine. U-Bahn Märkisches Museum. €109

Grosser Kurfürst Neue Rossstr. 11–12 ☎030/24 60 00, ⓦwww.deraghotels.de. Sleek hotel in a renovated turn-of-the-twentieth-century building, with straightforward, but spotless, rooms and more spacious suites. Facilities include laundry, wi-fi and a sauna and steambath. Discounts for longer stays offered. U-Bahn Märkisches Museum. €97

Luisenhof Köpenicker Str. 92 ☎030/241 59 06, ⓦwww.luisenhof.de. Restored 1822 coaching company building that's one of the best options in its price range. It's a little off the beaten track, though within walking distance of the U-Bahn and Nikolaiviertel. The rooms have all mod cons and are immaculate. Regular deals slash midweek rates by as much as half. U-Bahn Märkisches Museum. €160

Motel One Alexanderplatz ☎030/20 05 40 80, ⓦwww.motel-one.com. Countrywide hotel group whose stylish lobbies – flat-screen TV's and wacky modular 70s furniture – suggest far higher prices than its cheerfully straightforward en-suite rooms command. The location, a couple of minutes' walk from Alexanderplatz, helps make it a downtown bargain; the chain has five other locations in Berlin. Free wi-fi. U- & S-Bahn Alexanderplatz. €84

Park Inn Alexanderplatz ☎030/238 90 ⓦwww.parkinn-berlin.com. Big, ugly block bang in the middle of things, with unbeatable views over the city and hard to beat for convenience. Of the nine hundred en-suite rooms, the newly renovated business-class ones are a clear notch above the rest. U- & S-Bahn Alexanderplatz. €125

Radisson Blu Hotel Karl-Liebknecht-Str. 3 ☎030/23 82 80, ⓦwww.radissonblu.com /hotel-berlin. Impressive central modern hotel that offers the difficult choice between a room with views over the Spree and the

Accommodation prices

Hotels, pensions and hostels reviewed in this book are followed by a price that indicates the cost of the **standard double room midweek** in **high season** (May–Sept). Prices are also given for dorm beds in hostels.

Dom, or one facing inwards, onto a vast aquarium of 2500 tropical fish in the lobby-cum-atrium (part of the Sea-Life Center; see p.74). With spa and good restaurant. S-Bahn Hackescher Markt. €190

Spandauer Vorstadt

The following places are marked on the map on pp.82–83.

⚐ Circus Hotel Rosenthalerstr. 1 ☎030/20 00 39 39, ✆www.circus-berlin.de. A successful venture into the world of hotels from the excellent hostel over the road (see p.202). Plenty of smart, cheerful rooms and communal spaces, which include a beer garden. Free wi-fi. U-Bahn Rosenthaler Platz. €80

Dietrich-Bonhoeffer-Haus Ziegelstr. 30 ☎030/28 46 70, ✆www.hotel-dbh.de. This small, church-affiliated hotel and conference centre is where the first round of talks between the GDR regime and the opposition – which led to free elections and reunification – were held in December 1989. The airy en-suite rooms are simple, quiet and equipped with desks and TVs. A good buffet breakfast is included in the rate. U- & S-Bahn Friedrichstr. €137

⚐ Hackescher Markt Grosse Präsidentenstr. 8 ☎030/28 00 30, ✆www.hotel -hackescher-markt.com. Quirky little hotel on a quiet side street, in the midst of the Hackescher Markt bar scene. It has an eclectic mix of furnishings and some pleasant touches, including under-floor heating in the en-suite bathrooms and some non-smoking rooms. The rooms overlooking the courtyard are quieter. S-Bahn Hackescher Markt. €119

Honigmond Garden Hotel Invalidenstr. 122 ☎030/28 44 55 77, ✆www.honigmond-berlin .de. Downtown bargain in a charming 1845 building. The rooms are sparsely furnished, but their original wooden floors help generate an authentic elegance. Guests have access to the relaxing back garden. Breakfast included. U-Bahn Naturkundemuseum. €159

Kastanienhof Kastanienallee 65–66 ☎030/44 30 50, ✆www.kastanienhof.biz. Small hotel in a nineteenth-century tenement house, with spacious, well-appointed rooms, and convenient for the district's nightlife. Prices include breakfast. U-Bahn Senefelderplatz. €120

Märkischer Hof Linienstr. 133 ☎030/282 71 55, ✆www.maerkischer-hof-berlin.de. The location has the dual benefit of being on the doorstep of restaurants and nightlife at the western end of Oranienburger Str. and within strolling distance of Unter den Linden. The comfortable but unexciting rooms have a TV and mini-bar. U-Bahn Oranienburger Tor. €85

Merkur Torstr. 156 ☎030/282 95 23, ✆www .hotel-merkur-berlin.de. Budget place with vague Old Berlin styling and fairly comfortable rooms, most of which have showers and some toilets too. There are a small number of good-value singles; rates include breakfast. U-Bahn Rosenthaler Platz. €96

mitArt Hotel Linienstr. 139–140 ☎030/28 39 04 30, ✆www.mitart.de. A great choice for art lovers – this place is flanked by a couple of galleries. The hotel itself is dotted with enough art to make you wonder if it's an art gallery in a hotel or vice versa, and the landlady is a former curator. Not all the bright, airy and fairly basic rooms are en suite. Delicious organic breakfasts. U-Bahn Oranienburger Tor. €150

⚐ Hotel Taunus Monbijouplatz 1 ☎030/283 52 54, ✆www.hoteltaunus.com. No-frills budget hotel with clean and simple if cramped rooms but at extraordinarily low prices for the location – arguably as good as it gets in central Berlin. There are some en-suite rooms for an extra €10. S-Bahn Hackescher Markt. €59.

Tiergarten

The following places are marked on the map on pp.98–99.

Grand Esplanade Lützowufer 15 ☎030/25 47 80, ✆www.esplanade.de. Sleek and top-class hotel close to the Tiergarten park with all the facilities most people could want (including sauna, pool, fitness centre and spa) and a flashy New York-style cocktail bar. U-Bahn Nollendorfplatz. €89

Hansablick Flotowstr. 6 ⊕030/390 48 00, ⊛www.hotel-hansablick.de. A short hop from the Tiergarten, rooms sport cheerful multicoloured furnishings and preside over all the usual mod cons. The rate includes a good buffet breakfast. S-Bahn Tiergarten. €111

Intercontinental Budapester Str. 2 ⊕030/260 20, ⊛www.interconti.com. Modern luxury for high-powered business people and visiting rock stars. In a relatively dull corner of town, but with legion amenities, among them a fully equipped fitness centre, sauna and pool. U- & S-Bahn Zoologischer Garten. €105

Luise Kunsthotel Luisenstr. 19 ⊕030/28 44 80, ⊛www.luise-berlin.com. Each room here is an eccentric, and impressive, work of art: one comes with bananas all over the walls and hot-pink velvet bedding, while another is an *Alice in Wonderland*-themed room with oversized furniture. The elegant rooms at the front tend to suffer from train noise (earplugs provided) but the quieter rooms at the back are a bit blander. Not all are en suite and breakfast is extra. U- & S-Bahn Friedrichstr. €110

Hotel Spreebogen Alt-Moabit 99 ⊕030/39 92 00, ⊛www.hotel-spreebogen.de. A spirited hotel housed in a former dairy and filled with postmodern chic. Its position across the River Spree, though attractive, isolates it from most of the action. Free wi-fi. U-Bahn Turmstr. €99

City West

The following places are marked on the map on p.118.

Alsterhof Augsburgstr. 5 ⊕030/21 24 20, ⊛www.alsterhof.com. Central enough, though removed from the bustle of the Ku'damm, this is a pleasant modern hotel with a top-notch gym, pool and sauna. U-Bahn Augsburger Str. €101

art'otel Berlin City Centre West Lietzenburger Str. 85 ⊕030/887 77 70, ⊛www.artotel.de. This sleek hotel is one for Andy Warhol fans, with over two hundred originals of his scattered about the place. His style extends to the staff uniforms and the furniture: white leather beds and purple chairs. U-Bahn Uhlandstr. €79

Bogota Schlüterstr. 45 ⊕030/881 50 01, ⊛www.bogota.de. Pleasant down-to-earth place offering a touch of affordable luxury

in an historic nineteenth-century building – which once served as the Nazi Chamber of Culture. The photos on the third floor are by the photographer known only as YVA, who tutored Helmut Newton in the 1930s. The cheapest rooms share facilities; add €30 per night for an en-suite room. Rates include breakfast. S-Bahn Savignyplatz. €69

Brandenburger Hof Eislebener Str. 14 ⊕030/21 40 50, ⊛www.brandenburger-hof .com. This hotel is an architectural and design tour de force, a bright nineteenth-century mansion reworked with Bauhaus influences. The staff ooze suave attentiveness, and there's a Michelin-starred restaurant and a beautiful Japanese-influenced garden. U-Bahn Augsburger Str. €239

California Kurfürstendamm 35 ⊕030/88 01 20, ⊛www.hotel-california.de. Well-appointed hotel with huge chandeliers and elegant cornicing in the thick of the Ku'damm (and not particularly Californian). The large en-suite rooms have becoming nineteenth-century touches, though the cheaper rooms are dated and a little plain. An excellent buffet breakfast is included. U-Bahn Uhlandstr. €109

Dittberner Wielandstr. 26 ⊕030/884 69 50, ⊛www.hotel-dittberner.de. Friendly old-fashioned pension, boasting spacious rooms, stuccoed ceilings, antiques and plush upholstery. S-Bahn Savignyplatz. €97

Funk Fasanenstr. 69 ⊕030/882 71 93, ⊛www.hotel-pensionfunk.de. Interesting re-creation of a prewar flat, with furniture and objects from the 1920s and 1930s, when this was the home of Danish silent-movie star Asta Nielsen. Given this, its location, and the included breakfast buffet, it's a bargain. The cheapest rooms share bathrooms. U-Bahn Uhlandstr. €89

Hotel Gates Knesebeckstr. 8–9 ⊕030/31 10 60, ⊛www.hotel-gates.com. Slick modern business hotel with functional rooms. The main selling point is free high-speed internet access in every room, on flat-screen PCs. U-Bahn Ernst-Reuter-Platz. €75

Hecker's Grolmannstr. 35 ⊕030/889 00, ⊛www.heckers-hotel.de. Swanky boutique hotel close to the restaurants of Savignyplatz, with a range of classy suites and rooms. Pride of the hotel are its three luxuriously furnished, themed suites

(Bauhaus, Tuscany and Colonial), costing upwards of €350 per night. Free wi-fi. U-Bahn Uhlandstr. €100

Hollywood Media Hotel Kurfürstendamm 202 ☎030/88 91 00, ⓦwww.filmhotel.de. Owned by German film producer Artur Brauner (*Bridge Over the River Kwai*), this hotel is a shrine to films of all sorts. But it's all classily understated: rooms – themed by movie star – are tastefully decorated with just one headshot and bio in each. The modern hotel boasts predictably sound 4-star standards, has a sauna and steam room and a huge buffet breakfast included in the rates. Wi-fi costs extra. U-Bahn Uhlandstr. €96

🏃 **Kettler Bleibtreustr. 19** ☎030/883 49 49, ⓦwww.brunnenfee.de. A tiny, charming 1920s-style pension on a lively, café-lined street. A multitude of knick-knacks, Berlinana and patterned wallpaper give the place character. Rooms are themed by artist or performer (choose between the likes of Callas or Toulouse Lautrec) and have showers but share toilets. S-Bahn Savignyplatz. €55

Hotel Q! Knesebeckstr. 67 ☎030/810 06 60, ⓦwww.loock-hotels.com. Hotel full of minimalist Bauhaus-inspired elegance and quirks like bathtubs alongside many of the beds. Great buffet breakfast and extremely affable staff. S-Bahn Savignyplatz. €95.

Savoy Hotel Fasanenstr. 9–10 ☎030/31 10 30, ⓦwww.hotel-savoy.com. Luxury hotel whose traditional, old-world atmosphere has been happily married with some Cuban decorative flair – there's even a cigar shop in the lobby. U- & S-Bahn Zoologischer Garten. €93

Charlottenburg–Wilmersdorf

The following places are marked on the map on p.116.

Frauenhotel Artemisia Brandenburgische Str. 18 ☎030/873 89 05, ⓦwww.frauenhotel-berlin.de. Popular women-only hotel, with modern rooms (most en suite), a sociable roof garden and artworks as part of the decor. Fills quickly in high season, so book well in advance. Free wi-fi. U-Bahn Konstanzer Str. €78

Ibis Brandenburgische Str. 11 ☎030/86 20 20, ⓦwww.ibishotel.com. One of ten branches of this international chain in Berlin. Rooms are small but often aggressively priced. U-Bahn Fehrbelliner Platz. €88

München Güntzelstr. 62 ☎030/857 91 20, ⓦwww.hotel-pension-muenchen-in-berlin.de. Straightforward, unpretentious pension with simple, bright modern decor and friendly management. U-Bahn Günzelstr. €88

🏃 **Propeller Island City Lodge Albrecht-Achilles-Str. 58** ☎030/891 90 16, ⓦwww.propeller-island.de. Entertainingly wacky hotel where the furnishings in every room have been handcrafted by the owner according to individual themes: check the website to choose from among the likes of the Space Cube, the Mirror Room, Two Lions, Forest, Temple, Electric Wallpaper, Nudes or Upside Down. U-Bahn Adenauerplatz. €84

Schöneberg

The following places are marked on the map on p.128.

Altberlin am Potsdamer Platz Potsdamer Str. 67 ☎030/261 29 99, ⓦwww.altberlin-hotel.de. Large pension, recently refurbished with trappings from the turn of the nineteenth century, and just a few minutes' walk from the Tiergarten park. Large buffet breakfast is included. U-Bahn Kurfürstenstr. €106

Sylter Hof Berlin Kurfürstenstr. 116 ☎030/212 00, ⓦwww.sylterhof-berlin.de. Well-appointed eighteen-storey hotel just behind Wittenbergplatz and the Ku'damm. The suites are spacious and well priced, and come with kitchens. All accommodation has internet access and breakfast is included. U-Bahn Wittenbergplatz. €102

Western Kreuzberg

See map on p.132.

Hotel Am Anhalter Bahnhof Stresemannstr. 36 ☎030/258 00 70, ⓦwww.hotel-anhalter-bahnhof.de. Not a pretty hotel, but a pleasant one, with friendly staff. The cheaper rooms share bathrooms, but all the rooms are a good deal considering the location, just south of Potsdamer Platz and the Kulturforum. S-Bahn Anhalter Bahnhof. €90

Eastern Kreuzberg and Friedrichshain

The following places are marked on the map on pp.142–143.

Hotel 26 Grünberger Str. 26 ☎030/297 77 80, ⓦwww.hotel26.de. Simple, bright and modern hotel close to Friedrichshain's many bars. All rooms are en suite and rates include breakfast. U- & S-Bahn Warschauer Str. €89

Hotel Alameda Berlin Michaelkirchstr. 15 ☎030/30 86 83 30, ⓦwww.hotel-alameda -berlin.de. Small, modern hotel on the top floor of a commercial building in a quiet industrial area – a short walk from the action in Kreuzberg. Rooms are all clean, bright and attractive loft units: some with balcony, all with en-suite showers. Great breakfasts included but wi-fi costs extra. U-Bahn Heinrich-Heine-Str. €82

East Side Hotel Mühlenstr. 6 ☎030/29 38 33, ⓦwww.eastsidehotel.de. Small, laid-back modern hotel just over the Spree from Kreuzberg in southern Friedrichshain and overlooking the East Side Gallery. The service is exceptional and the absence of rules refreshing: you can check in or out, order room service, or have breakfast in the café 24 hours a day. Original artwork in the hotel includes quirky murals by Birgit Kinder, who famously painted the Trabant on the East Side Gallery. Breakfast included. U- & S-Bahn Warschauer Str. €99

Hotel Fredrichshain Warschauer Str. 57 ☎030/97 00 20 30, ⓦfriedrichshain.home -from-home.de. Straightforward modern hotel with uncluttered rooms – some share bathrooms – and a kitchen on every floor. A good deal for longer stays: prices drop after your third night and almost halve after your fifteenth. Reception is unmanned so you need to arrange in advance if you are arriving after 6pm. U- & S-Bahn Warschauer Str. €70

🏃 **IntercityHotel Berlin Am Ostbahnhof 5** ☎030/29 36 80, ⓦwww.berlin .intercityhotel.de. Sleek but budget-conscious business hotel at the Ostbahnhof, so very convenient for the S-Bahn and the Friedrichshain scene. Rooms are up to the usual international business standard, and rates include buffet breakfast and a ticket for Berlin's public transport network (zones A, B & C) for the duration of your stay. Rates vary wildly depending on events and demand. S-Bahn Ostbahnhof. €69

🏃 **Michelberger Hotel Warschauer Str. 39** ☎030/29 77 85 90, ⓦwww.michelberger hotel.com. Modern, trendy and urbane, this relaxed haunt with its cool warehouse-style interior provides anything but workaday hotel accommodation. Apart from enjoying the improvised feel of the interiors – cuckoo

clocks on raw concrete walls, exposed wiring – you'll also likely find the all-night bar and lobby friendly, relaxing and unpretentious hangouts. The buffet breakfast (€9) is excellent. U- & S-Bahn Warschauer Str. €80.

🏃 **Ostel Wriezener Karree 5** ☎030/25 76 86 60, ⓦwww.ostel.info. Step back into the GDR of the 1970s amid a haze of browns and oranges at this themed budget hotel a short walk from the Ostbahnhof. The rendition is creepily accurate, but thankfully the whole thing's done with a sense of humour and just the thing for those needing a fix of *Ostalgie* (see *Ostalgie* colour section). Some rooms share bathrooms; other GDR-era alternatives include a six-person apartment (€120/night); a "*Pionierlager*" or youth camp with dorms for €9; and good-value singles (€33). S-Bahn Ostbahnhof. €54

Upstalsboom Hotel Gubener Str. 42 ☎030/29 37 50, ⓦwww.upstalsboom-berlin.de. Upmarket hotel whose particular strong point is its spa. The rooms are bland, if spacious, and are available in four categories, the largest of which has a kitchenette. Wi-fi and breakfast included in rates. U- & S-Bahn Warschauer Str. €89

Prenzlauer Berg

The following places are marked on the map on pp.150–151.

🏃 **Acksel Haus Belforter Str. 21** ☎030/44 33 76 33, ⓦwww.ackselhaus.de. Small offbeat hotel on an attractive residential street in the midst of the lively Prenzlauer Berg scene. Besides rooms, it offers fully equipped and individually themed apartments with broadband access and spacious kitchens. U-Bahn Senefelderplatz. €110

Greifswald Greifswalder Str. 211 ☎030/442 78 88, ⓦwww.hotel-greifswald.de. An informal pension tucked away in a quiet rear courtyard. The en-suite rooms are tidy, if fairly basic. Breakfast is served right up until 1pm, though it isn't included in the rate. U-Bahn Senefelderplatz. €75

Myer's Hotel Metzer Str. 26 ☎030/44 01 40, ⓦwww.myershotel.de. Small upmarket hotel in the quiet courtyard of a renovated building from the turn of the nineteenth century. The rooms are elegant and taste-fully furnished, if a little small. U-Bahn Senefelderplatz. €72

Western suburbs

The following places are marked on the map on p.170.

Schlosshotel Im Grunewald Brahmsstr. 10 ☎030/89 58 40, ⓦwww.schlosshotelberlin .com. Escape the grittiness of Berlin in grand country house style in a peaceful and upmarket residential area where driveways are filled with Porsches. Much of the hotel's classical decor was given a modern design twist by Karl Lagerfeld and is matched by its seamless service. Meanwhile the large swathe of pleasant Grunewald woodland on the doorstep is perfect for a walk or run before enjoying the lovely spa, sauna, steam room and pool facilities. S-Bahn Hohenzollerndamm. €239

Hostels

Over the past decade Berlin has been hit by a tidal wave of new, independently run **hostels**, which have swept aside many of the old-fashioned, unfriendly pensions and overtaken the established IYH hostels in standards of service. The stock of scrupulously clean and functional private rooms at hostels is such that their presence threatens the livelihood of many traditional pensions.

Hostels reception desks are almost always bountiful sources of information and frequently double as a 24-hour bar for the communal area, where you'll generally find several internet terminals. Common rooms are usually available for relaxing and meeting other travellers, and the universal absence of curfews makes many real hubs for partying. Traditional facilities, such as a laundry and kitchens, are unusual in these places, but in Berlin the nearest launderette or snack bar is never far away.

All hostels welcome travellers of any age, though most cater mainly to twenty-somethings and larger ones are periodically overwhelmed by school groups. The actual accommodation tends to comprise various mixed-sex, multiple-occupancy dorms, plus a good stock of singles, doubles and triples. Prices reflect the number of people sharing: a twenty-bed dorm may be priced at around €10 per person, while five sharing a room might each pay double that; singles and doubles typically go for around €45–65. We list the range for each hostel. Bedding is provided in most instances, though sometimes there's a small one-off fee of around €3 for this, or you may be able use a sleeping bag. Most hostels offer a simple buffet breakfast for around €5, at some this is included.

Alexanderplatz

See map on p.71.

🏃 **Citystay Hostel** Rosenstr. 16 ☎030/23 62 40 31, ⓦwww.citystay.de. Probably Berlin's best-located hostel is in easy walking distance of the S-Bahn, Hackescher Markt and Museum Island. A large well-run place spreading over several immaculately clean floors, it also has a good stock of private rooms, some en suite, and pleasant communal areas including a leafy courtyard. Facilities include an all-night bar, restaurant, internet and wi-fi. The hostel's also a hub for

Booking hostel beds online

There are several websites where you can search and pay for a dorm bed or private room in advance. These take their commission from the hostels, so there is nothing extra to pay – you may even find that online deals beat what you'd be offered at a hostel reception. The following sites are all worth checking:

ⓦwww.gomio.com
ⓦwww.hostelbookers.com
ⓦwww.hostelberlin.com
ⓦwww.hostelz.com

various walking and cycling tours and bar crawls. S-Bahn Hackescher Markt. Dorms €17–21; singles €40; twins €50–64.

Spandauer Vorstadt

The following places are marked on the map on pp.82–83.

🏃 **Baxpax Downtown Ziegelstr. 28** ☏030/27 87 48 80, ⓦwww.baxpax.de. Great hostel with busy communal areas in a handy, yet relatively quiet location, with all the usual facilities – internet, bar, breakfast buffet, games room, bike rental – and a relaxed vibe. Avoid the fifty-bed dorm (€10) if you are a light sleeper in favour of an eight-bed (€13) or smaller (€16–21) dorm. S-Bahn Oranienburger Str. Dorms €10–21; singles €29; doubles €54.

🏃 **Circus Hostel Weinbergsweg 1a** ☏030/20 00 39 39, ⓦwww.circus-berlin.de. Top-notch hostel in fantastic location, with particularly helpful staff and good facilities. Rooms are plain though bright, with large windows and high ceilings, and with the advantage of not having bunk beds. The hostel has its own, decent bar, *Goldmans*, downstairs. U-Bahn Rosenthaler Platz. Dorms €19–25; singles €40; doubles €56.

Clubhouse Kalkscheunenstr. 4–5 ☏030/28 09 79 79, ⓦwww.clubhouse-berlin.de. Small, slightly grungy hostel with too few bathrooms, but whose faults are more than made up for by its fantastic location, close to the bars of Oranienburger Str. and a ten-minute walk from Unter den Linden. Dorms are spacious, and there are also apartments for up to ten (€180) people. Bedding, use of kitchen facilities and wi-fi and breakfast are all included. U- & S-Bahn Friedrichstr. Dorms €11–18; doubles €54.

Mittes Backpacker Chausseestr. 102 ☏030/28 39 09 65, ⓦwww.baxpax.de. Imaginatively decorated converted factory within walking distance of the Scheunenviertel bar scene. Facilities include bike rental and a communal kitchen. U-Bahn Naturkundemuseum. Dorms €14–26; singles €36; doubles €50.

🏃 **St Christopher's Hostel Rosa-** Luxemburg-Str. 39–41 ☏030/30 81 45 39 60, ⓦwww.st-christophers.co.uk. Well-run branch of a British hostel chain, with the perfect layout and 24-hour opening times for partying all night in its big bar, with chill-out areas and billiards. There's also

pub grub, free wi-fi and occasional live events, but the staff and guests are a motley international crew, so there's little to remind that you're in Germany. Rates include a basic breakfast and linen. U-Bahn Rosa-Luxemburg-Platz. Dorms (some single-sex) €15–21; singles €36; doubles & twins €50.

City West

See map on p.118.

🏃 **Jetpak City Hostel Pariserstr. 58** ☏030/784 43 60, ⓦwww.jetpak.de. Western Berlin's best hostel is scrupulously clean and in a quiet residential neighbourhood a short walk from the Ku'damm shops area and close to the U-Bahn. Amenities include free internet and wi-fi; access to printers, iPod chargers and speakers; and a common room with all sorts of film and gaming entertainment on a widescreen TV. Bike hire available. U-Bahn Spichernstr. Dorms €14–26.

Western Kreuzberg

See map on p.132.

Meininger Hallesches Ufer 30 & Tempelhofer Ufer 10 ☏030/66 63 61 00, ⓦwww.meininger -hotels.de. A pair of well-run hostels on either side of the Landwehrkanal, in one of Kreuzberg's duller corners. The dorms and private rooms come with a shower and toilet, while single and twins also have a TV and phone. U-Bahn Hallesches Tor. Dorms €15–21.50; singles €55; doubles €72.

Eastern Kreuzberg–Friedrichshain

The following places are marked on the map on pp.142–143.

All in Hostel Grünberger Str. 54 ☏030/288 76 83, ⓦwww.all-in-hostel.com. Clean, modern and well-managed hostel just yards from the nocturnal goings-on of Simon-Dach-Str. All the usual facilities are offered, with breakfast and linen included in rates. Though frequently beset by German school groups, it's a good choice for its hotel-standard private en-suite rooms and rock-bottom off-season prices, when dorm beds go for €7.77. U- & S-Bahn Warschauer Str. Dorms €26–35; singles €69; twins €80.

Baxpax Skalitzer Str. 104 ☏030/69 51 83 22, ⓦwww.baxpax.de. Cheerful and convivial beatnik hostel in a happening area of

Kreuzberg, whose claim to fame is its bed in a pink VW Beetle parked in one of the rooms. Otherwise it's unremarkable and the communal facilities are a bit overstretched. Besides dorms (€9–22), there are some doubles (€50) and one single (€37). U-Bahn Görlitzer Bahnhof.

Die Fabrik Schlesische Str. 18 ☎030/611 71 16, ⓦwww.diefabrik.com. Hip but quiet hostel in a converted factory. Unusually, the dorm beds aren't bunk beds. Bedding is included in the price, though the breakfasts aren't. U-Bahn Schlesisches Tor. Dorms €18; singles €38; doubles €58.

Eastern Comfort Mühlenstr. 73–77 ☎030/66 76 38 06, ⓦwww.eastern -comfort.com. Sleep swaying on the River Spree in a range of accommodation – from spacious doubles (€78), through cabin bunks (€16) all the way to bedding down on the deck in a tent (€12). All cabins except dorms are en suite and the boat has internet and wi-fi. Highly unconventional and lots of fun, and there's a social area and bar that's lively until the small hours. U- & S-Bahn Warschauer Str.

Hostel X Berger Schlesische Str. 22 ☎030/69 53 18 63, ⓦwww.hostelxberger.com. Dowdy, but clean and friendly hostel a hop, skip and a stagger from several of Berlin's best clubs. Common areas include a basic kitchen but little else. Free wi-fi. U-Bahn Schlesisches Tor. Dorms €12–19; singles €36; doubles €46.

Jetpak Alternative Görlitzerstr. 38 ☎030/62 90 86 41 ⓦwww.jetpak.de. The newest offering of Berlin's best hostel chain is up to its usual excellent standard, offering a pretty stark contrast to a gritty surrounding neighbourhood that's close to all the action in Kreuzberg and Friedrichshain. Transport links to Mitte and the airport are also good, while some rooms are en suite and have high-end fittings such as under-floor heating. Other perks include internet and wi-fi, a buffet breakfast and on-street parking – all free. Also available is bicycle hire, laundry facilities and cheap beer. U-Bahn Schle-sisches Tor. Dorms €27–35.

Odyssee Globetrotter Hostel Grünberger Str. 23 ☎030/29 00 00 81, ⓦwww.globetrotterhostel .de. Imaginatively decorated and sociable hostel hard by the Friedrichshain scene and with a happening bar of its own. Facilities include kitchen and free wi-fi. U-Bahn Frankfurter Tor. Dorms €13.50–19.50; single €36; doubles €47–54.

▲ Ostel

Ostel Wriezener Karree 5 ☎030/25 76 86 60, ⓦwww.ostel.info. Wacky GDR-themed budget hotel with dorm beds for only €9 each – see p.200.

Pegasus Str. der Pariser Kommune 35 ☎030/297 73 60, ⓦwww.pegasushostel.de. Well-run establishment set around a garden-cum-courtyard that comes into its own in the summer as a place to enjoy your free welcome drink. The location is a bit out of the way, though the U-Bahn is just a 5min walk away. Linen extra. U-Bahn Weberwiese. Dorms €13–19; singles €39; doubles €49.

Sunflower Hostel Helsingforserstr. 17 ☎030/44 04 42 50, ⓦwww.sunflower-hostel.de. Sociable hostel tucked away in a residential part of Friedrichshain. The reception doubles as a bar, while the hostel itself is fairly handy for transport and the local bar scene. The dorms are good value, but the singles (€35) and doubles (€45) are dingy and uninviting. U- & S-Bahn Warschauer Str. Dorms €13–19.

Prenzlauer Berg

The following places are marked on the map on pp.150–151.

Generator Storkower Str. 160 ☎030/417 24 00, ⓦwww.generatorhostels.com. This gargantuan place is part of an international chain and modern, clean, friendly and efficient, but rather out of the way. Some private rooms are en suite. S-Bahn Landsberger Allee. Dorms €16–22; singles €50; doubles €60.

Lette'm Sleep Lettestr. 7 ☎030/44 73 36 23, ⓦ www.backpackers.de. Quirky hostel with comfy if basic rooms, just steps away from the action in Prenzlauer Berg. A big plus point is the cosy living room with free internet, coffee and tea and a communal kitchen. There are discounts for stays of three nights or more. U-Bahn Eberswalder Str. Dorms €17–28; twins €49.

Transit Loft Greifswalder Str. 219 ☎030/48 49 37 73, ⓦ www.transit-loft.de. Part budget hotel, part hostel, this uncluttered establishment occupies the top floor of a converted factory building, the floors below housing a cinema, café, fitness club and billiard hall. Rooms are large and cheerful and the nightlife of Kollwitzplatz a stroll away. A buffet breakfast is included in the price. U-Bahn Rosa-Luxemburg-Platz. Dorms €21; singles €62; doubles €72.

The Grunewald

See map on p.173.

🏃 **Jetpak Ecolodge** Pücklerstr. 54 ☎030/832 250 11, ⓦ www.jetpak.de. One-of-a-kind hostel with a laid-back international vibe, in the woods on the southwestern edge of Berlin. The large communal spaces have plenty on offer, including free nightly big-screen movies, free internet access and lots of indoor and outdoor games. Bring supplies as there are no stores in the vicinity. Free internet and wi-fi; bike rental offered. U-Bahn Günzelstr. or Fehrberliner Platz then bus #115 to Pückerstr; night buses from the centre stop a 10min walk from the hostel. Dorms €15–18; twins €40; doubles €48.

Campsites

Of Berlin's campsites only *Tentstation* is close to the centre; if you're looking to cut costs, bear in mind that hostels will probably work out cheaper once you've added the cost of travel to a campsite. That said, all the campsites are well-run and inexpensive.

Campingplatz Am Krossinsee Wernsdorfer Str. 38 ☎030/675 86 87. Pleasantly located in the woods just outside the southeastern suburb of Schmöckwitz, Am Krossinsee offers easy access to local lakes. It's also possible to rent a bungalow here (€44 – substantial discounts for stays over one night). From S-Bahn Grünar take tram #68 to Schmöckwitz, and from there catch bus #733 to the grounds. Tents €5; plus €6 per person.

Campingplatz Kladow Krampnitzer Weg 111–117, Gatow ☎030/365 27 97; see map, **p.173.** Friendly campsite on the western side of the Havel lake, with good facilities including a crèche, bar, restaurant, shop and showers. U-Bahn Rathaus Spandau, then bus #X34 to Alt-Kladow stop, change to the #234 to "Selbitzer Strasse", walk west to the end of the road following "DCC"

signs. Bungalow rental €46 (substantial discounts for stays over one night). Tents €5; plus €6 per person.

🏃 **Tentstation** Seydlitzstr. 6 ☎030/39 40 46 50, ⓦ www.tentstation.de; see map, **pp.98–99.** Bohemian campsite surrounding a defunct open-air swimming pool in the fairly dreary residential district of Moabit – but an easy walk from the Hauptbahnhof. Facilities are basic, but are made up for by the chance to play basketball, football, volleyball and table-tennis or party until 1am in the groovy campsite bar whose programme of weekly events range from gigs to DJs to recitals and films. Rates are €11 per person in your own tent, or you can rent one for €4 per night (sleeping mats €1). Reception daily 8am–11pm. S-Bahn Hauptbahnhof. Open May–Sept.

Private rooms and apartments

Private rooms are usually of a good standard: clean and simple, often self-contained, and there's quite a lot of privacy – you may barely see your host. Breakfast is sometimes included in the price, in which event it's most likely a case of helping yourself to bread and what's in the fridge.

The typical charge for a private room is €25–35 per person per night, while monthly rents for a self-contained apartment start at €400, or about €300 if you're prepared to share kitchen and bathroom.

The accommodation agencies tend to specialize in either short-term – up to about a month – or long-term lets, for longer periods. In the case of the latter, there are often agency fees to pay on top, to a maximum of 25 percent of the monthly rent.

Mostly short term

Bed & Breakfast in Berlin ☎030/44 05 05 82, 🖰www.bed-and-breakfast-berlin.de. Single and double rooms and apartments with rates starting at around €28 a night.
Bed & Breakfast Privatzimmervermittlung 🖰www.bed-and-breakfast.de. Part of a national chain, offering rooms ranging from the simple to the luxurious.
Citybed ☎030/23 62 36 10, 🖰www.citybed.de. Primarily an online booking tool for accommodation, with prices starting at around €20 per person.
Stadtbett ☎030/69 56 50 00, 🖰www.stadtbett .de. Another good way of finding rooms and apartments online, via a request service.
Zimmervermittlung 24, 🖰www .zimmervermittlung24.com. Wide range of rooms and apartments all over the city with vast online search and booking engine; prices start from around €30 per person.

Mostly long term

Agentur Wohnwitz ☎030/861 82 22, 🖰www .wohnwitz.com. Agency offering rooms in shared flats and apartments.
Berlin Inn ☎030/339 88 77 82, 🖰www.berlin -inn.de. A good selection of rooms and apartments, short-and long-term lets.
Fine & Mine ☎030/235 51 20, 🖰www.fineand mine.de. Search engine of international agency with some short-term lets too.
Zeitraum Wohnkonzepte ☎030/441 66 22, 🖰www.zeit-raum.de. Helpful agency with rooms and apartments for short-and long-term let.

Eating and drinking

B erlin has all the restaurants, cafés and bars you'd expect from a major European capital, with virtually every imaginable cuisine: indeed, the national gastronomy generally takes a back seat to Greek, Turkish, Balkan, Indian and Italian specialities. Berliners tend to eat out regularly, so prices are reasonable – a main dish typically costs around €6 to €10 – though you can easily triple this figure by dining at top-end places serving **Neue Deutsche Küche**. In line with Berlin's rolling nightlife timetable, you can pretty much eat and drink around the clock. Most restaurants happily serve until around 11pm, and even later it's not hard to find somewhere in most neighbourhoods. Another common Berlin feature is how many places morph from one type of venue into another through the day. A good place to slurp a morning coffee and read a paper may well become a restaurant later on before bringing out the decks for a DJ until the wee small hours, then close only to repeat the cycle two or three hours later. The distinction between restaurants, cafés, bars and even clubs can be difficult to make: outside busy periods, many restaurants are perfectly happy to serve you just a coffee, and some of the tastiest food you'll eat on your trip may be from a café.

Our **listings** are divided into **cafés, bars and cheap eats** – all good daytime venues for hanging out or having a quick bite; **restaurants** – recommended for a full meal; and **microbreweries (Hausbrauereien) and beer gardens** – venues for the kind of concerted beer drinking Germany is famous for. Bars that are also good as part of a night out are mentioned again in the nightlife section (see p.223); other bars in that section may also do food, but not of the sort that you would go out of your way for.

You can find more or less every type of restaurant, café, bar and *Imbiss* (see box, p.208) in every Berlin district, but a few generalizations stand. Places around **Unter den Linden** and all the way to **Alexanderplatz** largely provide sightseers with coffee and large slabs of rich cake and traditional German meals, with the latter particularly well represented in the **Nikolaiviertel**, Berlin's old quarter. The **Spandauer Vorstadt**, particularly the stretch along Oranienburger Strasse, is far more eclectic and hip, but still caters primarily to visitors so the standards tend to be lower and prices higher than elsewhere in town, though it's still a good district for browsing if you're unsure what you're after. Outside Mitte, traditional coffee houses still congregate around the **Ku'damm**, while the scene in **Schöneberg** and **Kreuzberg** revolves around three distinct and fairly bohemian areas, which attract an older, less image-conscious crowd: Winterfeldplatz is a popular gay centre, Bergmann-strasse a relatively bohemian strip, and Oranienstrasse a grittier counter-cultural stronghold – you could spend weeks exploring these districts before exhausting the possibilities. The gastro scene in Berlin's club land and student nightlife quarter of **Friedrichshain** has started to come of age and is good for

Breakfast and Sunday brunch

Breakfast (*Frühstück*) will often be provided by your hotel, but many cafés serve it throughout the day. Prices start around €3 for a basic bread, eggs and jam affair, rising to €15 for more exotic, champagne-swigging delights.

Typically, you'll be offered a small platter of **cold meats** (usually sausage-based) and **cheeses**, along with a selection of marmalades, jams and honey, and, occasionally, muesli or another cereal. You're generally given a variety of **breads**, one of the most distinctive features of German cuisine. Both brown and white rolls are popular, often baked with caraway, coriander, poppy or sesame seeds. The rich-tasting black rye bread, known as *Pumpernickel*, is a particular favourite.

Freshly brewed **coffee** is the normal accompaniment, though plain or herbal **tea** and **hot chocolate** are common alternatives. A glass of orange **juice** is sometimes included as well.

Sunday brunch is a popular affair, offering first-class people-watching and often excellent food – they are particularly good value when offered as part of a **buffet**. Expect to pay €6–10 for unlimited food; drinks are paid for separately. Good places for brunch include *Restauration 1900* in Prenzlauer Berg (see p.221) and *Morgenland* (see p.221) in Kreuzberg, though trawling Friedrichshain's Simon-Dach-Strasse for an attractive spread also always yields good results.

inexpensive meals. As Berlin's bohemian yuppie district, **Prenzlauer Berg** has a particularly well-balanced mix of cafés, better restaurants and late-night nightlife.

Cafés, bars and cheap eats

The difference between many of Berlin's cafés, bars and snack places is slight, with distinctions blurred and labels often pointless. Traditionally the **Kneipe**, or pub, was a rather dowdy, male-orientated drinking hole and **cafés** the sort of self-consciously elegant coffee house where you'd treat yourself to mid-afternoon cakes, pastries and handmade chocolates in the Viennese tradition. Both still exist in Berlin and can be fun to seek out, but in recent decades they've fused into relaxed haunts where you're encouraged to linger over a coffee or a beer at virtually any time of day. Many of these places also serve breakfast and inexpensive full meals, usually with an international menu. Ethnic places in particular will focus on being **budget eateries** – many little more than a glorified *Imbiss* – where you'd go to chow down on a pile of noodles or plate of falafel rather than hang out. These are always more interesting than their international fast-food chain cousins which also dot the city, though the local *Nordsee* chain, which specializes in fish and seafood concoctions, is worth a try.

Unter den Linden and around

See map on pp.46–47.

Operncafé Operapalais, Unter den Linden 5
☎ 030/20 26 83. Located in a former royal palace, this elegant café evokes the atmosphere of Imperial Berlin, and its coffee and amazing cakes make it a good stopping-off point after seeing the local sights. U-Bahn Französische Str. Daily 8am–midnight.

Alexanderplatz and around

The following places are marked on the map on p.71.

Asia Snack Bahnhof Friedrichstr. For once dishes closely resemble the menu photos at this small place selling quick fixes of Thai and pan-Asian food to hungry diners. U- & S-Bahn Alexanderplatz. Daily 10am until late.

Käse Konig Panoramastr. 1. Join locals at this basic cafeteria serving decent

The Imbiss

The German term *Imbiss* was originally coined for the little food stalls at medieval markets, and Berliners are certainly past masters in serving inexpensive food for eating on the hoof. The city's recent immigrant population has built on the tradition, adapting recipes to produce quick portable meals. Today virtually every Berlin street has an *Imbiss*, with major concentrations in commercial areas and train stations. Some have a bit of seating, but many only a couple of high tables on which to lean.

The simple sausage has traditionally been the most popular *Imbiss* item and in Berlin it's been transformed into the local speciality **Currywurst** – a chubby smoked pork sausage smothered in curried ketchup – often served with French fries (*Pommes frites*). Another local *Imbiss* speciality is the *Boulette*, a hamburger pattie made from ground beef, eggs, butter and onions, which was first introduced into the city by the French Huguenots in the late 1600s.

But these days the most common of all are **Greek**, **Turkish** and **Middle Eastern** *Imbiss* stands selling *döner*, *gyros* or *swarma* respectively – all essentially kebabed meat or chicken bundled into pita, tortilla or ciabatta-style bread sandwich with salad and a sauce – usually hot (*scharf*), herb (*Kräuter*) or garlic (*Knoblauch*). All are likely to be delicious and fill you up for around €3.

The standard of *Imbiss* food throughout Berlin is very good since most rely on local business, so in general it's not worth going out of your way for one. But if you want to make sure you are having as good a *Currywurst* as the city can offer, try either the neonlit *Curry 195*, Kurfürstendamm 195 (Mon–Thurs 11am–5am, Fri & Sat 11am–6am, Sun noon–5pm; see map, p.118), which is famed for its popularity with German politicians and celebrities (you can even buy champagne here), although its prices remain everyday; or the family-run *Imbiss Konnopke*, Schönhauser Allee 44a (Mon–Fri 6am–8pm; U-Bahn Eberswalder Str; see map, pp.150–151), which has been serving *Pommes* and *Wurst* from a pre-fab cabin beneath the S-Bahn lines for 75 years – surviving fascism, communism and World War II.

simple German and Central European food at low prices off a small daily menu – such as schnitzel or goulash with boiled potatoes for around €6. Two branches share the same block, the larger of the two is further from the bustle of the street and has more outdoor seating. U- & S-Bahn Alexanderplatz. Mon–Sat 8am–7pm, Sun 10am–7pm.

Zum Nussbaum Am Nussbaum 3 ☎030/242 30 95. In the heart of the Nikolaiviertel, this is a convincing copy of a prewar bar – destroyed in an air raid – that stood on the Fischerinsel and was favoured by the artists Heinrich Zille and Otto Nagel. This replica verges on the expensive, but it's a good place to soak up a bit of ersatz old Berlin ambience. U- Bahn Klosterstr. Mon–Sat 9am–6pm.

Spandauer Vorstadt

The following places are marked on the map on pp.82–83.

Barcomi's Deli Sophienstr. 21 ☎030/28 59 83 63. Situated in a pleasant courtyard, accessible from both Sophienstr. and Gipsstr., *Barcomi's* is a nice place to rest while gallery-hopping; it serves interesting soups and American-style baked goodies, as well as great breakfasts. U-Bahn Weinmeisterstr. Mon–Sat 9am–9pm, Sun 10am–9pm.

Dada Falafel Linienstr. 132 ☎030/27 59 69 27. Tiny Middle Eastern *Imbiss* with sleek decor, some seating and excellent falafel and *schwarma* sandwiches – the best of a clutch of cheap and cheerful options at this end of Oranienburger Str. U-Bahn Oranienburger Tor. Sun–Thurs 10am–2am, Sat 10am–3pm.

Dolores Rosa-Luxemburg-Str. 7 ☎030/28 09 95 97. As good a burrito as you'll find in Berlin, dished up in a small, funky and generally overcrowded cafeteria at staggeringly low prices. You'll leave very full, €4–6 poorer and maybe a bit bewildered by the à la carte menu system. U-Bahn

Ostalgie

Nostalgia for the East, or rather *Nostalgie* for the *Osten*, has produced *Ostalgie*, a hybrid word for a phenomenon that's been gathering momentum throughout the old East Germany. Though the sentiment might originate with those who can remember the collapsed country, this nostalgia for the iconography of communist East Germany has also proved immensely popular with visitors, spawning a mini-industry in Berlin.

Old Stasi hats on sale ▲

Ampelmann deckchairs ▼

A Trabant car ▼

Ampelmann pedestrian sign ▼

Why look back?

The meaning of *Ostalgie* is a little nebulous as it's slowly redefined itself since the *Wende*. What started as a **melancholic craving** for the securities of life in a communist state by the 16 million East Germans thrust into the turbulent and uncertain world of capitalism, became an expression of both **discontent and identity**. It was a protest at the quick eradication of a unique East German culture and its absorption into the West – a process that implied that all things Western were superior, and tended to mock everything from the East as laughably backward and naive. So *Ostalgie* became a way of affirming that some aspects of the GDR were worth **celebrating**, that – despite the many shortcomings of the state – it had also produced happy and rewarding moments in people's lives.

Icons of kitsch

These days *Ostalgie* stretches far beyond political debates and the 2003 film *Good Bye Lenin!*, with its nostalgic and comedic celebration of 1970s GDR kitsch and innocence. Visiting Berlin you'll come across a swathe of cult GDR icons, for example the chubby, cheerful **Ampelmann** from East German pedestrian crossings and the cute fibreglass **Trabant** car. There's been a revival of some **utilitarian GDR products**, including foods, household products and cosmetics made by companies that had gone out of business when Western goods flooded the market. Some pop up in grocery stores and corner shops, but the entire range is most easily found online, in emporiums such as Ossiversand (Ⓦwww.ossiversand.de). But most of Berlin's *Ostalgie* shops concentrate on **souvenirs**, particularly the Ampelmann shop and Mondos Arts.

A fun Ostalgie day

▶▶ **Breakfast in the Fernsehturm**
Berlin's biggest GDR icon – where the
tell-tale smell of East German linoleum
glue still lingers – from where you can
try and work out from above where the
Berlin Wall once split the city. See p.72

▶▶ **Drive a Trabi** Unleash your inner
Ossi behind the wheel of the two-stroke
chariot and decide for yourself if this old
East German workhorse deserves its
cult status. See p.29

▶▶ **Shop at the Ampelmann Store,
Hackeshen Höfe** You can buy a whole
host of Ampelmann-branded items here
at its flagship store, from deck chairs
and diaries to T-shirts and toys – and
even a bicycle helmet. See p.244

▶▶ **Visit Karl-Marx-Allee** Try to take in
the vast dimensions of this communist
boulevard where monumentalist,
wedding-cake style architecture
produced "palaces for workers, not
American egg-boxes!" and pick a
cardboard kit to make your own model
version of these high-rises at the Karl
Marx Buchhandlung. See p.147

▶▶ **Coffee at Café Sybille** Along with
coffee with cake, this café also has an
informative exhibition on the building of
Karl-Marx-Allee. See p.211

▶▶ **Shop at Mondos Arts** The ultimate
GDR shopping temple – devoted to
the country where consumerism was
virtually outlawed. See p.244

▶▶ **Visit the DDR Museum** Explore
what daily life was like in old East
Germany and pick up a copy of the
funny satirical film *Good Bye Lenin!*, if
you haven't already seen it. See p.75

▶▶ **Drink at Verkehrsberuhigte
Ost-Zone** This bar is decked out in
GDR memorabilia. See p.225

▶▶ **Sleep at Ostel** Nod off at the
orange-and-brown furnished *Ostel*
lodging. Rooms come with spartan-
looking double beds or bunk beds,
and are kitted out with East German
furniture, lamps and radios. See p.203

▲ Old East German toy

▼ Trabi safari

▼ Inspecting tourists' hands during a Trabi safari

▼ Ostel

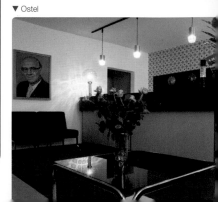

Das Leben
der Anderen

The Lives of Others▲

Stasi bugging device ▼

Peering through the Wall to the Death Strip ▼

Ostalgie's critics

Most agree that *Ostalgie* is just a good laugh, but the sentiment has its critics. Whistle-blowers warn of the dangers of posthumously glorifying any aspect of a totalitarian dictatorship and so glossing over a dreadful chapter of Germany's history. Among them is Berlin's mayor Klaus Wowereit (see p.252) who bluntly warned of the "need to be careful that the GDR does not achieve cult status". Certainly, cheerful as the Ampelmann and Trabi may be, and as refreshing as cravings for simple pleasures in a frugal existence may seem, a **balanced view** of East Germany is essential. Some counterbalance may come from the film **The Lives of Others**, winner of the 2006 best foreign film Oscar, which reminded Germany and the world of the oppression, censorship, secret police and intimidation that really underpinned life in communist Europe.

A serious Ostalgie day

▶▶ **Visit the Berlin Wall Memorial** Remind yourself what the Cold War really meant to the city. See p.95

▶▶ **Head to the Mauermuseum** The Wall Museum shows the extraordinary lengths to which people went to overcome the division. See p.135

▶▶ **Explore the Stasi: The Exhibition** Full of Stasi bugging devices that piece together evidence against former informers and operatives. See p.51

▶▶ **Take a tour at Hohenschönhause** Former detainees lead you on a tour round the prison and interrogation centre, and will impress upon you the extent of the psychological horror. See p.159

▶▶ **Watch The Lives of Others** Award-winning film that helps form an insight into how people's lives were touched and destroyed by the communist secret police. See p.302

Rosa-Luxemburg-Platz. Mon–Sat 11.30am–10pm, Sun 1pm–10pm.

Fischers Friedrichstr. 136 ☎030/28 87 93 13. Deli with counters and bar stools for quick sit-down meals. The chalk-board menu changes daily but pasta and fish dishes often feature and rarely cost more than €5, even though the quality is spot on. U-Bahn Oranienburger Tor. Mon–Fri 8am–8pm, Sat noon–6pm.

Gorki Park Weinbergsweg 25 ☎030/448 72 86. Tongue-in-cheek Soviet-themed café with 1970s Eastern Bloc-style furnishings and tasty and affordable Russian dishes like *blini* and *pelmeni* (mains average €8). A large *Milchcafé* comes with a delicious molasses cookie, and the weekend brunch buffet (€9) is a treat. Free wi-fi. U-Bahn Rosenthaler Platz. Daily 9.30am–2am.

Hackbarths Auguststr. 49a ☎030/282 77 04. Dominated by a huge triangular bar, *Hackbarths* attracts a very mixed crowd. The good choice of food includes tasty breakfasts and excellent tapas (from €2). U-Bahn Weinmeisterstr. Daily 10am until late.

Kapelle Zionskirchplatz 22–24 ☎030/44 34 13 00. High ceilings and apricot walls in the shadow of the hulking Zionskirche. A little off the beaten track but worth the detour particularly if you're heading to the flea-market on the Arkona-platz. Breakfasts, snacks, cakes and great frozen fruit juices available. U-Bahn Rosenthaler Platz. Daily 9am–3am.

Kilkenny Irish Pub Am Zwirngraben 17–20 ☎030/283 20 84. Large, very "oirish" pub, sprawling across several rooms, with a menu that includes Irish stew. S-Bahn Hackescher Markt. Daily 10am until late.

Oscar Wilde Irish Pub Friedrichstr. 112a ☎030/282 81 66. Generic Irish bar and something of a social club for Berlin's English-speaking community. The all-day breakfasts are good if you're craving a fry-up and the Irish stews aren't bad either. U-Bahn Oranienburger Tor. Mon–Fri noon–1am, Sat 1pm–3am, Sun 1pm–2am.

Strandbad Mitte Kleine Hamburger Str. 16 ☎030/24 62 89 63. At the end of a small street off the beaten tourist track, this inviting café and bar, with some outdoor seating, makes a good and calm retreat. Excellent breakfasts served 9am–4pm. U-Bahn Rosenthaler Platz. Daily 9am–2am (kitchen until midnight).

Tiergarten and around

The following places are marked on the map on pp.98–99.

Café Buchwald Bartningallee 29 ☎030/391 59 31. This old-fashioned *Konditorei* has been serving its famed *Baumkuchen* since 1852 (€2.80), and is good for a respite from a hard stroll around the Tiergarten. S-Bahn Bellevue. Mon–Sat 9am–6pm, Sun 10am–6pm.

Salomon Bagels Potsdamer Platz Arkaden, 1st floor. Good selection of bagels, sandwiches and desserts, but as with all the cheap eateries in this mall – they're concentrated in the basement – the noise and bustle don't exactly create a relaxing atmosphere. U- & S-Bahn Potsdamer Platz. Daily 9am–9pm.

City West

The following places are marked on the map on p.118.

Café Savigny Grolmanstr. 53 ☎030/31 51 96 12. Bright café serving superb coffee to an arty/media, mixed gay and straight crowd. Excellent for breakfast, served 9am–4pm. U-Bahn Ernst-Reuter-Platz. Daily 9am until late.

Dicke Wirtin Carmerstr. 9 ☎030/312 49 52. Traditional Berlin *Kneipe*, here since the 1920s and spruced up to make it more attractive to visitors who can pick from nine draught beers and basic snacks like *Schmalzbrot* (lard on bread €2.20). S-Bahn Savignyplatz. Daily noon until late.

Einhorn Mommsenstr. 2 ☎030/881 42 41. Vegetarian wholefood at its best, with a daily changing international menu and a fabulous lunch bar. Low prices (€4–7 per dish) mean it's often packed to standing, but the atmosphere remains friendly and relaxed. U-Bahn Uhlandstr. Mon–Fri 10am–5pm.

Gorilla Knesebeckstr. 5 ☎030/34 66 44 88. Vegetarian cafeteria, with bar-stool seating, which serves fresh quick meals using only organic ingredients. There's usually little more than a couple of potato- or pasta-based dishes of the day and some soups, but it's all excellent and well priced. S-Bahn Savignyplatz. Mon–Fri 8am–8pm, Sat & Sun 9am–8pm.

Lubitsch Bleibtreustr. 47 ☎030/882 37 56. Slick bistro-style café that's a bit on the expensive side and very popular with business people. U-Bahn Uhlandstr. Mon–Sat 10am–1am, Sun 8pm–1am.

Piccola Taormina Uhlandstr 29 ☏030/881 47 10. Enduringly popular wafer-thin pizza specialist with a strange setup: order what you want and pay at the bar, find a seat in the back room, listen up for a tannoy announcement when it's ready, then head back to the bar to collect. It's all a bit chaotic and very Italian, but well worth it for the food – slices from €1. U-Bahn Uhlandstr. Daily 11am–2am.

Tomasa Motzstr. 60 ☏030/213 23 45. Rather tacky 1970s-style interior, but excellent Mediterranean food and popular for breakfast (until 4pm) and brunch. Reservations essential. U- & S-Bahn Viktoria-Luise-Platz. Daily 8am–2am (kitchen until 11pm).

Zwiebelfisch Savignyplatz 7 ☏030/312 73 63. Corner bar that's a bit of a 1970s throwback for would-be arty and intellectual types. Jazz, earnest debate and good cheap grub (€5–11), like goulash and Swabian *Maultaschen* (ravioli), served until 1am. S-Bahn Savignyplatz. Daily noon–6am.

Schöneberg

The following places are marked on the map on p.128.

Baharat Falafel Winterfeldtstr. 37 ☏030/216 83 01. The best falafels this side of Baghdad in a bare-bones vegetarian *Imbiss*, with some seating. U-Bahn Nollendorfplatz. Daily noon–2am.

Café Einstein Kurfürstenstr. 58 ☏030/261 50 96. Housed in a seemingly ancient German villa, this is about as close as you'll get to the ambience of the prewar Berlin *Kaffeehaus*, with international newspapers and breakfast served until 2pm. Occasional live music, and a good garden. Expensive, though, and a little snooty. U-Bahn Nollendorfplatz. Daily 9am–midnight.

Café M Goltzstr. 33 ☏030/216 70 92. Though littered with tatty plastic chairs and precious little else, *M* is Berlin's most favoured rendezvous for self-styled creative types and the conventionally unconventional. Usually packed, particularly for its famous breakfasts; happy hour lasts from 8–10pm when cocktails cost €5.50. U-Bahn Nollendorfplatz. Mon–Fri 8am until late, Sat & Sun 9am until late.

Felsenkeller Akazienstr. 2 ☏030/781 34 47. An unpretentious old bar, recently discovered by a young hip crowd. Unchanged by the experience, it continues to pour beer and dish up cheap food. S-Bahn Julius-Leber-Brücke. Mon–Fri 4pm–2am, Sat noon–2am, Sun 6pm–2am.

Habibi Goltzstr. 24 ☏030/215 33 32. Amiable late-night falafel shop with seating. U-Bahn Nollendorfplatz. Fri & Sat 11am–5am, Sun–Thurs 11am–3am.

Kleisther Hauptstr. 5 ☏030/784 67 38. Neighbourhood institution perennially crowded with style-conscious alternative types, which does a good Sun buffet brunch (10am–4pm; €8.50). U-Bahn Kleistpark. Thurs–Sat 9am–5pm, Sun–Wed 9am–1pm.

Tori Katsu Winterfeldtstr. 7 ☏030/216 34 66. Slightly chaotic Japanese *Imbiss* – here long before sushi became popular – specializing in dishes with breaded chicken. U-Bahn Büllowstr. Mon–Fri 11am–1pm, Sat & Sun noon–11pm.

Toronto Crellestr. 17 ☏030/781 92 30. A classy wood-panelled café that spills out onto a large leafy plaza – perfect on a fine summer day. It serves excellent home-made cake and a Sun brunch buffet (10am–3pm; €10). S-Bahn Julius-Leber-Brücke. Mon–Sat 8.30am–11.30pm, Sun 10am–11pm.

Western Kreuzberg

The following places are marked on the map on pp.132.

Atlantic Bergmannstr. 100 ☏030/691 92 92. Kreuzberg's attempt at an upmarket and chic New York bar, it's good for people-watching along Bergmannstr. from the outside tables, busy at any time of day and also serves good snacks. U-Bahn Mehringdamm. Daily 9am until late.

Barcomi's Bergmannstr. 21 ☏030/694 81 38. American-style coffee house with exotic blends accompanied by bagels, brownies and other oversized American baked goods – great cheesecake and carrot cake. Scattered copies of the *New Yorker* as well. U-Bahn Gneisenaustr. Mon–Sat 8am–9pm, Sun 9am–9pm.

Milagro Bergmannstr. 12 ☏030/692 23 03. Superb café-cum-restaurant that's become fiercely popular for its imaginative food and huge breakfasts (until 4pm). Kloster beer on tap. U-Bahn Gneisenaustr. Daily 9am–1am.

Pagode Bergmannstr. 88 ☎030/619 26 40. The
Thai meals dished up here enjoy a high
reputation among Berlin's *Imbiss*
aficionados. U-Bahn Gneisnaustr. Daily
noon–midnight.

Sale e Tabacci Kochstr. 18 ☎030/25 29 50 03.
Authentic and beautiful Italian café near
Checkpoint Charlie where journalists and
architects linger over espresso and
cigarettes. Food is contemporary and uses
top-notch ingredients, but is a little overpriced, with mains around €9–25. U-Bahn
Kochstr. Mon–Fri 9am–2am, Sat & Sun
10am–2am.

Eastern Kreuzberg and Friedrichshain

The following places are marked on the
map on pp.142–143.

Ankerklause Kottbusser Damm 104 ☎030/693
56 49. This nautically themed pub
overlooking a bucolic canal has been transformed into a hip bar playing a mixture of
techno and easy listening. Great breakfast
choice (served until 4pm) with first-class
French toast and a Mexican breakfast that
will tide you over until dinner. Usually
packed by 11pm. U-Bahn Kottbusser Tor.
Tues–Sun 10am–4am, Mon 4pm–4am
(kitchen open until 11pm).

🔥 Burgermeister Oberbaumstr. 8. Cult
burger joint in a converted old
Prussian public toilets, by the elevated
underground station at Schlesisches Tor,
serving fresh and delicious burgers
(€2–3.50) that could hold their own in far
classier surroundings. Has a couple of
places to sit, but mostly it's standing room
only and often packed. U-Bahn Schlesisches Tor. Mon–Thurs 11am–2am, Fri &
Sat 11am–4am, Sun 3pm–2am.

Café am Uter Paul-Lincke-Ufer 43 ☎030/61 82
92 00. A fun place with good views of the
Landwehrkanal if you sit outside and
reasonable bar food and €7 breakfast
buffets at weekends. U-Bahn Kottbusser
Tor. Daily 9am until late.

Café Sybille Karl-Marx-Allee 72 ☎030/29 35 22
03. Airy café with a fin-de-siècle feel – it's
been here over a century – and a diverting
exhibition about Karl-Marx-Allee in the back.
Worth a visit for the cakes and ice creams
alone. U-Bahn Strausberger Platz. Daily
10am–8pm.

Café V Lausitzer Platz 12 ☎030/612 45 05.
Cosy, dimly lit, bohemian place beside a

▲ Café Sybille

leafy Kreuzberg park and as good a
hangout as restaurant. Though serving
fish, everything else is vegetarian, with
plenty of tofu and seitan (wheat gluten)
on offer – find them on pizzas and in
salads; the fennel nut salad is particularly
good (mains €8–12). Menus change
weekly. U-Bahn Görlitzer Bahnhof.
Daily 10am–2am.

Freischwimmer Vor dem Schlesischen Tor
2a ☎030/61 07 43 09. An old boathouse
on a feeder canal near the River Spree
has become a lovely waterside pre- and
post- club hangout with a good range of
snacks on offer. U-Bahn Schlesiches Tor.
Tues–Fri 4pm until late, Sat & Sun
10am until late.

Kvartira Nr. 62 Lübbener Strasse 18.
☎0179/134 33 43. Atmospheric Russian café
in 1920s-era dark red and gold decor
serving Russian classics such as *borscht*
(stew; €3), delicious *pelimi* (dumplings;
€4.50) and tea flavoured with jam – as well
as some great chocolate cake. U-Bahn
Schlesisches Tor. Sun–Wed 11am–midnight,
Thurs–Sat 11am–midnight.

Nachtigall Imbiss Ohlauerstr. 10 ☎030/611 71 15. Arab specialities, including the delicious *schwarma* kebab – lamb and hummus in pita bread. Good salads for vegetarians as well. U-Bahn Görlitzer Bahnhof. Daily 11am–midnight.

Yellow Sunshine Wiener Str. 19 ☎0178/21 46 00 66. Vegetarian self-service burger bar, with set meals including fries and a drink from €5.10. The toasties are good for breakfast. U-Bahn Görlitzer Bahnhof. Fri & Sat noon–1am, Sun–Thurs noon–midnight.

Prenzlauer Berg

The following places are marked on the map on pp.150–151.

Al Hamra Raumerstr. 16 ☎030/42 85 00 95. Comfortable Arab café with shabby decor but decent Mediterranean food, beer, water pipes, backgammon and chess, plus internet terminals and wi-fi. U-Bahn Eberswalder Str. Daily 10am–3am.

Duy Thai Kollwtizstr. 89 ☎030/44 04 74 44. Inexpensive and tasty Thai cuisine, including crispy duck with fruit, as well as many vegetarian and noodle dishes. U-Bahn Senefelderplatz. Mon–Fri noon–midnight, Sat & Sun 1pm–midnight.

Intersoup Schliemannstr. 31 ☎030/23 27 30 45. Mellow den with an encyclopedic collection of excellent soups (€3.50–5) and a relaxing vibe. The place's trademark soup – Thai lemon grass, bean sprouts, noodle, coconut milk with chicken, tofu, fish or shrimp – is well worth a try. DJs play until late. S-Bahn Prenzlauer Allee. Daily noon–4am.

Kietzkantine Oderberger Str. 50 ☎030/448 44 84. Choose from just two or three excellent daily specials at rock-bottom prices in this hugely popular bistro.

There's always something vegetarian, and students get a discount – order and pay at the till, the food will then be brought to your seat. U-Bahn Eberswalder Str. Mon–Fri 9am–4pm.

Metzer Eck Metzer Str. 33 ☎030/442 76 56. Founded in 1913, this *Kneipe* was a well-known haunt during GDR times, as the signed celebrity photos that adorn the walls attest. Its old-fashioned feel makes a change from the slicker, newer places in the neighbourhood, and it serves inexpensive traditional dishes like sausages, *Boulette* and fried potatoes (€5–9). U-Bahn Senefelderplatz. Mon–Fri 4pm–1am, Sat & Sun 6pm–1am.

Morgenrot Kastanienallee 85 ☎030/44 31 78 44. Bohemian Berlin hits its stride in this collective café where G8 riots are planned and vegan breakfasts consumed. Everything is organic and the vegetarian buffet breakfast (until 3pm) is excellent and costs between €4 and €8: pay according to how wealthy you consider yourself. U-Bahn Eberswalder Str. Tues–Fri 10am until late; Sat & Sun 11am until late.

November Husemannstr. 15 ☎030/442 84 25. Uncluttered, exposed wood place, just north of Kollwitzplatz, with imaginative German daily specials (€7–13), a reasonable Sun brunch (9am–4pm; €9) and outdoor seating in a pleasantly quiet residential street. U-Bahn Senefelderplatz. Daily 9am–2am (kitchen until 11.30pm).

Pasternak Knaackstr. 24 ☎030/441 33 99. Authentic upmarket Russian place that recalls the cafés and restaurants founded by Berlin's large Russian émigré community during the 1920s. A nice spot for caviar and champagne, a *Milchcafé* or a more substantial meal from the good selection of Russian dishes, including

Will Berliners butt out?

With one-third of Berliners smoking, and typically puffing on their first cigarette aged 13, Germany's smoking ban, introduced after much deliberation in 2008 would always prove hard to enforce. Technically this introduced a general **ban on smoking** in bars and restaurants, except in separate smoking rooms, though small local pubs smaller than 75 square metres are exempt. So too are clubs, though there is technically a ban on lighting up on the dancefloor. Many other places have elected to continue to allow smoking, by declaring themselves a *Raucherclub* (smokers' club) with a sign in the window. An illegal compromise, but one the police seem happy to tolerate.

borscht, pelmeni and blini. The range of vodkas is suitably extensive. U-Bahn Senefelderplatz. Daily 9am until late, kitchen until midnight.

Wohnzimmer Lettestr. 6 ☎030/445 54 58. The rumpled and ramshackle living room atmosphere helps make this a relaxed and sociable hangout at any time of day – and the comfy sofas make leaving hard. Breakfast served until 4pm. U-Bahn Eberswalder Str. Daily 9am–4am.

Zuckerfee Greifenhagener Str. 15 ☎030/52 68 61 44. Gastronomic concept based on Tchaikovsky's The Nutcracker and named after the Sugar Plum fairy. Most items are whipped up with sweet tooths in mind, and it's a great spot for breakfast – choose from fluffy blueberry pancakes and croissants with home-made jams. Otherwise there's a good line in soups, salads, waffles and ice creams later on. U-Bahn Schönhauser Allee. Tues–Sun 10am–6pm.

Köpenick

The following places are marked on the map on p.165.

Braustübel Müggelseedamm 164 ☎030/645 57 16. Waterside pub of the Berliner Bürgerbräu brewery, serving German and well-priced international dishes (mains around €8) and the fine local beer Rot Händel. S-Bahn Friedrichshagen and tram #60 or #61. Tues–Sat noon–midnight, Sun 11am–midnight.

Josef Heinrich Bölschestr. 11 ☎030/64 09 28 19. Simple modern café-bar, at the southern end of Friedrichshagen's

main drag, with basic modern pub grub – soups, nachos and a cheese platter (all at around €6), and a good Sun buffet brunch (€8.50). S-Bahn Friedrichshagen and tram #60 or #61. Mon–Fri 5pm until late; Sat 2pm until late; Sun 10pm until late.

Schlosscafe Köpenick Schlossinsel ☎030/65 01 85 85. Elegant café beside Schloss Köpenick, with lake views and excellent fresh daily dishes (mains €8–17), good cakes and a wonderful Sun brunch (10am–2pm; €14). S-Bahn Köpenick and bus M69, tram #67 or #68. May–Sept Tues–Sun 10am–11pm; Oct & April Tues–Sun 10am–7pm; Nov–March Mon–Sun 10am–6pm.

Spandau

The following places are marked on the map on p.177.

Barfly Brüderstr. 47 ☎030/331 55 55. Laidback, living room-style café with a good, ever-changing selection of food. All meats are organic and the weekend brunch buffet (10am–2pm; €10.50) is a winner. U- & S-Bahn Rathaus Spandau. Mon–Fri 8am–3am, Sat & Sun 9am–3am.

Florida Eiscafe Klosterstr. 15 ☎030/331 56 66. Ice cream parlour with a Berlin-wide reputation; you'll need to wait in line to see what the fuss is all about but that gives you time to choose from the 41 flavours. U- & S-Bahn Rathaus Spandau. Daily noon–11pm.

Microbreweries and beer gardens

By German standards Prussian beers aren't famous, yet Berlin, like the rest of Germany, has seen a mini renaissance of its **microbreweries (Hausbrauereien)**. The house beers in these places are generally top quality, and the decor is suitably shiny vat brewery-chic. **Beer gardens** in Berlin play a significant role as convivial outdoor gathering points, once they emerge from hibernation around the end of March. Some of the best places are out in the suburbs though, particularly along the shores of the city's lakes in **Köpenick** and **Zehlendorf**.

Alexanderplatz and around

The following places are marked on the map on p.71.

Brauhaus Georgbräu Spreeufer 4 ☎030/242 42 44. A merry touristy clientele, also popular

among locals for its excellent beer and traditional German food. U-Bahn Klosterstr. Daily 10am–midnight.

Brauhaus Mitte Karl-Liebknecht-Str. 13 ☎030/24 78 38 31 11. All the trappings of a Bavarian beer hall including the excellent

Berliner Weisse

Berlin's most famous and distinctive beer is **Berliner Weisse**. The brew is only just fermented and still quite watery and sour, so it's traditionally drunk with a shot of fruity syrup, or *Schuss*. Ask for it *mit grün* and you get a dash of woodruff, creating a green beverage with a herby taste; *mit rot* secures a raspberry-flavoured drink that works wonders on a breakfast time hangover.

beers – try the delicious Weissen, a cloudy Bavarian speciality – re-created in the heart of Berlin. Good for basic pub-food with well-priced lunch specials for €6. U- & S-Bahn Alexanderplatz. Mon–Sat 10am–midnight, Sun 10am–11pm.

Tiergarten and around

The following places are marked on the map on pp.98–99.

Café am Neuen See Lichtensteinallee 2 ☏ **030/254 49 30**. A little piece of Bavaria smack in the middle of the Tiergarten; this beer garden is next to a picturesque lake where you can rent a rowing boat. The usual snacks are served alongside frothing jugs. S- & U-Bahn Zoologischer Garten. Daily 10am–11pm.
Schleusenkrug Müller-Breslau-Str. ☏ **030/313 99 09**. Wedged between a canal lock, the zoo and Tiergarten, this is a great spot to spend a last hour before hopping on a train at Zoo Bahnhof. Chairs are easy to manoeuvre for optimal sunning, and

▲ Café Am Neuen See

anything off the small daily menu is a safe bet. Inside, it is modern diner chic. S- & U-Bahn Zoologischer Garten. Daily: March–Oct 10am until late; Nov–Feb 10am–6pm.

Charlottenburg-Wilmersdorf

See map on p.122.
Brauhaus Lemke Luisenplatz 1 ☏ **030/30 87 89 79**. Large microbrewery, which is almost a German cliché for its muscular bar staff carrying large numbers of frothing mugs. The menu of traditional staples – sausage salad, pepper steak, pork chops – fits in perfectly, is reasonably priced and available until 11pm. Note that the beer will keep coming unless you put your beer mat on the glass. U-Bahn Richard-Wagner-Platz. Mon–Thurs & Sun 9am–1am, Fri & Sat 9am–2am.

Western Kreuzberg

See map on p.132.
Golgotha Dudenstr. 48–64 ☏ **030/785 24 53**. Enormous and hugely popular summer-only beer garden and disco (from 10pm) perched in the Viktoriapark near the top of Kreuzberg's hill. Breakfast served until 3pm. U- & S-Bahn Yorckstr. April–Sept daily 10am until late.

Prenzlauer Berg

The following places are marked on the map on pp.150–151.
Pfefferberg Schönhauser Allee 176 ☏ **030/44 38 34 04**. This popular outdoor beer garden, in the courtyard of a former brewery, offers Czech and Bohemian tipples among its range of draught beers. Food is limited to meaty items from a couple of stalls. U-Bahn Senefelderplatz. Daily 11.30am–3.30pm & 5.30pm until late.
Prater Kastanienallee 7–9 ☏ **030/44 48 56 88**. In summer you can swig beer, feast on Bratwurst and other native food, and listen to Seventies German rock in the traditional beer garden; in winter the beer hall offers a

similarly authentic experience. U-Bahn Eberswalder Str. Mon–Sat 6pm until late, Sun noon until late.

Treptow

See map on p.144.
Haus Zenner in der Eierschale Alt-Treptow 14–17 ☎030/533 72 11. A large and popular beer garden by the shore of the Spree River. S-Bahn Treptower Park. Daily 10am–midnight.

Köpenick

See map on p.165.
Schrörs am Müggelsee Josef-Nawrocki-Str. 16, Friedrichshagen ☎030/64 09 58 80. Waterfront beer garden, at the northern end of the Spreetunnel, ideally placed for a beer before or after a wander along the lake shore. After 7pm you can buy cheap local specialities like herring and fried potatoes (€5.50). S-Bahn Friedrichshagen and tram #60 or #61. Daily 11am until late.

Zehlendorf

The following places are marked on the map on p.173.

Alter Krug Königin-Luise-Str. 52 ☎030/84 31 95 40. Rustic pub opposite Domäne Dahlem and close to the U-Bahn station; the large beer garden makes it an ideal counterbalance to the nearby museums, or prepare yourself for your culture fix with breakfast or the Sun brunch buffet (10am–2pm; €9). Later on there's lots of traditional meat-and-potatoes fare to choose from: mains around €12. U-Bahn Dahlem-Dorf. Daily 9am–11pm.
Loretta am Wannsee Kronprinzessinweg 260 ☎030/803 51 56. Inviting tree-lined beer garden with Wannsee views enjoyed by a mixed crowd digging into snacks and beer – let down by a confusing ordering system that requires items to be ordered at different tills. S-Bahn Wannsee. Daily 11pm until late.

Spandau

See map on p.177.
Brauhaus Spandau Neuendorfer Str. 1 ☎030/353 90 70. Brewery with beer garden and various beer halls. U-Bahn Altstadt Spandau. Mon 4pm–1am, Tues–Thurs 11am–1am, Fri 11am–2am, Sat 10am–2am, Sun 10am–midnight.

Restaurants

Eating at Berlin's restaurants is inexpensive by international standards: main courses start at around €6, and drinks aren't much pricier than in bars. When it comes to **tipping**, add a euro or so to the bill, since a fifteen percent service charge is already added. A tip should be given directly to your server when paying, rather than left on the table.

Italian, Greek and Asian restaurants often provide the best bargains, while traditional German places tend to be pricey and their food served is heavy and old-fashioned – dumplings, roast pork, sauerkraut and the like.

For most of the restaurants listed below you can just walk in, though on weekend nights or at the most expensive places, **booking** is recommended.

Unter den Linden and around

The following places are marked on the map on pp.46–47.
Borchardt Französische Str. 47 ☎030/81 88 62 62. A re-creation of an elegant prewar French restaurant of the same name, with original high ceilings and tile floors, and widely considered one of the top restaurants in the city. Delectable beef dishes

(€20–30) make regular appearances, though the menu changes every day. U-Bahn Französische Str. Daily noon–midnight.
🏃 **Käfer Dachgarten Platz der Republik 1** ☎030/22 62 99 33. Famous for its location on the roof of the Reichstag and its 180-degree view of eastern Berlin, this restaurant specializes in gourmet renditions of regional German dishes (mains €8–30). A reservation here also means you get to nip

German cuisine

To enjoy traditional **German cuisine**, it does help if you share the national penchant for solid, fatty food accompanied by compensatingly healthy fresh vegetables and salad.

The **pig** is the staple of the German menu – it's prepared in umpteen different ways, and just about every part eaten. Sausages are the country's most popular snack, while *Kassler Rippen* (smoked and pickled pork chops) and *Eisbein* (pigs' trotters) are Berlin favourites – although the fatty *Eisbein* tends to be more of a winter speciality. *Königsberger Klopse* (meat dumplings in a caper- and lemon-flavoured sauce) also appear on many menus.

Potatoes are used imaginatively, too: try *Kartoffelpuffer* (flour and potatoes mixed into a pancake) or *Pellkartoffeln mit Quark und Leinöl*, a combination of baked potatoes, low-fat cheese and linseed oil that's best digested with lashings of beer or schnapps.

Surprisingly for a country known for its cakes, **desserts** in Berlin's German restaurants are something of an anticlimax. *Rote Grütze* (mixed soft berries eaten hot or cold with vanilla sauce) is one of the few distinctive dishes. Otherwise, it's the usual selection of fresh and stewed fruits, cheeses and ice creams; if you have a sweet tooth, you're best off heading for a café that serves one of the delicious cakes or *gateaux* of which Germans are so fond.

in a side entrance and avoid the consistently long line at the front entrance. S-Bahn Unter den Linden. Daily 9am–midnight, with last orders taken at 10pm.

Margaux Unter den Linden 78, entrance on Wilhelmstr. ☎030/22 65 26 11. Onyx walls, marble floors and burgundy upholstery set the stage for this upscale restaurant, whose daily menu is dictated by the quality of available supplies. The gracious maitre d' will happily recommend wines from their selection of seven hundred; prices are harder to swallow, with mains from €26–42, but a good-value alternative is offered in the form of set meals, with three-course lunches (€35) and dinners (€95). S-Bahn Unter den Linden. Mon–Sat 7pm until late (kitchen until 10.30pm).

Umatoo Friedrichstr. 71 ☎030/20 94 61 50. Japanese joint underneath the huge spiral staircase of the Quartier 206 shopping mall. It serves dishes like *sashimi* and *bento* boxes (mains average €11) and is great for lunch specials, which include salads and ice-tea. U-Bahn Französiche Str. Mon–Fri 11am–8pm, Sat 11am–6pm.

VAU Jägerstr. 54–55 ☎030/202 97 30. Sleek and fiercely popular high-end restaurant that specializes in utilizing ingredients from the Berlin area. The menu changes often, but expect to see intriguing combinations such as scallops, red beets, dove and polenta, or halibut, spiced *taboule*, carrot and apple –

with prices hovering around the €35 mark. For a cheaper sample, try the selection of €12 lunchtime specials. U-Bahn Hausvogteiplatz. Mon–Sat noon–2.30pm & 7–10.30pm.

Alexanderplatz and around

The following places are marked on the map on p.71.

Emmas Heiligegeistkirchplatz 1 ☎030/24 63 17 32. Smart bistro specializing in simple fresh German food of the meat and potatoes variety, but with the addition of fresh veggies and modern twists to make things less stodgy. It's a particularly good choice for inexpensive lunches (€6.50), such as carrot and ginger soup followed by a rich goulash. S-Bahn Hackescher Markt. 11.30am–midnight.

Zille-Stube Spreeufer 3 ☎030/242 52 47. Traditional German restaurant and homage to Berlin life – and to artist Heinrich Zille. Zille used to drink nearby at Zum Nussbaum (see p.77), and his illustrations line the wood-clad walls. Particularly good on the menu of old Berlin favourites are the *Rinderroulade* (beef-stuffed cabbage leaves) and *Sauerbraten* (marinated pot roast), both for around €12. U-Bahn Klosterstr. Daily noon–10pm.

Zur letzten Instanz Waisenstr. 14–16 ☎030/242 55 28. Berlin's oldest *Kneipe*, with a wonderfully old-fashioned interior, including a classic tiled oven, and a great beer garden. Reasonably priced traditional dishes, all with legal-themed names like *Zeugen-Aussage* ("Eyewitness account"), a reminder of the days when people used to drop in on the way to the nearby courthouse. Considered so authentically German that foreign heads of state are often brought here: Mikhail Gorbachev dined at *Zur letzten* in 1989, as has, more recently, Jacques Chirac. If all the meaty dishes (€9–14) look too heavy, try the simple *Boulette*, Berlin's home-made mince and herb burger, done here to perfection. U-Bahn Klosterstr. Mon–Sat noon–11pm, Sun noon–9pm.

Spandauer Vorstadt

The following places are marked on the map on pp.82–83.

Amrit Oranienburger Str. 45 ℡030/28 88 48 40. A cut above most of Berlin's very average Indian restaurants, delivering good-quality ingredients and fresh spices at reasonable prices (mains €7–12) and in clean-cut contemporary surroundings. Lots of veggie choices. U-Bahn Oranienburger Tor. Sun–Thurs 11am–midnight, Fri & Sat noon until late.

Beth Café Tucholskystr. 40 ℡030/281 31 35. Small and spartan, yet slightly snooty, vegetarian kosher café run by a small Orthodox Jewish congregation, with pretty courtyard seating outside and no-smoking inside. The snacks and light meals are mostly Israeli and traditional eastern European specialities, most for about €6. S-Bahn Oranienburger Str. Sun–Thurs noon–8pm.

Hasir Oranienburger Str. 4 ℡030/28 04 16 16. One of Europe's finest Turkish restaurants with liveried waiters, tucked away in a courtyard near the Hackeschen Höfe. Predictably, you can't go wrong with any of the many lamb dishes – prepared either over a wooden coal grill or in a stone oven – and there are plenty of veggie options too. Main courses are mostly around the €15 mark, which is very reasonable, given the quality. S-Bahn Hackescher Markt. Daily 11.30am–1am.

Kasbah Gipsstr. 2 ℡030/27 59 43 61. Fabulous little Moroccan eatery with atmospheric dimness, and a certain Arabic charm – not least when the waiter washes your hands in rosewater. Pick from an unusual mix of starters that include *zaalouk*, a fruity aubergine dip, and *pastilla*,

Berlin ohne Speck – a guide for vegetarians

In the 1930s, Berlin had over thirty vegetarian restaurants, and while the city can't field anything like that amount today, it's still the best place for a vegetarian in a country that seems overwhelmingly to sustain itself on dead pig. There's a list of exclusively vegetarian places below: otherwise, you should generally steer clear of pubs and German restaurants, whether traditional or Neue Deutsche Küche – lard and beef stock are used ubiquitously, and there's an unwritten convention that no meal is really complete until sprinkled with small pieces of *Speck* (bacon). Thankfully, the city's cosmopolitan spread of cuisines means that choosing an Italian, Indian or Thai option will usually yield something without meat on the menu, and most upmarket cafés have a flesh-free option.

Useful phrases

Ich bin Vegetarier(in). I am a vegetarian (feminine ending in parenthesis).
Ich esse keinen Fleisch oder Fisch. I don't eat meat or fish.
Ich möchte keinen Speck oder Fleischbrühe essen. I don't want to eat bacon or meat stock.
Gibt's Fleisch drin? Has it got any meat in it?
Gibt's was ohne Fleisch? Do you have anything without meat in it?

Vegetarian restaurants

Beth Café (see p.217)
Café V (see p.211)
Einhorn (see p.209)
Gorilla (see p.209)

a flaky pastry filled with chicken and onion and coated with cinnamon and icing sugar. The choice of mains (€8–13) revolves around couscous variations and a number of first-class tajines (clay-pot stews). Clubby music and cocktails encourage lingering after dinner. U-Bahn Weinmeisterstr. Tues–Sun 6pm–midnight.

Kellerrestaurant im Brechthaus Chausseestr. 125 ☏ **030/282 38 43**. Atmospheric restaurant in the basement of Brecht's old house, decorated with Brecht memorabilia, including models of his stage sets. The Viennese specialities (mains €9–15) are from recipes dreamt up by Brecht's wife Helene Weigel, a busy actress with only East German ingredients at her disposal, so don't expect anything too elaborate or expensive. Reservations recommended. U-Bahn Oranienburger Tor. Daily 6pm until late.

Monsieur Vuong Alte Schönhauser Str. 46 ☏ **030/30 87 26 43**. Snazzy Vietnamese place with delicious soups and noodle dishes (€7–10) from a tiny menu – look out also for the daily specials on the blackboard, which are available without meat. Bench dining means you'll sometimes have to squeeze together with other diners – expect queues at peak times. Don't miss the delicious jasmine and artichoke teas, or the zesty fruit smoothies. U-Bahn Weinmeisterstr. Daily noon–midnight.

Pan Asia Rosenthaler Str. 38 ☏ **030/27 90 88 11**. Large, hip Asian restaurant, with long communal tables and simple modern decor, hidden in a courtyard beside the Hackeschen Höfe. The pan–Asian menu (mains €5–14) is huge, but avoid the pricey sushi, dull soups and bland Thai options and stick to the outstanding Chinese choices, such as *Pad Puk* (noodles with duck and vegetables). S-Bahn Hackescher Markt. Sun–Thurs noon–midnight, Fri & Sat noon–1am.

Unsicht-bar Gormannstr. 14 ☏ **030/24 34 25 00**. Hugely successful novelty restaurant (run by an organization of the blind and visually impaired), where you eat in total darkness. First, pick from one of several three- or four-course fixed menus (€37–54), including a vegetarian option, then follow your blind or partially sighted waiter into the pitch black for your meal. The idea is that without your eyesight, your other senses will be heightened, but you're likely to make other discoveries, too, including how hard it is to judge the amount of food that's on your plate or fork, or even down your front. U-Bahn Weinmeisterstr. Fri & Sat 6pm–1am, Sun–Thurs 5pm–1am.

Viva Mexico Chausseestr. 36 ☏ **030/280 78 65**. Authentic, family-owned Mexican restaurant with a vivacious vibe, fresh ingredients, moderate prices and salsa to die for. U-Bahn Naturkundemuseum. Mon–Thurs noon–11pm, Fri noon–midnight, Sat & Sun 5pm–midnight.

Yosoy Rosenthaler Str. 37 ☏ **030/28 39 12 13**. Inexpensive tapas bar, with beautiful tile work and Spanish staff, perfectly placed for before-drinking or after-clubbing dinners (€9–15). S-Bahn Hackescher Markt. Daily 11am until late.

Tiergarten

The following places are marked on the map on pp.98–99.

Angkor Wat Paulstr. 22 ☏ **030/393 39 22**. Excellent place, serving subtle variations on traditional Cambodian food at moderate prices (mains €10–15). The two-person set meals (from €30) are a great way to sample a cross-section of delicious dishes. S-Bahn Bellevue. Mon–Fri 6pm–midnight, Sat & Sun noon–midnight.

Paris-Moskau Alt-Moabit 141 ☏ **030/394 20 81**. Housed in a former train station on the Paris to Moscow line, this French gourmet restaurant is popular with politicians and civil servants from the nearby government district and manages to be elegant without being too snooty. But it's expensive: dishes such as the rack of lamb with roasted artichokes and gnocchi, or the pigeon-breast pie with fired goose liver on chicory with new potatoes, cost around €25; the six-course menu €72. S-Bahn Lehrter Bahnhof. Mon–Fri noon–3pm & 6–11pm, Sat & Sun 6pm–midnight.

City West

The following places are marked on the map on p.118.

Diekmann Meinekestr. 7 ☏ **030/883 33 21**. Longstanding Berlin bistro, with French colonial touches in the decor and on the menu; the €10 three-course business lunches are a bargain, otherwise you'll pay €17–23 for oft-changing mains that are

Wine

Traditionally many people's knowledge of German wine has started and ended with *Liebfraumilch*, the medium-sweet easy-drinking wine. Sadly, its success has obscured the quality of other German wines, especially those made from the *Riesling* grape, and it's worth noting that the *Liebfraumilch* drunk in Germany tastes nothing like the bilge swilled abroad.

The vast majority of German wine is white, as the grapes are better suited to the northern climate. If you're pining for a glass of red, try a *Spätburgunder* (Germany's answer to the *Pinot Noir* of Burgundy).

First step in any exploration of German wine should be to understand what's on the label: the predilection for Gothic script and gloomy martial crests makes this an uninviting prospect, but the division of categories is intelligent and helpful – if at first a little complex.

Wine categories

Like most EU wine, German wine is divided into two broad categories: *Tafelwein* ("table wine", for which read "cheap plonk") and *Qualitätswein* ("quality wine"), equivalent to the French *Apellation Controllée*.

TAFELWEIN

Tafelwein can be a blend of wines from any EU country; *Deutscher Tafelwein* must be 100-percent German. Like all German wines, *Tafelwein* can be *trocken* (dry), *halbtrocken* (medium dry) or *lieblich* (sweet). *Landwein* is a superior *Tafelwein*, equivalent to the French *Vin de Pays*, and medium dry.

QUALITÄTSWEIN

There are two basic subdivisions of *Qualitätswein*: **QbA** (*Qualitätswein eines bestimmten Anbaugebietes*) and **QmP** (*Qualitätswein mit Prädikat*). "QbA" wines come from eleven delimited regions and must pass an official tasting and analysis. "QmP" wines are further divided into six grades:

Kabinett The first and lightest style.

Spätlese Must come from late-picked grapes, which results in riper flavours.

Auslese Made from a selected bunch of grapes, making a concentrated medium-sweet wine. If labelled as a *trocken*, the wine will have lots of body and weight.

Beerenauslese Wine made from late-harvested, individually picked grapes. A rare wine, made only in the very best years, and extremely sweet.

Trockenbeerenauslese Trocken here means dry in the sense that the grapes have been left on the vine until some of the water content has evaporated. As with *Beerenauslese*, each grape will have been individually picked. This is a very rare wine that is intensely sweet and concentrated.

Eiswein Literally "ice wine", this is made from *Beerenauslese* grapes – a hard frost freezes the water content of the grape, concentrating the juice. Eiswein is remarkably fresh, due to its high acidity.

---

always fresh and reliable – the oysters are particularly good. U-Bahn Kurfürstendamm. Mon–Sat noon until late, Sun 6pm until late.

Florian Grolmanstr. 52 ☎030/313 91 84. Leading light of the Neue Deutsche Küche movement in Berlin, this is as much a place for Berlin's beautiful people to be seen as it is a place to eat. The food, similar to French nouvelle cuisine, is light and flavourful and only moderately expensive at €14–22 for

main courses. S-Bahn Savignyplatz. Daily 6pm–3am (kitchen until 2am).

Good Friends Kantstr. 30. ☎030/313 26 59. One of Berlin's few really authentic Cantonese restaurants, with many unusual items (mains €7–19). Always busy; evening bookings recommended. S-Bahn Savignyplatz. Daily noon–2am.

Paris Bar Kantstr. 152 ☎030/313 80 52. Once the city's most famous meeting place for artists, writers and intellectuals, high prices mean that it's now wholly the preserve of the moneyed middle classes – and visiting celebrities including Madonna, Robert de Niro and Mikhail Gorbachev. The food is French and Viennese in style and the service immaculate. Mains are around €18–26; weekday lunches, however, are a bargain at €8–12 each. U-Bahn Uhlandstr. Daily noon–1am.

Zwölf Apostel Bleibtreustr. **49** ☎**030/312 14 33.** This deluxe pizzeria has been packing them in for years, with out-of-the-ordinary toppings like smoked salmon and cream cheese and five types of calzone (mains €7–20). The €6.60 weekday lunch (11.30am–4pm) is excellent. Booking recommended. S-Bahn Savignyplatz. Daily 8am–1am.

Schöneberg

The following places are marked on the map on p.128.

Aroma Hochkirchstr. **8** ☎**030/782 58 21.** Quality Italian restaurant and one of the best options in this part of town, so it's advisable to book ahead. Mains cost between €7 and €15; the top-notch Sun brunch buffet (until 4pm) costs €9.50. Also has a small photo gallery and shows Italian films on Tues nights. U- & S-Bahn Yorckstr. Mon–Fri from 6pm, Sat from noon, Sun from 11am until late.

Edd's Thailändisches Lutzowstr. **81** ☎**030/215 52 94.** Huge portions of superbly cooked fresh Thai food make this a sumptuous place, popular all week. Bearing in mind the quality and authenticity – many family recipes stem from Edd's gran, who cooked in Bangkok's Royal Palace – the prices are very reasonable, with mains around €16. Booking is essential and credit cards not accepted. U-Bahn Kurfürstenstr. Tues–Fri 11.30am–3pm & 6pm–midnight, Sat 5pm–midnight, Sun 2pm–midnight.

Maharadscha Fuggerstr. **21** ☎**030/21 00 21 51.** Though the ambience is that of a German farmhouse, the food is pure Indian, with dishes (€7–11) from every part of the subcontinent. It gets packed out for the Sun buffet (noon–5pm; €7.90). U-Bahn Nollendorfplatz. Daily noon–midnight.

Petite Europe Langenscheidtstr. **1** ☎**030/781 29 64.** Unpretentious Italian place that dishes up filling home-made pastas and stone-oven pizzas (average €7) in an informal, lively atmosphere. Usually full, so booking is advised. U-Bahn Kleistpark. Daily 5pm–1am.

Renger Patzsch Wartburgstr. **54** ☎**030/784 20 59.** Rustic eatery serving cuisine from the Alsace region in what was once – they claim – a brothel. The excellent food, a mix of French and German, often including wild boar (mains €14–18), is served at long communal tables. Bookings advisable. U-Bahn Eisenacher Str. Daily 6pm until late (kitchen until 11.30pm).

Western Kreuzberg

The following places are marked on the map on p.132.

Altes Zollhaus Carl-Herz-Ufer **30** ☎**030/692 33 00.** Very classy place located in an old half-timbered building overlooking a canal, serving modern German food such as duck from Brandenburg with *Kartoffelpuffer*, and *zander*, a pike-like fish, from the Havel. The three-course set menus cost €38. U-Bahn Prinzenstr. Tues–Sat 6pm–1am.

Austria Bergmannstr. **30** ☎**030/694 44 40.** Generous portions of excellent Austrian food – particularly *Wiener Schnitzel* – are served up on solid wood tables in dark, rustic surrounds. Mains range between €9 and €18. U-Bahn Gneisenaustr. Daily 6pm until late.

Bar Centrale Yorckstr. **82** ☎**030/786 29 89.** Chic Italian locale, popular with the affluent young, and exiled Italians. Lots of fresh antipasti, pasta, fish and meat dishes (mains €14–23) and an international wine list. U-Bahn Mehringdamm. Daily noon–1am, kitchen opens at 2pm.

Osteria No. 1 Kreuzbergstr. **71** ☎**030/786 91 62.** Classy and popular Italian, run by a collective, dishing up quality pizzas and oft-changing pastas (€7.50–17) in a lush courtyard. Very child-friendly. U-Bahn Mehringdamm. Daily noon until late.

Eastern Kreuzberg and Friedrichshain

The following places are marked on the map on p.142–143.

Amrit Oranienstr. **202** ☎**030/612 55 50.** The seating is always a bit of a squeeze at this busy Indian restaurant, where the huge portions are inexpensive (mains €8–15) and delicious. Not the sort of place to linger after a meal, and reservations are recommended in the week and essential at weekends. U-Bahn Görlitzer Bahnhof. Daily noon–midnight.

Café Jacques Maybachufer 8, ☎030/694 10 48. Traditional French cuisine is the mainstay here on the leafy banks of the Landwehrcanal, but other foods like pasta and couscous also make an appearance as do seasonal ingredients, such as asparagus and globe artichokes; with most mains around €10. U-Bahn. Schönleinstr. Daily 6pm–midnight.

Gorgonzola Club Dresdener Str. 121 ☎030/615 64 73. Classy pizzas and freshly made pasta (€8–14) – choose any sauce with any pasta – in a rustic, fun atmosphere. U-Bahn Kottbusser Tor. Daily 6pm until late.

Henne Leuschnerdamm 25 ☎030/614 77 30. Pub-style restaurant serving the best fried chicken (€7.50) in Berlin. The interior is original – it hasn't been changed, the owners claim, since 1905. U-Bahn Mortizplatz. Reservations essential. Tues–Sat 7pm until late, Sun 5pm until late.

Kuchen Kaiser Oranienplatz 11–13 ☎030/61 40 26 97. Well-rounded café, overlooking a green platz, serving a mixed bag of items in a laidback atmosphere. Great for cakes at any time, but otherwise at its best during the Sun brunch buffet (10am–3pm; €9). U-Bahn Moritzplatz. Daily 9am until 2am.

🏃 **Morgenland Skalitzer Str. 35** ☎030/611 32 91. Relaxed café with a welcoming vibe, which serves a mix of European snacks. The amazing brunch buffet (Sat & Sun 10am–4pm; €9.50) seems to attract most of the neighbourhood. U-Bahn Görlitzer Bahnhof. Mon–Fri 9am until late, Sat & Sun 10am until late.

Weltrestaurant Markthalle Pücklerstr. 34 ☎030/617 55 02. Spacious restaurant that attracts a young crowd with its long communal tables and German food in hearty portions. Look out for the €7.50 daily special and leave space for the phenomenal cakes. U-Bahn Görlitzer Bahnhof. Daily 10am–midnight.

Prenzlauer Berg

The following places are marked on the map on pp.150–151.

The Bird Am Falkplatz 5 ☎030/51 05 32 83. Hugely popular American restaurant with punk-rock attitude, an international staff and gigantic portions of all the American classics. Steaks with hand-cut fries come in around the €20 mark, burgers start at around half that. Finish off with a sumptuous cheesecake, if you can manage it. U-Bahn Schönhauser Allee. Mon–Thurs 6–11pm, Fri & Sat 6pm–midnight, Sun noon–11pm.

Chez Maurice Botzowstr. 39 ☎030/425 05 06. A little out of the way but worth it for the authentic food and theatrics of the manic French chef Maurice. Service can be slow, so count on spending the better part of an evening here. Mains €14–27; reservations recommended. S-Bahn Griefswalder Str. Tues–Sat noon–4pm, daily 6.30pm until late.

Gugelhof Knaackstr. 37 ☎030/442 92 29. Lively Alsatian restaurant put on the map by Bill Clinton's surprise visit in 2000, and successful ever since. It serves inventive and beautifully presented German, French and Alsatian food (mains €8–18) – worth trying is the unusual *Flammekuchen*, a thin-crust Alsatian pizza. U-Bahn Senefelderplatz. Mon–Fri 4pm–1am, Sat & Sun 10am–1am.

Mao Thai Wörther Str. 30 ☎030/441 92 61. Perhaps a bit overpriced, but the Thai food is excellent, garnished with delightful little sculpted vegetables, and the staff, in traditional garb, unfailingly polite. Mains €10–20. U-Bahn Senefelderplatz. Daily noon until late.

Ostwind Husemannstr. 13 ☎030/441 59 51. Serene setting for superb modern and traditional (and MSG-free) Chinese dining; great for hotpots and Dim Sum. Prices are a little above average (mains €6.50–13.50), but justified by the quality of the ingredients and preparation. The Sun five-course brunch (11am–2pm; €8) is as good as it is unusual. U-Bahn Eberswalder Str. Mon–Sat 6pm–midnight, Sun 10am–11pm.

🏃 **Restauration 1900 Husemannstr. 1** ☎030/442 24 94. A Kollwitzplatz culinary highlight, serving traditional German dishes that spring a few surprises, as well as some pasta and vegetarian options (€9–18). It's also another excellent option for a Sun buffet brunch (10am–4pm; €10). Check out the photographs of the neighbourhood before and after reunification. U-Bahn Eberswalder Str. Daily 10am until late.

Trattoria Paparazzi Husemannstr. 35 ☎030/440 73 33. Top-rated place with outstanding Italian food and a large wine list. Prices are reasonable, given the quality, with mains

€11–17. U-Bahn Eberswalder Str. Daily 8pm–1am (kitchen until 11.30pm).

Treffpunkt Bangkok Prenzlauer Allee 46 ☏030/443 94 05. The authentic and very good Thai food here makes it the first choice in Prenzlauer Berg for inexpensive dining (dishes from €3.60), and consequently often a bit too busy for its own good. U-Bahn Senefelderplatz. Daily noon–11pm.

Zum Schusterjungen Danziger Str. 9 ☏030/442 76 54. Large portions of no-nonsense German food served in the back room of a locals' *Kneipe*. The plastic and formica decor has echoes of the GDR and, at around €8 per dish, the prices are almost as cheap as back then, too. U-Bahn Eberswalder Str. Daily noon–midnight.

Köpenick

See map on p.165.

Ratskeller Köpenick Alt Köpenick 21 ☏030/655 56 52. Authentic *Ratskeller* full of locals and

serving decent, good-value German food from €6 per dish. Regular live jazz on Fri and Sat. S-Bahn Köpenick. Daily 11am–11pm.

Spandau

The following places are marked on the map on p.177.

Kolk Hoher Steinweg 7 ☏030/333 88 79. Popular family-run restaurant in an old fire station, serving regional dishes, including good vegetarian versions (mains €8–16). Its outdoor seating is beside the old city walls. U-Bahn Altstadt Spandau. Daily 11.30am–midnight.

Sapore Divino Breite Str. 2–4 ☏030/49 80 65 12. Unpretentious Italian trattoria with exceptional food and prices for every budget: mains are in the €7 to €18 range. U-Bahn Altstadt Spandau. Mon–Sat 10am–midnight.

Nightlife

Since the days of the Weimar Republic, and even through the lean postwar years, Berlin's nightlife had the reputation for being some of the best – and steamiest – in Europe, an image fuelled by the drawings of George Grosz and films like *Cabaret*. Today's big draw are the clubs that have grown out of the city's techno scene. In a remarkably short space of time these places, many in abandoned East German industrial buildings, have spawned one of the most exciting scenes in Europe. Berlin also has a wide range of more traditional clubs, ranging from slick hangouts for the trendy to raucous punky dives – where you'll find live music of just about every sort.

To find out what's on where check **listings magazines** *Tip* (www.tip-berlin .de) and *Zitty* (www.zitty.de), available at any news stand, and the free magazine *030* (www.berlin030.de), distributed in bars and cafés, clubs and record shops. Like most major cities, Berlin's nightspots change rapidly: expect the following clubs and bars to have changed at least slightly by the time you arrive.

Bars and clubs

The distinction between cafés, bars, clubs and arts venues is notoriously fluid in Berlin, with **considerable overlap** between each, meaning that many cafés, bars and beer gardens listed in "Eating and drinking" (see p.206) may well double as venues of some sort into the small hours. Those listed below are particularly good for a night out.

Opening times are also very relaxed and there are no last-orders in Berlin. Typically bars will close between 1am and 5am, often depending on how busy they are and the mood of the staff, then may reopen around 9am for breakfast. Opening times for clubs are even more open-ended – it's rare for any to get going before midnight and some stay open beyond 6am, a common time to shut. Berlin's **clubs** are smaller, cheaper and less exclusive than their counterparts in London or New York. **Admission** is often free – though cover charges tend to run from €5 to €11 on weekends and can change dramatically depending on the event. And don't worry too much about dress code as the prevalence of a shabby-chic aesthetic in Berlin means you can get into most places without making much of an effort.

Several distinct nightlife areas have evolved in Berlin, making it easiest to spend an evening trawling a particular area before ending up in a late-night club nearby. Most really in places are to the east, where glitz is out and raving in. **Friedrichshain** and **eastern Kreuzberg** are good areas for the grungiest and most cutting-edge clubs. More established places are in **Prenzlauer Berg** and the **Spandauer Vorstadt**, and also in **Schöneberg** and **western Kreuzberg**, where they tend to attract a slightly older crowd.

Pub crawls

If the idea of venturing into Berlin's legendary nightlife seems overwhelming, or you fancy the company of young travellers, consider joining a **pub crawl tour**. For around €12 you'll be taken to around half-a-dozen watering holes and a club (cover charges included) at the end of it all. You'll be watered with free shots on the street along the way, so it's not the most dignified way to spend an evening, but it can be good fun if the crowd's right. Pub crawls trawl Berlin every night of the week and companies include: New Berlin Tours (Ⓦwww.newberlintours.com); Insider Tours (Ⓦwww.insider berlintours.com); Insomniac Tours (Ⓦwww.insomniactours.com); and Alternative Berlin (Ⓦwww.alternativeberlin.com). The last offers something a bit different, hitting more unusual nightspots than the competition and trying to keep group sizes smaller.

But with the **U- & S-Bahn** running nonstop on Friday and Saturday nights – and restarting from about 4am on other nights – jumping between areas of town could hardly be easier.

Unter den Linden and around

See map on pp.46–47.
Newton Bar Charlottenstr. 57
Ⓣ030/20 61 29 99. Helmut Newton's life-size shots of nude Amazons stare out at the black leather and dark-green marble interior of this highly chic bar: perfect for watching Berlin's sharp dressers smoking cigars and sipping expertly made cocktails. U-Bahn Stadtmitte. Daily 10am until late.

Alexanderplatz and around

See map on p.71.
Weekend Alexanderplatz 5 Ⓣ030/24 63 16 76, Ⓦwww.week-end-berlin.de. Using the former premises of the GDR state travel agency, this is another of Berlin's creative transfor-mations, and the twelfth-floor views over central Berlin are spectacular. All this makes up for the coolly offhand manner of most of its patrons as they groove to a steady diet of electronica. Entry €10–12. U- & S-Bahn Alexanderplatz. Thurs–Sat 11pm until late.

Spandauer Vorstadt

The following places are marked on the map on pp.82–83.
Acud Veteranenstr. 21 Ⓣ030/44 35 94 99, Ⓦwww.acud.de. Rock and blues are the mainstay of this ramshackle venue, with hip-hop and drum 'n' bass thrown in for good measure. There's also a gallery and movie theatre tucked inside. U-Bahn Rosenthaler Platz. Daily 9pm until late.

am to pm Am Zwirngraben 2 Ⓣ030/24 08 53 01. Open nonstop, this café-cum-bar-cum-club under the Hackescher Markt S-Bahn station helps support Berlin's reputation for 24-hour nightlife. It's a good people-watching spot during the day, and a convenient way to start, or finish, a night out. U- & S-Bahn Hackescher Markt. Open 24hr.
Bangaluu Invalidenstr. 30 Ⓣ030/809 69 30 77, Ⓦwww.bangaluu.com. Stylish and inventive spot where you can snack while reclining on mattresses and watching a live show, then take to the dancefloor or chill on the roof terrace. S-Bahn Nordbahnhof. Thurs–Sat 7.30pm until late.
Café Silberstein Oranienburger Str. 27 Ⓣ030/281 20 95, Ⓦwww.silbersteincafe.de. Great place – celebrated for its weird welded chairs (for sale) – that's usually packed and mutates into a club from 11pm at weekends. U-Bahn Oranienburger Tor. Daily 10am until late.
Clärchens Ballhaus Auguststr. 24 Ⓣ030/282 92 95, Ⓦwww.ballhaus.de. First opening in 1913 and providing a hedonistic venue throughout the 1920s before just about surviving fascism and communism, this dancehall is back in style. It now hosts a range of dance nights, with instruction provided (times on website): Mon salsa, Tues Tango, Wed swing, Thurs waltz, disco or rumba; while weekends its a bit of everything. Sun after-noons see the upstairs mirror room – unused during GDR days for being too glitzy – acting as the venue for concerts. Also dishes up good pizzas. S-Bahn Hackescher Markt, Daily 10am until late.

Delicious Doughnuts Rosenthaler Str. 9
☎030/28 09 92 74, ⊛www.delicious
-doughnuts.de. With beautiful party people
grooving to acid jazz, trip-hop and funk
beats, this place is best as a pre- or
post-club venue, though the little dancefloor can be busy until 10am on weekend
nights. Entry €3–5. U-Bahn Rosenthaler
Platz. Daily 10pm until late.

Grüner Salon Rosa-Luxemburg-Platz 2
☎030/24 59 89 36, ⊛www.gruener-salon.de.
Club beside the *Roter Salon* that preserves
something of the 1920s in its chandeliers
and velvet. Renowned for its salsa courses
and Fri tango evenings, but with a varied
programme of live music, comedy and
cabaret besides. Entry €4–15. U-Bahn
Rosa-Luxemburg-Platz. Thurs 9pm–4am,
Fri & Sat 11pm–4am.

Kaffee Burger Torstr. 60 ☎030/28 04 64 95,
⊛www.kaffeeburger.de. Russian-owned
smoky 1970s retro-bar legendary for its
Russian-themed disco nights, but good
anytime, not least for the mad mix of genres
– Balkan, surf rock, samba, rockabilly – that
fills the small dancefloor. Readings and
poetry often start evenings off, but it really
fills up later on. Entry €1–5. U-Bahn Rosa-
Luxemburg-Platz. June–Aug daily 10pm
until late, Sept–May Fri & Sat 9pm until late,
Sun–Thurs 7pm until late.

Kilkenny Irish Pub Am Zwirngraben 17–20
☎030/283 20 84. Lively, if generic, Irish-
theme pub, with several convivial rooms and
regular live rock. U- & S-Bahn Hackescher
Markt. Daily 10am until late.

Kingkongklub Brunnenstr. 173 ☎030/91 20 68
60, ⊛www.king-kong-klub.de. Rock club with
massive dark leather sofas and DJs
spinning just about any genre of rock from
Elvis through Hendrix to the sounds of
contemporary local bands, drawing a thirty-
something crowd. Popular rock 'n' roll
nights on Fri. Entry €8. U-Bahn Rosenthaler
Platz. Tues–Sun 10pm–3am.

Oscar Wilde Irish Pub Friedrichstr. 112a
☎030/282 81 66, ⊛www.oscar-wilde-irish
-pub.de. Sociable Irish bar and hub for
Berlin's English-speaking expats, with quiz
nights (Mon), karaoke (every other Fri),
SkySports on the big screen and live music
on most Fri & Sat nights. U-Bahn
Oranienburger Tor. Mon–Fri noon–1am, Sat
1pm–3am, Sun 1pm–2am.

Reingold Novalisstr. 11 ☎030/28 38 76 76.
Sophisticated Art Deco cocktail lounge with

a twenty- and thirty-something clientele
lounging on the leather and velvet seating.
U-Bahn Oranienburger Tor. Tues–Sat
7pm–4am.

Roter Salon Rosa-Luxemburg-Platz. 2 ☎030/24
06 58 06 ⊛www.volksbuehne-berlin.de. Tatty
club within the Volksbühne theatre, with
lurid red decor and chintzy furniture giving it
the feel of a 1950s brothel. Readings,
concerts and club nights are held here. Wed
is soul and funk night, other nights a mix of
electronica, ska and Brit-pop. Entry €5–6.
U-Bahn Rosa-Luxemburg-Platz. Mon &
Wed–Sat 11pm–4am.

Schokoladen Ackerstr. 169 ☎030/282 65 27,
⊛www.schokoladen-mitte.de. The spartan,
bare-brick interior of this former chocolate
factory is a hangover from its time as a
squatted building in the early post-*Wende*
days. Now a venue for theatrical and art
events, live music and decent contemporary
cabaret – particularly recommended if your
German's up to it. U-Bahn Rosenthaler
Platz. Mon–Thurs 8pm–4am, Fri & Sat
9pm–4am, Sun 7pm–4am.

Sophienclub Sophienstr. 6 ⊛www.sophienclub
-berlin.de. Small, functional and rather
nondescript club with a couple of cramped,
well-populated dance floors and a mixed
crowd. At its best on Tues Brit-pop nights,
otherwise patrons survive on a mixed
medley of soul, funk, house and indie. Entry
€3–5. S-Bahn Hackescher Markt. Tues &
Thurs–Sun 10pm until late.

Tacheles Oranienburger Str. 54 ☎030/282 61 85,
⊛www.tacheles.de. This one-time
department store became an artists' squat
after the *Wende* and now has several very
busy bars and clubs on its many levels.
Among them is a beer garden, the *Café
Zapata* club (⊛www.cafe-zapata.de) which
has regular live music, a cinema and
several late-night art galleries. Don't be put
off by the heavily graffitied stairwell, it
leads up to some of the best spots.
U-Bahn Oranienburger Tor. Daily 10am
until late.

Verkehrsberuhigte Ost-Zone Monbijouplatz,
S-Bahnbogen 153 ☎030/24 62 87 81, ⊛www
.veboz.de. Great little bar if you are looking
for a dose of *Ostalgie* with your beer, as the
decor is composed entirely of GDR
memorabilia. It's hidden away in the arches
of the S-Bahn overlooking the Spree, which
might be what keeps it from being touristy.
S-Bahn Hackescher Markt. Daily 8pm–3am.

Zosch Tucholskystr. 30 ☎030/280 76 64
🌐 www.zosch-berlin.de. Alternative place that
started as a squat when the Wall came
down, and has retained much of the feel. A
good place for gigs and club nights in the
cellar, where a fun-loving local Creole jazz
band often plays amid the smoky ambience
and constant chatter. U-Bahn Oranienburger
Tor. Daily 4pm–5am.

Tiergarten

The following places are marked on the
map on pp.98–99.
2BE Club Heidestr. 73 ☎030/89 06 84 10,
🌐 www.2be-club.de. Arguably Berlin's premier
hip-hop club, spread over two big dance
floors. Many big names come here. Entry
€10. U- & S-Bahn Hauptbahnhof. Thurs, Fri
& Sat 11pm until late.
Tape Club Heidestr. 140 ☎030/28 48 48 73,
🌐 www.tapeberlin.de. Hip new nightspot in
an old warehouse behind the Hamburger
Bahnhof that's perfect for those who like
their clubs to be a labyrinth of rooms and
nooks on several levels – the music's
generally a mix of disco, techno but is
particularly strong on house. S- & U-Bahn
Hauptbahnhof. Cover €10. Fri midnight
until late.

City West

The following places are marked on the
map on p.118.
Gainsbourg Savignyplatz 5 ☎030/313 74 64.
The name may pay homage to the master
of risqué chanson, but the cocktails (€8–10)
and food are more like An American in
Paris. Nevertheless, they're some of the
best drinks in the neighbourhood. S-Bahn
Savignyplatz. Daily 5pm until late.
Galerie Bremer Fasanenstr. 37 ☎030/881
49 08. Pricey cocktail bar in a 1950s gallery
– with interior features by Hans Scharoun,
architect of the Berlin Philharmonic, see
p.102 – that's a meeting point for actors
and artists. U-Bahn Spickernstr. Mon–Sat
8pm until late.
Puro Sky Lounge Tauentzienstr. 11 ☎030/26 36
78 75, 🌐 www.puro-berlin.de. Perhaps Berlin's
snazziest club has as its main selling point
its twentieth-storey location in the Europa
Centre, with great views of the City West
nightscape. But it's an elitist place and one
of the few clubs in Berlin with any kind of
dresscode: if it's not designer, you won't get

in. U-Bahn Zoologischer Garten. Tues–Sat
8pm until late.

Schöneberg

The following places are marked on the
map on p.128.
Bar am Lützowplatz Lützowplatz 7 ☎030/262
68 07. Distinguished by having the longest
bar in the city, this place also has Berlin's
best selection of whiskies (63 kinds), 150
kinds of champagne and a superb range of
moderately priced cocktails (€6–14); a
dangerously great bar. U-Bahn Nollendorfplatz. Daily 2pm–4am.
E&M Leydicke Mansteinstr. 4 ☎030/216 29 73.
Claiming to be the oldest Kneipe in western
Berlin – though some of the decor looks
suspiciously modern – this place is famed
for its fruit wines and theme nights:
rockabilly to belly-dancing. U- & S-Bahn
Yorckstr. Sat 4pm until late, Sun–Fri
9pm–1am.
Green Door Winterfeldtstr. 50 ☎030/215 25 15.
Somewhat snobby, dimly lit cocktail bar,
attracting a well-dressed crowd of young
professionals and party-goers. Press the
buzzer to get in; once you're past the
pretension the place can be fun, and they
mix a really good cocktail. U-Bahn Nollendorfplatz. Fri & Sat 6pm–4am, Sun–Thurs
6pm–3am.
Havanna Hauptstr. 30 ☎030/784 85 65, 🌐 www
.havanna-berlin.de. Upbeat Latin disco, with
seven bars and four dance floors: one for
salsa and merengue, and the others to
groove to funk and R&B. Dance classes
available; entry €3–7. S-Bahn Julius-Leber-
Brücke. Wed 9pm–4am, Fri & Sat
10pm–4am.
Kumpelnest 3000 Lützowstr. 23
☎030/261 69 18, 🌐 www.kumpelnest
3000.com. Carpeted walls and a mock-
Baroque effect attract a rough-and-ready
crew of thirty-somethings to this erstwhile
brothel, which gets going around 2am,
when there's standing room only. The best
place in the area, it's good fun and infamous
as a hook-up bar for people of all sexual
orientations. U-Bahn Kurfürstenstr. Daily
7pm–5am.
Mister Hu Goltzstr. 39 ☎030/217 21 11. Warm
red cocktail bar with a great range of drinks
(€6–11) that are mixed by some of the city's
best bartenders. U-Bahn Eisenacher Str. Fri
& Sat 6pm–4am, Sun–Thurs 6pm–3am.

Pinguin Club Wartburgstr. 54 ☎ **030/781 30 05.** Tiny and friendly bar – with 1950s and 1960s Americana decor – which doesn't really get going until after midnight. U-Bahn Eisenacher Str. Daily 7pm–4am.

Zoulou Bar Hauptstr. 4, ☎ **030/70 09 47 37,** ⓦ **www.zouloubar.de.** Wonderfully low-key bar packed after 11pm with sociable Schönebergers, quaffing draught *Kölsch*, Cologne's famous beer, and a few good cocktails. U-Bahn Kleistpark. Sun–Thurs 8pm–5am, Fri & Sat 8pm–6am.

Western Kreuzberg

The following places are marked on the map on p.132.

Golgotha Dudenstr. 48–64 ☎ **030/785 24 53.** Kreuzberg's popular hillside café hosts a daily al fresco disco from 10pm April–Sept, which is good fun on warm evenings. U- & S-Bahn Yorckstr. April–Sept daily 10am until late.

Junction Bar Gneisenaustr. 18, Kreuzberg ☎ **030/694 66 02,** ⓦ **www.junction-bar.de.** Nightly live music covering the full spectrum of sounds, played to a very mixed crowd in a basement club. Always busy, and DJs keep the night going after the bands finish. Entry €3–6. U-Bahn Gneisenaustr. Sun–Thurs 9pm–4am, Fri & Sat 10pm–4am.

Solar Stresemannstr. 76 ☎ **0163/765 27 00, www.solarberlin.com.** Swanky lounge bar whose seventeenth-floor location provides exceptional views over the city. There's also a pricey restaurant here, but the place to be is among the beautiful people grooving to ambient techno in the bar above. The entrance is slightly hidden at the back of a small parking lot opposite Anhalter Bahnhof and the door policy can be relatively stringent by Berlin standards: no need to dress up, but don't dress down either. S-Bahn Anhalter Bahnhof. Mon–Thurs noon–2am, Fri noon–4am, Sat 6pm–4am, Sun 6pm–2am.

Eastern Kreuzberg and Friedrichshain

The following places are marked on the map on pp.142–143, except *Insel* which is on p.144.

Ankerklause Kottbusser Damm 104 ☎ **030/693 56 49.** This little café, perched by the Landwehr canal, turns into a funk and soul club by night, and is very trendy and very crowded. Thurs is Sixties night. U-Bahn Kottbusser Tor. Mon 4pm–4am, Tues–Sun 10am–4am.

Berghain Am Wriezener Bahnhof ⓦ **www .berghain.de.** It's regarded by many as the best club in the world, and this vast, artfully scuzzy old power plant is happy to play up to its reputation: at its 3am peak-entry time, you can queue for well over an hour to get in, and have a good chance of getting knocked back by the notoriously picky bouncers (trying not to look too much like a tourist helps). Minimal techno and house from a phenomenal DJ roster cannonball around the gigantic dancefloors, while more laidback bars and murky back rooms cater to the wants of the evenly balanced gay and straight crowd. Photography strictly prohibited; you won't get in with a camera, but you should be fine if it's part of your phone. Entry around €10. S-Bahn Ostbahnhof. Fri & Sat midnight until late (usually the next afternoon).

Cassiopeia Reveler Str. 99 ☎ **030/47 38 59 49,** ⓦ **www.cassiopeia-berlin.de.** Another former squat where the shambolic vibe has been preserved to produce a venue that's as odd, grungy and as hip and nebulous as any: on-site there's a skate-park, climbing wall, cinema, beer garden and four dance floors. Always worth a look. Entry €3–7, extra when bands play. S- & U-Bahn Warschauer Str. Tues–Fri 6pm until late, Sat–Mon 3pm until late.

Dachkammer Simon-Dach-Str. 39 ☎ **030/296 16 73.** The largest and arguably most sociable place on the strip – the

▲ DJs at Tresor club

combination of a rustic bar downstairs and retro bar upstairs has made this a local classic. U- & S-Bahn Warschauer Str. Mon–Fri noon–1am, Sat & Sun 10pm–1am.

Habermeyer Gärtnerstr. 6 ☎030/29 77 18 87. Another of Berlin's 1970s spots but with free nibbles and an unusual mix of music from the DJ – from rockabilly to electronica – that give it the edge over similar places nearby. U- & S-Bahn Warschauer Str. Daily 7pm until late.

Insel Alt-Treptow 6, Treptow; see map, p.144. ☎030/20 91 49 90. Reliable venue for thrash/punk gigs and club nights, with occasional outdoor raves on the large terrace in summer. On a Spree island that's part of Treptower Park. S-Bahn Plänterwald. Times vary, usually Sat and Sun from 3pm.

Kantine am Berghain Rüdersdorfer Str. 70 ☎030/29 36 02 10. Its friendly atmosphere and tiny but jolly summer beer garden, mean this venue's started to go well beyond just offering a haven to those rejected by the strict but indefinable entry codes of the neighbouring Berghain club – to which its music and vibe is similar. S-Bahn Ostbahnhof. Sat noon until late, Sun 9am until late. Cover €5–10.

Kit-Kat Club Köpenicker Str. 76, entrance Brückenstr. No phone, ⓦwww.kitkatclub.de. Famously debauched club, sharing premises with the *Sage Club* (see below). Not for voyeurs but those looking for casual and public liaisons. The door policy is strict: wear something revealing or fetishistic – check the website for guidelines, and for details of theme evenings. U-Bahn Heinrich-Heine-Str. Fri & Sat 11pm until late, Sun 8am until late.

Konrad Tönz Falckensteinstr. 30 ☎030/612 32 52, ⓦwww.konradtoenzbar.de. Cheesy bar with 1970s trappings; sip cocktails (€3–7) while grooving to retro sounds and easy listening. U-Bahn Schlesisches Tor. Tues–Sun 8.15pm until late.

Kptn. A. Müller Simon-Dach-Str. 32. Ramshackle, sociable and very popular budget bar on the Simon-Dach-Str. strip, with free table football – though you'd better be good to challenge the locals. U- & S-Bahn Warschauer Str. Daily 6pm until late.

Madonna Wiener Str. 22 ☎030/611 69 43. It might have a grimy paint job, sparse interior and waning popularity, but this remains one of Berlin's "in" places. Check out the ceiling fresco of the seven deadly sins, pick from the extensive whisky selection and vibrate to the loud music. U-Bahn Görlitzer Bahnhof. Daily 3pm until late.

Maria am Ostbahnhof An der Schillingbrücke ☎030/21 23 81 90, ⓦwww.clubmaria.de. Cutting-edge club whose electronic music is mirrored by the industrial minimalism of its interior. There's a good live music programme, too. Entry €10–12. S-Bahn Ostbahnhof. Fri & Sat 11pm until late.

Matrix Warschauer Platz. 18 ☎030/29 36 99 90, ⓦwww.matrix-berlin.de. Once a temple for pill-poppers, the club has now gone mainstream with top-forty, hip-hop and reggae entertaining three colourful dance floors beneath vaulted stone-and-brick arches and Warschauer Str. train station. U- & S-Bahn Warschauer Str. Tues & Thurs from 9pm, Wed, Fri & Sat from 10pm until late.

Privatclub Pücklerstr. 34 Kreuzberg ☎030/611 30 02, ⓦwww.privatclub-berlin.de. Cellar club below Weltrestaurant Markthalle, which is notable for weekend theme parties – attracting a wide range of ages – ranging from 1970s disco trash and new wave to blaxploitation funk. Local bands often play here as well. €6–7. U-Bahn Görlitzer Bahnhof. Fri & Sat 11pm until late.

Sage Club Köpenicker Str. 76 ☎030/278 98 30, ⓦwww.sage-club.de. One of Berlin's premier clubs, with multiple dance floors and a good range of sounds – particularly rock, but also hip-hop, R&B, mainstream and techno. Always a good vibe, but perhaps a bit too popular with teenagers – the bouncers sometimes dress in drag to scare them away. U-Bahn Heinrich-Heine-Str. Thurs–Sun 11pm–5am.

Tresor Köpenicker Str. 70 ☎030/695 37 70, ⓦwww.tresorberlin.de. A key player in Berlin's dance music scene with trouser-shaking techno booming in every nook of the convoluted bunker-style club and attracting clubbers from all over Europe. The volume, intensity and light-show all have to be experienced to be believed. Entry Wed €5–8, Fri & Sat €10–15. U-Bahn Heinrich-Heine-Str. Wed–Sat midnight until late.

Watergate Falckensteinstr. 49 ☎030/61 28 03 95, ⓦwww.water-gate.de. Contender for top spot among Berlin's club scene, with a glorious location by the Oberbaumbrücke overlooking the waters of the Spree. The futuristic club with its impressive light installations sprawls over two levels with a large main floor and a floor with a lounge, and the music is varied but mostly electronic. Entry €8–12. U-Bahn Schlesisches Tor. Wed, Fri & Sat midnight until late.

Wiener Blut Wiener Str. 14 ℡ 030/618 90 23. A former studenty bar that has aged along with its clientele, though there's still table football and a buoyant, spirited atmosphere. U-Bahn Görlitzer Bahnhof. Daily 6pm until late.

Wild at Heart Wiener Str. 20 ℡ 030/611 70 10, ⓦ www.wildatheartberlin.de. Cornerstone live music venue for rock 'n' roll, indie and punk, with something always going on well into the small hours. U-Bahn Görlitzer Bahnhof. Daily 8pm until late.

WMF Klosterstr. 44 ⓦ www.wmf-club.com. Currently in an old telephone exchange – its eighth location in seventeen years, *WMF's* a difficult club to track down and may well have moved by the time you read this. Yet, partly because of this nomadic existence it's always worth the effort tracking it down for one of Berlin's most legendary nights out. U-Bahn Klosterstr. Sat 11pm until late, occasional Thurs & Fri. €8–10

Prenzlauer Berg

The following places are marked on the map on pp.150–151.

August Fengler Lychener Str. 11 ℡ 030/44 35 66 40. Classic neighbourhood bar – with table football and even a

▲ August Fengler

Kegelbahn (German nine-pin bowling; call ahead to book, €14 per hour) – that's been taken over by a trendy set who dance in the small back room to soul, disco and funk. U-Bahn Eberswalder Str. Daily 7pm–5am.

Dunckerclub Dunckerstr. 64 ℡ 030/445 95 09 ⓦ www.dunckerclub.de. Indie, industrial and unashamedly Goth refuge from the mainstream and techno. €3–5. S-Bahn Prenzlauer Allee. Mon–Thurs 10pm until late, Fri & Sat 11pm until late.

Geburtstagsklub Am Friedrichshain 33 ℡ 030/42 02 14 05, ⓦ www.geburtstagsklub.de. Hit-and-miss club that's always reinventing itself, though the Mon reggae night is one of Berlin's best, otherwise it's mostly house and disco. S-Bahn Greifswalder Str. Mon, Fri & Sat 11pm–6am.

Icon Cantianstr. 15 ℡ 030/322 97 05 20, ⓦ www.iconberlin.de. The finest drum 'n' bass club in town, with local DJs being regularly joined by international bigwigs. The club is divided into several bars, lounges and dance areas, making it easy to find your niche. Admission €4–7. U-Bahn Eberswalder Str. Tues 11pm until late, Fri & Sat 11.30pm until late.

Knaack Greifswalder Str. 224 ℡ 030/442 70 60, ⓦ www.knaack-berlin.de. One-time GDR youth centre that pioneered the clubland explosion in the east. Now a bit past its prime and pretty average, but excellent to see some of the local band scene, with indie acts regularly dropping in. Oddly, half the club is a karaoke bar. Entry €3.50–6. S-Bahn Greifswalder Str. Mon–Thurs 7pm until late, Fri & Sat 10pm until late.

Kulturbrauerei Knaackstr. 97 ℡ 030/48 49 44, ⓦ www.kulturbrauerei-berlin.de. Nineteenth-century brewery that's been turned into a multi-venue arts and cultural centre attracting frequent visits by local and mid-level bands. U-Bahn Eberswalder Str.

Magnet Club Greifswalder Str. 212–213 ℡ 030/44 00 81 40, ⓦ www.magnet-club.de. Exceptionally friendly club where up-and-coming bands often play for exposure. DJs spin after the gig and there's another dancefloor, too. Music styles vary, but the crowd is always in its twenties. Entry €3–8. S-Bahn Greifswalder Str. Tues, Thurs & Fri 11pm until late Mon, Wed, Sat & Sun 7pm until late.

nbi Schönhauser Allee 36 ℡ 030/67 30 44 57, ⓦ www.neueberlinerinitiative.de. The residential neighbourhood keeps the volume of the music here down, which the lounge-cum-club has used to its advantage, creating a comfortable environment for the appreciation of cutting-edge electronic music. DJs come here to hear each other experiment. Entry €3. U-Bahn Eberswalder Str. Daily 8pm until late.

Pavillon Friedenstr. in Volkspark ☎0172/750 47 24, ⒲www.pavillon-berlin.de. Beer garden by day and club by night in the laidback greenery of Volkspark Friedrichshain, this venue is best in the summer months when its hundred-person dancefloor packs out to the sounds of funk, Nu Jazz and soul. U-Bahn Strausberger Platz. March–Oct Mon–Fri 11am until late, Sat & Sun 10am until late.

Pfefferberg Schönhauser Allee 176 ☎030/282 92 89, ⒲www.pfefferberg.de. Club and cultural venue where non-European beats will regularly whisk you away from hectic Berlin,

at least mentally. U-Bahn Senefelderplatz. Daily 11am–3.30pm & 5.30pm until late.

Soda Knaackstr. 97 ☎030/44 31 51 44, ⒲www.soda-berlin.de. Club in the Kulturbrauerei cultural centre located in the grounds of a former brewery. The usual diet of soul, house and funk is interrupted on Thurs & Sun by well-attended salsa nights, and occasional live acts, too. Marred by some of Berlin's highest bar prices. U-Bahn Eberswalder Str. Thurs 8pm until late, Fri & Sat 11pm until late, Sun 7pm until late.

Zu mir oder zu dir Lychener Str. 15 ☎0176/24 42 29 40. Groovy, very Seventies lounge-bar with a sociable vibe and lots of sofas to crash out on. With a cheeky name – translating as "your place or mine?" – this is a good place to start an evening before heading down the road to the clubs of the Kulturbrauerei (see p.229). U-Bahn Eberswalder Str. Daily 8pm until late.

Live music

Lively, varied and cheap, Berlin's live music scene, is, as ever, bolstered by the city's grittiness. All tastes are catered to, and the best way of finding out what's on is in the local listings magazines (see p.39), or by checking the websites of some of the clubs and bars listed above. All except the most hardcore techno clubs frequently have **live music**; particularly good are *Magnet Club, Acud, Schokoladen*, the *Kulturbrauerei, Knaack* and *Wild at Heart*.

International **big-name acts** visiting town will tend to play at one of several stadiums and larger venues around town. The act will probably decide your choice, but particularly impressive venues include the Olympic Stadium (see p.126) and the nearby open-air Waldbühne on Glockenturmstrasse/Passenheimer Strasse (☎030/305 72 50; S-Bahn Pichelsberg), a natural amphitheatre that's great fun on summer evenings. Another fine outdoor venue is the small Parkbühne Wuhlheide (☎030/53 07 95 30, ⒲www.wuhlheide.de; S-Bahn Wuhlheide), which is tucked away in the forest near Köpenick and a favourite for summertime festivals.

Only **jazz and blues** and world music have dedicated clubs separate from the rest of Berlin nightlife, so they're listed below; the city's biggest jazz festival is the late-October or early November Jazz Fest Berlin (⒲www.berlinerfestspiele.de).

Jazz and blues

A-Trane Bleibtreustr./Pestalozzistr., Charlottenburg – City West; see map, p.118 ☎030/313 25 50, ⒲www.a-trane.de. Slick forum for the Berlin jazz scene and a good place to see both up-and-coming and well-known jazz artists in a comfortable, intimate setting. Best during Sat-night jams, when musicians arrive from other venues and join in at will throughout the evening.

Entry €5–20. U-Bahn Savignyplatz. Daily 9pm until late.

Badenscher Hof Badensche Str. 29, Wilmersdorf; see map, p.116 ☎030/861 00 80, ⒲www .badenscher-hof.de. Lively café-restaurant and long-standing jazz venue that draws in the Schöneberg crowd for its frequent concerts. Expect any type of jazz – from mainstream to modern – or some blues. U-Bahn Blissestr. Mon–Fri 4pm until late, Sat 6pm until late.

b-flat Rosenthaler Str. 13, Mitte; see map, pp.82–83 ☎030/283 31 23, ⓦwww.b-flat -berlin.de. Roomy and modern with live jazz and acoustic music every night; Wed is reserved for the local jam session and Sun for dancing tango. Entry usually €10. U-Bahn Weinmeister Str. Daily 8pm until late.

Quasimodo Kantstr. 12a, Charlottenburg – City West; see map, p.118 ☎030/312 80 86, ⓦwww .quasimodo.de. Casual cellar bar that's one of Berlin's best jazz spots, with nightly programmes starting at 10pm. A high-quality mix of international, usually American stars and up-and-coming names. Small, with a good atmosphere but a bit hard to find: go up to the terrace next to Theatre des Westens and follow the stairwell to the left of the café. Often free on weekdays, otherwise €5–26. U- & S-Bahn Zoologischer Garten. Daily 9pm–2am.

Yorckschlösschen Yorckstrasse 15 see map, p.132 ☎030/215 80 70, ⓦwww .yorckschloesschen.de. Century-old local institution and still famous as an artists' drinking den and a place to enjoy free live jazz, swing and blues. U-Bahn Mehringdamm. Daily 10am–3am.

World

Haus der Kulturen der Welt John-Foster-Dulles-Allee 10, Mitte; see map, pp.98–99 ☎030/39 78 70, ⓦwww.hkw.de. The city's number one venue for world music is always worth checking out. S-Bahn Hauptbahnhof.

The Arts

W
hen Berlin was a divided city, the West German government poured subsidies for all kinds of **art** into their half of the city: at DM550 million it was over half the federal budget for culture for the entire United States. Unification left it with a "doubling" of facilities, three magnificent opera houses and one of the liveliest arts scenes of any European city. Then, in the mood of glum post-unification realism, things changed: almost all subsidies disappeared and many companies folded. Nevertheless, the scene in Berlin remains buoyant: high-quality **dance and theatre groups** perform everything from classic to avant-garde experimental works; mainstream and art-house **cinemas** thrive; the **art gallery** scene is particularly vibrant and the city is slowly becoming one of the main international centres; and the city still has one of the world's finest **symphony orchestras**.

Contemporary art

The Hamburger Bahnhof (see p.113) may be the flagship venue for contemporary art in Berlin, but investigating the local scene can be much more astounding and rewarding. Many of Berlin's estimated 5000 artists regularly open their studios or put on shows at the hundreds of galleries around town. For a long time, the city's art scene was divided between east and west, the latter containing more expensive and established galleries in **Charlottenburg**, while the former reflected the current energy and attention. Immediately after the *Wende*, the area around

---

Tickets and information

As usual, listings magazines *Zitty* and *Tip* (see p.39) are good for what's on information, but so is the city's tourist information (ⓦ www.btm.de). You can book for most events through the site and at BTM offices (see p.39). Otherwise **ticket offices** (*Theaterkassen*) are usually the easiest way of buying tickets for all major arts events; open during working hours (or longer), they charge a hefty commission (up to 17 percent) on the ticket price. The first place to try, especially for fringe-type theatre, less popular classical concerts and dance, is *Hekticket*, which sells **half-price tickets** from 2pm.

Ticket offices

Hekticket Charlottenburg Hardenberg Str. 29a, Charlottenburg ☏ 030/230 99 33 33, ⓦ www.hekticket.de. U- and S-Bahn Zoologischer Garten.

Hekticket am Alex Karl-Liebknecht-Str. 12, Mitte ☏ 030/24 31 24 31, ⓦ www .hekticket.de. U- & S-Bahn Alexanderplatz.

Ko Ka 36 Oranienstr. 29, Kreuzberg ☏ 030/61 10 13 13, ⓦ www.koka36.de. U-Bahn Kottbusser Tor.

Berlin's art and fashion events

Berlin loves nothing more than being cutting edge, and its big annual art and fashion events are often just that, drawing in hundreds of international curators and designers to feel the city's pulse.

The first major date on Berlin's **contemporary art** calendar is **Gallery Weekend Berlin** (ⓦ www.gallery-weekend-berlin.de) in early May, when some forty galleries co-ordinate their efforts to startle and impress. But the big dates all fall close together in early October when the **Berliner Kunstsalon** (ⓦ www.berlinerkunstsalon.de) occupies the Humboldt Umspannwerk in Prenzlauer Berg; while collectors from around the world throng to the even larger Art Forum Berlin (ⓦ www.art-forum-berlin .de) at the ICC, Charlottenberg's trade fair hall; meanwhile the artist-led and more offbeat **Berliner Liste** (ⓦ www.berliner-liste.org) tends to focus on showcasing new local talent in a different venue each year.

July is the key month for **fashion shows**; the headline act tends to be **Mercedes Benz Fashion Week Berlin** (ⓦ www.mercedes-benzfashionweek.com), a big glitzy spectacular dominated by self-important big-name international designers and their funky retinue, but also with slots for new names. Held in tandem, the **Premium** (ⓦ www.premiumexhibitions.com) trade fair also showcases a lot of fashion, along with many sundry lifestyle products. More offbeat and arguably more in step with Berlin is the **Bread & Butter** (ⓦ www.breadandbutter.com) fashion festival, which takes over the defunct Tempelhof airport to showcase streetwear of the sort that you'll probably see in Berlin's subway the following month. There's more rebellious vernacular fashion at the **Spirit of Fashion** (ⓦ www.spirit-of-fashion.de) festival, an ode to punk, glam rock and gothic underground duds. Meanwhile the smallest, least predictable, but often most interesting event is **Projektgalerie** (ⓦ www.projektgalerie .net), when many city art galleries open their doors to fashion designers of all stripes.

Another spate of fashion excitement takes place in Berlin in **mid-January**, with Bread and Butter, the Berlin Fashion Week and Spirit and of Fashion, all reappearing in smaller form and with different seasonal collections.

Auguststrasse in the Spandauer Vorstadt (see p.91), became a breeding ground of experimental art, but now it's as settled and commercialized as the Charlottenburg galleries, which have tended in recent years to become more avant-garde and daring. Meanwhile the city's rough-and-ready art scene is on the move, looking for more improvised spaces. The railway arches at **Jannowitzbrücke** (see p.78), a new frontier in 2006 is now old hat. The newest gallery districts are developing around the Karl-Marx-Allee; behind the Hamburger Bahnhof and just north of Kreuzberg's Jüdisches Museum. A useful and comprehensive source of information about **what's on** in the city's galleries is the English/German monthly magazine *artery berlin* (€3; ⓦ www.artery-berlin.de), found in most galleries where you can usually pick up the free *Galerien Berlin* listings brochure put out by the Berlin Art Dealers Association (ⓦ www.berliner-galerien.de) and a similar leaflet produced by Index (ⓦ www.indexberlin.de). *Zitty* and *Tip* (under "Galerien" in "Ausstellungen") are also worth checking for up-to-the-minute details.

Galleries

Art Center Berlin Friedrichstr. 134, Mitte ☎030/27 87 90 27, ⓦ www.art-center-berlin.de. Berlin's largest exhibition space with international art spreading over several floors. The work usually covers the full range of modern art, paintings, sculptures, photography and video

art and there are exhibitions of local interest too. Entry €4.50. U-Bahn Oranienburger Tor. Daily 11am–9pm.

Atelier Brandner Helmholtzstr. 2–9, Entrance E, Charlottenburg ☎030/30 10 05 75, ⓦ www .atelier-brandner.de. Southern German Matthias Brandner is among the most successful of the many painters who have flocked to

Berlin's energetic, liberal atmosphere and cheap studio space. Though famed for his murals on buildings, it's his powerful abstract watercolours and oils that are on show at his studio. U-Bahn Turmstr. Daily noon–8pm.

Camera Work Kantstr. 149, Charlottenburg ☏030/310 07 73, ⊛www.camerawork.de. Hidden in a courtyard and blessed with huge north-facing windows and wonderfully even light, this photography gallery spreads over two floors and offers a relaxed atmosphere uncommon to many galleries. Exhibitions often focus on big names like Man Ray, Irving Penn, Horst P. Horst, Peter Lindbergh and Helmut Newton but the occasional up- and -coming name also gets a look-in too. U-Bahn Uhlandstr. Tues–Sat 11am–6pm.

Capitain Petzel Karl-Marx-Allee 45, Friedrichshain ☏030/24 08 81 30, ⊛www.capitainpetzel.de. This joint venture between a Cologne and a New York art dealer is most eye-catching for its location in a Soviet modernist glass cube. In GDR days, this is was a showcase for the Eastern Bloc. It's now far more international and the cornerstone of a new area in the Berlin art scene. U-Bahn Strausberger Platz. Tues–Sat 11am–6pm.

Carlier Gebauer Markgrafenstr. 67, Mitte ☏030/280 81 10, ⊛www.carliergebauer.com. Superb art gallery where you never quite know if you'll find home-grown or international art, but it's sure to be cutting-edge. U-Bahn Kochstr. Tues–Sat 11am–6pm.

Contemporary Fine Arts Am Kupfergraben 20, Mitte ☏030/288 78 70, ⊛www.cfa-berlin.com. Contemporary art and sculpture specialist founded in Charlottenburg, but now conveniently close to Museum Island. The large gallery offers a great place to feel the pulse of the Berlin art scene and see the work of local artists like Marc Brandenburg as well as international big names like Daniel Richter and Georg Baselitz. U- & S-Bahn Friedrichstr. Tues–Fri 11am–6pm, Sat 11am–4pm.

DAAD Galerie Zimmerstr. 90/91, Mitte ☏030/261 36 40, ⊛www.daad-berlin.de. Exhibitions and occasional readings by big-name artists working in the city on fellowships awarded by the Berlin Artist Exchange of the Deutsche Akademischer Austausch Dienst (German Academic Exchange Service). U-Bahn Kochstr. Mon–Sat 11am–6pm.

EIGEN+ART Auguststr. 26, Mitte ☏030/280 66 05, ⊛www.eigen-art.com. Run by Gerd Harry Lybke, who opened the first private gallery in the GDR back in the 1980s, this is one of the most important Auguststr. galleries. Though originally a showcase for East German talent, the programme now covers painting, installations and photography by predominantly young international artists. S-Bahn Hackescher Markt. Tues–Sat 11am–6pm.

Fine Art Rafael Vostell Knesebeckstr. 30, Charlottenburg ☏030/885 22 80, ⊛www.vostell.de. Showing a mix of international artists of the 1960s and some young Berlin painters. S-Bahn Savignyplatz. Mon–Fri 11am–7pm, Sat 11am–4pm.

Galerie Anselm Dreher Pfalzburger Str. 80, Wilmersdorf ☏030/883 52 49, ⊛www.galerie-anselm-dreher.com. Long-standing top city gallery, showing international avant-garde artists and particularly keen on sound installations. U-Bahn Hohenzollernplatz. Tues–Fri 2–6pm, Sat 11am–2pm.

Galerie Barbara Thumm Markgrafenstr. 68, Mitte ☏030/128 39 03 47, ⊛www.bthumm.de. British and Berlin-based artists working in all media. U-Bahn Kochstr. Tues–Sat 11am–6pm.

Galerie Springer & Winckler Fasanenstr. 13, Charlottenburg ☏030/315 72 20, ⊛www.springer-winckler.de. Top-class contemporary painting. One of the galleries foremost in establishing the Berlin art scene after World War II. U- & S-Bahn Zoologischer Garten. Tues–Fri 10am–2pm & 3–6pm, Sat noon–3pm.

Galerie Thomas Schulte Charlottenstr. 24, Charlottenburg ☏030/20 60 89 90, ⊛www.galeriethomasschulte.de. Well-presented conceptual art, photography and sculptures; frequently featuring established artists from America. S-Bahn Charlottenburg. Tues–Sat noon–6pm.

Galerie Wohnmaschine Invalidenstr. 50/51, Mitte ☏030/30 87 20 15, ⊛www.wohnmaschine.de. Young gallery owner Friedrich Loock opened his first gallery in his flat in the Spandauer Vorstadt and he now specializes in promoting the works of young, predominantly local, artists. S- & U-Bahn Hauptbahnhof. Tues–Sat 11am–6pm.

Haunch of Venison Heidestr. 46, Mitte ☏030/39 74 39 63, ⊛www.haunchofvenison.com. With galleries in London and New York, this provides a good example of how international Berlin's scene has become. It's one of a number of start-ups in the promising warehouse district behind the Hamburger Bahnhof (see p.113). U- & S- Bahn Hauptbahnhof. Tues–Sat 11am–6pm.

Kunst-Werke Berlin Auguststr. 69, Mitte ☎030/243 45 90, ⓦwww.kw-berlin.de. Large gallery in a former factory building, where exhibits vary from has-been American artists carpetbagging their way into the city arts scene to astute reflections on contemporary Berlin. Principal organizer of the Berlin Biennale (ⓦwww.berlinbiennale.de). U-Bahn Oranienburger Tor. Entry €6. Tues–Wed & Fri–Sun 2–7pm, Thurs noon–9pm.

Kunstraum Bethanien Mariannenplatz 2, Kreuzberg ☎030/902 98 14 55, ⓦwww .kunstraumkreuzberg.de. One wing of a giant old hospital in a Kreuzberg park, tries to match offbeat neighbourhood art. There's space for graffiti art, local fashion and artists from developing countries who'd struggle to get space elsewhere. U-Bahn Görlitzerbahnhof. Daily noon–7pm.

Raab Galerie Fasanenstr. 72, Charlottenburg ☎030/261 92 17, ⓦwww.raab-galerie.de. Avant-garde and contemporary art on show at this popular meeting place for the art in-crowd. S-Bahn Savignyplatz. Mon–Fri 10am–7pm, Sat 10am–4pm.

Zwinger Galerie Gipsstr. 3, Mitte ☎030/28 59 89 07, ⓦwww.zwinger-galerie.de. One of the city's most important galleries, presenting a mixture of the avant-garde and conventional art. U-Bahn Weinmeisterstr. Tues–Fri 2–7pm, Sat noon–6pm.

Classical music

For years classical music in Berlin meant one man and one orchestra: Herbert von Karajan and the Berlin Philharmonic. Since his death in 1989, the **Philharmonie** has had its former supremacy questioned by the rise of the excellent **Deutsches Symphonie Orchester**. Yet the Philharmonic still remains arguably the world's best orchestra, directed since 2002 by Simon Rattle. In addition, many smaller orchestras play at sites in and around the city, and museums and historic buildings often host chamber concerts and recitals.

A major annual music festival is the **Festtage** in the first half of April, which is organized by the Staatsoper, but staged at the Berlin Philharmonic for its superior acoustics. Also popular is the Musikfest Berlin (ⓦwww.berlinerfestspiele.de), an acclaimed international music festival during the first half of September, when guest orchestras arrive from around the world to take part in a programme that features innovative works by modern composers.

Year-round it's possible to pick up inexpensive tickets for many performances from *Hekticket* (see box, p.54). As ever, see *Zitty* and *Tip* for full and up-to-date listings.

Orchestras and venues

Berliner Symphoniker ⓦwww.berliner -symphoniker.de. Founded in 1952 and based in the Konzerthaus (see below), this used to be East Berlin's main symphony orchestra, and it maintains its fine reputation today, conducted by Lior Shambadal, though it does not compare to the Philharmonic. Tickets €13–35.

Deutsche Oper Bismarckstr. 35, Charlottenburg; box office ☎030/34 38 43 43, ⓦwww.deutsche operberlin.de. Formerly West Berlin's premier opera house, built in 1961 after the Wall cut access to the Staatsoper. Once the city's most prestigious venue in terms of visiting performers, it now shares that honour with its eastern cousin. Tickets €12–118. U-Bahn Deutsche Oper.

Deutsches Symphonie Orchester ⓦwww .dso-berlin.de. Currently under conductor Ingo Metzmacher and with no permanent base, though often at the Philharmonie. Tickets €10–80.

Komische Oper Behrenstr. 55–57, Mitte ☎030/47 99 74 00, ⓦwww.komische-oper -berlin.de. Less traditional than the Staatsoper, but a reliable venue for well-staged operatic productions. The building doesn't look like much from the outside, but the interior is a wonderful 1890s frenzy of red plush, gilt and statuary and a great place to enjoy cutting-edge interpretations of modern works alongside the usual fare. Tickets €8–93. S-Bahn Unter den Linden.

Konzerthaus Berlin (Schauspielhaus) Gendarmenmarkt, Mitte; box office ☎030/20 30 90, ⓦwww.konzerthaus.de. A super venue mainly for visiting musicians, orchestras and ensembles. Two concert spaces occupy the Schinkel-designed building: the Grosser Konzertsaal for orchestras and its Kammermusiksaal for smaller groups and chamber orchestras. Look out for performances on the Konzerthaus's famed organ. Tickets €10–99. U-Bahn Stadtmitte.

Philharmonie Herbert-von-Karajan-Str. 1, Mitte; box office ☎ 030/25 48 80, ⊛ www.berlin -philharmonic.de. Home to the world-famous Berlin Philharmonic, Hans Scharoun's indescribably ugly building is acoustically near-perfect, and while you'll have to be near-loaded to enjoy it, it's definitely worth it. Conductor Simon Rattle has created his own distinctive sound with the orchestra, moving them away from their traditional Germanic comfort zone of Brahms and Beethoven and into more contemporary music like that of the Finnish composer Magnus Lindberg. At first this caused the orchestra concern, but the tremendous success of the eventual execution of these pieces has strengthened the relationship between the director and orchestra. The Philharmonie also contains the smaller Kammermusiksaal for more intimate performances, and your best chance of getting a ticket is when guest orchestras are playing. Tickets €8–138. U- & S-Bahn Potsdamer Platz.

Rundfunk Symphonieorchester Berlin ⊛ www .rsb-online.de. After the Philharmonic, the second-oldest orchestra in Berlin and a little more daring than its older sister. The orchestra appears at both the Philharmonie and the Konzerthaus, and director Marek Janowski often lends his baton to talented guest conductors.

Staatsoper Unter den Linden 5–7, Mitte; box office ☎ 030/20 35 45 55, ⊛ www.staatsoper -berlin.de. The city's oldest and grandest music venue, built for Frederick the Great in 1742 to a design by Knobelsdorff. During the GDR years, political isolation meant that performers didn't match the glamour of the venue, but the appointment of Daniel Barenboim in 1992 as musical director was an attempt to bring the Staatsoper to the forefront of the international opera scene and it certainly seems to be working. Tickets €5–160. U-Bahn Friedrichstr.

Theatre

Mainstream **civic and private theatres** in Berlin tend to be dull, unadventurous and expensive – though last-minute tickets can cut costs – yet the **fringe** scene is exciting. The thousands of eager young Germans that flock to the city every year, rent a space, and stage their work, make Berlin a major venue for **experimental work**, and if your German is up to it, a number of groups are worth the ticket price. The scene is active, though it's worth remembering that many theatre companies take a break in August; check under "Off-Theater" in *Tip* or *Zitty* for up-to-the-minute listings. Groups that have the word *Freie* in their name are not dependent on city or state subsidies, which often impose creative constraints on a group's output.

Civic and private theatres

Admiralspalast Friedrichstr. 101, Mitte ☎ 030/47 99 74 99, ⊛ www.admiralspalast.de. The Admiralspalast provides the round-the-clock entertainment it did in its 1920s heyday – though without the brothel it incorporated then. These days it's the eclectic events programme, including comedy, live music, burlesque and operas, plus a casino, that draws punters. Tickets €10–60. U- & S-Bahn Friedrichstr.

Berliner Ensemble Bertolt-Brecht-Platz 1, Mitte ☎ 030/28 40 81 55, ⊛ www.berliner-ensemble .de. Brecht's old theatre still features a lot of his work, though thankfully the productions are a little livelier than in GDR days and much of the rest of the programme is given over to a range of reliable pieces by Henrik Ibsen, Friedrich Schiller and the like. There are also occasional experimental productions on the Probebühne (rehearsal stage). Tickets €4–32. U- & S-Bahn Friedrichstr.

Deutsches Theater Schumannstr. 13a, Mitte ☎ 030/28 44 12 25, ⊛ www.deutsches-theater .de. Good, solid productions taking in everything from Schiller to Mamet make this one of Berlin's best theatres and invariably sold out. Also includes a second theatre, the Kammerspiele des Deutschen Theaters, and Die Baracke, an experimental stage. Tickets €5–45. U-Bahn Oranienburger Tor.

Maxim-Gorki-Theater Am Festungsgraben 2, Mitte ☎030/20 22 11 15, ⓦwww.gorki.de. Consistently good productions of modern works like Tabori's Mein Kampf and Schaffer's Amadeus. More experimental works are staged on the Studiobühne (studio stage). Tickets €12–30. U- & S-Bahn Friedrichstr.

Prater der Volksbühne Kastanienallee 7–9, Prenzlauer Berg ☎030/24 06 57 77, ⓦwww.volksbuehne-berlin.de. Second stage of the Volksbühne (see below), showing experimental works and modern adaptations of classics. Tickets €10–20. U-Bahn Eberswalder Str.

Renaissance Theater Knesebeckstr. 100, Charlottenburg ☎030/312 42 02, ⓦwww.renaissance-theater.de. Contemporary pieces of theatre from Ayckbourn to Reza, readings and musical revues. Tickets €14–42. U-Bahn Ernst-Reuter-Platz.

Schaubühne am Lehniner Platz Kurfürstendamm 153, Wilmersdorf ☎030/89 00 23, ⓦwww.schaubuehne.de. State-of-the-art theatre that hosts performances of the classics and some experimental pieces, with plenty of young energy and an accent on dance. Its good reputation means booking ahead is advisable. Tickets €7–39. U-Bahn Adenauerplatz.

Theater des Westens Kantstr. 12, Charlottenburg ☎030/319 030, ⓦwww.theater-des-westens.de. Musicals and light opera, the occasional Broadway-style show, sometimes in English. Housed in a beautiful fin-de-siècle building. Tickets €30–100. U- & S-Bahn Zoologischer Garten.

Theater im Palais Am Festungsgraben, Mitte 1 ☎30/201 06 93, ⓦwww.theater-im-palais.de. Traditional theatre pieces performed with a contemporary spin – conversational delivery, music, storytelling – while preserving theatrical simplicity. Expect pieces by the likes of Fontane, Heine or E.T.A. Hoffmann. Beside the Maxim-Gorki-Theatre. Ticket €20. U- & S-Bahn Friedrichstr.

Volksbühne Linienstr. 227, Mitte ☎030/24 06 57 77, ⓦwww.volksbuehne-berlin.de. One of Berlin's most adventurous and interesting theatres, often with highly provocative performances: nudity and throwing things at audiences crop up fairly regularly and there's a high chance of witnessing a partial audience walkout. Tickets €10–25. U-Bahn Rosa-Luxemburg-Platz.

Experimental and free theatre

BAT Studiotheater Belforter Str. 15, Prenzlauer Berg ☎030/755 41 77 77, ⓦwww.bat-berlin.de. Originally a "workers' and students' theatre", founded in 1975, this can usually be relied on to come up with challenging experimental offerings. A meeting point for everyone interested in theatre. Tickets €8. U-Bahn Senefelder Platz.

English Theatre Berlin Fidicinstr. 40, Kreuzberg ☎030/691 12 11, ⓦwww.etberlin.de. Tiny courtyard theatre specializing in English-language fringe productions. Tickets €14. U-Bahn Platz der Luftbrücke.

Hebbel Am Ufer Hallesches Ufer 32, Kreuzberg ⓦwww.hebbel-am-ufer.de. Hosts short runs of a variety of theatre, performance and dance productions, sometimes in English. Often interesting, modern and experimental. The theatre also features four major annual contemporary dance festivals. Tickets €8–19. U-Bahn Hallesches Tor.

Schaubude Greifswalder Str. 81–84, Prenzlauer Berg ☎030/423 43 14, ⓦwww.schaubude-berlin.de. Former GDR puppet theatre now presenting shows for adults and children – from Hansel and Gretel to Faust and performances on atomic physics. Tickets €9.50–12.50. S- & U-Bahn Greifswalder Str.

Theater 89 Torstr. 216, Mitte ☎030/282 46 56, ⓦwww.theater89.de. A small venue putting on modern works in a simple and unaffected style. Tickets €12. U-Bahn Oranienburger Tor.

Cabaret

In the 1920s and 1930s, Berlin had a rich and intense **cabaret scene**: hundreds of small clubs presented acts that were often deeply satirical and political. When the Nazis came to power these quickly disappeared, to be replaced by anodyne entertainments in line with Party views. Sadly, the cabaret scene has never recovered: most of what's on show today is either semi-clad titillation for tourists or drag shows. However, a few places are worth trying, notably the **Chamäleon**, which plays host to some very eclectic acts. Be warned though that most cabaret venues make their money by charging very high prices at the bar.

Cabaret venues

Bar Jeder Vernunft Scharperstr. 24, Wilmersdorf ☏030/883 15 82, ⓦwww.bar-jeder-vernunft.de. Hip young venue for all manner of modern cabaret and comedy with the occasional chanson act too. Tickets €15–30. U-Bahn Spichernstr.

Chamäleon Rosenthaler Str. 40–41 (in the Hackeschen Höfe), Mitte ☏030/400 05 90, ⓦwww.chamaeleonberlin.de. Lively, innovative cabaret and vaudeville shows with jugglers, acrobats and the like. Seating is around tables and there's a bar, so there's no harm in turning up early. Tickets €31–42. S-Bahn Hackescher Markt.

Friedrichstadtpalast Friedrichstr. 107, Mitte ☏030/23 26 23 26, ⓦwww.friedrichstadtpalast .de. Big, flashy variety shows with leggy chorus girls, but the real stuff is to be found in their small café theatre. Tickets €22–102. U-Bahn Oranienburger Tor.

Kleine Nachtrevue Kurfürstenstr. 116, Schöneberg ☏030/218 89 50, ⓦwww .kleine-nachtrevue.de. Berlin burlesque, intimate and dimly lit, going for that 1920s feel. Tickets €15. U-Bahn Wittenbergplatz.

La Vie en Rose Flughafen Tempelhof, Kreuzberg ☏030/69 51 30 00, ⓦwww.lavieenrose-berlin .de. A drag variety revue with lots of glitter and lots of skin in one of the old Tempelhof airport buildings. There's also a piano bar. Tickets €25–32. U-Bahn Platz der Luftbrücke.

Mehringhof Theater Gneisenaustr. 2a, Kreuzberg ☏030/691 50 99, ⓦwww.mehringhoftheater.de. Mixed bag of alternative cabaret. Tickets €15–20. U-Bahn Mehringdamm.

Roter Salon and Grüner Salon in the Volksbühne (see p.237), Rosa-Luxemburg-Platz, Mitte. Lots of interesting and varied goings on, with occasional performances in English.

Scheinbar Variete Monumentenstr. 9, Schöneberg ☏030/784 55 39, ⓦwww .scheinbar.de. Experimental and fun; open stage on many nights. Tickets €7–11. U- & S-Bahn Yorckstr.

Wintergarten Potsdamer Str. 96, Tiergarten ☏030/588 43 40, ⓦwww.wintergarten-variete .de. A glitzy attempt to re-create the Berlin of the 1920s, with live acts from all over the world – cabaret, musicians, dance, mime, magicians. Tickets €20–54. U-Bahn Kurfürstenstr.

Dance

Though there are few **dance groups** in the city, those that exist are of a high quality: you can expect to see plenty of original, oddball and unusual perform-ances. Apart from those regular venues listed below, expect dance performances to pop up at various theatres, particularly the more experimental ones.

Dance companies and venues

Die Etage Ritterstr. 12–14, Kreuzberg ☏030/691 20 95, ⓦwww.dieetage.de. Contemporary dance and mime; also runs dance classes. Tickets €5–8. U-Bahn Moritzstr.

Komische Oper Behrenstr. 55–57, Mitte ☏030/47 99 74 00, ⓦwww.komische-oper -berlin.de. Modern ballet and experimental works, arguably the most interesting of the established heavyweights. Tickets €10–74. U-Bahn Französische Str.

Staatsballett ⓦwww.staatsballett-berlin.de. Berlin's premier ballet company performs at the Staatsoper and Deutsche Oper; see p.235. Tickets €16–66

Tanzfabrik Berlin Möckernstr. 68, Kreuzberg ☏030/786 58 61, ⓦwww.tanzfabrik-berlin.de. Experimental and contemporary works, usually fresh and exciting. This is also Berlin's biggest contemporary dance school. Tickets €10. U- & S-Bahn Yorckstr.

Film

When the all-night drinking starts to get too much, it's always possible to wind down in front of the silver screen. Art-house cinemas are unfortunately facing hard times, but for those who like the mainstream, the rise of the multiplex theatres mean more English-language screenings.

Tip and *Zitty* have listings of all the films showing each week and give you cinema addresses and tell you which language the film is in. If a film is listed as **OF** or **OV** (*Originalfassung*) it's in its original language; **OmU** (*Originalfassung mit Untertiteln*) indicates German subtitles. Otherwise, the film will have been dubbed into German. You may occasionally see films listed as **OmE** – original with English subtitles. The small selection of cinemas below are either particularly strong on screening English-language versions of films or just particularly atmospheric cinemas.

Ticket prices range from €7 to €11, but there are always reductions for children and sometimes for students, too. Also one day a week, designated *Kinotag* (KT in the listings magazines), normally a Monday, Tuesday or Wednesday, the price generally halves.

In February, the **Berlinale** (ⓦ www.berlinale.de) Film Festival dominates the city's cultural life. Second only to Cannes among European festivals, it offers a staggering number of films from all around the world and is much more accessible to the public. A limited number of season tickets (around €150) go on sale a week before the opening. Otherwise, advance tickets can be purchased at the ticket booths centrally located in the Potsdamer Platz Arkaden shopping mall, the second floor of the Europa Center or at the International (see below). Tickets for the day of the show must be purchased at the cinema box office. During the festival, programming information is available in the regular listings magazines or the festival's own daily magazine, **Berlinale**, available at all participating theatres. A much smaller event, but equally global, is the **Jewish Film Festival** (ⓦ www .jffb.de) held in Berlin and Potsdam in late April.

Cinemas

Babylon Dresdener Str. 126, Kreuzberg ☎ 030/61 60 96 93, ⓦ ww.yorck.de. New films in English, with and without subtitles. *Kinotag* Mon. U-Bahn Kottbusser Tor.

Babylon Mitte Rosa-Luxemburg-Str. 30, Mitte ☎ 030/242 59 69, ⓦ www.babylonberlin.de. Central Berlin's best repertory cinema in a landmark theatre. Occasional films with English subtitles. U-Bahn Rosa-Luxemburg-Platz.

Central Rosenthalerstr. 39, Mitte ☎ 030/28 59 99 73, ⓦ www.kino-central.de. Main programme is almost all German, but bizarre midnight events are often held and are often in English. Located beside Hackeschen Höfe. *Kinotag* Tues & Wed. S-Bahn Hackescher Markt.

Cinestar Sony Center Potsdamer Str. 4, Tiergarten ☎ 030/26 06 62 60, ⓦ www.cinestar .de. Eight-screen cinema in the bowels of the Sony Center, with almost every screen in the original (usually English) language; most films are of the Hollywood blockbuster variety. U- & S-Bahn Potsdamer Platz.

Hackesche Höfe Rosenthalerstr. 40–41 (in Hackeschen Höfe), Mitte ☎ 030/283 46 03,

ⓦ www.hoefekino.de. Five-screen multiplex on the top floor of the busy Hackeschen Höfe. Upscale independent foreign films and documentaries, sometimes in English. Often sold out at weekends, but they take phone reservations. *Kinotag* Mon & Tues. S-Bahn Hackescher Markt.

High End 54 Oranienburgerstr. 54–56 (in Tacheles), Mitte ☎ 030/283 14 98. Mostly foreign and indie films, sometimes in English. *Kinotag* Mon & Tues. U-Bahn Oranienburger Tor.

International Karl-Marx-Allee 33, Mitte ☎ 030/24 75 60 11, ⓦ www.yorck.de. A big, comfortable GDR landmark cinema showing new releases. The Mon-night gay programme often shows films in their original language. U-Bahn Schillingstr.

Odeon Hauptstr. 116, Schöneberg ☎ 030/78 70 40 19, ⓦ www.yorck.de. If you're after the more intelligent English-language releases, the Odeon will have them first. *Kinotag* Mon, Tues & Wed. U-Bahn Innsbrucker Platz.

Zeughaus-Kino Unter den Linden 2, Mitte ☎ 030/20 30 44 21, ⓦ www.dkm.de/kino. Cinema in the Zeughaus, which often unearths fascinating films from the pre- and postwar years. S-Bahn Hackescher Markt.

16

Shopping

Most Berliners visit the city's many multistorey **department stores** for much of their shopping, but that's not to say that Berlin doesn't have more interesting shops. In fact, a remarkable number of small and quirky specialist shops thrive, and some of the more interesting are listed below. The list is far from exhaustive, so the yellow pages (*Gelbe Seiten*) can be useful in finding further specialist shops, but better still is to ask around at similar shops. The level of shop-assistant training is invariably excellent – and if a shop can't supply your needs they will not hesitate to suggest alternatives. If you like browsing and foraging you'll find a second home in the city's many **flea markets** – generally replete with Eastern Bloc relics – and **secondhand clothes shops**.

Glitz and dazzle are the prerogatives of **City West**, with its two miles of large chain stores on or around the **Kurfürstendamm**, while **Friedrichstrasse** in the east, though more modest in size, is as opulent. The largest and best central malls are the Potsdamer Platz Arkaden and the Alexa Centre just southeast of Alexanderplatz. Many of the city's funkiest speciality shops and expensive boutiques are concentrated in **Charlottenburg**, **Mitte** and **Prenzlauer Berg**. Ethnic foods and "alternative" businesses are mostly in **Kreuzberg**, along Oranienstrasse and Bergmannstrasse.

Large shops in central Berlin are **open** Monday to Saturday from 10am to 8pm, while smaller shops or those outside the centre usually close two hours earlier, and a few department stores will stay open until 10pm on Thursday, Friday and Saturday. Supermarkets and other shops in main stations, particularly the Hauptbahnhof, are open longer hours, mostly daily 8am to 10pm. Most other shops are closed on Sundays. Except for chains and the larger places, **credit cards** are slowly becoming more widely accepted, but don't rely on being able to use them.

Books, newspapers and magazines

Berlin boasts a great variety of new and secondhand bookstores, and it's an ideal city for leisurely browsing. There are quite a few places to find **English-language books**, most of them on or around Knesebeckstrasse, the street with Berlin's highest concentration of bookstores.

Almost any decent-sized magazine shop in the central districts of Berlin will stock a few English-language newspapers, usually at least *The Guardian, Financial Times* and *The New York Herald-Tribune*. But you'll probably find the best selection at the Hauptbahnhof.

English-language and general

Another Country Riemannstr. 7, Kreuzberg ☎030/69 40 11 60, ⓦwww.anothercountry.de. A living-room atmosphere pervades this intimate shop of English-language secondhand books, where you can borrow any book for €1.50. U-Bahn Gneisenaustr. Mon–Fri 11am–8pm, Sat & Sun noon–4pm.

Books in Berlin Goethestr. 69, Charlottenburg ☎030/313 12 33, ⓦwww.booksinberlin.de. Small bookstore with a good selection of English-language history and popular fiction, some secondhand. U-Bahn Ernst-Reuter-Platz. Mon–Fri noon–8pm, Sat 10am–4pm.

Dussmann Friedrichstr. 90, Mitte ☎030/20 25 11 11, ⓦwww.kulturkaufhaus.de. A huge emporium of books, CDs, videos and software. U- & S-Bahn Friedrichstr. Mon–Sat 10am–midnight.

Hugendubel Branches at Potsdamer Platz Arkaden, Mitte (U- & S-Bahn Potsdamer Platz); and Tauentzienstr. 13, Charlottenburg (U-Bahn Kurfürstendamm) ☎0181/48 44 84, ⓦwww .hugendubel.de. Huge general bookstore with a section devoted to English-language paperback fiction. Potsdamer Platz branch Mon–Sat 9.30am–9pm; Tauentzienstr. Branch Mon–Sat 9.30am–8pm.

Marga Schoeller Knesebeckstr. 33, Charlottenburg ☎030/881 11 12, ⓦwww .margaschoeller.de. Small shop, packed with English fiction and nonfiction: the best place for esoteric topics in English. S-Bahn Savignyplatz. Mon–Wed 9.30am–7pm, Thurs & Fri 9.30am–8pm, Sat 9.30am–6pm.

Local interest

Berlin Story Unter den Linden 26, Mitte ☎030/20 45 38 42, ⓦwww.berlinstory.de. The city's most extensive bookshop on itself, with everything from travel guides to specialist histories, and offered in a range of languages. U- & S-Bahn Friedrichstr. Daily 10am–8pm.

The arts

Artificium Rosenthaler Str. 40–41, in the Hackeschen Höfe, Mitte ☎030/30 87 22 80, ⓦwww.artificium.com. Nineteenth- and twentieth-century art, architecture, photography and the like. S-Bahn Hackescher Markt. Mon–Thurs 10am–9pm, Fri 10am–11pm, Sat 10am–midnight.

Bücherbogen Stadtbahnbogen 593, Charlottenburg ☎030/31 86 95 11, ⓦwww .buecherbogen.com. Situated under the S-Bahn arches, a nevertheless airy and spacious setting for specialist books on art, architecture, film and photography. S-Bahn Savignyplatz. Mon–Fri 10am–8pm, Sat 10am–6pm.

Museum für Fotografie Jebensstr. 2 Charlottenburg ☎030/20 90 55 66. Small bookshop in the foyer of the museum where you can browse a glut of books on photography, art and design – many at reduced prices – without paying admission. U- & S-Bahn Zoologischer Garten. Wed & Fri–Sun 10am–6pm, Thurs 10am–10pm.

Comics and science fiction

Grober Unfug Zossener Str. 32, Kreuzberg ☎030/69 10 14 90, ⓦwww.groberunfug.de. Large display of international comics, plus T-shirts and cards on sale. Often has exhibitions of cartoonists' work in the small gallery upstairs. U-Bahn Gneisenaustr. Mon–Fri 11am–7pm, Sat 11am–4pm.

Travel

Chatwins Goltzstr. 40, Schöneberg ☎030/21 75 69 04, ⓦwww.chatwins.de. Friendly bookshop run for and by travellers with a vast array of guidebooks and travel writing. U-Bahn Nollendorfplatz. Mon–Fri 10am–8pm, Sat 10am–4pm.

Schropp Hardenbergstr. 9a, Schöneberg ☎030/23 55 73 20, ⓦwww.landkartenschropp .de. Specialist store with a large, well-chosen selection of travel books and maps, including detailed cycling maps of Berlin and Germany. U- & S-Bahn Zoologischer Garten. Mon–Fri 10am–8pm, Sat 10am–6pm.

Music

Berlin doesn't have a large number of general record stores but there are plenty of smaller shops dedicated to just one style.

DaCapo Kastanienallee 96, Prenzlauer Berg
☎030/448 17 71, ⓦwww.da-capo-vinyl.de.
Vinyl-only new and used record shop with a
wide selection of jazz, 1960s–80s rock and
releases on East German label Amiga.
U-Bahn Eberswalderstr. Tues–Fri
11am–7pm, Sat 11am–4pm.
Dussmann Friedrichstr. 90, Mitte ☎030/20 25
11 11, ⓦwww.kulturkaufhaus.de. Good
selection of rock, jazz, dance, world and
international vocalists. The basement is
devoted entirely to classical. You can spend
a whole afternoon listening to CDs without
being interrupted by a salesperson if you
like. U- & S-Bahn Friedrichstr. Mon–Sat
10am–midnight.
Hard Wax Paul-Lincke-Ufer 44a, Kreuzberg
☎030/61 13 01 11, ⓦwww.hardwax.com.
Premier dance music specialist. Techno,
trance: you name it, they should have it.

And if they haven't, they'll get it for you.
U-Bahn Görlitzer Bahnhof. Mon–Sat
noon–8pm.
L&P Classics Welserstr. 28, Charlottenburg
☎030/88 04 30 43, ⓦwww.lpclassics.de. Store
devoted entirely to classical music. U-Bahn
Wittenbergplatz. Mon–Sat 10am–8pm.
Mr Dead & Mrs Free Bülowstr. 5, Schöneberg
☎030/215 14 49, ⓦwww.deadandfree.com.
Primarily pop, folk, indie and country
records on independent labels, mostly on
vinyl. U-Bahn Nollendorfplatz. Mon–Fri
noon–7pm, Sat 11am–4pm.
Soultrade Sanderstr. 29, Kreuzberg ☎030/694
52 57, ⓦwww.soultrade.de. Specialists in
black music including soul, hip-hop, funk,
house and jazz. U-Bahn Schönleinstr. Mon
& Wed 11am–7pm, Tues, Thurs & Fri
11am–8pm, Sat noon–6pm.

Fashion

Although they like to think of themselves as such, Berliners aren't exactly trend-
setters, and despite the many innovative fashion designers in the city their work is
mostly small-scale and tends to lack international impact. Still, it's possible to pick
up superb **bargains** at the many **secondhand** clothes stores: you'll find unusual
(and trendy) items here at very low prices. Easy access to the discarded wardrobes
of the East has brought many odd items of official uniform and clothing into the
shops since the Wall fell.

The main shopping areas at Wilmersdorferstrasse U-Bahn, Wilmersdorf and
Walter-Schreiber-Platz U-Bahn, Steglitz, have plenty of inexpensive name-brand
styles. Ku'damm and Friedrichstrasse boast designer clothes shops targeting the
rich and conservative, as well as several leather outlets with cheap and good-quality
jackets, and some excellent and stylish shoe shops. For the most cutting-edge
boutiques head to the area around the Hackescher Markt: styles throughout the
district have more in common with the functional and urbane look of the Bauhaus
movement than with the chic Parisian-style glamour, with funky trainers winning
out over glamorous heels. Many specialize in a sort of 1970s-revival-meets-GDR-
Ostalgie look.

Secondhand

Garage Ahornstr. 2, Schöneberg
☎030/211 27 60, ⓦwww.kleidermarkt.de.
Largest secondhand clothes store in Europe
– good for jackets, coats and jeans. Prices
are according to weight (the clothes', not
yours), with a 30 percent discount offered
Wed 11am–1pm. U-Bahn Nollendorfplatz.
Mon–Fri 11am–7pm, Sat 11am–6pm.
Humana Frankfurter Tor 3, Friedrichshain
☎030/422 20 18, ⓦwww.humana-de.org.
Gigantic branch of a local secondhand

chain that has a dozen stores in Berlin,
offers great bargains on items that are
(again) in style. Mon–Fri 10am–7pm,
Sat 10am–4pm.
ReSales branches at Pestalozzzistr. 82,
Charlottenburg, U-Bahn Wilmersdorfer Str.;
Potsdamer Str. 105, Schöneberg, U-Bahn
Kurfürstenstr.; Turmstr. 72, Mitte, U-Bahn
Turmstr.; ⓦwww.jeden-tag-was-neues.de.
Nationwide chain of secondhand stores with
four branches in central Berlin and huge
vast array of garments that range from hip
streetwear to silky evening wear at each. All

tend to be fair prices too. Opening times vary between stores, but approx Mon–Sat 10am–7pm.

Secondo Mommsenstr. 61, Charlottenburg ☎030/881 22 91, ⓦwww.secondoberlin.de. Exclusively designer clothes at massively knock-down prices: most items are in top condition, though of course many designs are a bit dated. You'll find a number of similar shops further up and down the street. S-Bahn Savignyplatz. Mon–Fri 11am–6.30pm, Sat 11am–3.30pm.

Sgt. Peppers Kastanienallee 91, Prenzlauer Berg ☎030/448 11 21, ⓦwww.sgt-peppers-berlin.de. Mixed bag of vintage 1960s and 1970s, and the store also has its own label of retro-wear. U-Bahn Eberswalder Str. Mon–Fri 11am–8pm, Sat 11am–6pm.

Designer labels

Great times to browse are during the **sales** in January (*Winterschluss verkauf*) and August (*Sommerschluss verkauf*). To find as many local designers as possible, try the area around Hackescher Markt, (see p.81); and check the website ⓦwww.berlinerklamotten.com, where many local designers have congregated to promote their wares.

🏃 **Berlinomat Frankfurter Allee 89, Friedrichshain** ☎030/42 08 14 45, ⓦwww.berlinomat.com. The showcase for more than thirty Berlin designers, Berlinomat stocks a large and varied assortment of clothing, accessories and unique souvenirs. The prices, considering they're designer, are reasonable. U- & S-Bahn Frankfurter Allee. Mon–Sat 11am–8pm.

Claudia Skoda Alte Schönhauser Str. 35, Mitte ☎030/280 72 11, ⓦwww.claudiaskoda.com. Berlin's knit-master and most famous designer. U-Bahn Weinmeisterstr. Mon–Fri noon–8pm, Sat 11am–7pm.

Eisdieler Kastanienallee 12, Prenzlauer Berg ☎030/28 38 12 91, ⓦwww.eisdieler.de. Innovative, international collection of urban streetwear. U-Bahn Eberswalder Str. Mon–Fri noon–8pm, Sat noon–7pm.

Flagship Store Oderberger Str. 53 ☎030/43 73 53 27, ⓦwww.flagshipstore-berlin.de. Great one-stop shop to peruse the urbane collections of some thirty local designers. U-Bahn Eberswalderstr. Mon–Sat noon–8pm.

Lisa D. Rosenthaler Str. 40–41 (in the Hackeschen Höfe), Mitte ☎030/282 90 61,

▲ Lisa D.

ⓦwww.lisad.com. One of Berlin's very few local designers to have made a name for herself, Lisa D. favours fitted dresses in muted colours. S-Bahn Hackescher Markt. Mon–Sat 11am–7pm, Sun 11am–5pm.

Mientus Wilmersdorfer Str. 73, Charlottenburg ☎030/323 90 77, ⓦwww.mientus.com. Casual and formal up-to-the-minute menswear, ranging in price from reasonable to outrageously expensive. U-Bahn Wilmersdorfer Str. Mon–Sat 10am–7pm.

Nix Oranienburger Str. 32, Mitte ☎030/281 11 80 44, ⓦwww.nix.de. Unusual, robust and practical designs for women from a couple of young east Berliners. S-Bahn Oranienburger Str. Mon–Sat 11am–8pm.

🏃 **Respectmen Neue Schönhauser Str. 14, Mitte** ☎030/283 50 10, ⓦwww.respectmen.de. Good tailoring and nice design mark out the suits and casual wear of this men's store. S-Bahn Hackescher Markt. Mon–Fri noon–8pm, Sat noon–7pm.

Soma Alte Schönhauser Str. 27, Mitte ☎030/281 93 80, ⓦwww.soma-berlin.de. Young Berlin designers and club-wear in the front of the shop, secondhand in the rear. S-Bahn Hackescher Markt. Mon–Fri noon–8pm, Sat noon–6pm.

Shoes

Budapester Schuhe Kurfürstendamm 43, Charlottenburg ☎030/88 62 42 06, ⓦwww.budapester.eu. World-class, expensive designer shoes such as Prada and Dolce & Gabbana. U-Bahn Uhlandstr. Mon–Fri 10am–7pm, Sat 10am–6pm.

Luccico Bergmannstr. 8, Kreuzberg ☎030/216 65 17, ⓦwww.luccico.de. Wild and wacky Italian shoes, plus plainer varieties; also at Oranienburger Str. 23. U-Bahn Mehringdam. Mon–Fri noon–8pm, Sat 11am–8pm.

Ludwig Reiter Kurfürstendamm 50, Charlottenburg ☎030/88 68 17 76, ⓦwww.ludwig-reiter.com. Luxurious formal wear and well-made sports shoes. U-Bahn Uhlandstr. Mon–Fri 11am–7pm, Sat 11am–4pm.

Mad Flavor Solmsstr. 33, Kreuzberg ☎030/312 49 63, ⓦwww.madflavor.de. Trendy sneakers for the hip-hop and club crowd. U-Bahn Gneisenaustr. Mon–Sat noon–8pm.

🏃 **Trippen Hackeschen Höfe, Rosenthaler Str. 40, Mitte** ☎030/28 39 13 37, ⓦwww.trippen.com. Hot Berlin design company specializing in wooden-soled shoes with a rounded toe. S-Bahn Hackescher Markt. Mon–Fri 11am–7pm, Sat 10am–5pm.

Underwear

Körpernah Massanenstr. 8 ☎030/215 74 71, ⓦwww.koerpernah-berlin.de. Fashionable underwear and lingerie for both sexes in every possible size. U-Bahn Nollendorfplatz. Mon–Fri 10am–6.30pm. Sat 10am–3pm.

Accessories

Fiona Bennett Grosse Hamburger Str. 25, Mitte ☎030/28 09 63 30, ⓦwww.fionabennett.com. Unique and avant-garde designer hats for men and women. S-Bahn Hackescher Markt. Mon–Wed 10am–6pm, Thurs & Fri noon–8pm, Sat noon–6pm.

Rio Bleibtreustr. 52, Charlottenburg ☎030/313 31 52, ⓦwww.rio-modeschmuck-berlin.de. Decorative costume jewellers, with lots of unusual offerings from Paris and Milan, as well as its own line. Also specializes in earrings at affordable prices. S-Bahn Savignyplatz. Mon–Wed & Fri 11am–6.30pm, Thurs 11am–7pm, Sat 11am–6pm.

Souvenirs

Ach Berlin Markengrafstr. 39, Mitte ☎030/92 12 68 80, ⓦwww.achberlin.de. Good source of offbeat Berlin memorabilia where classy designs celebrate local landmarks and life: among them cookie-cutters of the TV tower, brooms that look like the Brandenburg Gate and many stylish souvenir T-shirts. U-Bahn Stadtmitte. Mon–Sat 11am–7pm.

Ampelmann Galerie Shop Hackeschen Höfe V, Mitte ☎030/44 72 64 38, ⓦwww.ampelmann.de. Celebration of the traffic-light man (Ampelmann) that reigns supreme on the eastern side of the city. He was threatened by replacement with the svelte West Berlin counterpart and has since become a cult object. Pick up T-shirts, mugs, lights and so on here. S-Bahn Hackescher Markt. Mon–Sat 9.30am–10pm, Sun 10am–7pm.

Mondos Arts Schreinerstr. 6, Friedrichshain ☎030/42 01 07 78, ⓦwww.ost-shop.de. GDR-kitsch heaven devoted to cult of the Amplemann, Sandmann (a cult character from children's TV) and the Trabi and stockist of virtually every other imaginable piece of *Ostalgie*. Lots of fun, even if you can't reminisce. U-Bahn Samariterstr. Mon–Fri 10am–7pm, Sat 11am–4pm.

Flowers, cards & gifts

Flowers are frequently given as gifts, and are almost a prerequisite for birthdays and other special occasions. It's most fun choosing your own bouquet. Simply explain roughly what colours you'd like and your budget – around €10 should get you a respectable bunch. The city's many open-air markets sell interesting arrangements at affordable prices, but should you get stuck for a florist head to the main train stations, where there's always one, even open on a Sunday.

Ararat Bergmannstr. 99a, Kreuzberg ☎030/693 50 80, ✆www.ararat-berlin.de. Huge selection of greetings cards and postcards; posters and prints are across the street at Bergmannstr. 9. U-Bahn Gneisenaustr. Mon–Sat 10am–8pm.

Küchenladen Knesebeckstr. 26, Charlottenburg ☎030/881 39 08, ✆www.kuechenladen.com. Everything for the foodie, from tortoiseshell teaspoons to Italian cookbooks. S-Bahn Savignyplatz. Mon–Fri 11am–7pm, Sat 10am–6pm.

Travel equipment

Bannat Lietzenburger Str. 69, Charlottenburg ☎030/882 72 42, ✆www.bannat-berlin.de. A great selection of travel equipment, particularly for the backpacker and camper. U-Bahn Uhlandstr. Mon–Fri 10am–8pm, Sat 10am–6pm.

Fahrradbüro Berlin Hauptstr. 46, Schöneberg ☎030/78 70 26 01, ✆www.fahrradbuero.de. Every conceivable piece of equipment for bikes. U-Bahn Kleistpark. Mon–Fri 10am–3pm, Sat 10am–2pm.

Globetrotter Schloßstr. 78–82, Steglitz-Zehlendorf ☎030/850 89 20 ✆www.globetrotter.de. Massive outdoor shop with several gimmicks – like the pool to try out kayaks and a freezer at –25°C to try out jackets and sleeping bags – as well as lots of well-priced stock. A bit of a trek from the centre, but directly above the station. U- & S-Bahn Rathaus Steglitz. Mon–Fri 10am–8pm, Sat 9am–8pm.

Electricals

Saturn Alexanderplatz 3, Mitte ☎030/263 99 70, ✆www.saturn.de. Giant electrical superstore with aggressively priced mobile phones, cameras, memory cards, iPods and the like.

You can find branches in the Europa Center and the Potsdamer Arkaden. U-Bahn Alexanderplatz. Daily 10am–9pm.

Department stores

There are no surprises inside Berlin's **department stores** and, with the exception of KaDeWe and Galeries Lafayette, they're only worth popping into to stock up on essentials. Listed below are the most central ones.

Galeria Kaufhof Alexanderplatz 9, Mitte ☎030/24 74 30, ✆www.galeria-kaufhof.de. Once the location of the GDR's showcase department store, this is now a quite typical emporium. U- & S-Bahn Alexanderplatz. Mon–Wed 9.30am–8pm, Thurs–Sat 9.30am–10pm.

Galeries Lafayette Friedrichstr. 76, Mitte ☎030/20 94 80, ✆www.lafayette-berlin.de. Branch of the upscale Paris-based department store. Surprisingly small, but packed with beautiful and expensive things and including a food department with imports from France. U-Bahn Französische Str. Mon–Sat 10am–8pm.

KaDeWe Tauentzienstr. 21, Schöneberg ☎030/212 10, ✆www.kadewe-berlin.de. Content rather than flashy interior decor

rules the day here. From designer labels to the extraordinary displays at the international delicatessen, where you can nibble on some piece of exotica, there's everything the consumer's heart desires at this, the largest department store on the continent. U-Bahn Wittenbergplatz. Mon–Thurs 10am–8pm, Fri 10am–9pm, Sat 9.30am–8pm.

Karstadt Kurfürstendamm 231, Charlottenburg ☎030/88 00 30, ✆www.karstadt.de. A smaller and cheaper version of KaDeWe. Everything is beautifully laid out, with a particularly good menswear department. Other branches dot the rest of Berlin. U-Bahn Kurfürstendamm. Mon–Thurs & Sat 10am–8pm, Fri 10am–9pm.

Food and drink

Of the city's **supermarket chains** Pennymarkt, Lidl, Aldi and Plus, are by far the cheapest for food and drink, although they offer limited choice. Ullrich, on Hardenbergstrasse, underneath the railway bridge by Zoo Station, has an excellent selection of foods, wines and spirits and is cheap despite its central location. You'll also find several **food markets** with well-priced good quality fruit, veg and local produce within each quarter of Berlin, and small neighbourhood bakeries scattered throughout the city: **wholemeal bread** fresh from the oven is one of the delights of Berlin.

The city's **speciality food shops** are spread throughout the city, though the majority of Turkish shops are in Kreuzberg. But probably the single best place to head for is the food court of a luxurious **department store**. The sixth floor of KaDeWe (see p.245) is devoted to a mind-boggling array of gourmets' delights: 400 types of bread, 1200 cheeses and 1400 meats, a bewildering number of cakes and even a counter of high-end confectioner Leysieffer. But probably its best feature is its many counters where you can sample goodies on sale. Galeries Lafayette (see p.245) also has a good gourmet food section with delectables from around the world.

Coffee and tea

Barcomi's Bergmannstr. 21, Kreuzberg ☎030/28 59 83 63, ⓦwww.barcomis.de. A good selection of top-notch, house-roasted coffee, including organic and caffeine-free varieties. U-Bahn Gneisenaustr. Mon–Sat 8am–9pm, Sun 9am–9pm.

Tchibo Alexanderplatz 2, Mitte ☎030/24 72 06 96 (many other branches around the city). The city's most popular stand-up coffee place with good-quality beans and the chance to mix your own blend from a small choice at the counter. U-Bahn Kurfürstendamm. Mon–Sat 8am–8pm.

Teesalon Invalidenstr. 160 ☎030/28 04 06 60, ⓦwww.tee-import.de. Offers a glut of exotic teas and all the paraphernalia they cry out for to be enjoyed in style. U-Bahn Rosenthaler Platz. Mon–Fri 10am–7pm, Sat 10am–4pm.

Delicatessen

Alimentari e Vini Skalitzer Str. 23, Kreuzberg ☎030/611 49 81, ⓦwww.alimentari.de. A slick shop in scruffy Kreuzberg offering wines, pastas and other Italian deli items. U-Bahn Kottbusser Tor. Mon–Fri 9am–6pm, Sat 9am–1pm.

Health food

Health food is very popular in Berlin, particularly organic fruit, vegetables and meats (look for the "Neuland" logo for the latter), and almost every neighbourhood has its own health-food shop (*Naturkostladen*), with vegetarian goodies, chemical-free beers and wines.

Einhorn Wittenbergplatz 5, Schöneberg ☎030/218 63 47. Excellent wholegrain breads and cakes, baked in-house, at this popular veggie eatery (see p.209). U-Bahn Uhlandstr. Mon–Fri 10am–6pm.

Himmel und Erde Naturkost Skalitzer Str. 46, Kreuzberg ☎030/611 60 41, ⓦwww.himmel erde.de. Excellent organic supermarket, that's been around for over two decades. U-Bahn Görlitzer Bahnhof. Mon–Fri 9am–7pm, Sat 9am–4pm.

LPG Bio-Markt Kollwitzstr. 17, Prenzlauer Berg ☎030/322 97 14 00, ⓦwww.lpg-naturkost.de. Europe's largest organic supermarket with a staggering 18,000 products, many from the countryside surrounding Berlin. U-Bahn Senefelderplatz. Mon–Sat 9am–9pm.

Food markets

Türken-Markt Kottbusser Damm/Maybachufer, Neukölln. Definitely worth a visit, especially on Fri when there's a real Oriental flavour. Handy for all things Turkish, especially cheese, bread, olives and dried fruits, all at rock-bottom prices. U-Bahn Kottbusser Tor. Tues & Fri noon–6pm.

Wines and spirits

Wein & Glas Compagnie Prinzregentenstr. 2, Wilmersdorf ☎030/235 15 20, ⓦwww.wein undglas.com. German and French wines (and some glasses). U-Bahn Eisenacher Str. Mon–Fri 10am–6.30pm, Sat 9.30am–4pm.
Wein & Whisky Eisenacher Str. 64 ☎030/784 50 10, ⓦwww.world-wide-whisky.de. Though far from the source, this whisky specialist has

an almost definitive collection encompassing over 2000 varieties of the water of life. U-Bahn Eisenacher Str. Mon 1–6pm, Tues–Fri 11am–6pm, Sat 10am–2pm.
Weinkeller Blücherstr. 22, Kreuzberg ☎030/693 46 61, ⓦwww.weinkeller-berlin.de. Spanish, French, Italian and German wines, and sherries and whiskies from the cask. U-Bahn Gneisenaustr. Mon–Fri 10am–8pm, Sat 10am–4pm.

Markets and junk shops

Listed below is a selection of Berlin's best **flea markets** and **junk shops**. For the latter, and **antiques**, try also browsing Suarezstrasse in Charlottenburg, Gotzstrasse in Schöneberg and Bergmannstrasse in Kreuzberg.

Flea markets

Berliner Kunst- und Nostalgiemarket by the Bode and Pergamon museums, Mitte. A good mix of real antiques, schlock souvenirs, used books and bootleg CDs. S-Bahn Hackescher Markt. Sat & Sun 11am–4pm.
Flohmarkt am Boxhagener Platz Boxhagener Platz, Friedrichshain. Small flea market catering to the needs of the student quarter and good for old Eastern Bloc memorabilia. U- & S-Bahn Warschauer Str. Sun 9am–4pm.
Flohmarkt am Moritzplatz Moritzplatz. An integral part of Kreuzberg's social fabric, with all that entails. Lots of Turkish goods and some pretty rough-and-ready clutter to sift through for gems. U-Bahn Moritzplatz. Sun 8am–4pm.
Flohmarkt Schöneberg in front of the Schöneberg City Hall, Schöneberg. Some professionals here selling books and collectables, but also a good number of amateur vendors who have cleared out the garage or attic and are selling the motley results. U-Bahn Rathaus Schöneberg. Sat & Sun 8am–4pm.
Flohmarkt am Tiergarten Strasse des 17 Juni, north side of road near Ernst-Reuter-Platz, Charlottenburg. Pleasant enough for a Sun morning stroll, but the most expensive of the flea markets, and with tourist-oriented wares. Good for embroidery and lace, though. S-Bahn Tiergarten. Sat & Sun 10am–5pm.

Hallentrödelmarkt Treptow Eichenstr. 4, Treptow. Ideal rainy-day option: there's something of everything in this huge indoor flea market. The stalls are all permanent fixtures and thoroughly chaotic. S-Bahn Treptower Park – head north along Hoffmannstr. parallel to the Spree River. Sat & Sun 10am–5pm.
Trödelmarkt am Arkonaplatz Arkonaplatz, Prenzlauer Berg, ⓦwww.troedelmarkt -arkonaplatz.de. Popular flea market in the city's yuppie district, thick with 1960s and 70s junk and cult objects in equal measure. U-Bahn Bernauer Str. Sun 10am–4pm.

Junk shops

Antiquitäten- und Flohmarkt Bahnhof Friedrichstr. under the railway arches 190–203, Mitte ☎030/208 26 55, ⓦwww.antikmarkt -berlin.de. Tending more towards the antique end of things, with several shops selling everything from books to jewellery. Not particularly cheap. U- & S-Bahn Friedrichstr. Daily 11am–6pm.
Zille-Hof Uhlandstr. 19, Charlottenburg. Not so much a flea market as an overgrown junkshop with reproduction curios, old street signs and a miscellany of interesting junk. Not especially cheap, but the pleasure is in rummaging as much as in buying. U-Bahn Uhlandstr. Mon–Fri 8am–5pm, Sat 8am–1pm.

(17)

Sport

W hile Berliners go in for healthy eating in a big way, they're not famous for being fitness fanatics – they need all their energy for the frenetic nightlife. Nonetheless there is a surprising variety of **participatory sports** available in the city and, despite a shortage of top-flight teams, the **spectator sports** scene is vibrant, with some fanatical support for virtually every team. Major and some minor sporting events are listed in the *Tip* and *Zitty* what's on magazines (see p.39), but the best index of facilities and events is on the web on the German-only Ⓦ www.citysports.de.

Participatory sports

Municipal facilities for many sports are excellent across the city, as this is one area the GDR was always keen to invest in. Wherever you are in the city, it shouldn't be hard to find somewhere to jog and swim – with many outdoor pools opening for the summer. Berlin is also a cycle-friendly city (see p.29).

Jogging

With so many parks it's easy to find a good place to jog in Berlin. Best are the Tiergarten, Volkspark Friedrichshain, Treptower Park and the gardens of Schloss Charlottenburg. The lakes around the city are also popular with joggers: try the Schlachtensee, Krumme Lanke or Grunewaldsee. If you're into long-distance running there's always the **Berlin Marathon** (see p.32) on the last weekend in September.

Ice-skating

Small open-air rinks sprout up near Christmas markets in the centre of town, but the proper rinks are all a little way out. These usually have several three-hour sessions per day which cost around €4 and the same again to rent skates. The city's largest

rink is the Horst-Dohm-Eisstadion, Fritz-Wildung-Strasse 9, Wilmersdorf (☏030/89 73 27 34, Ⓦ www.eissport -service.de; U-Bahn Heidelberger Platz), an outdoor facility, with a track surrounding the central rink.

In-line skating and skateboarding

In-line skating is extremely popular in Berlin, as evidenced by the success of Skate Night (June–Sept; Ⓦ berlin .skatebynight.de) when thousands take to cordoned-off streets in the city centre. The event costs €2, starts at 7pm on selected summer Sundays and runs until dusk, returning skaters back to the start point. It's a magnificent opportunity to see some of Berlin's streets from an unusual viewpoint. If you need to rent skates try Ski Shop Charlottenburg, Schustehrusstrasse 1 (☏030/341 48 70; Ⓦ www.ski -shop-charlottenburg.de; U-Bahn

Richard-Wagner Platz), who rent out skates for €8 per day.

The most obvious place for skateboarders to head to is the Skatehalle Berlin, Revaler Strasse 99 (Mon 2–8pm, Tues, Wed & Fri 2pm–midnight, Thurs 2–10pm, Sat noon–midnight, Sun noon–8pm; €5; no phone, ⓦwww .skatehalle-berlin.de), within the Cassiopeia complex in Friedrichshain (see p.227) – though check web in advance as some times are reserved for BMXers. Other skateparks, ramps and pipes are scattered around the city's parks, with some of the best at the old Radrennbahn in Weissensee and Grazer Platz in Schöneberg. A full overview is given on the website ⓦwww .skate-spots.de.

Sports centres

Berlin's private gyms are generally members-only and you'll usually need to be a guest of a member to qualify for a day pass, which is likely to be around €25.

Ars Vitalis Hauptstr. 19, Schöneberg ☎030/311 65 94 70, ⓦwww.ars-vitalis.de. Excellent private gym, with all the usual equipment as well as a good range of classes, and three different saunas. Masseurs are on standby. Day pass €28, ten-day pass €59. U-Bahn Kleistpark. Mon–Sun 8am–11.30pm.

FEZ Wuhlheide An der Wuhlheide 197, Köpenick ☎030/53 07 10, ⓦwww.fez-berlin.de. Large leisure complex some way out of town with some unusual facilities, such as a BMX track, that makes the trek out of town worthwhile. S-Bahn Wuhlheide. Tues–Fri 9am–10pm, Sat 1–6pm, Sun 10am–6pm – all times are extended during school holidays.

Freisportanlage Am Südpark 51, Spandau. Massive outdoor sports complex on the edge of town, with lots of free facilities including basketball and volleyball courts, table tennis, tennis and an in-line skating area. Also crazy golf (€4 per round). May–Sept. S-Bahn Spandau. Opening hours vary but generally daily 8am–11pm.

Swimming pools, saunas and spas

Most districts throughout the city have both indoor and outdoor **swimming**

pools (not necessarily in the same place). Most municipal pools (ⓦwww .berlinerbaederbetriebe.de) charge around €4 for a swim and have complicated opening hours – from as early as 7am to as late as 10pm on some days, with some closing in the summer and some offering men- and women-only times and family times. Look out too for **Warmbädetag**, when the water is warmer than usual – and admission usually more. Many pools also have saunas which cost around €14 for three hours, and require you to leave any Anglo-Saxon prudishness at home, for they are inevitably naked and mixed-sex. Women who feel uncomfortable with this arrangement should look out for women-only sessions offered regularly at most facilities, while men should be aware that somewhere advertising itself as a men's sauna is a gay venue (see p.254), where some cruising is likely.

Bad am Spreewaldplatz Wiener Str. 59h, Kreuzberg ☎030/69 53 520, ⓦwww .berlinerbaederbetriebe.de. Popular indoor pool complete with sauna and wave machine. U-Bahn Görlitzerbahnhof.

Hamam Mariannenstr. 6, Kreuzberg ☎030/615 14 64, ⓦwww.hamamberlin.de. Women-only (but not lesbian) Turkish-style bathhouse in women's centre Schokofabrik. Various beauty treatments are also available. U-Bahn Kottbusser Tor. Mon 3–11pm, Tues–Sun noon–11pm.

Liquidrom Möckernstr. 10, Kreuzberg ☎030/258 00 78 20, ⓦwww .liquidrom-berlin.de. Cutting-edge health spa, whose claim to fame is its atmospheric saltwater pool into which ambient music is piped. The amazing underwater sound experience is complemented by mildly psychedelic projections on the ceiling and floors. There's also a couple of hot tubs – one outdoor – a sauna and steam room and civilized bar. S-Bahn Anhalter Bahnhof. Sun–Thurs 10am–midnight, Fri & Sat 10am–1am.

Sommerbad Olympia-Stadion Olympischer Platz (Osttor), Charlottenburg ☎030/663 11 42, ⓦwww.berlinerbaederbetriebe.de. Outdoor pool that's part of the impressive 1930s-era Olympic Stadium complex. U-Bahn Olympia Stadion.

Badeschiff

A dip in the River Spree might not sound like such a good idea until you visit **Badeschiff**, an old industrial barge converted into a clear blue twenty-metre-long swimming pool that bobs in the river. A wooden jetty that's perfect for sunbathing connects the pool to a beach – complete with beach bar – that's been constructed on the bank. Look out for early morning yoga sessions. The entrance is hidden behind a maze of old tram sheds beside the Arena complex. In winter the pool gets a roof and its two saunas are popular. Open daily noon–midnight; entry €3 pool, €12 sauna; ℡030/533 20 30, ⓦwww.arena-berlin.de. U-Bahn Schlesiches Tor.

▲ Olympic Stadium

Stadtbad Charlottenburg (Alte Halle) Krumme Str. 10, Charlottenburg ℡030/34 38 38 60, ⓦwww.berlinerbaederbetriebe.de. A delightful, old-fashioned tiled pool with sauna, which is seldom crowded. U-Bahn Bismarckstr.

Stadtbad Mitte Gartenstr. 5, Mitte ℡030/308 80 90, ⓦwww.berlinerbaederbetriebe.de. Centrally located old-fashioned fifty-metre pool. S-Bahn Nordbahnhof.

Stadtbad Neukölln Ganghoferstr. 3, Neukölln ℡030/68 24 98 12, ⓦwww.berlinerbaederbetriebe.de. Swim and relax in a setting that resembles a Hungarian spa. Two pools (one heated, one cool) decorated with fountains and mosaic tiles, encased in a maze of archways and colonnades. Sauna and steamroom available. U-Bahn Rathaus Neukölln.

Strandbad Wannsee Wannseebadweg 25, Zehlendorf ℡030/70 71 38 33, ⓦwww.berlinerbaederbetriebe.de. Outdoor pool with beach nearby, lots of activities in the summer and which is usually packed. S-Bahn Nikolassee.

Thermen am Europa-Center Nürnberger Str. 7, Charlottenburg ℡030/257 57 60, ⓦwww.thermen-berlin.de. Big sauna complex with no less than nine saunas, as well as indoor and outdoor saltwater pools, fitness rooms and beauty treatments. Towels available for rent. U-Bahn Wittembergplatz. Mon–Sat 10am–midnight, Sun 10am–9pm.

Spectator sports

Though none of Berlin's sporting teams is world-class, all play in competitive leagues and have a loyal and entertaining fan base. The most high-profile is Hertha BSC, the city's major **football team**, though virtually all of Berlin's other teams tend to do better in their leagues. The biggest sporting spectacles, however, are the city's annual events, including the **Six-day Non-stop Cycle Race** (see p.31) in late January and the late-September **Berlin Marathon** (see p.32).

Teams and venues

Alba Berlin ℡030/300 90 50, tickets ℡01805/57 00 11, ⓦwww.albaberlin.de. Berlin's premier basketball team, and one of the top dozen in Europe, competes in the German League and the Euroleague, and plays in the O2 World Arena in Friedrichshain. Oct–June; tickets €10–35. S-Bahn Ostbahnhof.

EHC Eisbären ☎ 030/97 18 40 40, ⓦ www
.eisbaeren.de. Fanatically supported eastern
Berlin ice hockey team, which has been
competing at the very top of the premier
German division for some years. The
razzmatazz surrounding the teams and
players brings it close to the likes of the
NHL and the game quality is not too far off
either. The Eisbären, or polar bears, play in
tho O2 World Arena. Season Sept–March;
tickets €15–30. S-Bahn Ostbahnhof.
Hertha BSC ☎ 01805/18 92 00, ⓦ www
.herthabsc.de. Berlin's Bundesliga also-rans,
who always seem to evade real glory,
despite lots of promise and the occasional
successful European outing. But the
Olympic Stadium is glorious whatever the
team or result. Tickets are generally easy to
come by, either online or via the Hertha
fan-shop in the Europa Center (see p.119).

Season Aug–May; tickets €15–56. U-Bahn
Olympia Stadion.
Trabrennbahn Karlshorst Treskow allee 129,
Lichtenberg ☎ 030/740 12 12, ⓦ www
.berlintrab.de. Enjoy a day at the races
Berlin-style, watching harness racing. The
racetrack is to the left of Treskow allee, just
south of the S-Bahn bridge. Year-round;
tickets €3. S-Bahn Karlshorst.
Union Berlin ☎ 030/656 68 80, tickets ☎ 030/65
66 88 93, ⓦ www.fc-union berlin.do. Eastern
Berlin's football team, with a fiercely loyal
working-class following, plays in the second
division. Despite some shock success in
German cup matches and even in Europe,
the day-to-day picture is less exciting.
Matches are played in the Stadion An der
Alten Försterei, An der Wuhlheide In
Köpenick. Season Aug–May; tickets €9–25.
S-Bahn Köpenick.

Gay and lesbian Berlin

Berlin's gay and lesbian scenes are world-class – certainly on a par with those of San Francisco or New York – and so a huge magnet for gay men and women from all over Germany and Europe. This has been the case since the 1920s, when Christopher Isherwood and W.H. Auden both came here, drawn to a city where, in sharp contrast to the oppressiveness of London, the gay community did not live in fear of harassment and legal persecution.

The easy-going, easy-living attitude stretches into the straight community, too, and it's not uncommon to see transvestites at their glitziest dancing atop tables at even conservative bashes. The best time to arrive and plunge yourself into the hurly-burly is during **Gay Pride Week**, centred around the **Christopher Street Day parade** (Ⓦ www.csd-berlin.de) in late June every year.

Information and resources

The German/English-language **Berlin von Hinten** (€12) is the city's most useful gay guide. **Siegessäule** (Ⓦ www.siegessaeule.de), a monthly gay magazine, has listings of events and an encyclopedic directory of gay and lesbian contacts and groups; it's available free from the resources below and most gay bars. They also

> ### Wowi
>
> Oozing can-do attitude, Berlin's flashy and openly gay mayor **Klaus Wowereit** or "Wowi", as Berliners call him, is used to courting controversy. In June 2001 he became Germany's first high-level politician to announce his homosexuality, coining the now famous German phrase "Ich bin schwul, und das ist auch gut so" ("I'm gay, and that's all right, too"). But he caused quite a stir when he zealously welcomed Folsom-Europe, a sado-masochism festival, to Berlin in 2005. Attracting 10,000 leather- and chain-clad revellers to the city, it caused outrage among conservatives in the city's parliament, but Wowi shot back that Berlin in particular must, above all, be tolerant. Berliners appear to agree, and Wowi was re-elected as mayor in 2006, despite widespread dissatisfaction with his mainstream political party the SPD. His personality seemed to have carried the show: according to polls at the time, two-thirds of Berliners said they would have voted for him if there had been a direct vote for mayor.

produce an online city guide in both German and English: **Ⓦ**www.out-in-berlin
.de. **Blattgold** (**Ⓦ**www.blattgold-berlin.de), a monthly publication listing all
lesbian groups and events, is available from feminist meeting places and bookshops.
The gay and women's centres listed here are also a good resource for information
and contacts.

Mann-O-Meter Bülowstr. 106, Schöneberg
☎030/216 80 08, **Ⓦ**www.mann-o-meter.de.
One of the city's main gay information
centres and meeting points. U-Bahn
Nollendorfplatz. Tues–Fri 5–10pm, Sat &
Sun 2–8pm.

Vorspiel Martin-Luther-Str. 56, Schöneberg
☎030/44 05 77 40, **Ⓦ**www.vorspiel-berlin.de.
Berlin's gay and lesbian sports club, offering
a variety of activities for every level of fitness
and ability. S-Bahn Papestr. Mon 1 0pm,
Tues 5–7pm, Thurs 10am–1pm.

Accommodation

Most **accommodation** in Berlin is gay-friendly, though there are some places,
listed below, that are run for and by the gay community. There are no hotels or
pensions in Berlin specifically for lesbians, though there are two women-only
hotels, the **Artemisia** (see p.199) and **Intermezzo** (see p.195).

Art Hotel Charlottenburger Hof Stuttgarter
Platz 14, Charlottenburg; see map, p.116
☎030/32 90 70, **Ⓦ**www.charlottenburger
-hof.de. Bright contemporary hotel, replete
with modern art, Bauhaus design and
multicoloured furniture. Perks include free
internet access in every room and a 24hr
café. Rates can often be slashed by
booking specials online. S-Bahn Charlottenburg. €65
Art Hotel Connection Fuggerstr. 33, Schöneberg;
see map, p.128 ☎030/210 21 88 00, **Ⓦ**www
.arthotel-connection.de. Located above the
well-known *Connection* club. Most rooms
are large and en suite; breakfast is included
in the rate. U-Bahn Wittenbergplatz. €89

Le Moustache Gartenstr. 4, Mitte; see map,
pp.82–83 ☎030/281 72 77, **Ⓦ**www
.lemoustache.de. Basic hotel next door to the
leather bar of the same name (see p.255).
Rooms share bathrooms. U-Bahn
Oranienburger Tor. €50
Tom's Hotel Motzstr. 19, Schöneberg; see map,
p.128 ☎030/219 66 04, **Ⓦ**www.toms-hotel.de.
One of the largest gay hotels in town and
has a great location in Berlin's gay village.
Bright simple rooms, with free wi-fi and a
bowl of fruit provided along with a pass for
discounts at a number of local businesses.
Also operates the *Gay Hostel* over the road
– dorms €26–31; singles €51. U-Bahn
Nollendorfplatz. €120

Bookshops, cinemas, galleries and museums

Ana Koluth Schönhauser Allee 124, Prenzlauer
Berg ☎030/87 33 69 80, **Ⓦ**www.anakoluth.de.
Well-stocked lesbian bookstore, which also
puts on regular exhibitions and readings: as
listed on the website. U-Bahn Schönhauser
Allee. Mon–Fri 10am–8pm, Sat 10am–6pm.
Bad Boy'z Schliemannstr. 38, Prenzlauer Berg
☎030/440 81 65 **Ⓦ**www.badboyz.de. Gay
cinema, toyshop and bookshop. Lesbians
also welcome, but the cinema is men-only.
U-Bahn Eberswalder Str. Daily 1pm–1am.
Das Verborgene Museum Schlüterstr. 70,
Charlottenburg ☎030/313 36 56, **Ⓦ**www
.dasverborgenemuseum.de. A gallery founded

by women artists for the research,
documentation and exhibition of women's
art. Entry €2. S-Bahn Savignyplatz. Thurs &
Fri 3–7pm, Sat & Sun noon–4pm.
Kino International Karl-Marx-Allee 33,
Friedrichshain ☎030/24 75 60 11, **Ⓦ**www
.yorck.de. The Mongay event every Mon
involves a screening of a cult gay or lesbian
film – the bar opens at 9pm, the film is at
10pm and the party only really starts afterwards. U-Bahn Schillingstr.
Prinz Eisenherz Buchladen GmbH Lietzenburger.
9a, City West ☎030/313 99 36, **Ⓦ**www
.prinz-eisenherz.com. Friendly and informative

gay bookstore with helpful assistants. Excellent for relaxed browsing, free magazines and what's-on posters and leaflets about current gay happenings in the city. U-Bahn Wittenbergplatz. Mon–Sat 10am–8pm.

Schwules Museum Mehringdamm 61, Kreuzberg ☎030/69 59 90 50, ⓦwww.schwulesmuseum .de. Interesting, but relatively low-profile gay museum with changing exhibitions (entrance €5) on local and international gay history, and library material to browse through.

U-Bahn Mehringhamm. Wed–Fri & Sun 2–6pm, Sat 2–7pm.

Spinnboden Anklamer Str. 38, Mitte ☎030/448 58 48, ⓦwww.spinnboden.de. A comprehensive archive of every aspect of lesbian experience, with a beautifully housed collection of books, videos, posters and magazines. U-Bahn Bernauer Str. Wed & Fri 2–7pm.

Xenon Kolonnenstr. 5, Schöneberg ☎030/78 00 15 30, ⓦwww.xenon-kino.de. Gay cinema that often screens English-language independent films. Tickets €6. U-Bahn Kleistpark.

Saunas

Treibhaus Sauna Schönhauser Allee 132, Prenzlauer Berg ☎030/448 45 03, ⓦwww .treibhaussauna.de. Sauna with excellent facilities and opportunities for wicked

cruising; you can even rent a cabin. Therapeutic massages available from €25. Entry €20. U-Bahn Eberswalder Str. Mon–Fri 1pm–7am.

Cafés and venues

Berlin's gay hotspots of Schöneberg, Kreuzberg and Prenzlauer Berg are where you'll find the majority of gay and lesbian hangouts. In addition to the small number of cafés there are several very active and convivial mixed-use venues, popular within the lesbian scene.

AHA–Lesben- und Schwulenzentrum Mehringdamm 61, Western Kreuzberg; see map, p.132 ☎030/692 36 00 ⓦwww .aha-berlin.de. Non-profit cooperative that organizes workshops and events for gay and lesbian groups. U-Bahn Mehringdamm.

Begine Potsdamer Str. 139, Schöneberg; see map, p.128 ☎030/215 14 14, ⓦwww.begine .de. Women's centre with a programme of earnest lectures and films, and excellent performances by women musicians and dancers. U-Bahn Bülowstr. Mon–Fri 5pm–late, Sat 7pm–late.

Café Berio Maassenstr. 7, Schöneberg; see map, p.128 ☎030/216 19 46. Ideal spot for *Kaffee und Kuchen* in the Viennese tradition, but later on the drinks specials (7–9pm) are the main draw. Exhibitions grace the place occasionally, too. U-Bahn Nollendorfplatz. Mon–Thurs & Sun 8am–midnight, Fri & Sat 8pm–1am.

Café Seidenfaden Dircksenstr. 47, Mitte; see map, pp.82–83 ☎030/283 27 83, ⓦfrausuchtzukunft.de. Calm women-only café with inexpensive lunch specials (€3–5). No alcohol. U-Bahn Weinmeisterstr. Mon–Sat noon–8pm.

EWA Prenzlauer Allee 6, Prenzlauer Berg; see map, pp.150–151 ☎030/442 55 42, ⓦwww .ewa-frauenzentrum.de. The first post-Wall women's centre in east Berlin, EWA offers courses and counselling, as well as various cultural events and computer and media facilities. It also has an airy women-only café-gallery with a children's play area. Good for what's-on information and flyers. U-Bahn Rosa-Luxemburg-Platz. Mon–Thurs 10am–11pm, Fri–Sun varies according to programme on website.

Frauenzentrum Schokofabrik Mariannenstr. 6, Eastern Kreuzberg; see map, pp.142–143 ☎030/615 29 99, ⓦwww.schokofabrik.de. One of Europe's largest women's centres, with a café/gallery, sports facilities (including a women-only Turkish bath; see p.249) and diverse events. U-Bahn Kottbusser Tor. Mon–Thurs 10am–2pm, Fri noon–4pm.

Melitta Sundström Mehringdamm 61, Kreuzberg; see map, p.132 ☎030/692 44 14. Small and pleasant mixed café that's low-key and comfortable – often a warm-up for the basement, location of the legendary *SchwuZ* club (see p.256). Food served until 11pm. U-Bahn Mehringdamm. Daily 10am–4am.

Bars and clubs

The longest-standing and most concentrated area of **gay bars** is in Schöneberg between Wittenbergplatz and Nollendorfplatz, though in the last decade or so the area south of Kleiststrasse, along Schönhauser Allee in Prenzlauer Berg, has become an eastern gay centre. Many mainly straight clubs have gay nights – see *Tip*, *Zitty* or *Siegessäule* for details. **Berghain** (see p.227), **Kit Kat Club** (see p.228) and **Kumpelnest 3000** (see p.226) are all mixed venues with a strong gay presence that have become legendary. Other nights not to miss are the **GMF** events (ⓦ www.gmf-berlin.de), which pop up at different venues around town, and have over the years become a stalwart of the Berlin scene – think stripped-to-the-waist revellers dancing to pounding house-music.

As in many other large cities, **lesbians** in Berlin have a much lower profile than gay men. Perhaps because of this, there's no real distinction between bars and cafés for lesbians and straight women, and many of Berlin's women-only bars have a strong lesbian following.

Mitte

Mostly men

Le Moustache Gartenstr. 4; see map, pp.82–83 ⓉT 030/281 72 77, ⓦ www.lemoustache.de. Men-only leather bar in the tiled surroundings of an old butcher's shop. Quite average, but a popular haunt in a part of town with few other gay venues. Doesn't usually get going until around 11pm. Has a guesthouse attached (see p.253). U-Bahn Oranienburger Tor. Wed–Sun from 9pm.

Schöneberg

The following places are marked on the map on p.128.

Mostly men

Connection Fuggerstr. 33 ⓉT 030/23 62 74 44. Gay entertainment complex including refined American sports bar – Prinzknecht – all bare brick and gleaming chrome, attracting a broad range of middle-aged gay men and some women. Very popular house and techno club at weekends. U-Bahn Wittenbergplatz. Daily 3pm–late.

Heile Welt Motzstr. 5 ⓉT 030/21 91 75 07. The youngest and trendiest bar in Schöneberg provides a second living room for many locals; great cocktails and convivial atmosphere. U-Bahn Nollendorfplatz. Daily 6pm–late.

Neues Ufer Hauptstr. 157 ⓉT 030/78 95 97 00. Lovely neighbourhood gay bar, where Bowie used to drink in the 1970s when it was

Anderes Ufer. U-Bahn Kleistpark. Daily 11am–2am.

Prinzknecht Fuggerstr. 33 ⓉT 030/23 62 74 44. A refined version of an American sports bar, all bare brick and gleaming chrome, attracting a broad range of middle-aged gay men and some women. The men-only cellar darkroom is underused. U-Bahn Wittenbergplatz. Daily 3pm–3am.

Scheune Motzstr. 25 ⓉT 030/213 85 80. Very popular leather club with regular theme parties for devotees of rubber, uniforms or sheer nakedness. Darkroom, baths and other accoutrements. U-Bahn Nollendorfplatz. Mon–Thurs 9pm–7am, non-stop Fri 9pm–Mon 7am.

Tom's Bar Motzstr. 19 ⓉT 030/213 45 70, ⓦ www.tomsbar.de. Dark, sweaty and debauched cruising establishment with a large darkroom. Possibly Berlin's most popular gay bar, and a great place to finish off an evening. Drinks are two for the price of one on Mon night. Men only. U-Bahn Nollendorfplatz. Daily 10pm–late.

Mixed

Hafen Motzstr. 19, Schöneberg ⓉT 030/211 41 18. Adjacent to *Tom's Bar* (see p.128), this mixed cruisey place is a long-established bar for thirty- and forty-somethings, and always packed – a great place to start a night out. U-Bahn Nollendorfplatz. Daily 8pm until late.

Western Kreuzberg

The following places are marked on the map on p.132.

Mixed

SchwuZ Mehringdamm 61 ☎030/69 50 78 89, ⓦwww.schwuz.de. Dance club well loved by all stripes of the gay community, and always crowded and convivial. One floor has the usual Eighties and disco mixes, the other more experimental tunes. Highly recommended. U-Bahn Mehringdamm. Fri & Sat 11pm–late.

Women

Serene Bar Schwiebusser Str. 2 ☎030/69 04 15 80 ⓦwww.serenebar.de. Great lesbian hangout, particularly on Sat when the big dance floor packs out; the bar is also used by many special interest groups as a meeting point: table tennis, amateur photography and so on. The entrance is a little tucked away down an alley. U-Bahn Platz-der-Luftbrücke. Tues 6pm until late, Wed & Thurs 8pm until late, Sat 9pm until late.

Eastern Kreuzberg

See map on pp.142–143.

Mixed

Roses Oranienstr. 187 ☎030/615 65 70. Kitsch gay club with a strong lesbian presence. One of the venues of choice for a solo night out for either sex. U-Bahn Kottbusser Tor. Daily 9.30pm–5am.

Prenzlauer Berg

The following places are marked on the map on pp.150–151.

Mostly men

Schoppenstube Schönhauser Allee 44 ☎030/442 82 04. The best-known gay place in eastern Berlin, this is really two very different bars: a pleasant wine bar upstairs, and a steamy cruisers' haven downstairs. Knock for entry, and if the doorman likes the look of you you're in. U-Bahn Eberswalder Str. Daily 10pm until late.
Stiller Don Erich-Weinert-Str. 67 ☎0172/182 01 68. Slightly intellectual neighbourhood bar with a gay clientele running right across the age spectrum. U-Bahn Schönhauser Allee. Daily 8pm until late.

Mixed

Schall und Rauch Gleimstr. 23 ☎030/443 39 70. Tasteful, designer elegance in this hip young mixed bar. A place to see and be seen – and eat, thanks to an imaginative and everchanging menu. U-Bahn Schönhauser Allee. Daily 9am–2am.

19

Kids' Berlin

A ttitudes to young children in Berlin strike the outsider as oddly ambivalent. While the city has a large number of single-parent families and excellent social-service provisions for them, Berliners aren't too tolerant of kids in "adult" places, such as restaurants or bars, and though the city consists of a higher proportion of lakes, parks and woodland than any other European capital, there's little in them directly geared to entertaining children. If you're bringing kids, be prepared to do Berlin versions of the obvious things – zoos, museums and shops – rather than anything unique to the city. On a day-to-day basis, check the listings in *Tip* and *Zitty* (under "Kinder") for details of what's on.

Parks and zoos

With over a third of Berlin being forest or parkland, often with playgrounds dotted around, there's no shortage of spaces for children to go and let off steam. The most central and obvious choice is the **Tiergarten**, northeast of Zoo Station, though this is rather tame compared to the rambling expanses of the **Grunewald** (S-Bahn Grunewald). In both parks, paddle and rowing boats can be rented. The Grunewald borders the **Wannsee** lake, and it's fun to take the ferry over to the **Pfaueninsel** (Peacock Island; see p.175), where there's a castle and strutting peacocks. Alternatively, **Freizeitpark Tegel** (U-Bahn Alt-Tegel, walk to the lake, then turn right) has playgrounds, trampolines, table tennis and paddle boats, while the **Teufelsberg** (Devil's Mountain; a twenty-minute walk south down Teufelsseechaussee from S-Bahn Heerstr.), a large hill to the west of the city, is the place to go kite-flying at weekends. On the southeastern edge of the city, the woods around the **Grosser Müggelsee** (S-Bahn to

Babysitting and child care

Berlin has a couple of reliable agencies that can supply English-speaking **babysitters** and a multilingual **day-care centre** where kids can stay overnight. Aufgepasst (☎030/851 37 23, ⓦwww.aufgepasst.de) is a babysitting and day-care agency in Wilmersdorf whose rates are around €10 per hour, plus a €10 booking fee. Meanwhile, at Kinderinsel, Eichendorffstrasse 17 (☎030/41 71 69 28, ⓦwww .kinderinsel.de; U-Bahn Naturkundemuseum), parents can leave their children (0–14 years) in good hands for anything from a couple of hours to several days. The programme of outings and activities offered by the friendly and dynamic centre ensures the kids won't get bored; rates are €13 per hour, €69 for an overnight stay.

Friedrichshagen) offer lakeside walking trails, and there's also a good nature trail around the **Teufelssee** (S-Bahn to Köpenick, then bus #X69 for five stops), just south of the Müggelsee.

Kinderbauernhof auf dem Görlitzer Görlitzer Park, Wiener Str. 59, Kreuzberg ⓦwww .kinderbauernhofberlin.de. The most central of several of Berlin's educationally oriented children's farms, which can all still be fun without knowing the language. You can find others, together with information on the location of Berlin's many adventure playgrounds, at the excellent German-only website ⓦwww.akib.de. Mon, Tues, Thurs & Fri 10am–7pm (5pm in winter), Sat & Sun 11am–6pm (5pm in winter).

Sea-life Center Spandauer Str. 3 ⓣ030/99 28 00, ⓦwww.sealifeeurope.com. An educational and entertaining aquarium (see p.74); kids can test their knowledge with quiz questions dotted around the facility (in English) and touch manta rays and starfish in a tank. The elevator ride through the Aquadom, a gigantic tubular tank, is also a sure-fire hit. S-Bahn Hackescher Markt. Daily 10am–7pm.

Tierpark Friedrichsfelde ⓣ030/51 51 10, ⓦwww.tierpark-berlin.de. This sprawling zoo with all the usual suspects as well as modern monkey enclosures that are likely to provide most of the entertainment. U-Bahn Tierpark. Daily 9am–7pm.

Zoologischer Garten Hardenbergplatz 8, Charlottenburg ⓣ030/25 40 10, ⓦwww .zoo-berlin.de. Near the train station of the same name (see p.118), kids will likely love the monkeys, orang-utans and gorillas; the hippo house; the nocturnal rooms (a dark area where varieties of gerbil-like creatures, and bats, do their thing); pony and horse-and-trap rides around the zoo; a playground and a children's zoo where farm animals can be petted and fed. The aquarium is also well worth the money, with a dazzling array of fish and a humid crocodile hall. U- & S-Bahn Zoologischer Garten. Daily 9am–7pm.

Circuses, leisure complexes and funfairs

Professional circus troupes and small funfairs visit the city regularly during the summer months, setting up in the parks that dot the city.

Cabuwazi Zirkus Weiner Str. 59h, Kreuzberg ⓣ030/611 92 75, ⓦwww.cabuwazi.de. Resident circus, but one in which young-sters perform. Also a popular venue for visiting circuses. U-Bahn Görlitzer Bahnhof. Opening hours vary according to performances.

FEZ Wuhlheide An der Wuhlheide 197, Köpenick ⓣ030/53 07 10, ⓦwww.fez-berlin.de. A large GDR-era recreation park, packed with play- and activity-areas for kids of all ages and including a popular narrow-gauge railway, the seven-kilometre-long Berliner

Parkeisenbahn (ⓦwww.parkeisenbahn.de), which is operated by children. S-Bahn Wuhlheide. Hours vary according to school terms, but core times: Tues–Fri & Sun 9am–10pm, Sat 1–6pm, Sun noon–6pm.

UFA-Fabrik Viktoriastr. 10, Tempelhof ⓣ030/75 50 30, ⓦwww.ufafabrik.de. Residential circus offering an inventive alternative – jugglers, acrobats, magicians – to the usual lions-and-clowns stuff. U-Bahn Ullsteinstr. Mon–Sat 10am–7pm, Sun 2–7pm.

Museums and sights

Almost all museums give a discount for children; the following are the most interesting for kids, mainly thanks to fun interactive exhibits. Depending on your children's level of interest, some sightseeing might also be enjoyable; a ride on the #100 or #200 bus will take in all the main sights between Alexanderplatz and Bahnhof Zoo and also connect several places with superb **views** of Berlin from on high. The Siegessäule (see p.109) is fun but has a lot of steps, making it hard work for little legs; the Reichstag dome (see p.48) is of some interest; but the Fernseh-turm (see p.72) and the Panorama Punkt (see p.107) are probably going to go down better – though the exposed outdoor nature of the latter might unnerve some smaller children.

Deutsches Technikmuseum Berlin Trebbiner Str. 9 ☎030/902 05 40, ⊛www.dtmb.de. The German Technology Museum of Berlin (see p.139) has lots of highly diverting gadgets to experiment with, plus a great collection of old steam trains and carriages. U-Bahn Möckernbrücke. Tues–Fri 9am–5.30pm, Sat & Sun 10am–6pm.

Domäne Dahlem Königin-Luise-Str. 49, Zehlendorf ☎030/666 30 00, ⊛www.domaene-dahlem.de. This working farm and craft museum has plenty to entertain kids besides farmyard animals, especially at weekends when craft fairs are held here, and there are games and shows especially for children. U-Bahn Dahlem-Dorf. Daily 10am–6pm (closed Tues).

Düppel Museum Village Clauertstr. 11, Zehlendorf ☎030/802 66 71, ⊛www.dueppel.de. Reconstruction of a medieval country village, with demonstrations of the handicrafts and farming methods of those times. Better for older children. Bus #115 from U-Bahn Fehrberliner Platz or S-Bahn Hohenzollern. Mid-March to late Oct Thurs 3–7pm, Sun 10am–5pm.

Juniormuseum im Ethnologischen Museum Lansstr. 8, Dahlem, ☎030/830 14 38, ⊛www.juniormuseum-berlin.de. A section of the Ethnological Museum in Dahlem (see p.171), this museum teaches children about different cultures through playful activities and interactive temporary exhibits. U-Bahn Dahlem-Dorf. Tues–Fri 10am–6pm, Sat & Sun 11am–6pm.

Labyrinth Kindermuseum Berlin Osloer Str. 12, Wedding ☎030/800 93 11 50,

⊛www.kindermuseum-labyrinth.de. A converted factory building that offers temporary exhibits, usually very inventive and thoughtful, geared towards hands-on learning and fun. U-Bahn Pankstr. Outside school holidays Fri & Sat 1–6pm, Sun 11am–6pm; in school holidays Mon–Fri 9am–6pm, Sat 1–6pm, Sun 11am–6pm; admission €4.50, children €4.

Museum für Kommunikation Berlin Leipziger Str. 16, Mitte ☎030/20 29 40, ⊛www.museumsstiftung.de. Robots career around the main lobby in this hands-on communications museum (see p.135) that offers older kids lots of computers and devices to play with. U-Bahn Stadtmitte. Tues–Fri 9am–5pm, Sat & Sun 10am–6pm.

Museum für Naturkunde Invalidenstr. 43, Mitte ☎030/20 93 85 91, ⊛www.naturkundemuseum-berlin.de. Natural history museum (see p.94) whose main attraction is a gigantic Brachiosaurus skeleton, and there's plenty more to keep animal-crazy kids happy for an hour or so. U-Bahn Naturkundemuseum. Tues–Fri 9.30am–6pm, Sat & Sun 10am–6pm.

The Story of Berlin Kurfürstendamm 207–208, Charlottenburg-Wilmersdorf, ☎030/88 72 01 00, ⊛www.story-of-berlin.de. Easily the most captivating of the city's history museums (see p.121), with lots of multimedia gimmicks to help bring the experience alive for kids. U-Bahn Uhlandstr. Daily 10am–8pm.

Theatres and cinemas

Most cinemas show **children's films** during the school holidays but these are likely to be German-language only. The one time you're likely to catch English-language kids' films is during the Berlinale Film Festival in February (see p.31), which always offers a children's programme (*Kinderprogramm*). Berlin supports an aston-ishing number of **puppet theatres**, most of which put on worthwhile perform-ances that kids don't need a knowledge of German to enjoy. For details of children's films and theatre performances, check the listings magazines.

Die Schaubude Greifswalder Str. 81–84, Prenzlauer Berg ☎030/423 43 14, ⊛www.schaubude-berlin.de. Puppet theatre for kids aged 4 and over. S-Bahn Greifswalder Str.

Grips Theater Altonaer Str. 22, Tiergarten ☎030/39 74 74 77, ⊛www.grips-theater.de. Top-class children's/young people's theatre; often improvised. U-Bahn Hansaplatz.

Shops

There's a fair but not overwhelming selection of **children's shops** in Berlin, with an emphasis on wooden toys, ecological themes and multicultural education.

Anagramm Mehringdamm 50, Kreuzberg
℡030/785 95 10, ⓦwww.anagramm-buch.de.
Neighbourhood bookstore with an excellent children's section and a reading corner. U-Bahn Mehringdamm. Mon–Fri 9am–7pm, Sat 10am–4pm.

Bella, Boss & Bulli Trafohaus auf dem Helmholtzplatz ℡030/44 67 41 34. Café, playground and secondhand children's wear all in one: very Prenzlauer Berg bohemian. U-Bahn Eberswalder Str. Daily 2–7pm; opens at noon when the weather's good.

Emma & Co Niebuhrstr. 2 ℡030/88 67 67 87, ⓦwww.emmaundco.de. Designer knitwear and other children's fashions, lots of unique and interesting pieces and a good selection of shoes. S-Bahn Savignyplatz. Mon–Fri 11am–7pm, Sat 11am–4pm.

Flying Colors Eisenacher Str. 81, Schöneberg ℡030/78 70 36 36, ⓦwww.flying-colors.de. Kite shop – the place to come before heading off for the Teufelsberg hill. U-Bahn Eisenacher Str. Mon–Fri 10am–6.30pm, Sat 10am–2pm.

Grober Unfug Zossener Str. 32, Kreuzberg ℡030/69 10 14 90, ⓦwww.groberunfug.de. Large display of international comics. U-Bahn Gneisenaustr. Mon–Fri 11am–7pm, Sat 11am–6pm.

Levy's Tabularium Rosenthalerstr. 40–41, Mitte ℡030/280 82 03. One half of this store is dedicated to Judaica, the other half to wooden toys, sophisticated puzzles and children's books. S-Bahn Hackescher Markt. Mon–Sat 11am–7pm.

Spielbrett Körtestr. 27, Kreuzberg ℡030/692 42 50. Massive selection of games and puzzles with some picture books too. U-Bahn Südstern. Mon–Fri 10am–6.30pm, Sat 10am–2pm.

Zauberkönig Hermannstr. 84, Neukölln ℡030/621 40 82, ⓦwww.zauberkoenig-berlin.de. Illusions and tricks for magicians and their apprentices. U-Bahn Leinestr. Mon–Thurs 1–6pm, Fri 10am–6pm, Sat 10am–1pm.

Contexts

Contexts

History

As the heart of the Prussian kingdom, cultural centre of the Weimar Republic, headquarters of Hitler's ruthless Third Reich and a key frontline flashpoint in the Cold War, Berlin has long been a weather vane of European and even world history. But World War II left the city devastated, with bombs razing 92 percent of all its shops, houses and industry, so it's the latter half of the twentieth century that shaped much of what's visible today. This was a period when the world's two most powerful military systems stood face to face, glaring at one another over that most tangible object of the Iron Curtain, the Berlin Wall. As the Wall fell in November 1989, Berlin was again at the forefront of world events, ushering in a period of change as frantic, confused and significant as any in the city's history.

All this historic turmoil provides a troubling fascination, and understanding it unlocks the secrets of a cityscape that is only just beginning to settle down from the slew of post-unification building work as Berlin once again became Germany's capital. In the wake of this, the city has successfully cultivated a fashionable and cosmopolitan outlook, and is now firmly established as a hothouse of contemporary European trends and dilemmas, where the hopes and challenges of eastern and western Europe collide.

Beginnings

Archeologists reckon that people have lived around the area of modern-day Berlin for about 60,000 years. Traces of hunter-gatherer activity dating from about 8000 BC and more substantial remains of Stone Age farming settlements from 4000 BC onwards have been discovered. The Romans regarded this as barbarian territory and left no mark on the region. Although **Germanic tribes** first appeared on the scene during the fifth and sixth centuries AD, many of them left during the great migrations of later centuries, and the vacated territories were occupied by **Slavs**. Germanic ascendancy only began in the twelfth and thirteenth centuries, when Saxon feudal barons of the Mark (border territory) of Brandenburg expelled the Slavs. The **Saxons** also granted municipal charters to two humble riverside towns – where the Berlin story really begins.

The twin towns

Sited on marshlands around an island (today's Spreeinsel) at the narrowest point on the River Spree, **Berlin** and **Cölln** were on a major trade route to the east and began to prosper as municipalities. Despite many links (including a joint town hall built in 1307), they retained their separate identities throughout the fourteenth century, when both received the right to mint their own coinage and pronounce death sentences in local courts.

Black Death struck the twin towns in 1348 – the first of many major devastations Berlin was to endure – killing ten percent of the population and unleashing anti-Jewish pogroms. Things looked up twenty years later with the admission of Berlin and Cölln to the powerful **Hanseatic League** of city-states in 1369, confirming their economic and political importance. Powerful trade guilds and prosperous burghers ran the towns and, by 1391, made them virtually autonomous from the Mark of Brandenburg, which grew ever more chaotic in the early fifteenth century.

Order was eventually restored by **Friedrich Hohenzollern**, burgrave of Nürnberg, when in 1411 the Holy Roman Emperor invited him to take over – the start of a dynasty that would rule Berlin for half a millennium. Friedrich's subjugation of the province was initially welcomed by the burghers of Berlin and Cölln. However, when his son Johann attempted to treat them likewise, they forced him to withdraw to Spandau. It was only divisions within their ranks that enabled **Friedrich II**, "Irontooth" Johann's brother, to take over the two cities. Some of the guilds offered him the keys of the gates in return for taking their part against the Berlin-Cölln magistrates. Friedrich obliged, then built the Berliner Schloss (see p.62) and instituted his own harsh rule, forbidding any further union between Berlin and Cölln.

After swiftly crushing a **rebellion** in 1448, Friedrich imposed new restrictions. To symbolize the **consolidation of Hohenzollern power**, a chain was placed around the neck of Berlin's heraldic symbol, the bear, which remained on the city's coat of arms until 1875. After the Hohenzollerns moved their residence and court here, Berlin-Cölln assumed the character of a *Residenzstadt* (royal residence) and rapidly expanded, its old wattle-and-daub dwellings replaced with more substantial stone buildings – culminating in a Renaissance Schloss finished in 1540. Yet life remained hard, for despite being involved in the Reformation, Berlin-Cölln lagged behind the great cities of western and southern Germany, and in 1576 it was ravaged by plague.

The **Thirty Years' War** (1618–48) marked another low point: Europe was riven by Protestant-Catholic conflicts and national rivalries, and leaders who could ill-afford to pay their mercenary armies promised them loot instead. Both Catholic Imperial troops and Protestant Swedes occupied and ransacked the twin towns and by the end of the war they had lost half their population and one-third of their buildings.

The Great Elector

The monumental task of postwar reconstruction fell to the Mark's new ruler, Elector **Friedrich Wilhelm of Brandenburg** (1620–88), who was barely out of his teens. Massive fortifications were constructed, besides the residences and public buildings necessary to make Berlin-Cölln a worthy capital for an Elector. (Seven Electors – three archbishops, a margrave, duke, count and king – were entitled to elect the Holy Roman Emperor.) In recognition of his achievements, Friedrich Wilhelm came to be known as the **Great Elector**. After defeating the Swedes at the Battle of Fehrbellin in 1675, the Mark of Brandenburg was acknowledged as a force to be reckoned with, and its capital grew accordingly. Recognizing the value of a cosmopolitan population, the Elector permitted Jews and South German Catholics to move here and enjoy protection as citizens.

A later wave of immigrants affected Berlin-Cölln even more profoundly. Persecuted in France, thousands of **Protestant Huguenots** sought new homes in England and Germany. The arrival of five thousand immigrants – mostly skilled craftsmen or traders – revitalized Berlin-Cölln, whose own population was only twenty thousand. French became an almost obligatory second language, indispensable for anyone looking for social and career success. Another fillip to the city's development was the completion of the **Friedrich Wilhelm Canal**, linking the Spree and the Oder, which boosted it as an east–west trade centre.

Carrying on from where his father had left off, Friedrich III succeeded in becoming king of Prussia to boot (thus also gaining the title Friedrich I), while

Berlin continued to expand. The **Friedrichstadt** and **Charlottenburg** quarters and the **Zeughaus** (now the Deutsches Historisches Museum) were created during this period, and Andreas Schlüter revamped the Elector's palace. In 1709, Berlin-Cölln finally became a single city named **Berlin**. None of this came cheap, however. Both Berlin and the Mark of Brandenburg were heavily in debt by the end of Friedrich's reign, to the point where he even resorted to alchemists in the hope of refilling his treasury.

Berlin under the Soldier King

The next chapter in the city's history belongs to Friedrich I's son, **Friedrich Wilhelm I** (1688–1740). Known as the **Soldier King** and generally reckoned to be the father of the Prussian state, he dealt with the financial chaos by enforcing spartan conditions on his subjects and firing most of the servants at court. As much as eighty percent of state revenues were then directed to building up his army, and culture took a back seat to parades (eventually he even banned the theatre). While the army marched and drilled, the populace had a draconian work ethic drubbed into them – Friedrich took to walking about Berlin and personally beating anyone he caught loafing.

Friedrich tried to introduce conscription but had to make an exception of Berlin when the city's able-bodied young men fled en masse to escape the army. Despite this, Berlin became a **garrison town** geared to maintaining the army: the Lustgarten park of the royal palace was transformed into a parade ground, and every house was expected to have space available for billeting troops. Much of modern Berlin's shape and character can be traced back to Friedrich – squares like **Pariser Platz** (the area in front of the Brandenburg Gate) began as parade grounds, and **Friedrichstrasse** was built to link the centre with Tempelhof parade ground. When Friedrich died after watching rehearsals for his own funeral (and thrashing a groom who made a mistake), few Berliners mourned.

Frederick the Great and the rise of Prussia

His son, Friedrich II – known to historians as **Frederick the Great** (1712–86) and to his subjects as "Der alte Fritz" – enjoyed a brief honeymoon as a liberalizer, before reverting to his father's ways. Soon Prussia was drawn into a series of wars that sent Berlin taxes through the roof, while the king withdrew to Sanssouci Palace in Potsdam, where only French was spoken, leaving the Berliners to pay for his military adventurism. Friedrich's saving grace was that he liked to think of himself as a philosopher king, and Berlin's **cultural life** consequently flourished during his reign. This was thanks in part to the work of the leading figures of the German Enlightenment, like the playwright Gotthold Ephraim Lessing and the philosopher Moses Mendelssohn, both of whom enjoyed royal patronage.

It was the **rise of Prussia** – particularly the invasion of and subsequent annexation of Silesia in 1740 – that alarmed Austria, Saxony, France and Russia into starting the **Seven Years' War** in 1756. Four years later they occupied Berlin and demanded a tribute of four million thalers, causing city president Kirchstein to faint on the spot. This was later reduced to 1.5 million when it was discovered that the city coffers were empty. Berlin was eventually relieved by Frederick, who, with British aid, went on to win the war (if only by default) after Russia and France fell out. A general peace was concluded in 1763 and victory confirmed Prussia's power in Central Europe, but keeping the peace meant maintaining a huge standing army.

Besides direct taxation, Frederick raised money by establishing **state monopolies** in the trade of coffee, salt and tobacco. (For a time he even banned coffee and vigorously promoted beer as an alternative.) Citizens were actually required to buy set quantities of these commodities whether they wanted them or not. This was the origin of some of Berlin's most celebrated dishes: sauerkraut, *Kassler Rippchen* (salted pork ribs) and pickled gherkins were all invented by people desperate to use up their accumulated salt. Popular discontent was muffled by Frederick's **secret police** and **press censorship**.

Unter den Linden came into its own during Frederick's reign, as grandiose new edifices like the **Alte Bibliothek** sprang up. Just off the great boulevard, the **Französischer Dom** was built to serve the needs of the Huguenot population, while the construction of Schloss Bellevue in the Tiergarten sparked off a new building boom, as the wealthy flocked into this newly fashionable area.

Decline and occupation

After Frederick's death Prussia went into a **decline**, culminating in the defeat of its once-invincible army by French revolutionaries at the Battle of Valmy in 1792. The decline went unchecked under Friedrich Wilhelm II (1744–97), continuing into the Napoleonic era. As Bonaparte's empire spread across Europe, the Prussian court dithered, appeasing the French and trying to delay the inevitable invasion. Life in Berlin continued more or less as normal, but by August 1806 citizens were watching Prussian soldiers set off on the march westwards to engage the Napoleonic forces. On September 19, the king and queen left the city, followed a month later by Count von der Schulenburg, the city governor, who had assured Berliners that all was going well right up until he learned of Prussia's defeat at Jena and Auerstadt.

Five days later French troops marched through the **Brandenburg Gate** and Berlin was occupied. On October 27, 1806, Napoleon himself arrived to head a parade down Unter den Linden – greeted as a liberator by the Berliners, according to some accounts. **French occupation** forced state reform: ministries were streamlined, nobles could engage in trade and guild membership became more accessible. And during this time Berlin embraced the Romantic movement – a rebellious celebration of German spirit and tradition in opposition to the cold rationality of the French Enlightenment. From the movement sprouted notions of what it meant to be German and the idea that all Germans should be unified in a single state – though this wouldn't happen until 1871.

The rebirth of Prussia

After his defeats in Russia and at the Battle of Leipzig in 1813, Napoleon's empire began to collapse, allowing Prussia to pull out of their forced alliance and resume self-rule. Symbolically, the Quadriga (the Goddess of Victory in her chariot) was restored to the Brandenburg Gate, but despite high hopes for reform the people of Berlin gained only the promise of a constitution for Prussia, which never materialized. Otherwise the pre-Napoleonic status quo was restored, and the real victor was the **Prussian state**, which acquired tracts of land along the Rhine, including the Ruhr, that contained the iron and coal deposits on which its military might was to be rebuilt.

The war was followed by an era of reaction and oppression, which did so much to stifle intellectual and cultural life in Berlin that the philosopher Wilhelm von Humboldt resigned from the university in protest at the new authoritarianism. Gradually this mellowed out into the **Biedermeier years**, characterized by the retreat into private and family life, tranquil art and Neoclassical architecture. Meanwhile, Prussia's industrial fortunes began to rise, laying the foundation of its Great Power status. Berlin continued to grow: factories and railways and the first of the city's *Mietskaserne*, or **tenement buildings**, were constructed – foreshadowing what was to come with full industrialization.

Revolution and reaction

Berlin enjoyed more than thirty years of peace and stability after 1815, but it shared the revolutionary mood that swept Europe in **1848**. Influenced by events in France and the writings of Karl Marx (who lived here from 1837 to 1841), Berliners demanded a say in the running of their own affairs. King Friedrich Wilhelm IV (1795–1861) refused to agree. On March 18, citizens gathered outside his palace to present their demands. The soldiers when accidentally fired two shots and the demonstration became a **revolution**. Barricades went up and a fourteen-hour battle raged between insurgents and loyalist troops. According to eyewitness accounts, rich and poor alike joined in the rebellion. During the fighting 183 Berliners and eighteen soldiers died.

Aghast at his subjects' anger, Friedrich Wilhelm IV ordered his troops to withdraw to Spandau, leaving the city in the hands of the revolutionaries, who failed to take advantage of the situation. A revolutionary parliament and citizens' militia were established, but rather than assaulting Spandau or taking other measures to consolidate the revolution, the new assembly concerned itself with protecting the royal palace from vandalism. No attempt was made to declare a republic or seize public buildings in what was turning out to be an unusually orderly – and ultimately doomed – revolution.

On March 21, the king appeared in public wearing the black, red and gold tricolour emblem of the revolution. Having failed to suppress it, he now proposed to join it, along with most of his ministers and princes. The king spoke at the university, promising nothing much but paying lip service to the idea of German unity, which impressed the assembled liberals. Order was fully restored, then in October, a Prussian army under General Wrangel entered Berlin and forced the **dissolution of parliament**. The Berliners either gave up the fight or followed millions of their fellow Germans into exile.

Suppression followed. Friedrich gave up the tricolour and turned to persecuting liberals, before going insane shortly afterwards. His brother Prince Wilhelm – who had led the troops against the barricades – became king. **Otto von Bismarck** was appointed to the chancellorship (1862), despite the almost universal loathing he inspired among Berliners.

Meanwhile, Berlin continued to grow apace, turning into a cosmopolitan, modern industrial city. Its free press and revolutionary past exerted a liberal influence on Prussia's emasculated parliament, the **Reichstag**, to the irritation of Bismarck and the king (who was soon to proclaim himself emperor, or kaiser). However, Bismarck became a national hero after the Prussian victory at the **Battle of Königgrätz** (1866) had smashed Austrian military power, clearing the way for

Prussia to unite – and dominate – Germany. Although militaristic nationalism caused liberalism to wither elsewhere, Berlin continued to elect liberal deputies to the Reichstag, which became the parliament of the whole nation after **German unification** in 1871.

Yet Berlin remained a maverick city. It was here that three attempts were made to kill Emperor Wilhelm I; the final one on Unter den Linden (1878) left him with thirty pieces of shrapnel in his body. While the kaiser recovered, Bismarck used the event to justify a **crackdown on socialists**, closing newspapers and persecuting trade unionists. The growth of unionism was a direct result of relentless urbanization. Between 1890 and 1900, Berlin's population doubled to two million and thousands of tenement buildings sprang up in working-class districts like **Wedding**. The poor conditions here meant its residents were solidly behind the Social Democratic Party (**SPD**), whose deputies were the chief dissenters within the Reichstag.

By 1890 Wilhelm II had become kaiser and dropped Bismarck, but the country continued to be militaristic and authoritarian. While Berlin remained defiantly liberal, it steadily acquired the attributes of a modern capital. Now an established centre for commerce and diplomacy, it boasted electric trams, an underground railway, and other technical innovations of the age. In the arts Berlin also moved forward, developing its own form of Modernism, particularly as the Berlin Secession movement, which rejected the art establishment and included artists Max Liebermann, Edvard Munch and Walter Leistikow.

World War I and its aftermath

The arms race and alliances that polarized Europe during the 1890s and the first decade of the twentieth century led inexorably towards **World War I**. Its outbreak in 1914 was greeted with enthusiasm by civilians everywhere – only confirmed pacifists or communists resisted the heady intoxication of patriotism. In Berlin, Kaiser Wilhelm II spoke "to all Germans" from the balcony of his palace, and shop windows across the city were festooned with national colours. Military bands played *Heil dir im Siegerkranz* ("Hail to you in the Victor's Laurel") and *Die Wacht am Rhein* ("The Watch on the Rhine") in cafés, while Berliners threw flowers to the Imperial German army, or Reichswehr, as it marched off to war. The political parties agreed to a truce, and even the Social Democrats voted in favour of war credits.

The General Staff's calculation that France could be knocked out before Russia fully mobilized soon proved hopelessly optimistic, and Germany found itself facing a war on two fronts – the very thing Bismarck had dreaded. As casualties mounted on the stalemated western front, Berliners gathered around public lists of the dead looking for the names of sons or husbands, 350,000 of whom were to perish in the war. Rationing and food shortages began to hit poorer civilians and **disillusionment** set in. By the summer of 1915 housewives were demonstrating in front of the Reichstag, a portent of more serious popular unrest to come. Ordinary people were beginning to see the war as an exercise staged for the benefit of the rich at the expense of the poor, who bore the brunt of the suffering.

In December 1917, nineteen members of the SPD announced that they could no longer support their party's backing of the war and formed an independent socialist party known as the USPD. This party joined the "International Group" of **Karl Liebknecht** and **Rosa Luxemburg** – later known as the

Spartacists – which had opposed SPD support for the war since 1915. This grouping later formed the nucleus of the postwar Kommunistische Partei Deutschlands, or **KPD**. Meanwhile, fuel, food and even beer shortages added to growing hardships on the home front.

Defeat and revolution

With their last great offensive spent, and America joining the Allied war effort, even Germany's supreme warlord, Erich von Ludendorff, recognized that **defeat** was inevitable by the autumn of 1918. Knowing the Allies would refuse to negotiate with the old absolutist system, he declared (on September 9) a democratic, **constitutional monarchy**, whose chancellor would be responsible to the Reichstag and not the kaiser. A government was formed under Prince Max von Baden, which agreed to extensive reforms. But it was too little, too late for the bitter sailors and soldiers on the home front, where the contrast between privilege and poverty was most obvious. At the beginning of November the Kiel Garrison led a **naval mutiny** and revolutionary **Workers' and Soldiers' Soviets** mushroomed across Germany. Elements of this revolutionary unrest were mirrored in the Dada art movement, which put down firm roots in the city in 1919, while the fresh, functional design of the Bauhaus movement (see p.109) began to tidy some of the chaos.

Caught up in this wave of unrest, Berliners took to the streets on November 8–9, where they were joined by soldiers stationed in the capital. Realizing that the game was up, **Kaiser Wilhelm II abdicated**, which produced a situation of dual power: almost at the same time as Philipp Scheidemann of the SPD declared a **"German Republic"** from the Reichstag's balcony, Karl Liebknecht was proclaiming a "Free Socialist Republic" from a balcony of the royal palace, less than a mile away. In the face of increasing confusion, SPD leader Friedrich Ebert took over as head of the government. A deal was struck with the army, which promised to protect the republic if Ebert would forestall the full-blooded socialist revolution demanded by the Spartacists. Ebert now became chairman of a Council of People's Delegates that ruled Berlin for nearly three months. However, many of the revolutionary soldiers, sailors and workers who controlled the streets favoured the establishment of Soviet-style government and refused to obey Ebert's orders. Things came to a head with the **Spartacist uprising** in Berlin during the first half of January 1919. This inspired lasting dread among the bourgeoisie, who applauded when the Spartacists were eventually crushed by the militarily superior **Freikorps**: armed bands of right-wing officers and NCOs from the old Imperial army, dedicated to protecting Germany from "Bolshevism". The torture and **murder of Liebknecht and Luxemburg** by Freikorps officers (who threw their bodies in the Landwehrkanal) was never punished once the fighting was over. This hardly augured well for the future of the **new republic**, whose National Assembly elections were held on January 19.

The Weimar Republic

The elections confirmed the SPD as the new political leaders of the country, with 38 percent of the vote; as a result, Ebert was made president, Scheidemann chancellor. **Weimar**, the small country town that had seen the most glorious flowering of the German Enlightenment, was chosen as the place to draft a national constitution in preference to Berlin, which was tinged by its monarchic and military associations.

The **constitution** drawn up was hailed as the most liberal, democratic and progressive in the world. While it incorporated a highly complex system of checks and balances to prevent power becoming too concentrated in either particular parts of government or regions, it crucially lacked any clauses for outlawing parties hostile to the system. This opened the way for savage attacks on the republic by extremists at both ends of the political spectrum. With public opinion divided between a plethora of parties promoting sectional interests, all Weimar-era governments became unwieldy coalitions that often pursued contradictory policies in different ministries and had an average life of only about eight months, providing a weak framework that later readily allowed the Nazis to take control.

1920s Berlin

Much of Germany's **1920s** history was being dictated by the Allies and the harsh terms imposed by the **Treaty of Versailles:** Alsace-Lorraine was handed back to France. In the east, Germany lost a large chunk of Prussia to Poland, giving the latter access to the Baltic, but cutting the German province of East Prussia off from the rest of the country. The overseas empire was dismantled and the Rhineland occupied. But what aggrieved Germans most was the treaty's war guilt clause that held Germany responsible "for causing all the loss and damage" suffered by the Allies in the war. This was seen as a cynical victors' justice, yet provided the validation for a gigantic bill of reparation payments: a total of 132 billion gold marks.

The early 1920s was a bad time for Berlin. As the mark began to plunge in value, the government was shocked by the **assassination of Walter Rathenau**. As foreign minister, he had just signed the Treaty of Rapallo, aimed at promoting closer economic ties with the Soviet Union, since the western powers remained intransigent. Rathenau was killed at his own house in the Grunewald by Freikorps officers. When France and Belgium occupied the Ruhr in response to alleged defaults in the reparations payments, a general strike was called across Germany in January 1923.

The combination of reparations and strikes sent the mark plummeting, causing the worst **inflation** ever known. As their savings were wiped out and literally barrowloads of paper money wasn't enough to support a family, Berliners experienced the terrors of hyperinflation. In working-class districts, street fighting between right and left flared up. Foreigners flocked in to pay bargain prices for carpets and furs that even rich Germans could no longer afford, and fortunes were made and lost by speculators. In the midst of all this, on November 8, Berliners' attention was briefly diverted to Munich, where a motley crew of right-wing ex-army officers including General Ludendorff attempted to mount a putsch. It failed, but Berliners were to hear of one of the ringleaders again – **Adolf Hitler**.

The mark was finally stabilized under the supremely able foreign minister, **Gustav Stresemann**, who believed relief from reparation payments was more likely to come from cooperation than stubborn resistance. The Allies too moderated their stance, realizing Germany needed to be economically stable in order to pay. So, under the **1924 Dawes Plan**, loans poured into Germany, particularly from America, leading to an economic upsurge.

Nightlife and the arts

Economic recovery transformed the social life of Berlin. For many people the centre of the city had shifted from Friedrichstrasse and Unter den Linden, to the cafés and bars of the Kurfürstendamm. Jazz hit the **nightclubs** in a big way, like drug abuse (mainly cocaine) and all kinds of sex. There were clubs for transvestites, clubs where you could watch nude dancing, or dance naked yourself – and usually the police didn't give a damn. This was the legendary era later to be celebrated by Isherwood and others, when Berlin was briefly the most open, tolerant city in Europe, a Mecca for all those who rejected conventions and traditions.

The 1920s was also a boom time for the arts, as the Dada shockwave rippled through the decade. **George Grosz** satirized the times in savage caricatures, while **John Heartfield** used photomontage techniques to produce biting political statements. Equally striking, if less didactic, was the work of artists like **Otto Dix** and **Christian Schad**.

Producer **Max Reinhardt** continued to dominate Berlin's theatrical life, as he'd done since taking over at the Deutsches Theater in 1905. **Erwin Piscator** moved from propaganda into mainstream theatre at the Theater am Nollendorfplatz, without losing his innovative edge, and in 1928 **Bertolt Brecht**'s *Dreigroschen Oper* ("Threepenny Opera") was staged for the first time. Appropriately, Berlin also became a centre for the very newest of the arts. Between the wars the **UFA film studios** (see p.189) at Babelsberg was the biggest in Europe, producing legendary films like **Fritz Lang**'s *Metropolis*, *The Cabinet of Doctor Caligari* and *The Blue Angel* (starring Berlin-born **Marlene Dietrich**).

Middle- and lowbrow tastes were catered for by endless all-singing, all-dancing **musicals**, featuring platoons of women in various states of undress. This was also the heyday of the Berlin cabaret scene, when some of its most acidic exponents were at work.

Political extremism and the rise of the Nazis

Germany's economic upsurge the late 1920s would last only until the **Wall Street Crash** in October 1929. That suddenly ended all American credit and wiped out Germany's economic stability. The poverty of the immediate postwar period returned with a vengeance. Everyone suffered: hyperinflation wiped out middle-class savings, while the Wall Street Crash made six million unemployed by 1932. Increasingly people sought radical solutions in political extremism, and started supporting two parties that bitterly opposed one another but shared a desire to end democracy: the **Communists** and the **National Socialist German Workers' Party** (NSDAP), or Nazis. While red flags and swastika banners hung from neighbouring tenements, gangs from the left and right fought in the streets in ever-greater numbers, with the brown-shirted Nazi **SA** (Sturmabteilung) Stormtroopers, fighting endless pitched battles against the communist **Rote Frontkämpferbund** (Red Fighters' Front). The threat of a return to the anarchy of the postwar years increased Nazi support among the middle-classes and captains of industry (who provided heavy financial support) who feared for their lives and property under communist rule. Fear of the reds also helped the Nazis ensure little or nothing was done to curb SA violence against them. The growth of Nazi popularity was also attributable to Hitler's record as a war veteran, his identification of Jews as scapegoats and a charisma that promised to restore national pride. Meanwhile, the Communists found it difficult to extend support beyond the German working classes.

By September 1930, the Communists and Nazis together gained nearly one of every three votes cast and in the July 1932 **parliamentary elections** the Nazis took 37 percent of the vote – their largest total in any free election – making them the largest party in the Reichstag; while the Communists took 15 percent. Nazi thugs began attacking Jewish shops and businesses and intimidating liberals into muted criticism or silence.

But what eventually brought the Nazis to power in 1933 was in-fighting among conservatives, who persuaded a virtually senile Hindenburg to make Hitler chancellor. This move was based on a gamble that the Nazis would usefully crush the left but fail to form an effective government – so that within a few months Hitler could be nudged aside. Hitler became chancellor on January 4, 1933 and Berlin thronged with Nazi supporters bearing torches. For the vast majority

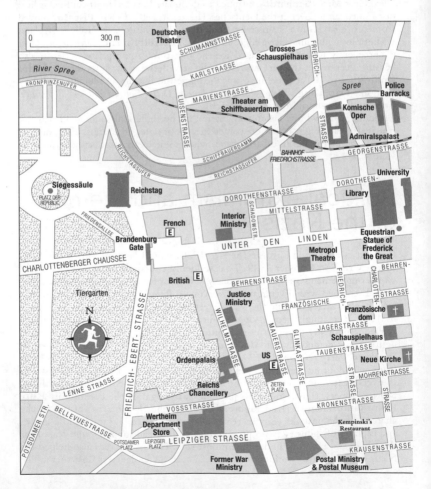

of Berliners it was a nightmare come true: three-quarters of the city had voted against the Nazis at the last elections.

Nazi takeover

With inflation under control, Germany returned to relative **political stability**. The 1924 elections demonstrated increased support for centre-right and republican parties. When President Ebert died (February 28, 1925) and was succeeded by the former commander of the Imperial army, **General Field Marshal von Hindenburg**, monarchists and conservatives rejoiced. Nevertheless, it was now that the extreme right, particularly the **National Socialist German Workers' Party** (NSDAP), or Nazis, began gradually gaining ground, starting in Bavaria.

The pretext for an all-out **Nazi takeover** was provided by the **Reichstag fire** (February 28, 1933), which was likely started by them, rather than the simple-minded Dutch communist Marius van der Lubbe on whom blame fell. An **emergency decree** the following day effectively legalized a permanent state

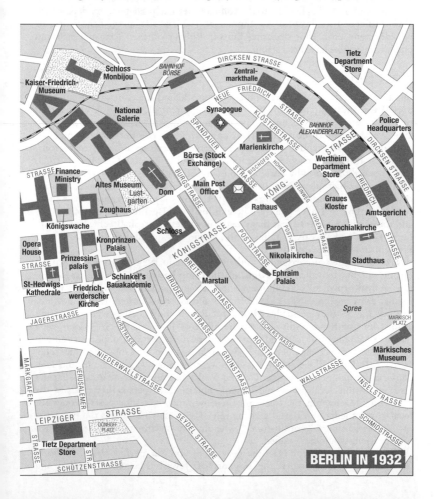

Jewish Berlin

Though commonly thought of as a history of persecution, and marginalization, in fact Berlin was one of the most accepting and progressive cities in Europe which is why it had fostered such a large Jewish population before the Nazis came to power. For a history of the difficult relationship that Jews have had with Berlin, see the box on p.88.

of emergency, which the Nazis quickly used to start crushing the communists and manipulate the 1933 **elections** in which the Nazis won 43.9 percent of the vote. Though short of a majority, this need was quickly rendered unnecessary by the arrest of communist deputies and SPD leaders to pass an **Enabling Act** that gave the Nazis dictatorial powers. Hitler was only just short of the two-thirds majority he needed to legally abolish the Weimar Republic. The SPD salvaged some self-respect by refusing to accede to this, but the Catholic centrists meekly supported the Bill in return for minor concessions. It was passed by 441 votes to 84, hammering the final nails into the coffin of German parliamentary democracy. With Hindenburg's death in the summer of 1934, Hitler merged the offices of president and chancellor declaring himself **Führer** of the German Reich and producing an absolute dictatorship.

Nazi Berlin

Once in absolute power Hitler quickly consolidated his control by removing opposition and tightening the Nazi grip on all areas of society. Rival political parties were effectively banned, unions quickly disbanded, and leaders of both arrested and sent to **concentration camps**. Then the persecution of Nazi opponents was extended to embrace "active church members, freemasons, politically dissatisfied people…abortionists and homosexuals". On May 11, 1934, they shocked the world by burning thousands of books that conflicted with Nazi ideology on Opernplatz (now Bebelplatz) in central Berlin. After the concentration camps, the **book-burnings** (Büchverbrennung) remain one of the most potent symbols of Nazi brutality. The **exodus from Berlin** of known anti-Nazis and those with reasons to fear them began in earnest. Bertolt Brecht, Kurt Weill, Lotte Lenya and Wassily Kandinsky all left the city, joining the likes of Albert Einstein and George Grosz in exile.

Nazi ruthlessness also extended to their own, and in 1934 the party was purged during a night later called the "**Night of the Long Knives**". Under **Ernst Röhm**, the SA had grown to 500,000 men and their power worried big business, the regular army and rival Nazis like Himmler and Göring. United in their hostility towards the SA they persuaded Hitler that Röhm and his allies were conspiring against him with the result that on the night of June 30, the SA leaders were taken to Stadelheim Prison and shot in the courtyard by SS troopers; it came as such a surprise that some believed it was an army coup, and died shouting "Heil Hitler!". In Berlin alone, 150 SA leaders were executed. Other victims included conservative politicians such as General Schleicher and several of von Papen's assistants, while local police and Gestapo chiefs added personal enemies to the death lists. Meanwhile, the Nazis put their own men into vital posts throughout local governments – in Berlin and the rest of Germany. This was the first stage of Gleichschaltung ("coordination"), whereby the machinery of state, and then society itself, would be Nazified.

The other big night of Nazi savagery in the prewar period was *Kristallnacht* (November 9, 1938) when the **boycott of Jewish** businesses, medical and legal practices in Berlin – enforced by the SA since April 1, 1934 – turned into bare-faced **attacks on Jewish shops and institutions**. Just as the Reichstag fire was used as an excuse to consolidate power, the Nazis used the assassination of Ernst vom Rath, a German official in Paris, by Herschel Grynszpan, a young German-Jewish refugee, as an excuse to unleash a general pogrom on German Jews. Grynszpan was protesting his parents' forced deportation to Poland with ten thousand other Jews. (Ironically, vom Rath was an anti-Nazi whom Grynszpan had mistaken for his intended target, the German ambassador.) In retaliation the Nazis organized "spontaneous" anti-Jewish demonstrations – directing the police to ensure that attacks on the Jewish community, mainly by SA men in civilian clothes, were not hindered. After *Kristallnacht* the Nazi government enacted anti-Semitic laws confiscating property and making life difficult and dangerous for German Jews, paving the way for the greater horrors to come.

Daily life and the Olympics

Given the suppression, fear, exodus and the tightening grip of Nazi control on all areas of life, the atmosphere in Berlin changed irrevocably. The unemployed were drafted into labour battalions, set to work on the land or building autobahns; the press and radio were orchestrated by Goebbels; children joined Nazi youth organizations; and every tenement building had Nazi-appointed wardens who doubled as Gestapo spies. It was even decreed that women should eschew make-up as an "un-German" artifice – one of the few edicts that wasn't taken seriously. Anti-Nazi criticism – even of the mildest kind – invited a visit from the Gestapo. Although Germans might avoid joining the NSDAP itself, it was difficult to escape the plethora of related organizations covering every aspect of life, from riding clubs and dog breeders to the "Reich Church" or "German League of Maidens". This was the second stage of *Gleichschaltung* – drawing the entire population into the Nazi net.

As the capital of the Reich, Berlin became a showcase city of banners, uniforms and parades. An image of order and dynamism, of a "new Germany" on the march, was what the Nazis tried to convey. This reached its zenith during the **1936 Olympics** (see p.126), held at a vast purpose-built stadium in the Pichelsdorf suburb of Berlin, which helped raise Germany's international standing and temporarily glossed over the realities of Nazi brutality.

World War II

Throughout the 1930s the Nazis made **preparations for war**, expanding the army and gearing the economy for war readiness by 1940, to dovetail with Hitler's foreign policy of obtaining Lebensraum ("living space") from neighbouring countries by intimidation. From 1936 onwards Hitler even spent much time with his favourite architect, **Albert Speer**, drawing up extensive plans for a remodelled and grandiose Berlin, to be called "Germania", that would reflect a postwar role as world capital of the "Thousand Year Reich". His megalomania inspired hours of brooding on how future generations might be awed by Germania's monumental ruins – hence the need to build with the finest materials on a gigantic scale.

The road to war was swift. In 1936 the German army occupied the Rhineland (demilitarized under the terms of the Treaty of Versailles) to token protests from the League of Nations. The Anschluss ("annexation") of Austria in 1938 was likewise carried off with impunity, and a few months later Britain and France agreed to dismember Czechoslovakia.

Encouraged by their appeasement, Hitler made new demands on Polish territory in 1939, probably hoping for a similar collapse of will by the western powers, the more so since he had pulled off the spectacular coup of signing a nonaggression pact with his ultimate enemy, the Soviet Union, thus ensuring that Germany could avoid a war on two fronts. But two days after the German invasion of Poland began on September 1, Britain and France declared war in defence of their treaty obligations.

Outbreak and early success

The outbreak of **World War II** was greeted without enthusiasm by Berliners, despite German victories in Poland. There were few signs of patriotic fervour as the troops marched off to war through the streets of Berlin, and Hitler cancelled further parades out of pique. Only the spectacle of the military parade to mark the fall of France (July 18, 1940), when German troops marched through the Brandenburg Gate for the first time since 1871, really attracted the crowds.

Initially, Berlin suffered little from the war. Although citizens were already complaining of meagre rations, delicacies and luxury goods from occupied Europe gravitated towards the Reich's capital. What remained of the diplomatic and foreign press community, and the chic lifestyles of Nazi bigwigs, passed for high life. Open dissent seemed impossible, with Gestapo informers believed to lurk everywhere. The impact of wartime austerity was also softened by Nazi welfare organizations and a blanket of propaganda.

Air raids

Göring had publicly boasted that Germans could call him "Meyer" (a Jewish surname) if a single bomb fell on Berlin – notwithstanding that the British RAF dropped some for the first time on August 23, 1940. A further raid on the night of August 28–29 killed ten people – the first German civilian casualties. These raids had a marked demoralizing effect on Berliners, who had counted on a swift end to the war, and Hitler had to reassure the populace in a speech at the Sportpalast. Holding up a Baedeker guide to Britain, he thundered that the Luftwaffe would raze Britain's cities to the ground one by one.

However, these early **bombing raids** caused scant real damage and it wasn't until March 1, 1943 – when defeat in the Western Desert and difficulties on the eastern front had already brought home the fact that Germany was not invincible – that Berlin suffered its first heavy raids. While the RAF bombed by night, the Americans bombed by day, establishing a pattern that would reduce Berlin to ruins in relentless stages. "We can wreck Berlin from end to end if the USAAF will come in on it. It will cost us between 400 and 500 aircraft. It will cost Germany the war," the head of Bomber command, Sir Arthur "Bomber" Harris, had written to Churchill in 1943. The first buildings to go were the Staatsoper and Alte Bibliothek on Unter den Linden. On December 22, the Kaiser-Wilhelm-Gedächtniskirche was reduced to a shell. By the year's end, daily and nightly bombardments were a feature of everyday life.

During the 363 air raids until the end of the war, 75,000 tons of high-explosive or incendiary bombs killed between 35,000 and 50,000 people and rendered 1,500,000 Berliners homeless. Yet despite the colossal destruction that filled the streets with 100 million tons of rubble, seventy percent of the city's industrial capacity was still functioning at the war's end.

Apart from chipping away at Nazi power, the destruction also intensified **underground resistance** – despite the Gestapo stranglehold making this almost impossible. Yet some groups managed minor successes and several failed attempts on Hitler's life were made, particularly notable the **July Bomb Plot** (see p.106). But much of the resistance was piecemeal and included the assistance given to **Jews** to help them evade being rounded up onto trains bound for **concentration camps**.

The fall of Berlin

Enjoy the war while you can! The peace is going to be terrible...

Berlin joke shortly before the fall of the city.

By autumn 1944, it was obvious to all but the most fanatical Nazis that the end was approaching fast. Even so, Hitler would brook no talk of surrender or negotiation. But by January 1945, distance between the Allied forces was narrowing inexorably and on January 27, Soviet forces crossed the Oder a hundred miles from Berlin. Only Hitler now really believed there was any hope for Germany. The Nazis threw all they could at the eastern front and mobilized the Volkssturm, an ill-equipped home guard of old men, boys and cripples. Thirteen- and fourteen-year-old members of the **Hitler Youth** were briefly trained in the art of using the Panzerfaust bazooka, then sent into the fray against tanks and battle-hardened infantrymen. As thousands died at the front to buy a little time for the doomed Nazi regime, life in Berlin became a nightmare. The city was choked with refugees and terrified of the approaching Russians; it was bombed day and night, and the flash of Soviet artillery could be seen on the horizon.

Behind the lines, **flying court martials** picked up soldiers and executed anyone suspected of "desertion" or "cowardice in the face of the enemy". On February 1, 1945, Berlin was declared *Verteidigungsbereich* (a "zone of defence") – to be defended to the last man and the last bullet. The civilian population – women, children and forced labourers – were set to work building tank traps and barricades; stretches of the U- and S-Bahn formed part of the fortifications. Goebbels trumpeted a **"fortress Berlin"**, while Hitler planned the deployment of **phantom armies**, which existed on battle charts, but hardly at all in reality.

As Berlin frantically prepared to defend itself, the Russians consolidated their strength. On April 16, at 5am Moscow time, the **Soviet offensive** began with a massive bombardment lasting 25 minutes. When the artillery fell silent, 143 searchlights spaced 200m apart along the entire front were switched on to dazzle the enemy as the Russians began their advance. Three army groups totalling over 1.5 million men moved forward under marshals Zhukov, Konev and Rokossovsky – and there was little the vastly outnumbered Germans could do to halt them. By April 20 – Hitler's 56th birthday (celebrated with tea and cakes in the *Führerbunker*) – the Red Army was on the edge of Berlin. Next day the city centre came within range of their guns, and several people queueing outside the Karstadt department store on Hermannplatz were killed by shells. On April 23, Soviet troops were in the Weissensee district, just a few miles east of the centre.

Hitler's birthday party was the last time the Nazi hierarchy assembled before going – or staying – to meet their respective fates. The dictator and his mistress Eva Braun chose to remain in Berlin, and Goebbels elected to join them in the **Führerbunker** with his family. It was a dank, stuffy complex of reinforced concrete cells beneath the garden of the Reich Chancellery. Here Hitler brooded over Speer's architectural models of unbuilt victory memorials, subsisting on salads, herbal tisanes and regular injections of dubious substances by one Dr Morell. To hapless generals and faithful acolytes, he ranted about traitors and the unworthiness of the German *Volk*, declaring that the war was lost and that he would stay in the bunker to the end, after learning that General Steiner's army group had failed to stop Zhukov's advance.

The final days

By April 25, Berlin was completely **encircled by Soviet troops**, which met up with US forces advancing from the west. Over the next two days, the suburbs of Dahlem, Spandau, Neukölln and Gatow fell to the Russians, and the city's telephone system failed. On April 27, the Third Panzer Army was completely smashed; survivors fled west, leaving Berlin's northern flank virtually undefended. The obvious hopelessness of the situation didn't sway the top Nazis' fanatical **refusal to surrender**. As the Red Army closed in, Goebbels called hysterically for "rücksichtslose Bekämpfung" – fight without quarter – and SS execution squads worked around the clock, killing soldiers, Volkssturm guards or Hitler Youth who tried to stop fighting.

In the city the horrors mounted. The **civilian population** lived underground in cellars and air-raid shelters, scavenging for food wherever and whenever there was a momentary lull in the fighting. Engineers blasted canal locks, flooding the U-Bahn to prevent the Russians from advancing along it. Scores of civilians sheltering in the tunnels were drowned as a result. On April 27, the Ninth Army was destroyed attempting to break out of the Russian encirclement to the south, and unoccupied Berlin had been reduced to a strip nine and a half miles long from east to west, and three miles wide from north to south, constantly under bombardment. Next the Russians captured the Tiergarten, reducing the **last pocket of resistance** to the *Regierungsviertel*, where fighting focused on the Reichstag and Hitler's Chancellery, and on Potsdamer Platz, only a few hundred metres from the *Führerbunker*, by now under constant shellfire.

Hitler still hoped that one of his phantom armies would relieve Berlin, but on April 28 his optimism evaporated when he heard that Himmler had been suing for unconditional surrender to the western Allies. In the early hours of the following day, he married Eva Braun, held a small champagne wedding reception, and dictated his will. As the day wore on, savage fighting continued around the Nazi-held enclave. At a final conference the commandant of Berlin, General Weidling, announced that the Russians were in the nearby *Adlon Hotel*, and that there was no hope of relief.

A breakout attempt was proposed, but Hitler declared that he was staying put. On the afternoon of April 30, after testing the cyanide on his pet German shepherd dog, **Hitler and Eva Braun committed suicide**: he with a revolver, she by poison. The bodies were taken to the Chancellery courtyard and doused with 200 litres of petrol; Hitler's followers gave the Nazi salute as the corpses burned to ashes. Meanwhile, Soviet troops were battling to gain control of the Reichstag, and at 11pm two Russian sergeants raised the red flag from its rooftop.

After Hitler's death, chief of staff Krebs was sent out to parley with the Russians. After hasty consultation with Stalin, General Chuikov replied that only unconditional surrender was acceptable. When Krebs returned to the bunker, Goebbels rejected this and ordered the fighting to continue. That night he and his wife killed themselves, having first poisoned their six children. Almost all the rest of the eight hundred or so bunker occupants decided to try and break out. Weidling agreed not to surrender until the following dawn in order to give the fugitives time to **escape** through the railway tunnels towards northern Berlin; about a hundred made it – the rest were either killed or captured.

Capitulation and surrender

At 5am, Weidling offered the **capitulation of Berlin** to General Chuikov, who broadcast his surrender proclamation from loudspeaker vans around the city. At 3pm, firing in the city centre stopped, although sporadic, sometimes fierce, fighting continued on the outskirts, where German troops tried to break out to the west to surrender to the more merciful British or Americans rather than the vengeful Russians. The **official surrender of German forces** occurred at a Wehrmacht engineers' school in the Berlin suburb of Karlshorst on May 8, 1945. By then Berliners had already emerged from their shelters and started to clear the dead and the rubble from the streets.

With the final act of surrender complete, it was time to count the cost of the Battle of Berlin. It had taken the lives of 125,000 Berliners (including 6400 suicides and 22,000 heart attacks), and innumerable German soldiers from the 93 divisions destroyed by the Red Army. The Soviets themselves had suffered some 305,000 casualties in the battle, while the city itself was left in ruins, without even basic services.

But for those civilians who remained in the city, this was just the start of the worst as the Soviets unleashed an **orgy of rape and looting** on the capital.

Occupation

During the immediate postwar months, civilian rations of food, fuel and medicine were cut to the bone to support the two-million-strong **Soviet occupation forces**. Survival rations were measured in ounces per day, if forthcoming at all, and civilians had to use all their wits to stay alive.

The Soviet Union had taken steps towards establishing a civilian, communist-dominated administration even before the war was over. On April 30, a group of exiled German communists arrived at Küstrin airfield and were taken to Berlin, where they established a temporary headquarters in Lichtenberg. Directed by **Walter Ulbricht**, the future leader of the GDR's communist party, they set about tracking down old Berlin party members and setting up a new **municipal administration**.

The **western occupation sectors** had been demarcated by the Allies as far back as 1943, but the troops didn't move in until July 1–4, 1945, when fifty thousand British, American and French soldiers replaced the Red Army in the western part of the city. Here, the food situation improved marginally once American supplies began to find their way through, but public health remained a huge problem. Dysentery and TB were endemic, and there were outbreaks of typhoid and paratyphoid, all exacerbated by an acute shortage of hospital beds. British and American soldiers had endless opportunities to profit from the burgeoning **black market**: trading cigarettes, alcohol, gas, NAAFI and PX supplies for antiques, jewellery or sexual favours. Huge black market centres sprang up around the Brandenburg Gate and Alexanderplatz.

From July 17 to August 3 the **Potsdam conference** took place at the Cecilienhof Palace. It was to be the last great meeting of the leaders of the Big Three wartime alliance. Churchill took the opportunity to visit the ruins of the Reich's Chancellery, followed by a mob of fascinated Germans and Russians. Mid-conference he returned to Britain to hear the results of the first postwar election – and was replaced by the newly elected Labour prime minister, Clement Attlee, who could do little but watch as Truman and Stalin settled the fate of postwar Europe and Berlin.

Starvation and unrest

For Germans, the worst was yet to come. Agriculture and industry had virtually collapsed, threatening acute **shortages of food and fuel** just as winter approached. In Berlin they dug mass graves and stockpiled coffins for the expected wave of deaths, and thousands of children were evacuated to the British occupation zone in the west of the country, where conditions were less severe. To everyone's surprise the winter turned out to be uncommonly mild. Christmas 1945 was celebrated after a fashion, and mothers took their children to the first postwar *Weihnachtsmarkt* (Christmas fair) in the Lustgarten.

Unfortunately the respite was only temporary, for despite the good weather, food supplies remained overstretched. In March rations were reduced drastically, and the weakened civilian population fell prey to typhus, TB and other **hunger-related diseases**; the lucky ones merely suffered enteric or skin diseases. The Allies did what they could, sending government and private relief, but even by the spring of 1947 rations remained at malnutrition levels. **Crime and prostitution** soared. In Berlin alone, two thousand people were arrested every month, many of them from juvenile gangs that roamed the ruins murdering, robbing and raping. Trains were attacked at the Berlin stations, and in the countryside bandits ambushed supply convoys heading for the city. The winter of 1946–47 was one of the coldest since records began. Wolves appeared in Berlin and people froze to death aboard trains. There were rumours of cannibalism and Berlin hospitals treated 55,000 people for frostbite.

Allied tensions

Meanwhile, **political developments** that were to have a lasting impact on Berlin were occurring. In March 1946, parts of the SPD were forced into a shotgun merger with the KPD, to form the **SED** (Sozialistische Einheitspartei Deutschlands – "Socialist Unity Party of Germany"), or future **communist party** of East Germany, underlining the political division of the city as the wartime alliance between the western powers (France had also been allotted an occupation zone) and the Soviet Union fell apart, ushering in a new era of conflict that would all too often focus on Berlin. The Allied Control Council met for the last time on March 20, when Marshal Sokolovsky, the Soviet military governor, protested about British and American attempts to introduce economic reform in their occupation zones.

Tension mounted over the next few months as the Allies went ahead with economic reform, while the Russians demanded the right to board Berlin-bound Allied trains, and on June 16 walked out of the four-power Kommandantura that had ultimate control over Berlin. Things came to a head with the **introduction of the D-Mark** in the western zone (June 23, 1948). On that day, the Soviets presented Berlin's mayor with an ultimatum, demanding that he accept their Ostmark as currency for the whole city. But the city's parliament voted overwhelmingly against the Soviet-backed currency.

Everyone knew that this was asking for trouble, and trouble wasn't long in coming. On the night of June 23–24, power stations in the Soviet zone cut off electricity supplies to the western half of Berlin, and road and rail links between the western part of Germany and Berlin were severed. This was the beginning of the **Berlin blockade**, the USSR's first attempt to force the western Allies out of Berlin. SPD politician Ernst Reuter, soon to be mayor of West Berlin, addressed a crowd at the Gesundbrunnen football field, promising that Berlin would "fight with everything we have". In the end the greatest weapon proved to be American and British support when on June 26, 1948, they began the Berlin airlift, flying supplies into the city to keep it alive against the odds for almost a year (see p.141).

The 1950s: the birth of the two Germanys

Within six months, the political division of Germany was formalized by the creation of two rival states. First, the British, French and American zones of occupation were amalgamated to form the **Federal Republic of Germany** (May 1949); the Soviets followed suit by launching the **German Democratic Republic** on October 7. As Berlin lay deep within GDR territory, its eastern sector naturally became the official GDR capital. However, much to the disappointment of many Berliners, the Federal Republic chose Bonn as their capital. West Berlin remained under the overall control of the Allied military commandants, although it was eventually to assume the status of a Land (state) of the Federal Republic.

Political tension remained a fact of life in a city that had become an arena for superpower confrontations. The Soviets and GDR communists had not abandoned the idea of driving the Allies out of Berlin, and mounted diverse operations against them, just as the Allies ran spying and sabotage operations against East Berlin. In this cradle of **Cold War espionage**, the recruitment of former Gestapo, SD or Abwehr operatives seemed quite justifiable to all the agencies concerned. On one side were Britain's SIS (based at the Olympic Stadium) and the American CIA, which fostered the Federal Republic's own intelligence service, the Gehlen Bureau, run by a former Abwehr colonel. Opposing them were the Soviet KGB and GRU (based at Karlshorst), and the GDR's own foreign espionage service and internal security police. The public side of this rumbling underground war was a number of **incidents** in 1952. An Air France plane approaching West Berlin through the air corridor was fired upon by a Russian MiG; the East German authorities blocked streets leading from West to East Berlin and expropriated property owned by West Berliners on the outskirts of the eastern sector.

The economic miracle and the Berlin Wall

Throughout the 1950s important events took place in **West Germany** under Chancellor Konrad Adenauer. Foremost among them was the so-called "**economic miracle**", which saw West Germany recover from the ravages of war astonishingly quickly and go on to become Europe's largest economy. Although West Berlin's **economic recovery** was by no means as dramatic as that of West Germany, the city did prosper, particularly in comparison to East Berlin. **Marshall Plan aid** and West German capital were transforming West Berlin into a glittering showcase for capitalism, whereas the GDR and East Berlin seemed to languish, partly the result of the Soviets' ruthless **asset-stripping** – removing factories, rolling stock and generators to replace losses in the war-ravaged USSR.

The **death of Stalin** on March 5, 1953, raised hopes that the situation in Berlin could be eased, but these were soon dashed. In the eastern sector, the communists unwittingly fuelled smouldering resentment by announcing a ten percent **rise in work norms** on June 16. For workers already hard-pressed to support their families, this demand to produce more or earn less was intolerable, causing workers to band together in an uprising on June 16 and 17, which was brutally suppressed (see p.138).

So as the economic disparity between East and West Germany (and their respective halves of Berlin) worsened throughout the 1950s, West Berlin became an increasingly attractive destination for East Berliners, who were able to cross the **zonal border** more or less freely at this time. Many came to stay, while others worked in the city, benefiting from the purchasing power of the D-Mark. And those who did neither used the city to enjoy the entertainment and culture lacking in the more spartan East. This steady **population drain** undermined prospects for development in the GDR, as young and often highly skilled workers headed west for higher living standards and greater political freedom. Roughly 2,500,000 people quit the GDR during the 1950s, mostly via the open border with West Berlin, where an average of 19,000 East Germans crossed over every month. Both the GDR and Soviet governments saw this as a threat to East Germany's existence.

On November 10, 1958, Soviet leader Nikita Khrushchev demanded that the western Allies relinquish their role in the "occupation regime in Berlin, thus facilitating the normalization of the situation in the capital of the GDR". Two weeks later, Khrushchev suggested the Allies should withdraw and make Berlin a free city – coupled with a broad hint that if no agreement was reached within six months, a blockade would be reimposed. The Allies rejected the ultimatum, and the Kremlin allowed the deadline to pass without incident. Tripartite **negotiations** at Geneva (May–Sept 1959) failed to produce a settlement. Meanwhile, tens of thousands of East Germans continued to cross the border into West Berlin.

By 1961, Ulbricht's regime was getting desperate, and rumours that the border might be sealed began to circulate. In mid-June Ulbricht felt compelled to assure the world that no one had "the intention of building a wall". Simultaneously, however, border controls were tightened. Yet the flood of people voting with their feet continued to rise, in what West Berlin's Springer press dubbed "mass escapes...of avalanche proportions". It was obvious that something was about to happen. Shortly after midnight on August 13, 1961, it did with the East German sealing of the border, dividing the city with the Berlin Wall (see p.136).

Reaction in the West

Despite public outrage throughout West Germany and formal **diplomatic protests** from the Allies, everyone knew that to take a firmer line risked nuclear war. The West had to fall back on symbolic gestures: the Americans sent over General Lucius Clay, organizer of the Berlin airlift, and Vice-President Lyndon Johnson on August 18. The **separation of families** plunged morale in East Berlin to new depths and **economic problems** hit West Berlin, which was suddenly deprived of sixty thousand skilled workers who formerly commuted in from the GDR. They could only be replaced by creating special tax advantages to attract workers and businesses from the Federal Republic into West Berlin. American support for West Berlin was reaffirmed in August 1963, by President **John F. Kennedy**'s "Berliner" speech (see p.130), but for all its rhetoric and rapturous reception, the West essentially had to accept the new status quo.

The 1960s

The **gradual reduction of political tension** that occurred after the Wall had been standing a couple of years was partly due to improved relations between the superpowers, but mostly to local efforts. Under SPD mayor **Willy Brandt**, talks were opened up between the West Berlin Senate and the GDR government, resulting in the **"Pass Agreement"** of December 1963, whereby 730,000 West Berliners were able to pay brief visits to the East at the end of the year. Three more agreements were concluded over the next couple of years until the GDR decided to use border controls as a lever for winning **diplomatic recognition** (which the Federal Republic and its Western allies refused to give). Access to West Berlin via routes through GDR territory was subject to official hindrance; on one occasion, deputies were prevented from attending a plenary session of the Bundestag, held in West Berlin in April 1965. New and more stringent **passport and visa controls** were levied on all travellers from June 1968 onwards.

As the direct threat to its existence receded, West Berlin society began to fragment along generational lines. Partly because Berlin residents could legally evade West German conscription, young people formed an unusually high proportion of the population – many gravitating towards Kreuzberg. The immediate catalyst was the wave of **student unrest** in 1967–68, when initial grievances over unreformed, badly run universities soon spread to embrace wider disaffection with West Germany's materialistic culture. As in West Germany, the APO, or **extra-parliamentary opposition**, emerged as a strong and vocal force in West Berlin, criticizing what many people saw as a failed attempt to build a true democracy on the ruins of Nazi Germany. Another powerful strand was anti-Americanism, fuelled by US policy in Southeast Asia, Latin America and the Middle East. Both these viewpoints tended to bewilder and enrage older Germans.

The police reacted to street demonstrations in Berlin with a ferocity that shocked even conservatives. On June 2, 1967, a student was shot by police during a protest against a state visit by the Shah of Iran. The right-wing **Springer press** (deliberately sited just near the Wall) absolved the police, pinning all the blame on "long-haired communists". When someone tried to kill student leader **Rudi Dutschke** (April 11, 1968), there were huge and violent demonstrations against the Springer press. Although the mass-protest movement fizzled out towards the end of the 1960s, a new and deadlier opposition would emerge in the 1970s – partly born from the West German establishment's violent response to what was initially a peaceful protest movement.

Ostpolitik and détente

The international scene and Berlin's place in it changed considerably around the turn of the decade. Both superpowers now hoped to thaw the Cold War and agree to a détente, while elections in the Federal Republic brought to power Willy Brandt, a chancellor committed to rapprochement with the GDR. On February 27, 1969, US President Richard Nixon called for an easing of international tension during his visit to Berlin. Soon afterwards, **Four Power Talks** were held in the former Allied Control Council building in the American sector. Participants decided to set aside broader issues in an effort to fashion a workable agreement on the status of the divided city resulting in the **Quadripartite Agreement** (September 3, 1971), followed in December by inter-German agreements regarding transit routes to West Berlin and travel and traffic regulations for West Berliners. In 1972, the Federal Republic and the GDR signed a **Basic Treaty**, which bound both states to respect each other's frontiers and de facto sovereignty. In return for diplomatic recognition, the GDR allowed West Germans access to friends and family across the border, which had effectively been denied to them (barring limited visits in the mid-1960s). However, the freedom to move from East to West was restricted to disabled people and senior citizens.

The 1970s

During the 1970s Berlin assumed a new identity, breaking with the images and myths of the past. Thanks to the easing of Cold War tensions, West Berlin was no longer a frontline city, and East Berlin lost much of its intimidating atmosphere. Throughout the decade, **West Berlin** had similar problems to those of West Germany: economic upsets triggered by the quadrupling of oil prices in 1974, and a wave of terrorism directed against the establishment. In addition, West Berlin suffered from a deteriorating stock of housing and rising unemployment – both alleviated to some extent by financial help from West Germany.

East Berlin remained relatively quiet. A new East German leader, **Erich Honecker**, who was regarded as a "liberal", succeeded Ulbricht in 1971. Under him, living standards improved and there was some relaxation of the tight controls of the Ulbricht days. However, most people regarded the changes as essentially trivial, and escapes continued to be attempted, although by now the Wall was formidably deadly. In 1977, a rock concert in Alexanderplatz turned into a brief explosion of street unrest, which the authorities suppressed with deliberate brutality.

The 1980s

Throughout the 1970s and early 1980s, the Quadripartite Agreement and the inter-German treaties formed the backdrop to relations between West and East Berlin. The main irritant was the **compulsory exchange** of D-Marks for Ostmarks, which the GDR raised in value from DM6.50 to DM25 in 1980, deterring significant numbers of visitors. But on the whole, a degree of stability and normality had been achieved, enabling both cities to run smoothly on a day-to-day basis, without being the focus of international tension. Even after the partial resumption of the Cold War, following the Soviet invasion of Afghanistan in 1979, Berlin remained relatively calm. The only notable event was the shooting of an American officer on an alleged spying mission in Potsdam in the spring of 1985.

As elsewhere in West Germany, Berlin witnessed a crystallization of issues and attitudes and the flowering of new radical movements. Concern about the arms race and the environment was widespread; feminism and gay rights commanded increasing support. Left-wing and Green groups formed an **Alternative Liste** to fight elections, and a left-liberal newspaper, *Tageszeitung*, was founded. Organized squatting was the radical solution to Berlin's **housing crisis**. In 1981, the new Christian Democrat administration (elected after a financial scandal forced the SPD to step down) tried to evict the squatters from about 170 apartment buildings, and police violence sparked rioting in Schöneberg. The administration compromised by allowing some of the squatters to become legitimate tenants, which had a big effect on life in West Berlin. For the first time since the late 1960s, the social divisions that had opened up showed signs of narrowing. Alternative Liste delegates were elected to the Berlin Senate for the first time in May 1981, and the same year witnessed a boom in **cultural life**, as the arts exploded into new vitality.

The **early 1980s** saw a resumption of frostiness in US–Soviet relations, which heightened concern about **nuclear weapons**. Anti-nuclear activists protested during the Berlin visit of President Ronald Reagan in June 1981. But the tension and sabre-rattling of the 1950s and 1960s Cold War didn't return to Berlin even though ideological hostility prevented the two halves of the city from jointly celebrating Berlin's 750th **anniversary** in 1987. In East Berlin anniversary celebrations were preceded by a massive **urban renewal project**, in both the city centre and the inner suburbs; the reconstructed Nikolaiviertel (see p.76) stems from this time. In West Berlin, the elections of spring 1989 swept the CDU administration from power, and an **SPD/Alternative Liste coalition** took over, with Walter Momper as mayor. In Kreuzberg, demonstrations against what many regarded as an Alternative Liste sell out were put down with unwarranted force, sparking running street battles.

The GDR resists perestroika

When, in 1985, **Mikhail Gorbachev** became the new the Soviet leader and began campaigns for *glasnost* and *perestroika*, their initial impact on East Germany was slight. The SED regarded them with deep suspicion, so while Poland and Hungary embarked on the road to democracy, Erich Honecker declared that the Berlin Wall would stand for another fifty or one hundred years if necessary. The authorities then banned pro-*glasnost* Soviet magazine *Sputnik* and several 1960s Russian films from the 1960s, that had only just been released from censorship.

Die Wende

The year 1989 ranks as both one of the most significant years in German history and one of the most unforeseeable. Yet within twelve months **Die Wende** ("the turn") transformed Germany. With little warning East Germany suddenly collapsed in the wake of the general easing of communism in the Eastern Bloc of the late-1980s. The Berlin Wall parted on November 9, 1989, symbolizing an end to the Cold War, making a lifetime's dream come true for most Germans – above all, for those living in the East. Several events then fairly logically and briskly followed: the union of the two Germanys; the reassertion of Berlin as capital; and the start of the lengthy process of putting those responsible for the GDR's crimes on trial.

The first holes in the Iron Curtain

Despite the unyielding position of the GDR government, as the decade wore on things started to happen. The **Protestant Church** provided a haven for **environmental and peace organizations**, whose members unfurled protest banners calling for greater freedom at an official ceremony in Berlin in January 1988. They were immediately arrested, imprisoned, and later expelled from the GDR. Through events like this, the end of the regime didn't seem nigh – so when Chris Gueffroy was shot dead trying to cross the Berlin border at Neukölln on February 6, 1989, no one fathomed that he would be the last person killed in such an attempt. However, the impetus for East German collapse came from other Eastern European countries: in 1988 Hungary began taking down the barbed wire fence along their Austrian border, creating a **hole in the Iron Curtain**, across which many East Germans fled. A similar pattern emerged in Czechoslovakia.

The October revolution

The East German government's disarrayed response to these goings on then galvanized into action thousands who had previously been content to make the best of things. Fledgling **opposition groups** like the **Neues Forum** emerged, and unrest began in Leipzig and Dresden and soon spread to Berlin.

Then, at the beginning of October, at the pompous official celebration of the GDR's **fortieth anniversary**, Gorbachev stressed the need for new ideas and stunningly announced that the USSR would not interfere in the affairs of fellow socialist states. Protests and scuffles along the cavalcade route escalated into a huge demonstration as the day wore on, which the police and Stasi brutally suppressed. Thousands of arrests were made, and prisoners were subjected to the usual degrading treatment and beatings.

The following week, **nationwide demonstrations** came close to bloodshed in **Leipzig**, where 70,000 people marched through the city, forcing the sudden replacement of Erich Honecker with **Egon Krenz** as party secretary, who immediately announced that the regime was ready for dialogue.

The final week of October saw a growing exodus of GDR citizens via other Eastern Bloc countries, while pressure on the streets kept rising. Then on November 4, East Berlin saw over one million citizens demonstrate, forcing authorities to make hasty **concessions**, including dropping the requirement for GDR citizens to get visas to visit Czechoslovakia – in effect, permitting emigration. People swarmed across the Czech border, and within two days fifteen thousand had reached Bavaria – bringing the number of East Germans who had fled the country in 1989 to 200,000.

The Wall opens

The **opening of the Berlin Wall** was announced almost casually, on the evening of Thursday November 9, when Berlin party boss Günter Schabowski told a press conference that East German citizens were free to leave the GDR with valid exit visas, which would henceforth be issued without delay. Hardly daring to believe the puzzling announcement, Berliners on both sides of the Wall started heading for border crossings.

Huge crowds converged on the **Brandenburg Gate**, where the Volkspolizei gave up checking documents and simply let thousands of East Germans walk into West Berlin. An impromptu **street party** broke out, with West Berliners popping champagne corks and Germans from both sides of the Wall embracing. The scenes of joy and disbelief flashed around a world taken by surprise. West German Chancellor **Helmut Kohl** interrupted a state visit in Warsaw to rush to West Berlin, where the international press was arriving in droves. Inside the GDR, disbelief turned to joy as people realized that the unimaginable had happened. On the first weekend of the opening of the Wall – November 11 and 12 – 2.7 million exit visas were issued to East Germans, who formed mile-long queues at checkpoints. West Germans – and TV-viewers around the world – gawped at streams of Trabant cars pouring into West Berlin, where shops enjoyed a bonanza as East Germans spent their DM100 "welcome money", given to each of them by the Federal Republic.

By the following weekend, **ten million visas** had been issued since November 9 – an incredible statistic considering the whole population of the GDR was only sixteen million.

The road to Reunification

Despite the opening of the border East German demonstrations continued and anti-government feelings still ran high, forcing the immediate dismantling of the formidable Stasi security service and an agreement to have free elections, for which the **SED** hastily repackaged itself as a new, supposedly voter-friendly **PDS**

– Partei des Demokratischen Sozialismus (Democratic Socialist Party), partly by firing the old guard. But the next initiative came from the West when **Chancellor Kohl** visited Dresden on December 19, addressing a huge, enthusiastic crowd as "dear countrymen", and declaring a **united Germany** his ultimate goal. East Germans began to agree as they discovered that West Germany's standard of living eclipsed anything in the GDR, found out exactly how corrupt their government had been – with the result that the GDR's first free elections on March 18, 1990 returned a victory for a right-wing alliance dominated by the CDU and Kohl.

The **economic union** was hammered out almost immediately and the GDR began rapidly to fade away. Eastern produce vanished from shops to be replaced by western consumer goods, and, superficially it seemed as though a second "economic miracle" had begun. Yet for many East Germans, the excitement was tempered by fears of rent increases and factory closures during the transformation to a market economy. Already the first legal claims by former owners of apartment buildings in East Berlin were being lodged.

With confirmation that a united Germany would respect its post World War II boundaries, the wartime allies agreed to reunification. After an all-night Volkskammer session on August 23 it was announced that the GDR would become part of the Federal Republic on **October 3, 1990**.

Street-level changes

The two Berlins, meanwhile, were already drawing together as the border withered away during the course of the year. Passport and customs controls for German citizens had ceased early in 1990 and, by the time of currency union, nationals of other countries, although nominally still subject to control, could cross the border unhindered. During the course of the year most of the central sections of **the Wall** were demolished and numerous cross-border streets linked up once again.

As border controls in Berlin and elsewhere throughout the former Soviet bloc eased, Berlin became a magnet for the restless peoples of eastern Europe. First arrivals had been the **Poles**, who set up a gigantic impromptu street market on a patch of wasteland near the Wall, much to the chagrin of Berliners, who felt the order of their city threatened by the influx of thousands of weekend street traders selling junk out of suitcases. They were followed by **Romanians**, mainly gypsies, fleeing alleged persecution at home and hoping, by taking advantage of visa-free access to what was still the GDR, to secure a place for themselves in the new Germany. Post-unification visa regulations were to be put a stop to the commuting activities of the Poles, but as asylum-seekers the Romanians had the right to remain, and the sight of gypsy families begging on the streets of Berlin became commonplace.

Reunification and the 1990s

On **October 3, 1990**, the day of **reunification**, Chancellor Kohl spoke to assembled dignitaries and massive crowds in front of the Reichstag. A conscious effort was made to rekindle the spontaneous joy and fervour that had gripped the city on the night the Wall was opened and during Berlin's first post-*Wende* new year, but for many ordinary people already experiencing the economic side-effects of the collapse of the GDR the celebrations left a bitter taste. On the sidelines anti-unification demonstrators marched through the streets, precipitating minor **clashes with the police**.

Just over a month later, on the night of November 13, the reunited Berlin experienced its first **major upheaval** when SPD mayor Walter Momper ordered the police to evict **West Berlin squatters** who had occupied a number of tenement blocks in the eastern Berlin district of Friedrichshain. The violent tactics of the police, coupled with the uncompromising stance of the radical Autonome squatters, who responded with petrol bombs and a hail of missiles from the rooftops, resulted in the fiercest **rioting** seen in the city since 1981, with dozens of police injured and over three hundred squatters arrested. Politically, the unrest resulted in the **collapse** of the fragile Red-Green SPD/Alternative Liste coalition that had governed West Berlin for the previous twenty months.

December 2, 1990 saw Germany's first nationwide elections since 1933. Nationally the CDU, in coalition with the FDP (Free Democrats), triumphed easily. One surprise was that the PDS secured 25 percent of the vote in eastern Berlin on an anti-unemployment and anti-social inequality ticket. At the start of 1991, with the celebrations of the first united Christmas and New Year over, it was time for the accounting to begin in earnest. The new year brought vastly unpopular **tax increases** in western Germany to pay for the spiralling **cost of unification**. As the year wore on, and **unemployment** continued to rise, Kohl's honeymoon with the East ended. He became reluctant to show himself there, and when he finally did, in April, he was greeted by catcalls and egg-hurlers.

Ill-feeling between easterners and westerners (nicknamed *Ossis* and *Wessis*) also became apparent and increased throughout the decade. West Germans resented the tax increases and caricatured easterners as naive and lazy. East Germans resented patronizing western attitudes and economic inequalities that made them second-class citizens, so mocked westerners for their arrogance and materialism. Feelings got worse as it became apparent that the ever-increasing cost of reunification had pushed the German economy into recession. As the instability of the transitional period began to ebb, witch-hunts for those responsible for the crimes of the GDR's repressive regime began in earnest, many the result of Stasi files to which people

The Love Parade

Nowhere was the spirit of unity and excess in a newly self-confident post-*Wende* Berlin celebrated as hard as at the **Love Parade**, the annual techno-fest that grew into an institution throughout the 1990s, before becoming a victim of its own success. The event spawned copy-cat parades around the globe – including Leeds, Vienna, Tel Aviv and Cape Town – and still soldiers on elsewhere in Germany (see ⓦwww .loveparade.de) but now seems to have more-or-less severed its links with Berlin.

The event began modestly enough in 1989, as a extravagant birthday party for local **DJ Dr Motte**. He played his records from a float followed down Berlin's streets by a hundred or so of his friends who chanted "Friede, Freude, Eierkuchen" (peace, joy and pancakes), bemusing onlookers. Later that year the Berlin Wall fell and somehow the event captured the mood of the time, gathering unbelievable momentum in subsequent years. By 1995 attendance was up to 300,000, grid-locking city-centre streets for the entire weekend. The following year the crowd doubled and the parade around town was re-routed to end in the Tiergarten, finding a natural home for the pill-popping party-goers gyrating to the thud of €15 million sound systems and indulging in generous amounts of no-holts-barred sexual activity of all types. The annual **cancellation rumours** were no more than that until 2004, when the organizers couldn't find the money demanded by the city for the immense clean-up operation needed in the aftermath of a million loved-up ravers. This continues to be the problem, so the parade's brief reappearance in 2006 may well go down as the city's last.

had increasing access. Trials throughout the 1990s brought Politbüro members, border guards, and even sports coaches who'd doped players without their knowledge, before the courts.

On June 20, 1991, a Bundestag decision to **relocate the national government to Berlin** ushered in a new era: a tremendous task, and one undertaken in the late 1990s with the usual German thoroughness.

Berlin today

Since the start of the twenty-first century Berlin has been a city on the move, with **building sites** everywhere, particularly along the old east-west border. The city is finally coming out of an era of transition and in some ways only now completing the rebuilding work in the areas destroyed by both the World War and Cold War. Magically this has almost wound back the clock to the 1920s, before Nazism struck, with Berlin once again a cosmopolitan and upbeat **party-loving city**. But also like the 1920s, the city is plagued by **economic and social problems** to which there are no easy solutions. Berlin's underperforming economy is perhaps the hardest nut to crack, though there are signs that things might be improving, with the hope that the knock-on effect will be to stem the small-scale resurgence of **neo-Nazism** and improve the lot of the city's marginalized **immigrants**, with their violence, restless gangs and occasional retreats into Islamic fundamentalism.

Party capital

As host of the 2006 football **World Cup finals**, Berlin, like much of the rest of Germany, was able to project its friendly and youthful dynamism to the world in an event that put the nation back at ease with being patriotic. The city hosted several games, including the final, in the fine old Olympic Stadium, and visiting fans quickly realized that the city deserved its reputation for partying hard. Since then barely a week has passed without a big event, and twenty-somethings from all over Europe jet in on low-cost airlines for the all-night club scene. The nightlife is again as wild and cutting edge as it ever was, even if the Love Parade (see box opposite) has fallen out with the city. The gay scene too is thriving, and Berlin's sociable, gay mayor **Klaus Wowereit** or "Wowi", as Berliners call him, has become one of Germany's best-known public figures (see box, p.252).

Economic woes and hopes

Greatly weakened by the costs of pulling the two Germanys together, and heavy investment in construction projects like the Hauptbahnhof and Berlin-Brandenburg International Airport, the city has long been teetering on the edge of recession. In recent years it has become an impoverished place with only the rich political ghetto at its heart showing signs of flourishing. You don't have to stray far from this smart central district to find the bedraggled likes of Wedding, Neukölln or Lichtenberg.

Part of the problem has been the **death of manufacturing**: after unification Berlin hoped to become an industrial hub again, but instead the city lost two-thirds of its jobs in manufacturing, which now employs fewer than 100,000 in a population of 3.4 million. But the city's **welfare mentality** has also been blamed for the stagnation. Not only do almost half of all Berliners live on benefits today, but the legacy of state subsidies shoring up uncompetitive firms is said to be almost as detrimental to entrepreneurialism in West Berlin as socialism was in the East – and new initiatives tend to be mired by the huge contemporary bureaucracy.

Even so, Berlin is helped by its location between eastern and western Europe, particularly with Poland and other eastern European countries absorbed into the European Union, and by the fact that Berlin has an increasingly hip image, helping firms lure skilled workers here so that both can benefit from the city's relatively **cheap real estate**. A clutch of small fashion designers have moved in around the Hackescher Markt and the banks of the River Spree have become the base for Universal Music, MTV and other media firms. Meanwhile information technology parks in the southern suburbs have grown fast, as has the research and development sector, thanks largely to the presence of three universities in the city. Growth in all these areas led to a **property market boom**, with sales rocketing since 2006.

Meanwhile **tourism** has become a major growth area, with Berlin overtaking Rome in terms of visitor numbers (making it third in Europe after London and Paris), and economic forecasters predicting modest growth for the city.

Neo-Nazis

One reason to improve Berlin's economy is to counter the right-wing extremism and xenophobic violence fuelled by youth unemployment. Of particular concern has been the growth in the **National Partie Deutschland** (National Party of Germany; NPD), which has seats in two east German state legislatures (another far right party has deputies in Brandenburg) and does well in local elections. Yet Berlin remains relatively untroubled by the **racist violence** that occurs fairly regularly in Brandenburg towns. Yet in 2006, a brutal and unprovoked attack on a German man of Ethiopian origin in Potsdam, which left him in a coma for weeks, put the problem on Berlin's doorstep. In the same year a politician of Turkish origin was badly beaten in Lichtenberg, a district of eastern Berlin known as a neo-Nazi stronghold.

Despite all the debate caused by such events these impromptu brutalities are hard to stop, while the country's constitutional court has blocked attempts to ban the NPD, which may be inadvisable anyway, since quashing free speech risks making martyrs of them.

Ethnic minorities and Islamic fundamentalism

While neo-Nazism tends to be a problem in the old east, in the west a greater concern is the growth of a subculture of disaffected descendants of immigrants who increasingly use Islam as a rallying point. Many are the children of Turkish "guest workers" who were invited to the country in the 1960s and preferred to settle in Germany rather than return home. Their children are now caught between two cultures: a Turkish one of which they are no longer a part and a German one that won't fully accept them. Living in the poorest neighbourhoods with the worst schools, much of their frustration and anger at society is voiced through petty crime, home-grown hip-hop and a guns and drugs culture. These problems have particularly grabbed headlines in Berlin, with the "honour killing" of 23-year-old **Hatun Sürücü,** a woman of Turkish origin killed by her brothers in 2005, as punishment for adopting a Western lifestyle: shortly before being killed, she had obtained a divorce from an arranged marriage, stopped wearing a headscarf and started to train as an electrician. Then in 2005 the press published a letter from teachers from the **Rütli** school – full of disadvantaged Turks – begging the city to close it down as they feared for their lives. Meanwhile, their students are statistically unlikely to finish school or get vocational training, and will struggle to find a job. Under the weight of these problems some feel attracted to radical Islam, a movement which has been linked to failed terrorist attacks in Germany in 2006 and 2007.

Milestones

Despite these threats of extremism, 2009 offered Berlin a moment to pause for thought and look back at its tremendous achievements in the twenty years since the Wall came down. The city celebrated the anniversary with an installation in which imitation pieces of wall toppled like dominoes between the Brandenburg Gate and Potsdamer Platz. Meanwhile world leaders past and present, including Mikhail Gorbachev, gathered to congratulate each other, mark the occasion and remind everyone that the economic and political freedom now enjoyed by the city should not be taken for granted.

Books

Huge numbers of books have been written about Berlin. The collection below shows a bias towards unravelling the evil mysteries of the Third Reich, the double-dealing of the Cold War and getting to grips with the *Wende*. But Berlin has also attracted dozens of specialist guides, the most useful of which are books on its architecture, new and old. Some books are out of print but should be easy to track down online or in secondhand bookshops. Books marked with a ✤ are particularly recommended.

History

General History and pre-Third Reich

Otto Friedrich *Before the Deluge: A Portrait of Berlin in the 1920s*. An engaging social history, full of tales and anecdotes, of the city when Dada and decadence reigned. An excellent history of Berlin's most engaging period.

Anton Gill *A Dance Between Flames*. Gill's dense but readable account of Berlin in the 1920s and 1930s has lots of colour, quotation and detail but leans so heavily on a single source – *The Diary of Henry Kessler* – that you feel he should be sharing the royalties. Even so, one of the best books on the period.

Mark Girouard *Cities and People*. A well-illustrated social and architectural history of European urban development that contains knowledgeable entries on Berlin, particularly the eighteenth- and nineteenth-century periods.

Alex De Jong *The Weimar Chronicle*. While not the most comprehensive of accounts of the Weimar Republic, this is far and away the most lively. A couple of chapters focus on Berlin, and the book is spiced with eyewitness memoirs and a mass of engaging detail, particularly on the arts in Berlin. Worth hunting the libraries for.

Giles MacDonogh *Berlin*. The book's thematic rather than chronological organization might be a bit baffling initially – and doesn't really work in uncovering themes from the city's past as it intends – but there's a wealth of fascinating anecdotes on aspects of daily life here that's ignored by traditional histories.

Andreas Nachama et al *Jews in Berlin*. Packed with source material of every kind, this well-illustrated book charts the troubled history of Berlin's Jewish community between 1244 and 2000 and is definitely worth getting hold of if you have a passing interest in the subject.

Alexandra Ritchie *Faust's Metropolis*. A thick and thorough general history of the city, beginning with the very first settlers and ending in the 1990s. Ritchie debunks a number of myths about the city – such as its supposed anti-Nazism – but her conservatism too often intrudes on the narrative.

Ronald Taylor *Berlin and Its Culture*. A profusely illustrated survey of the cultural movements and personalities that constituted the artistic life of the city; especially good on Weimar writing and cinematography.

Third Reich

Allied Intelligence Map of Key Buildings. This large, detailed map published by After The Battle is an excellent resource for anyone searching for Nazi and prewar remains in the city.

Anonymous *A Woman in Berlin*. The recent reissue of a remarkable war diary kept by a female journalist who vividly describes the pathetic lot of Berlin's vanquished in the closing days of the war, when looting and gang rape were part of daily life. Like most women in Berlin, the author was raped multiple times by different Russian soldiers, yet her exposure of this led to such an uproar when the book was first published in 1950s Germany – society was unprepared to face its recent trauma – that it wasn't reprinted again during the author's lifetime; she died in 2001.

Antony Beevor *Berlin the Downfall 1945*. It might take until halfway through this thick book to actually get to the fall of Berlin, but once there a fine job is done of synthesizing many sources to provide a riveting account of how the city's defences crumbled and its civilians suffered, with few harrowing details spared. Beevor was congratulated by many female victims of brutal rapes by Soviet troops for at last telling their story as related in *A Woman in Berlin* (see above), which for a long time was ignored as too difficult to face.

Christabel Bielenberg *The Past is Myself*. Bielenberg, the niece of Lord Northcliffe, married German lawyer Peter Bielenberg in 1934 and was living with her family in Berlin at the outbreak of the war. Her autobiography (serialized for TV as *Christabel*) details her struggle to survive the Nazi period and Allied raids on the city, and to save her husband, imprisoned in Ravensbrück as a result of his friendship with members of the Kreisau resistance group.

George Clare *Berlin Days 1946–1947*. "The most harrowing and yet most fascinating place on earth" is how Clare begins this account of his time spent as a British army translator. This is Berlin seen at what the Germans called the *Nullpunkt* – the zero point – when the city, its economy, buildings and society, began to rebuild almost from scratch. Packed with characters and observation, it's a captivating – if at times depressing – read.

D. Fisher and A. Read *The Fall of Berlin*. Superb account of the city's *Götterdämmerung*, carefully researched with a mass of anecdotal material you won't find elsewhere. An essential book for those interested in the period.

Bella Fromm *Blood and Banquets*. Fromm, a Jewish aristocrat living in Berlin, kept a diary from 1930 until 1938. Her job as society reporter for the *Vossische Zeitung* gave her inside knowledge on the top figures of Berlin society, and the diaries are a chilling account of the rise of the Nazis and their persecution of Berlin's Jews.

Tony Le Tissier *The Battle of Berlin*. Soldierly (the author is a retired lieutenant-colonel) shot-by-shot account of Berlin's final days. Authoritative, if a little dry. His *Berlin Then and Now* is a collection of photographs of sites in the city during the war years, contrasted with the same places today. This extraordinary book is the best way to find what's left of Nazi Berlin's buildings – a startling number have barely changed.

Martin Middlebrook *The Berlin Raids*. Superbly researched account of the RAF's campaign to destroy the capital of the Third Reich by mass bombing. Based on interviews with bomber crews, Luftwaffe fighter pilots and civilians who survived the raids – a moving, compassionate and exciting read.

🏃 **William Shirer** *The Rise and Fall of the Third Reich*. Shirer was an American journalist stationed in Berlin during the Nazi period, and his history of the German state before and during the war has long been recognized as a classic. Notwithstanding its length and occasionally outdated perceptions, this book is full of insights and is ideal for dipping into, with the help of its exhaustive index.

Hugh Trevor-Roper *The Last Days of Hitler*. A brilliant reconstruction of the closing chapter of the Third Reich, set in the Bunker of the Reich's Chancellery on Potsdamer Platz. Trevor-Roper subsequently marred his reputation as the doyen of British historians by authenticating the forged Hitler diaries, themselves the subject of several books.

Marie Vassiltchikov *The Berlin Diaries*. Daughter of a Russian émigré family and friend of the Bielenbergs, Vassiltchikov's diaries provide a vivid portrait of wartime Berlin and the July 1944 bomb-plot conspirators – whose members also numbered among her friends.

Peter Wyden *Stella*. Stella Goldschlag was a young, very "Aryan"-looking Jewish woman who avoided deportation and death by working for the SS as a "catcher", hunting down Jews in hiding in wartime Berlin – including her former friends and even relatives. The author, who knew the young Stella, traces her life story and tries to untangle the morality and find some explanation for the motives behind what seem incalculably evil actions. A gripping, terrifying story.

Postwar history and social studies

🏃 **Anna Funder** *Stasiland. True Stories From Behind the Berlin Wall*. Engrossing account of the experiences of those East Germans who found themselves tangled in the web of the State Security Service (Stasi) in the GDR.

🏃 **Timothy Garton Ash** *The File: A Personal History*. Garton Ash lived and worked as a journalist in East Berlin in 1980, making him the subject of surveillance and a Stasi file. In this book he tracks down the file and interviews informers using an informal style to weave everything together and marvellously evoke the era. His book *We the People* (US title: *The Magic Lantern*) is an equally enjoyable first-hand account of the fall of the Wall.

Norman Gelb *The Berlin Wall*. The definitive account of the building of the Wall and its social and political aftermath – as far as 1986. Includes a

wealth of information and anecdotes not to be found elsewhere.

Anne McElvoy *The Saddled Cow*. Thorough and witty analysis of the GDR by Berlin's *Times* correspondent who witnessed the fall of the Wall. The book also draws on the author's time in East Germany before and after the *Wende*: its title is a quote from Stalin, who once said that "Communism fits Germany as a saddle fits a cow".

David E. Murphy, Serfei A. Kondrashev and George Bailey *Battleground Berlin: CIA vs KGB in the Cold War*. A detailed account by participants of the tense, skirmishing in Berlin between the spies of the two superpowers.

Hermann Waldenburg *The Berlin Wall Book*. A collection of photographs of the art and graffiti the Wall inspired, with a rather self-important introduction by the photographer.

Art and architecture

Peter Adam *The Art of the Third Reich*. Engrossing and well-written account of the officially approved state art of Nazi Germany – a subject that for many years was ignored or deliberately made inaccessible. Includes over three hundred illustrations.

🏃 **Karl Baedeker** *Berlin and its Environs*. First published in 1903, the learned old Baedeker is an utterly absorbing read, describing a grand imperial city now long vanished. There's advice on medicinal brine-baths, where to buy "mourning clothes", the location of the Estonian embassy, and beautiful fold-out maps that enable you to trace the former course of long-gone streets. An armchair treat.

Wolf-Dieter Dube *The Expressionists*. A good general introduction to Germany's most distinctive contribution to twentieth-century art.

🏃 **Duane Philips and Alexandra Geyer** *Berlin: A guide to recent architecture*. Ideal little pocket guide for fans of modern architecture, with commentary and photographs of most of Berlin's key buildings – even if the text is occasionally mired by opaque architectural snobbery.

Michael Z. Wise *Capital Dilemma: Germany's Search for a New Architecture of Democracy*. An engaging discussion of the historical, political and architectural considerations in the rebuilding of Berlin.

Guides and travel writing

Stephen Barber *Fragments of the European City*. Written as a series of interlocking poetic fragments, this book explores the visual transformation of the contemporary European city, focusing on Berlin. An exhilarating evocation of the intricacies and ever-changing identity of the city.

🏃 **Heather Reyes, Katy Derbyshire (eds)** *City Lit Series Berlin*. Superb anthology that provides an intellectual tour of Berlin in some hundred pieces written by various historians, journalists and writers; among them Christopher Isherwood, Ian McEwan and David Bowie. Great for a quick sense of the city's historical context, its ongoing cultural and architectural evolution and its counter-cultural vibe.

Uwe Seidel *Berlin & Potsdam*. Illustrated guide to the city that has much detail on what you can't see anymore. Useful if you need more knowledge of the what-stood-where kind.

Ian Walker *Zoo Station*. A personal recollection of time spent in Berlin in the mid-1980s. Perceptive, engaging and well informed, it's the most enjoyable account of pre-*Wende* life in the city.

Fiction

Len Deighton *Winter: A Berlin Family 1899–1945*. This fictional saga traces the fortunes of a Berlin family through World War I, the rise of Nazism and the collapse of the Third Reich: a convincing account of the way in which a typical upper-middle-class family weathered the wars. Better known is *Funeral in Berlin*, a spy-thriller set in the middle of Cold War Berlin and based around the defection of an Eastern chemist, aided by hard-bitten agent Harry Palmer (as the character came to be known in the film starring Michael Caine). *Berlin Game* pits British SIS agent Bernard Samson (whose father appears in *Winter*) against an arch manipulator of the East Berlin secret service, and leaves you hanging for the sequels *Mexico Set* and *London Match*.

Alfred Döblin *Berlin-Alexanderplatz*. A prominent socialist intellectual during the Weimar period, Döblin went into exile shortly after the banning (and burning) of his books in 1933. This is his weightiest and most durable achievement, an unrelenting stream-of-consciousness epic of the city's proletariat.

Theodor Fontane *Effi Briest*. This story of a woman's adultery in the second half of the nineteenth century offers a vivid picture of Prussian mores, with the sort of terrible and absurd climax that's virtually unique to Fontane and to German literature. One of the few classics to come out of Berlin.

Hugo Hamilton *Surrogate City* is a love story between an Irish woman and a Berliner and is strongly evocative of pre-*Wende* Berlin. *The Love Test* is the tale of a journalist researching the history of a woman's involvement with the Stasi and gives a realistic account of 1990s Berlin.

Robert Harris *Fatherland*. A Cold War novel with a difference: Germany has conquered Europe and the Soviet Union, and the Cold War is being fought between the Third Reich and the USA. Against this background, Berlin detective Xavier March is drawn into an intrigue involving murder and Nazi officials. All this owes much to Philip Kerr (see opposite) but Harris's picture of Nazi Berlin in 1964 is chillingly believable.

Lillian Hellman *Pentimento*. The first volume of Hellman's memoirs contains "Julia", supposedly (it was later accused of being heavily fiction-alized) the story of one of her friends caught up in the Berlin resistance. This was later made into a finely acted, if rather thinly emotional, film of the same name.

Christopher Isherwood *Goodbye to Berlin*. Set in the decadent atmosphere of the Weimar Republic as the Nazis steadily gain power, this collection of stories brilliantly evokes the period and brings to life some classic Berlin characters. It subsequently formed the basis of the films *I Am a Camera* and the later remake *Cabaret*. See also Isherwood's *Mr Norris Changes Trains*, the adventures of the overweight eponymous hero in pre-Hitler Berlin and Germany.

Wladimir Kaminer *Russian Disco, Tales of Everyday Lunacy on the Streets of Berlin*. Collection of stories that are snapshots of Berlin through the eyes of a Russian immigrant from Moscow. Unusual, entertaining and well written: Kaminer has since become a local celebrity, DJing *Russendisko* nights at *Kaffee Burger* (see p.225).

Philip Kerr *Berlin Noir: March Violets, The Pale Criminal* and *A German Requiem*. Three great novels on Berlin in one omnibus edition. The first is a well-received detective thriller set in the early years of Nazi Berlin. Keen on period detail – nightclubs, the Olympic Stadium, building sites for the new autobahn – and with a terrific sense of atmosphere, the book rips along to a gripping denouement. Bernie Gunther, its detective hero, also features in the second title – a wartime Berlin crime novel. But the best, *A German Requiem*, has Gunther travelling from ravaged postwar Berlin to run into ex-Nazis in Vienna.

Ian McEwan *The Innocent*. McEwan's novel brilliantly evokes 1950s Berlin as seen through the eyes of a post office worker caught up in early Cold War espionage – and his first sexual encounters. Flounders in its obligatory McEwan nasty final twist, but laden with a superbly researched atmosphere.

Ulrich Plenzdorf *The New Sufferings of Young W.* A satirical reworking of Goethe's *Die Leiden des jungen Werthers* set in 1970s East Berlin. It tells the story of Edgar Wibeau, a young rebel without a cause adrift in the antiseptic GDR, and when first published it pushed against the borders of literary acceptability under the old regime with its portrayal of alienated, disaffected youth.

Holly-Jane Rahlens *Becky Bernstein Goes Berlin*. A young Jewish girl from Queens falls in love with a German, emigrates to Berlin and discovers a new love for the city. A bouncy and funny novel full of New York wit.

Film in Berlin

B
erlin's cinema history goes back to some of the very first tinkerings in the medium. It rapidly became the cornerstone of Germany's film industry, a position consolidated in the 1920s and then throughout the Nazi era, despite the mass exodus of many of the country's key stars and directors. After World War II East Germany quickly made the most of all the equipment that had fallen into their hands in the Soviet-controlled suburbs of Berlin to produce a programme of tightly controlled film-making. Meanwhile, in West Berlin subsidies lured many of Germany's most cutting-edge film-makers there. But it's since the *Wende* that film in the city has really begun to blossom again.

The beginnings: showmen and inventors

Berlin first whirred into cinema history on November 1, 1895 when former fairground showman Max Skladanowsky and his brother Emil put on a show with their home-made film projector – which they called a *Bioskop* – at the city's Wintergarten music hall. It was quickly replaced by better methods and techniques in Paris later that year, but Berlin continued to play a crucial role, with locals like Oskar Messter pioneering and setting standards for many production techniques.

Once established, Germany's early twentieth-century film industry grew steadily, particularly as a result of its relationship with politics and international events. The outbreak of World War I and subsequent boycott of French films stimulated growth, and Berlin consolidated its role in 1917 with the founding of the giant and partially nationalized **Universum Film AG** (UFA) studio – largely intended to imitate the very effective Allied propaganda films.

Boom in Weimar Germany

After the war, movies became a popular form of escapism in the hard times of **Weimar Germany**, with new genres emerging to portray forbidden love, myths, triviality and trashiness. The film industry boomed, churning out vast quantities of celluloid – 600 feature films a year in the 1920s – thanks partly to hyperinflation, which allowed film-makers to borrow money that would vastly devalue before repayment. Even so, studio bankruptcies were common and film budgets relatively tight, which helped prompt the rise of **German Expressionist cinema**. This relied heavily on symbolism and artistic imagery, as evidenced in the era's most famous film, *Das Kabinett des Doktor Caligari* (*The Cabinet of Dr Caligari*; 1920), shot in Berlin using wild, non-realistic and exaggeratedly geometric sets with images painted on floors and walls invoking objects, light and shadow – all complementing the dark, psychological yarn. The era's other great film-making landmark was Fritz Lang's futuristic **Metropolis** (1927), a gigantic project for which UFA was massively expanded and which included 750 extras, becoming Weimar Germany's most expensive film, and a commercial flop. The film's exploration and critique of social power structures and hierarchies was common to much of the overwhelmingly left-wing films made at the time, which the Nazis would quickly quash. The arrival of sound at the very end of the 1920s produced a final artistic flourish for German film before the collapse of the Weimar Republic. **Der Blaue Engel** (*The Blue Angel*; 1930), by Josef von Sternberg, was Germany's first talking film and, shot simultaneously in German and English, made an international star of Marlene Dietrich, a local girl discovered at a Berlin variety show.

Film in Nazi Germany

Marlene Dietrich was one of many performers to leave the country after the Nazi seizure of power in 1933. The uncertain economics and politics of Weimar Germany had already prompted many to leave the country, primarily for the USA, but after 1933 the trickle turned into a flood. Around 1500 directors, producers, actors and other film professionals fled the Third Reich, among them Fritz Lang. All those in exile were either excluded from or rejected the *Reichskulturkammer*, the Nazi cultural organization that excluded Jews and anyone politically questionable and defined who could work in the media, effectively bringing to an end the glory days of German cinema. Nevertheless, even the Nazi period produced a few cinematic masterpieces, particularly by **Leni Riefenstahl**: *Triumph des Willens* (*The Triumph of the Will*; 1935), which documented the 1934 Nuremberg Rally; and *Olympia* (1938), an awe-inspiring tribute to Berlin's 1936 Summer Olympics, both of which obviously remain controversial for propagandizing Nazi ideals.

Evolution in a divided Germany

After the war East Germany was quick to capitalize on the fact that much of Germany's film infrastructure, notably the former UFA studios, lay in the Soviet occupation zone. Film production quickly got off the ground with Soviet encouragement and Berlin's cinemas were reopened in May 1945, within three weeks of German capitulation. However, strict controls limited topics to those directly contributing to the communist state project. A particular strength turned out to be children's films, notably fairytale adaptations such as *Drei Haselnüsse für Aschenbrödel* (*Three Nuts for Cinderella*; 1973), but also genre works such as *Der schweigende Stern* (*The Silent Star*; 1960), an adaptation of a Stanislaw Lem sci-fi novel, or "red westerns" such as *The Sons of the Great Mother Bear* (1966) in which the heroes tended to be Native American.

Meanwhile the West German film industry of the 1950s could no longer measure up to that of France, Italy or Japan. German films were perceived as provincial and only rarely distributed internationally. Cinema attendance began to stagnate and drop in the 1950s, then ever more sharply in the 1960s. One reaction to this and a perceived artistic stagnation, was the 1962 **Oberhausen Manifesto** in which a group of young film-makers proclaimed "Der alte Film ist tot. Wir glauben an den neuen" ("The old cinema is dead. We believe in the new"), rejecting the commercial dictates of the German film industry and resolving to build a new industry based on artistic excellence. Many up-and-coming film-makers allied themselves with this group, among them Volker Schlöndorff, Werner Herzog, Wim Wenders, Hans-Jürgen Syberberg and Rainer Werner Fassbinder. The lure of new subsidies quickly brought many to Berlin, where the movement **New German Cinema** returned the country to international acclaim. The *Tin Drum* (1979), by Schlöndorff, became the first German film to win the Academy Award for Best Foreign Language Film, and *Das Boot* (1981) still holds the record for most Academy Award nominations for a German film (six).

A post-Wende renaissance

But during the 1980s the vitality of the New German Cinema movement ebbed and the country's film industry struggled against a glut of private TV channels, videos and then DVDs. Not until almost ten years after the *Wende* did it really begin to find its feet again. Unlike the more sober and artistic films of the 1970s, this time success has been based on an ability to marry arthouse sensibilities with a more commercial outlook, yet still addressing difficult topics from Germany's history and the country's contemporary issues. **Good Bye Lenin!** (see opposite) was a particularly important landmark in re-launching German cinema abroad, grossing $80m, most of it from overseas.

Appropriately the film was first screened at the city's own internationally recognized **Berlinale film festival**, where it won a coveted Golden Bear award as the best European film of 2003. The festival itself has also become a symbol of the city's cinematic prowess, steadily growing and attracting international talent, critics and filmgoers in increasing numbers.

But it's at ground-level that Berlin's cinema is arguably most vibrant; there are over 260 cinemas – not counting the dozens of venues where a projector is often set up for the occasional screening of avant-garde local works. Many have come from the city's burgeoning underground film scene, which is defined by overwhelmingly serious and social themes. Given their penetrating, realistic studies of relationships and characters, these films don't tend to travel far internationally, but have enjoyed critical success in France, where the term **Nouvelle Vague Allemande** is used for the work of a group of mostly Berlin-based directors, including Christian Petzold, Thomas Arslan, Valeska Grisebach and Christoph Hochhäusler.

A Berlin Filmography

Over the years Berlin has provided the inspiration and set for a great many films, which now repay their debt by being one of the few ways left to glimpse the Berlin that vanished in the mayhem of its twentieth century.

Berlin: Sinfonie einer Grosstadt (*Berlin: Symphony of a Great City*; Walter Ruttmann; 1927). Expressionist silent documentary that magnificently captures a day in the life of 1920s Berlin.

Metropolis (Fritz Lang; 1927). Futuristic classic and masterpiece of film architecture that was both inspired by and filmed in Berlin.

Mutter Krausens Fahrt ins Glück (*Mother Krause's Journey to Happiness*; Phil Jutzi; 1929) A film version of the working-class Berlin that Heinrich Zille (see p.77) portrayed and caricatured. Set in Wedding where most of the actors came from.

Berlin Alexanderplatz (Phil Jutzi; 1931). Epic portrayal – all 931 minutes of it – of 1920s Berlin, based on the Alfred Döblin novel.

M (Fritz Lang; 1931). Berlin thriller that pioneered film noir.

Olympia (Leni Riefenstahl; 1938). Olympic majesty as never captured

on film before or since, based on literally hundreds of kilometres of footage taken during the 1936 Berlin Olympics.

The Big Lift (George Seaton; 1950). Dramatized version of the Berlin Air Lift, starring Montgomery Clift.

Funeral in Berlin (Guy Hamilton; 1966). Spy film in which Michael Caine stars as a British agent sent to Berlin.

Cabaret (Bob Fosse; 1972). Weimar Berlin as glimpsed through the eyes of the Kit Kat Klub and Christopher Isherwood, then reinterpreted by Bob Fosse.

Die Legende von Paul und Paula (*The Legend of Paul and Paula*; Heiner Carow; 1973). Love story set in East Berlin and filmed in Marzahn. Good for dose of genuine *Ostalgie*.

Christiane F. – Wir Kinder vom Bahnhof Zoo (*We Children from Bahnhof Zoo* (US); *Zoo* (UK); Uli Edel; 1981). Gritty and dark film about heroin addiction in the underbelly of 1970s West Berlin. Disturbing and pulls no punches.

Berlin Tunnel 21 (Richard Michaels; 1981). Reasonable made-for-TV-movie about a former American officer who leads an attempt to build a tunnel underneath the Wall in 1961; not bad at providing a feel of early-1960s Berlin.

Taxi zum Klo (Frank Ripploh; 1981). Groundbreaking film documenting gay culture in West Berlin directed by the lead, who possibly plays himself: an oversexed shaggy-haired teacher who has an interest in film-making.

Octopussy (John Glen; 1983). Probably Roger Moore's best outing as James Bond – who arrives in Berlin to investigate 009's death.

Der Himmel über Berlin (*Wings of Desire*; Wim Wenders; 1987). Iconic classic – which infected the imaginations of countless film-makers – about love in a divided city, where angels swoop in on postwar and more modern-day Berlin.

Linie 1 (Reinhard Hauff; 1988). Musical based on a girl from the country arriving in the big city, meeting various oddball and low-life characters and travelling extensively up and down U-Bahn Line 1: based on a play created by the GRIPS theatre (see p.259).

Lola Rennt (*Run Lola Run*; Tom Tykwer; 1998). Fast-paced film set to a pounding techno soundtrack and speckled with wry examples of Berlin humour and urban living.

Sonnenallee (Leander Haussmann; 1999). Well-received teen comedy set in 1970s East Berlin, and one of the earliest examples of *Ostalgie*.

Berlin Babylon (Hubertus Siegert; 2001). Fascinating documentary film on the rebuilding projects after the fall of the Wall, based on four years of footage.

Invincible (Werner Herzog; 2001). True story of a Jewish strongman in Weimar Berlin who becomes convinced he's been chosen by God to warn his people of imminent danger.

Berlin is in Germany (Hannes Stöhr; 2001). A look back at the GDR era through the eyes of a convict released after the *Wende* and struggling to come to terms with the new Germany he faces.

Was Tun, Wenn's Brennt? (Gregor Schnitzler; 2002). A tale of anarchists squatting in 1980s Berlin, going their separate ways and then being reunited a dozen years later when charged with a crime. Neat insights into the time and Berlin's grittier aspects.

Good Bye Lenin! (Wolfgang Becker; 2003). Arguably the finest *Ostalgie* film with dozens of humorous moments, yet also with a melancholic look at the *Wende* and its influence on daily lives.

Der Untergang (*Downfall*; Oliver Hirschbiegel; 2004). Much-debated film portraying the last days of Hitler (played by Bruno Ganz) in his bunker, it also believably depicts scenes from the Battle of Berlin.

Die Fetten Jahre sind vorbei (*The Edukators*; Hans Weingartner; 2004). *Good Bye Lenin's* Daniel Brühl plays one of three activists who kidnap a businessman in one of Berlin's affluent suburbs. The film at times takes itself a bit too seriously but delivers some fun snatches of life in contemporary Berlin, as well as a plot with several interesting twists.

Gestpenster (*Ghosts*; Christian Petzold; 2005). Modern urban alienation in Mitte, focusing on the life of a late-teenage orphan with mental problems.

Das Leben der Anderen (*The Lives of Others*; Florian Henckel von Donnersmarck; 2005). Highly evocative Stasi drama set in an East Berlin that's riddled by agents, informers and bugging devices. The film's international success made it a potent way of telling the world about Stasi crimes.

Ich bin ein Berliner (Franziska Meyer Price; 2005) Fluffy but watchable comedy by one of Germany's foremost female directors.

Valkyrie (Bryan Singer; 2008) American dramatization of the July Bomb Plot (see p.106) in which Tom Cruise stars as Klaus Schenk von Stauffenberg.

Language

Language

German

German is not a language you can hope to master in a short time. As English was a compulsory subject in West Berlin's school curriculum, most Germans who have grown up in the West since the war have some familiarity with it, which eases communication a great deal. In the East, Russian was the language most often taught, but since the *Wende* everyone in the school system has been learning English from an increasingly early age. The subject is now a common part of Kindergarten education and certainly anyone under the age of thirty can be expected to have a reasonable grasp of English.

But wherever you are, a smattering of German will help. Of the many teach-yourself courses available, best is the BBC course, Deutsch Direkt. For the most useful travelling companion, look no further than the *Rough Guide to German*, a practical and easy-to-use **dictionary/phrasebook**.

Pronunciation

English speakers find the complexities of German grammar hard to handle, but pronunciation isn't as daunting as it might first appear. Individual syllables are generally pronounced as they're printed – the trick is learning how to place the stresses in the notoriously lengthy German words.

Vowels and umlauts

a as in **father**, but can also be used as in **hut**

e as in **day**

i as in **leek**

o as in **bottom**

u as in **boot**

ä is a combination of a and e, sometimes pronounced like **e** in b**e**t (eg L**ä**nder) and sometimes like **ai** in p**ai**d (eg sp**ä**t)

ö is a combination of o and e, like the French *eu*

ü is a combination of u and e, like t**rue**

Vowel combinations

ai as in **lie**

au as in **house**

ie as in **free**

ei as in **trial**

eu as in **oil**

Consonants

Consonants are pronounced as they are written, with no silent letters. The differences from English are:

j is pronounced similar to an English y

r is given a dry throaty sound, similar to French

s is pronounced similar to, but slightly softer than, an English z

v is somewhere between f and v

w is pronounced the same way as English v

z is pronounced ts

The German letter ß, the Scharfes S, occasionally replaces ss in a word: pronunciation is identical.

Gender

German words can be one of three genders: masculine, feminine or neuter. Each has its own ending and corresponding ending for attached adjectives. If you don't know any German grammar, it's safest to use either neuter or male forms.

Words and phrases

Basics

Yes, No	Ja, Nein	This one	Dieses
Please/You're welcome	Bitte	That one	Jenes
		Large, Small	Gross, Klein
A more polite form of Bitte	Bitte schön	More, Less	Mehr, Weniger
		A little	Wenig
Thank you, Thank you very much	Danke, Danke schön	A lot	Viel
		Cheap, Expensive	Billig, Teuer
Where, When, Why?	Wo, Wann, Warum?	Good, Bad	Gut, Schlecht
How much?	Wieviel?	Hot, Cold	Heiss, Kalt
Here, There	Hier, Da	With, Without	Mit, Ohne
Now, Later	Jetzt, Später	Where is...?	Wo ist...?
All mean "open"	Geöffnet, offen, auf	How do I get to (a town)?	Wie komme ich nach...?
Both mean "closed"	Geschlossen, zu		
Earlier	Früher	How do I get to (a building, place)?	Wie komme ich zur/ zumo...?
Over there	Da drüben		

Greetings and times

Goodbye (telephone only)	Auf Wiederhören	The day before yesterday	Vorgestern
Goodbye (informal)	Tschüs	The day after tomorrow	Übermorgen
Good morning	Guten Morgen		
Good evening	Guten Abend	Day	Tag
Good day	Guten Tag	Night	Nacht
How are you? (polite)	Wie geht es Ihnen?	Week	Woche
		Month	Monat
How are you? (informal)	Wie geht es dir?	Year	Jahr
		Weekend	Wochenende
Leave me alone	Lass mich in Ruhe	In the morning	Am Vormittag/ Vormittags
Get lost	Hau ab		
Go away	Geh weg	In the afternoon	Am Nachmittag/ Nachmittags
Today	Heute		
Yesterday	Gestern	In the evening	Am Abend
Tomorrow	Morgen		

Days, months and dates

Monday	Montag	September	September
Tuesday	Dienstag	October	Oktober
Wednesday	Mittwoch	November	November
Thursday	Donnerstag	December	Dezember
Friday	Freitag	Spring	Frühling
Saturday	Samstag/Sonnabend	Summer	Sommer
Sunday	Sonntag	Autumn	Herbst
January	Januar	Winter	Winter
February	Februar	Holidays	Ferien
March	März	Bank holiday	Feiertag
April	April	Monday, the first of May	Montag, der erste Mai
May	Mai		
June	Juni	the second of April	Der zweite April
July	Juli	the third of April	Der dritte April
August	August		

Some signs

Women's toilets	Damen/Frauen	Diversion	Umleitung
Men's toilets	Herren/Männer	Attention!	Vorsicht!
Entrance	Eingang	Speed limit	Geschwindig-keitsbegrenzung
Exit	Ausgang		
Emergency exit	Notausgang	Hospital	Krankenhaus
Arrival	Ankunft	Police	Polizei
Departure	Abfahrt	No smoking	Nicht rauchen
Exhibition	Ausstellung	No entrance	Kein Eingang
Motorway	Autobahn	Prohibited	Verboten
Motorway entrance	Auffahrt	Building works	Baustelle
Motorway exit	Ausfahrt	Traffic light	Ampel

Numbers

1	eins	16	sechszehn
2	zwei	17	siebzehn
3	drei	18	achtzehn
4	vier	19	neunzehn
5	fünf	20	zwanzig
6	sechs	21	ein-und-zwanzig
7	sieben	22	zwei-und-zwanzig
8	acht	30	dreissig
9	neun	40	vierzig
10	zehn	50	fünfzig
11	elf	60	sechzig
12	zwölf	70	siebzig
13	dreizehn	80	achtzig
14	vierzehn	90	neunzig
15	fünfzehn	100	hundert

Questions and requests

All enquiries should be prefaced with the phrase *Entschuldigen Sie bitte* (excuse me, please). Note that *Sie* is the polite form of address to be used with everyone except close friends, though young people often don't bother with it. The older generation will certainly be offended if you address them with the familiar *Du*, as will all officials.

Do you speak English?	Sprechen Sie Englisch?	Separately or together?	Getrennt oder Zusammen?
I don't speak German	Ich spreche kein Deutsch	The menu, please	Die Speisekarte, bitte
Please speak more slowly	Könnten Sie bitte langsamer sprechen	Hello! (to get attention of waiter/waitress)	Hallo!
I don't understand	Ich verstehe nicht	Have you got something cheaper?	Haben Sie etwas billigeres?
I understand	Ich verstehe		
How do you say that in German?	Wie sagt mann das auf Deutsch?	Is there a room available?	Haben Sie noch ein Zimmer frei?
Can you tell me where...is?	Können Sie mir bitte sagen wo...ist?	Where are the toilets?	Wo sind die Toiletten, bitte?
How much does that cost?	Wieviel kostet das?	I'd like that one	Ich hätte gern dieses
When does the next train leave?	Wann fährt der nächste Zug?	I'd like a room for two	Ich hätte gern ein Zimmer für zwei
At what time?	Um wieviel Uhr?	I'd like a single room	Ich hätte gern ein Einzelzimmer
What time is it?	Wieviel Uhr ist es?		
Are these seats taken?	Sind die Plätze noch frei?	Does it have a shower, bath, toilet...?	Hat das Zimmer eine Dusche, ein Bad, eine Toilette ... ?
The bill, please	Die Rechnung, bitte		

Food and drink terms

Basics

Frühstück	breakfast	Brötchen	bread roll
Mittagessen	lunch	Butter	butter
Abendessen	supper, dinner	Butterbrot	sandwich
Messer	knife	Belegtes Brot	open sandwich
Gabel	fork	Marmelade	jam
Löffel	spoon	Honig	honey
Speisekarte	menu	Käse	cheese
Teller	plate	Fleisch	meat
Tasse	cup	Fisch	fish
Glas	glass	Ei	egg
Vorspeise	starter	Gemüse	vegetables
Hauptgericht	main course	Obst	fruit
Nachspeise	dessert	Joghurt	yoghurt
Brot	bread	Sahne	cream

Zucker	sugar
Pfeffer	pepper
Salz	salt
Öl	oil
Essig	vinegar
Senf	mustard

Sosse	sauce
Reis	rice
Spätzle	shredded pasta
Maultaschen	form of ravioli
Rechnung	bill
Trinkgeld	tip

Soups and starters

Bohnensuppe	bean soup
Erbsensuppe	pea soup
Flädlesuppe, Pfannkuchensuppe	clear soup with pancake strips
Fleischsalat	sausage and onion salad
Fleischsuppe	clear soup with meat dumplings
Grüner Salat	mixed green salad
Gulaschsuppe	thick soup in imitation of goulash
Gurkensalat	cucumber salad
Hühnersuppe	chicken soup

Lachsbrot	smoked salmon on bread
Leberknödelsuppe	clear soup with liver dumplings
Leberpastete	liver pâté
Linsensuppe	lentil soup
Melone mit Schinken	melon and ham
Ochsen Schwanzsuppe	oxtail soup
Schnittlauchbrot	chives on bread
Sülze	jellied meatloaf
Suppe	soup
Zwiebelsuppe	onion soup

Meat and poultry

Aufschnitt	slices of cold sausage
Bockwurst	chunky boiled sausage
Bratwurst	grilled sausage
Broiler	chicken
Currywurst	sausage served with piquant sauce
Eisbein	pigs' trotters
Ente	duck
Fasan	pheasant
Frikadelle	meatballs
Froschschenkel	frogs' legs
Gans	goose
Geschnetzeltes	shredded meat, usually served with rice
Gyros	kebab
Hackbraten	mincemeat roast
Hackfleisch	mincemeat
Hammelfleisch	mutton
Hase	hare
Herz	heart
Hirn	brains
Hirsch, Reh	venison
Huhn, Hähnchen	chicken

Innereien	innards
Jägerschnitzel	cutlet in wine and mushroom sauce
Kaninchen	rabbit
Kassler Rippen	smoked and pickled pork chops
Kotelett	cutlet (cheapest cut)
Krautwickerl	cabbage leaves filled with mincemeat
Lamm	lamb
Leber	liver
Leberkäse	baked meatloaf
Lunge	lungs
Nieren	kidneys
Ochsenschwanz	oxtail
Rahmschnitzel	cutlet in cream sauce
Rindfleisch	beef
Sauerbraten	braised pickled beef
Saure Lunge	pickled lungs
Schaschlik	diced meat with piquant sauce
Schinken	ham
Schnecke	snail

Schnitzel Natur	uncoated cutlet	Wienerwurst	boiled pork sausage
Schweinebraten	roast pork	Wild	wild game
Schweinefleisch	pork	Wildschwein	wild boar
Speck	bacon	Wurst	sausage
Truthahn	turkey	Zigeunerschnitzel	cutlet in paprika
Wiener Schnitzel	thin cutlet in		sauce
	breadcumbs	Zunge	tongue

Fish

Aal	eel	Muscheln	mussels
Forelle	trout	Rotbarsch	rosefish
Hecht	pike	Sardinen	sardines
Hering, Matjes	herring	Scampi	scampi
Hummer	lobster	Schellfisch	haddock
Kabeljau	cod	Scholle	plaice
Karpfen	carp	Schwertfisch	swordfish
Kaviar	caviar	Seezunge	sole
Krabben	crab	Thunfisch	tuna
Lachs	salmon	Tintenfisch	squid
Makrele	mackerel	Zander	pike-perch

Vegetables

Blumenkohl	cauliflower	Paprika	green or red peppers
Bohnen	beans	Pellkartoffeln	jacket potatoes
Bratkartoffeln	fried potatoes	Pilze	mushrooms
Champignons	button mushrooms	Pommes frites	chips/French fries
Erbsen	peas	Reibekuchen	potato cake
Grüne Bohnen	green beans	Rosenkohl	Brussels sprouts
Gurke	cucumber	Rote Rübe	beetroot
Karotten, Möhren	carrots	Rotkohl	red cabbage
Kartoffelbrei	mashed potatoes	Rübe	turnip
Kartoffelpuree	creamed potatoes	Salat	salad
Kartoffelsalat	potato salad	Salzkartoffeln	boiled potatoes
Knoblauch	garlic	Sauerkraut	pickled cabbage
Knödel, Kloss	potato dumpling	Spargel	asparagus
Kopfsalat	lettuce	Tomaten	tomatoes
Lauch	leeks	Weisskohl	white cabbage
Maiskolben	corn on the cob	Zwiebeln	onions

Fruit

Ananas	pineapple	Brombeeren	blackberries
Apfel	apple	Datteln	dates
Aprikose	apricot	Erdbeeren	strawberries
Banane	banana	Feigen	figs
Birne	pear	Himbeeren	raspberries

Johannisbeeren	redcurrants		Pampelmuse	grapefruit
Kirschen	cherries		Pfirsich	peach
Kompott	stewed fruit or fruit mousse		Pflaumen	plums
			Rosinen	raisins
Mandarine	tangerine		Schwarze Johannis beeren	blackcurrants
Melone	melon			
Obstsalat	fruit salad		Trauben	grapes
Orange	orange		Zitrone	lemon

Cheeses and desserts

Apfelstrudel mit Sahne	apple strudel with fresh cream		Käseplatte	cheese board
Berliner	jam doughnut		Keks	biscuit
Dampfnudeln	large yeast dumplings served hot with vanilla sauce		Nüsse	nuts
			Nusskuchen	nut cake
			Obstkuchen	fruitcake
Eis	ice cream		Pfannkuchen	doughnut
Emmentaler	Swiss Emmental		Schafskäse	sheep's cheese
Gebäck	pastries		Schokolade	chocolate
Kaiserschmarrn	shredded pancake served with powdered sugar, jam & raisins		Schwarzwälder Kirschtorte	Black Forest gateau
			Torte	gateau, tart
			Weichkäse	cream cheese
Käsekuchen	cheesecake		Ziegenkäse	goat's cheese

Common terms

art	in the style of		gut bürgerliche	traditional German
blau	rare		hausgemacht	home-made
eingelegte	pickled		heiss	hot
frisch	fresh		kalt	cold
gebacken	baked		Küche	cooking
gebraten	fried, roasted		spiess	skewered
gedämpft	steamed		Topf, Eintopf	stew, casserole
gefüllt	stuffed		vom heissen Stein	raw meats you cook yourself on a red-hot stone
gegrillt	grilled			
gekocht	cooked			
geräuchert	smoked			

Glossaries

Art and architecture

Art Deco Geometrical style of art and architecture prevalent in the 1930s.

Art Nouveau Sinuous, highly stylized form of architecture and interior design; in Germany, mostly dates from the period 1900–15, and is known as Jugendstil.

Baroque Expansive, exuberant architectural style of the seventeenth and early eighteenth centuries, characterized by ornate decoration, complex spatial arrangements and grand vistas. The term is also applied to the sumptuous style of painting from the same period.

Bauhaus Plain, functional style of architecture and design, originating in early twentieth-century Germany.

Expressionism Emotional style of painting, concentrating on line and colour, extensively practised in early twentieth-century Germany; the term is also used for related architecture of the same period.

Gothic Architectural style with an emphasis on verticality, characterized by the pointed arch, ribbed vault and flying buttress, introduced to Germany around 1235 and surviving in an increasingly decorative form until well into the sixteenth century. The term is also used for paintings of this period.

Neoclassical Late eighteenth- and early nineteenth-century style of art and architecture, returning to classical models as a reaction against Baroque and Rococo excesses.

Renaissance Italian-originated movement in art and architecture, inspired by the rediscovery of classical ideals.

Rococo Highly florid, light and graceful eighteenth-century style of architecture, painting and interior design, forming the last phase of Baroque.

Romanesque Solid architectural style of the late tenth to mid-thirteenth centuries, characterized by round-headed arches and a penchant for horizontality and geometrical precision. The term is also used for paintings of this period.

Romanticism Late eighteenth- and nineteenth-century movement, particularly strong in Germany, rooted in adulation of the natural world and rediscovery of the achievements of the Middle Ages.

German terms

Altstadt Old part of a city.

Auskunft Information.

Ausländer Literally "foreigner", the word has come to be a pejorative term for any non-white non-German.

Ausstellung Exhibition.

Bäckerei Bakery.

Bahnhof Station.

Bau Building.

Berg Mountain or hill.

Berliner Schnauze Sharp and coarse Berlin wit.

Bezirk City district.

Brücke Bridge.

Burg Mountain or hill.

Bushaltestelle Bus stop.

Denkmal Memorial.

Dom Cathedral.

Dorf Village.

Einbahnstrasse One-way street.

Elector (Kurfürst) Sacred or secular prince with a vote in the elections to choose the Holy Roman Emperor. There were seven for most of the medieval period, with three more added later.

Feiertag Holiday.

Flughafen Airport.

Fluss River.

Fremdenzimmer Room for short-term let.

Gasse Alley.

Gastarbeiter "Guest worker": anyone who comes to Germany to do menial work.

Gasthaus, Gasthof Guesthouse, inn.

Gaststätte Traditional bar that also serves food.

Gemälde Painting.

Grünen, die Green political party.

Haupteingang Main entrance.

Hof Court, courtyard, mansion.

Insel Island.

Jugendherberge Youth hostel.

Jugendstil German version of Art Nouveau.

Junker Prussian landowning class.

Kaiser Emperor.

Kammer Room, chamber.

Kapelle Chapel.

Kaufhaus Department store.

Kino Cinema.

Kirche Church.

Kneipe Bar.

Konditorei Cake shop.

Krankenhaus Hospital.

Kunst Art.

Markt Market, market square.

Motorrad Motorbike.

Not Emergency.

Platz Square.

Quittung Official receipt.

Rathaus Town hall.

Reich Empire.

Reisebüro Travel agency.

Rundgang Way round.

Sammlung Collection.

Schickie Abbreviation of "Schicki-Micki": yuppie.

Schloss Castle, palace (equivalent of French *château*).

See Lake.

Staatssicherheitsdienst (STASI) The former "State Security Service" or secret police of the GDR.

Stadt Town, city.

Stammtisch Table in a pub or restaurant reserved for regular customers.

Stasi Slang term for the Staatssicherheitsdienst.

Stiftung Foundation.

Strand Beach.

Strassenbahn Tram.

Tankstelle Petrol station.

Tor Gate, gateway.

Trabi Conversational shorthand for the now famous Trabant, East Germany's two-cylinder, two-stroke people's car.

Turm Tower.

U-Bahn Network of underground trains.

Verkehrsamt, Verkehrsverein Tourist office.

Viertel Quarter, district.

Volk People, folk; given mystical associations by Hitler.

Vopo Slang for Volkspolizei, a member of the East German police force.

Wald Forest.

Weimar Republic Parliamentary democracy, established in 1918, which collapsed with Hitler's assumption of power in 1933.

Wende Literally, "turning point" – the term used to describe the events of November 1989 and after.

Zeitschrift Magazine.

Zeitung Newspaper.

Zeughaus Arsenal.

Zimmer Room.

Acronyms

BRD (Bundesrepublik Deutschlands) official name of former West Germany.

CDU (Christlich Demokratische Union) Christian Democratic (Conservative) Party.

DDR (Deutsche Demokratische Republik) official name of former East Germany.

GDR (German Democratic Republic) English equivalent of DDR.

NSDAP (National SozialistiSche Deutsche Abrbeiterparte) "National Socialist German Workers' Party", the official name for the Nazis.

SED (Sozialistische Einheitspartei Deutschlands) "Socialist Unity Party of Germany", the official name of the East German communist party before December 1989.

SPD (Sozialdemokratische Partei Deutschlands) Social Democratic (Labour) Party.

Small print and

Index

A Rough Guide to Rough Guides

Published in 1982, the first Rough Guide – to Greece – was a student scheme that became a publishing phenomenon. Mark Ellingham, a recent graduate in English from Bristol University, had been travelling in Greece the previous summer and couldn't find the right guidebook. With a small group of friends he wrote his own guide, combining a highly contemporary, journalistic style with a thoroughly practical approach to travellers' needs.

The immediate success of the book spawned a series that rapidly covered dozens of destinations. And, in addition to impecunious backpackers, Rough Guides soon acquired a much broader and older readership that relished the guides' wit and inquisitiveness as much as their enthusiastic, critical approach and value-for-money ethos.

These days, Rough Guides include recommendations from shoestring to luxury and cover more than 200 destinations around the globe, including almost every country in the Americas and Europe, more than half of Africa and most of Asia and Australasia. Our ever-growing team of authors and photographers is spread all over the world, particularly in Europe, the US and Australia.

In the early 1990s, Rough Guides branched out of travel, with the publication of Rough Guides to World Music, Classical Music and the Internet. All three have become benchmark titles in their fields, spearheading the publication of a wide range of books under the Rough Guide name.

Including the travel series, Rough Guides now number more than 350 titles, covering: phrasebooks, waterproof maps, music guides from Opera to Heavy Metal, reference works as diverse as Conspiracy Theories and Shakespeare, and popular culture books from iPods to Poker. Rough Guides also produce a series of more than 120 World Music CDs in partnership with World Music Network.

Visit www.roughguides.com to see our latest publications.

Rough Guide credits

Text editor: Lucy White
Layout: Anita Singh
Cartography: Jasbir Sandhu
Picture editor: Nicole Newman
Production: Rebecca Short
Proofreader: Anita Sach
Cover design: Nicole Newman, Daniel May, Chloë Roberts
Photographer: Roger d'Olivere Mapp, Diana Jarvis
Editorial: **London** Andy Turner, Keith Drew, Edward Aves, Alice Park, Jo Kirby, James Smart, Natasha Foges, Róisín Cameron, James Rice, Lara Kavanagh, Emma Beatson, Emma Gibbs, Kathryn Lane, Monica Woods, Mani Ramaswamy, Harry Wilson, Lucy Cowie, Alison Roberts, Eleanor Aldridge, Ian Blenkinsop, Joe Staines, Matthew Milton, Tracy Hopkins; **Delhi** Madhavi Singh, Jalpreen Kaur Chhatwal
Design & Pictures: **London** Scott Stickland, Dan May, Diana Jarvis, Mark Thomas, Sarah Cummins, Emily Taylor; **Delhi** Umesh Aggarwal, Ajay Verma, Jessica Subramanian, Ankur Guha, Pradeep Thapliyal, Sachin Tanwar, Nikhil Agarwal, Sachin Gupta

Production: Liz Cherry, Louise Daly, Erika Pepe
Cartography: **London** Ed Wright, Katie Lloyd-Jones; **Delhi** Rajesh Chhibber, Ashutosh Bharti, Rajesh Mishra, Animesh Pathak, Swati Handoo, Deshpal Dabas, Lokamata Sahu
Online: **London** Faye Hellon, Jeanette Angell, Fergus Day, Justine Bright, Clare Bryson, Aine Fearon, Adrian Low, Ezgi Celebi; **Delhi** Amit Verma, Rahul Kumar, Narender Kumar, Ravi Yadav, Debojit Borah, Rakesh Kumar, Ganesh Sharma, Shisir Basumatari
Marketing & Publicity: **London** Liz Statham, Jess Carter, Vivienne Watton, Anna Paynton, Rachel Sprackett, Laura Vipond;
New York Katy Ball; **Delhi** Aman Arora
Digital Travel Publisher: Peter Buckley
Reference Director: Andrew Lockett
Operations Assistant: Becky Doyle
Operations Manager: Helen Atkinson
Publishing Director (Travel): Clare Currie
Commercial Manager: Gino Magnotta
Managing Director: John Duhigg

Publishing information

This ninth edition published January 2011 by
Rough Guides Ltd,
80 Strand, London WC2R 0RL
11, Community Centre, Panchsheel Park, New Delhi 110017, India

Distributed by the Penguin Group

Penguin Books Ltd,
80 Strand, London WC2R 0RL

Penguin Group (USA)
375 Hudson Street, NY 10014, USA

Penguin Group (Australia)
250 Camberwell Road, Camberwell, Victoria 3124, Australia

Penguin Group (NZ)
67 Apollo Drive, Mairangi Bay, Auckland 1310, New Zealand

This paperback edition published in Canada in 2010. Rough Guides is represented in Canada by Tourmaline Editions Inc. 662 King Street West, Suite 304, Toronto, Ontario M5V 1M7

Cover concept by Peter Dyer.

Typeset in Bembo and Helvetica to an original design by Henry Iles.

Printed in Singapore
© John Gawthrop, Christian Williams and Rough Guides 2011
Maps © Rough Guides

Help us update

We've gone to a lot of effort to ensure that the ninth edition of **The Rough Guide to Berlin** is accurate and up-to-date. However, things change – places get "discovered", opening hours are notoriously fickle, restaurants and rooms raise prices or lower standards. If you feel we've got it wrong or left something out, we'd like to know, and if you can remember the address, the price, the hours, the phone number, so much the better.

Please send your comments with the subject line "**Rough Guide Berlin Update**" to ©mail @roughguides.com. We'll credit all contributions and send a copy of the next edition (or any other Rough Guide if you prefer) for the very best emails.

Find more travel information, connect with fellow travellers and book your trip on ®www .roughguides.com

Acknowledgements

Christian Williams wants to extend a big thank you to Neil Nadarajah in Berlin for all his help and his wonderful under-floor heating. At Rough Guides thanks go to all those involved in the book including Jo Kirby and Lucy White, whose editorial cuts were done with admirable energy and enthusiasm.

SMALL PRINT

Readers' letters

Thanks to all the readers who have taken the time to write in with comments and suggestions (and apologies if we've inadvertently omitted or misspelt anyone's name):

Nick Beattie; Veronica M. Brown; J.A. Clifford; T.D. Corlett; Gary Daniels; Dorian; Gustavo Ekelund; David & Helen Grant; John Lindsay; Katherine Lloyd; Linda Mullineux; Gerard Platt; Tony Le Tissier and Susannah Wright.

Photo credits

All photos © Rough Guides except the following:

Architecture colour section
Berlin's Olympic Stadium © Rachel Royse/Corbis

Ostaglie colour section
Ostel Hotel © Courtesy Ostel PR
Sandmaennchen figure sitting in his
Sandmaennchen car © Sean Gallup/Getty
Memorial Berlin Wall, Bernauer Strasse
© Photolibrary

Black and whites
p.153 Jewish cemetery in Berlin-Weinsee
© H. & D. Zielske/Getty
p.184 Sanssouci Castle © Svenja-Foto/Corbis
p.203 Ostel Hotel © Courtesy Ostel PR
p.227 Tresor Club © Courtesy Tresor Club PR

Index

Map entries are in colour.

J

K

L

M

Map symbols

maps are listed in the full index using coloured text

—··—	Provincial boundary	✈	Airport
— — —	Chapter division boundary	ⓘ	Tourist office
▬▬▬	Motorway	⊠	Post office
═══	Major road	🄴	Embassy
───	Minor road	◉	Accommodation
▬▬▬	Pedestrianized road	▣	Restaurant
───	Unpaved road	✡	Synagogue
━━━	Railway	▬	Building
-----	Path	▭	Church
───	River	▭	Market
··········	Wall	⬯	Stadium
≍	Bridge	⊞	Christian cemetery
✦	Place of interest	⬓	Jewish cemetery
⊙	Statue	▨	Park
Ⓤ	U-Bahn station	▨	Beach
Ⓢ	S-Bahn station		

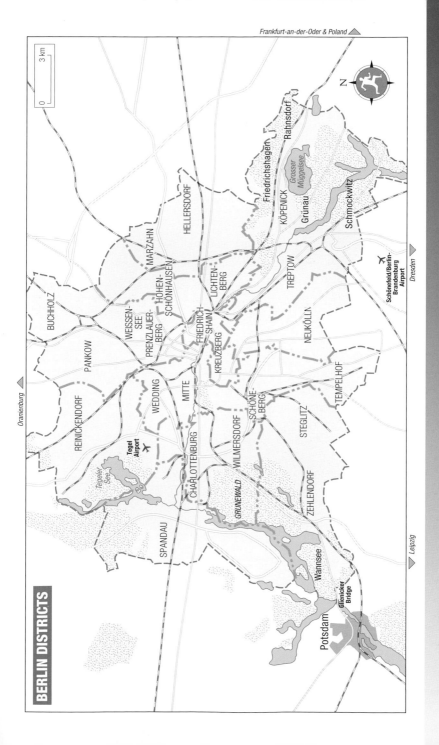

BERLIN DISTRICTS

Frankfurt-an-der-Oder & Poland

Oranienburg

Leipzig

Dresden

REINICKENDORF

PANKOW

BUCHHOLZ

WEISSEN-
SEE

PRENZLAUER-
BERG

HOHEN-
SCHÖNHAUSEN

HELLERSDORF

MARZAHN

LICHTEN-
BERG

FRIEDRICH-
SHAIN

KREUZBERG

NEUKÖLLN

TREPTOW

KÖPENICK

Grünau

Friedrichshagen

Rahnsdorf

Grosser
Müggelsee

Schmockwitz

TEMPELHOF

STEGLITZ

SCHÖNE-
BERG

WILMERSDORF

MITTE

WEDDING

CHARLOTTENBURG

GRUNEWALD

ZEHLENDORF

SPANDAU

Tegeler
See

Tegel
Airport

Wannsee

Potsdam

Glienicker
Bridge

Schönefeld/Berlin-
Brandenburg
Airport

0   3 km

N

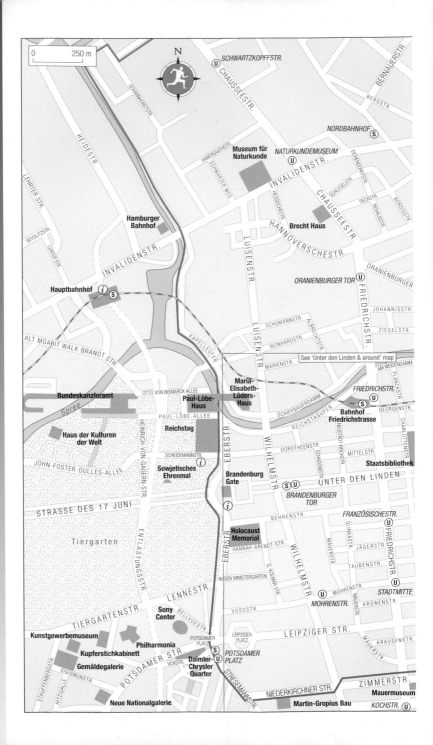

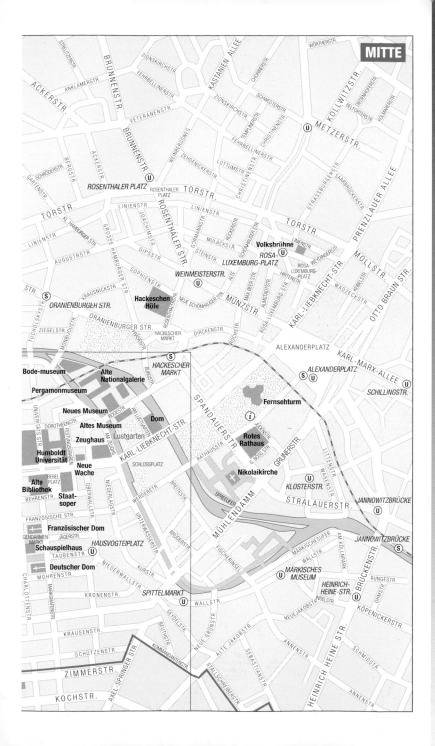

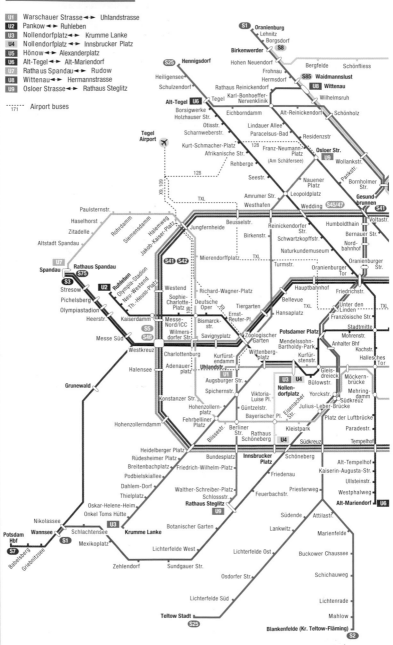

THE U- AND S-BAHN

U1	Warschauer Strasse ◄ ► Uhlandstrasse
U2	Pankow ◄ ► Ruhleben
U3	Nollendorfplatz ◄ ► Krumme Lanke
U4	Nollendorfplatz ◄ ► Innsbrucker Platz
U5	Hönow ◄ ► Alexanderplatz
U6	Alt-Tegel ◄ ► Alt-Mariendorf
U7	Rathaus Spandau ◄ ► Rudow
U8	Wittenau ◄ ► Hermannstrasse
U9	Osloer Strasse ◄ ► Rathaus Steglitz

171 ······· Airport buses

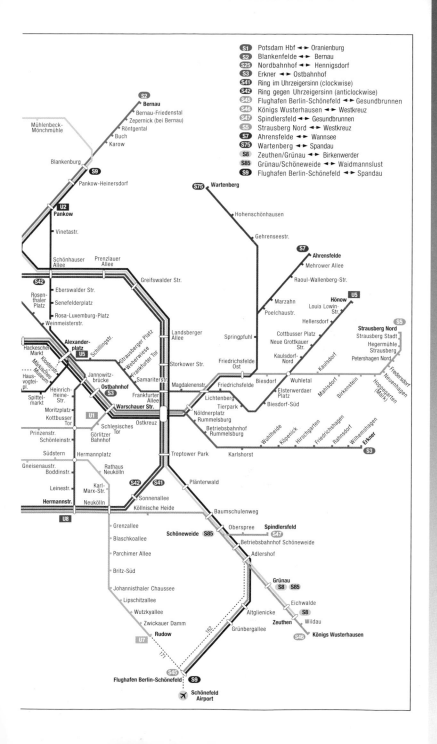

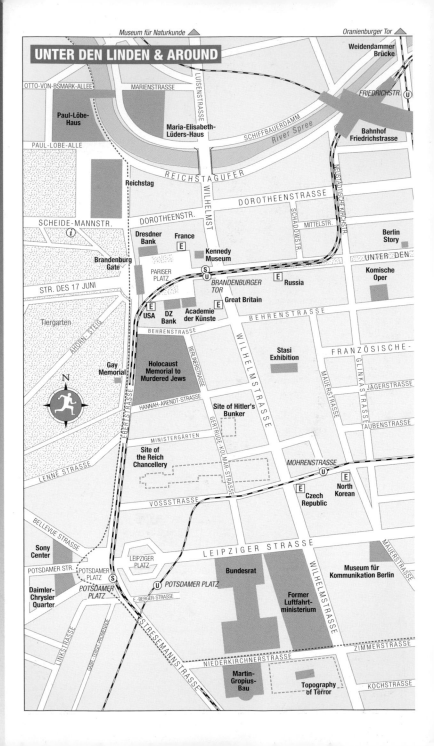

UNTER DEN LINDEN & AROUND

Weidendammer
Brücke

OTTO-VON-BSMARK-ALLEE   MARIENSTRASSE   LUISENSTRASSE   FRIEDRICHSTR. Ⓤ

Paul-Löbe-
Haus

Maria-Elisabeth-
Lüders-Haus

SCHIFFBAUERDAMM   River Spree

Bahnhof
Friedrichstrasse

PAUL-LOBE-ALLE

REICHSTAGUFER

Reichstag

WILHELMST.

DOROTHEENSTRASSE

SCHEIDE-MANNSTR.

DOROTHEENSTR.

SCHADOWSTR.

MITTELSTR.

Ⓘ

Berlin
Story

Dresdner
Bank

France
Ⓔ

Kennedy
Museum

Brandenburg
Gate

PARISER
PLATZ

Ⓢ

UNTER DEN

STR. DES 17 JUNI

BRANDENBURGER
TOR

Ⓔ

Russia

Komische
Oper

Tiergarten

Ⓔ
USA

DZ
Bank

Academie
der Künste

Ⓔ

Great Britain

BEHRENSTRASSE

FRANZÖSISCHE-

BEHRENSTRASSE

N

Gay
Memorial

Holocaust
Memorial to
Murdered Jews

BERLINERSTRASSE

WILHELMSTRASSE

Stasi
Exhibition

MAUERSTRASSE

GLINKASTRASSE

JÄGERSTRASSE

HANNAH-ARENDT-STRASSE

TAUBENSTRASSE

MINISTERGÄRTEN

Site of Hitler's
Bunker

GERTRUDE-KOLMAR-STRASSE

Site of
the Reich
Chancellery

MOHRENSTRASSE Ⓤ

Ⓔ
North
Korean

LENNÉ STRASSE

VOSSSTRASSE

Ⓔ
Czech
Republic

BELLEVUE STRASSE

LEIPZIGER STRASSE

Sony
Center

LEIPZIGER
PLATZ

Bundesrat

MAUERSTRASSE

Museum für
Kommunikation Berlin

POTSDAMER STR.   POTSDAMER
PLATZ Ⓢ

Ⓤ POTSDAMER PLATZ

Daimler-
Chrysler
Quarter

POTSDAMER
PLATZ

E.-BERGER-STRASSE

Former
Luftfahrt-
ministerium

WILHELMSTRASSE

ZIMMERSTRASSE

LINKSSTRASSE

STRESEMANNSTRASSE

NIEDERKIRCHNERSTRASSE

Martin-
Gropius-
Bau

Topography
of Terror

KOCHSTRASSE

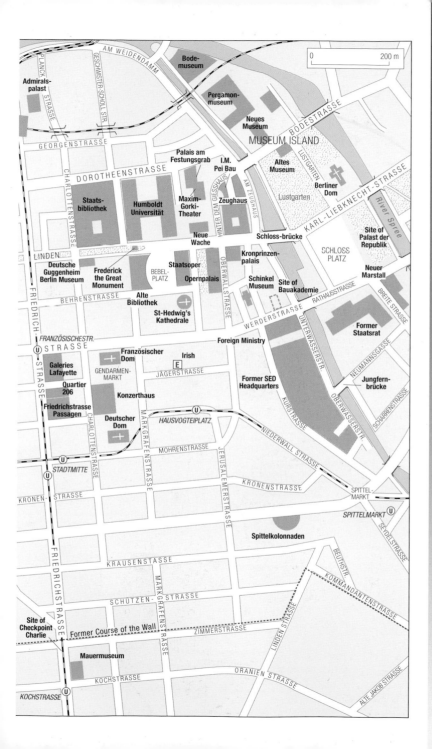

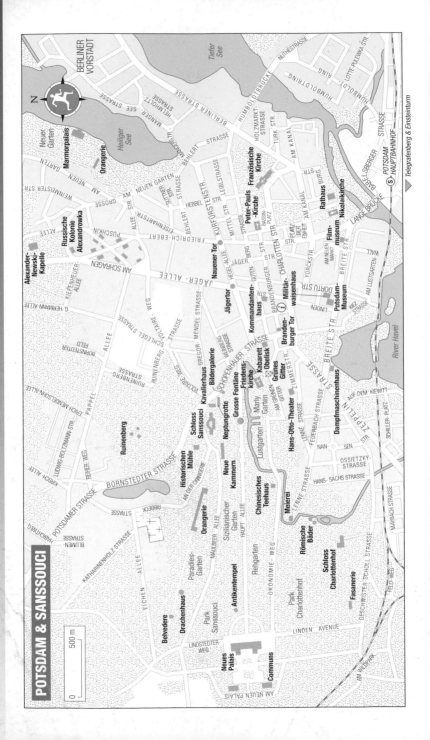

POTSDAM & SANSSOUCI

N

0 — 500 m

BERLINER VORSTADT

Tiefer See

Heiliger See

Neuer Garten

Marmorpalais

Orangerie

Alexander-Newski-Kapelle

Russische Kolonie Alexandrowka

Französische Kirche

Peter-Pauls-Kirche

Rathaus

Nikolaikirche

Nauener Tor

Film-museum

Jägertor

Kommandanten-haus

Militär-waisenhaus

Potsdam-Museum

Bildergalerie

Kavalierhaus

Brandenburger Tor

Kabarett

Obelisk

Grünes Gitter

Friedens-kirche

Ruinenberg

Schloss Sanssouci

Neptungrotte

Grosse Fontäne

Marly Garten

Hans-Otto-Theater

Dampfmaschinenhaus

Historischen Mühle

Neue Kammern

Lustgarten

Orangerie

Sizilianischer Garten

Chinesisches Teehaus

Meierei

Paradies-Garten

Rehgarten

Römische Bäder

Schloss Charlottenhof

Belvedere

Drachenhaus

Antikentempel

Park Sanssouci

Park Charlottenhof

Fasanerie

Neues Palais

Communs

POTSDAM HAUPTBAHNHOF

River Havel

Telegrafenberg & Einsteinturm